# EMO BOY

## Volume 2:
### Walk Around With Your Head Down

by steve
emond

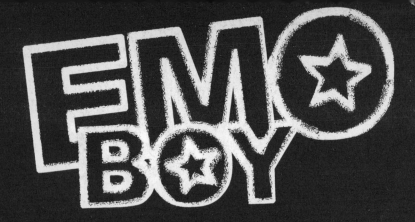

Emo Boy Volume Two: Walk Around with Your Head Down collects issues #7 - 12 of the SLG Publishing series *Emo Boy*.

www.slgcomic.com

First Printing: September 2007
ISBN-13: 978-1-59362-075-2

**Published by
SLG Publishing**

**President and Publisher
Dan Vado**

**Editor in Chief
Jennifer de Guzman**

**Production Artist
Eleanor Lawson**

**P.O. Box 26427
San Jose, CA 95159**

# PREVIOUSLY, IN EMO BOY

IT STARTED WITH A BOY. A BOY WITH POWERS. SUPER POWERS. EMO SUPER POWERS! POINTLESS EMO SUPER POWERS. HE ANGERED THE TOWN HE LIVED IN. HE HAD NO FRIENDS BEYOND SWEET MAXINE, WHO TOOK HIM IN WITH HER MOTHER TO LIVE WITH THEM. HE GOT BAD GRADES. HE GOT BEAT UP. HE FANCIED HIMSELF A MISUNDERSTOOD GENIUS, A GENTLE SOUL, A POET, AN ARTIST. HE LOVED A GIRL, HER NAME WAS PENNY, SOME WOULD SAY IT STILL IS. PENNY DIDN'T KNOW EMO BOY EXISTED, UNTIL ONE DAY SHE DID KNOW HE EXISTED. SHE DID NOT LIKE HIM. BUT THEN SHE DID! THEY KISSED. HE WAS HAPPY. 'A HAPPY EMO BOY?!' YOU SAY. WELL, THAT IS WHERE OUR STORY BEGINS...

# EMO ☆ BOY

## issue number 7

### by Steve Emond

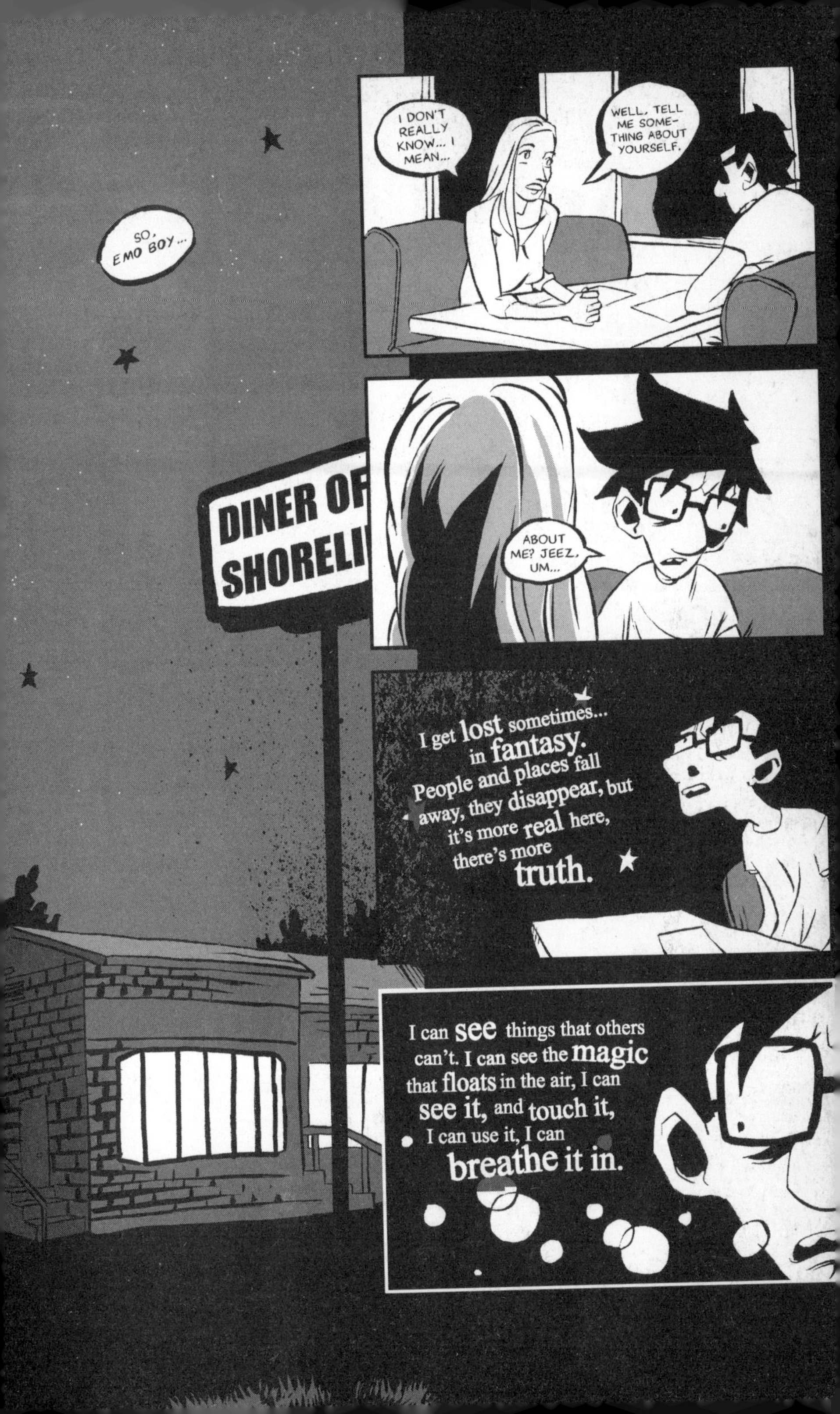
SO, EMO BOY...
I DON'T REALLY KNOW... I MEAN...
WELL, TELL ME SOME-THING ABOUT YOURSELF.
DINER OF SHORELI
ABOUT ME? JEEZ, UM...
I get lost sometimes... in fantasy. People and places fall away, they disappear, but it's more real here, there's more truth.
I can see things that others can't. I can see the magic that floats in the air, I can see it, and touch it, I can use it, I can breathe it in.

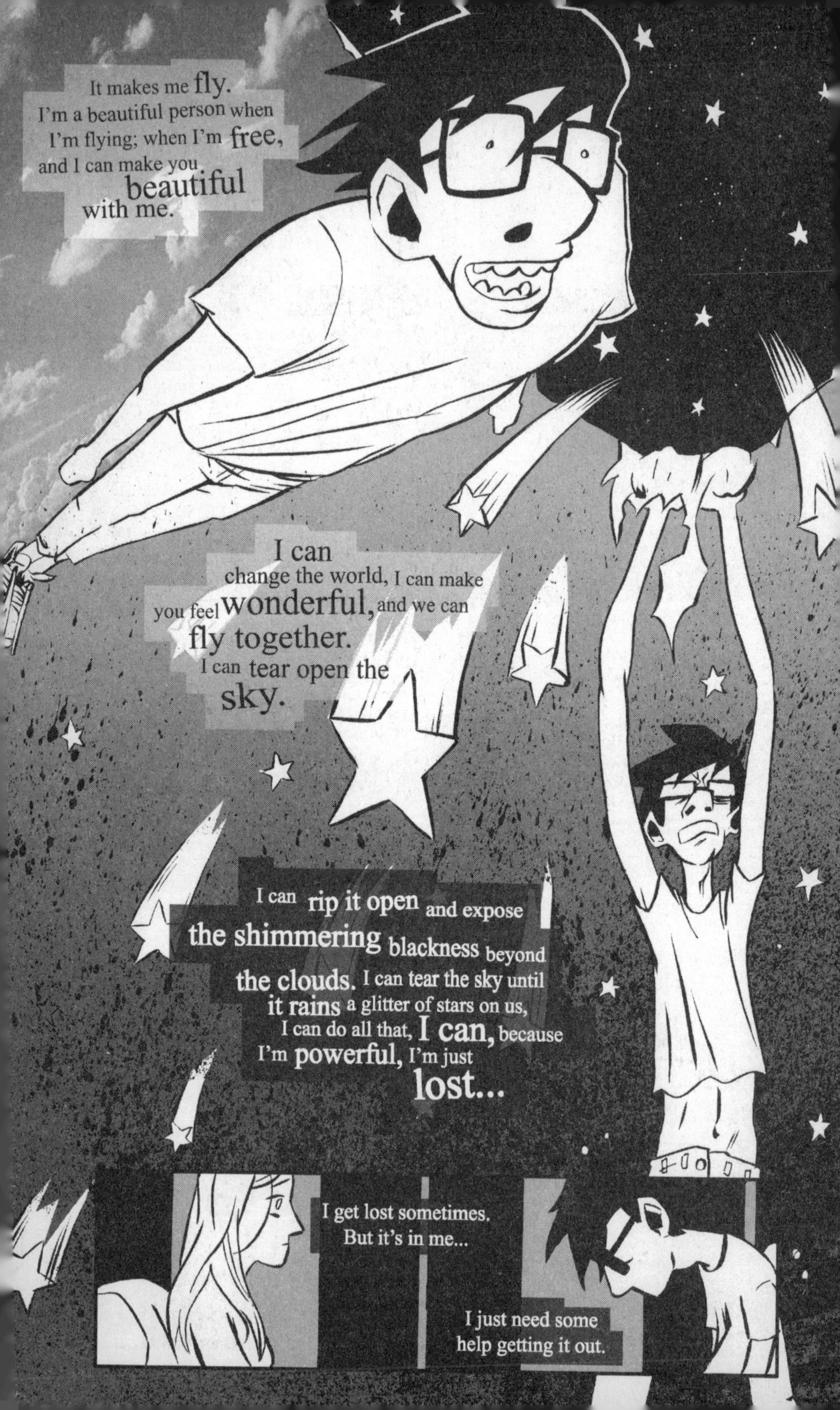

It makes me fly. I'm a beautiful person when I'm flying; when I'm free, and I can make you beautiful with me.
I can change the world, I can make you feel wonderful, and we can fly together. I can tear open the sky.
I can rip it open and expose the shimmering blackness beyond the clouds. I can tear the sky until it rains a glitter of stars on us, I can do all that, I can, because I'm powerful, I'm just lost...
I get lost sometimes. But it's in me...
I just need some help getting it out.

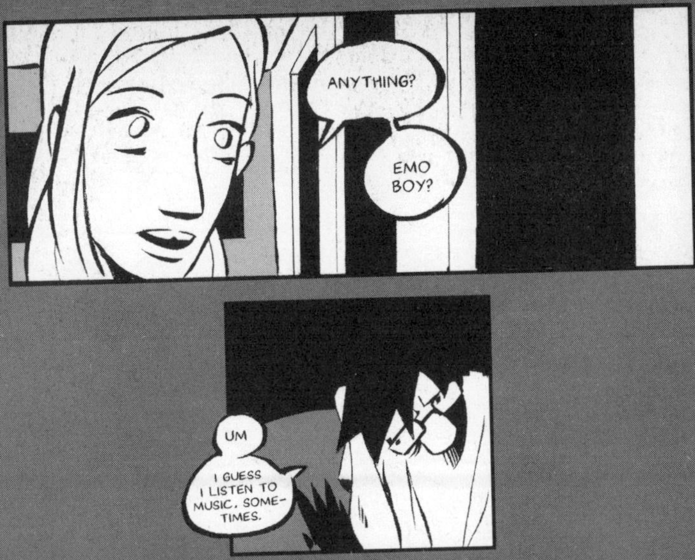
ANYTHING?
EMO BOY?
UM
I GUESS I LISTEN TO MUSIC. SOME-TIMES.

## Emo Boy #7

# "Disconnected"

Story and Art by Steve Emond

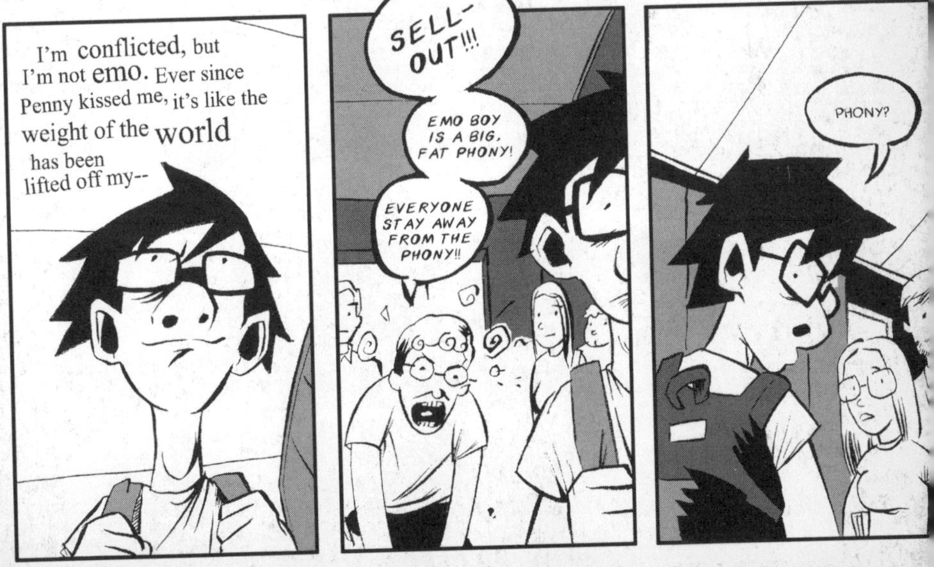
I'm conflicted, but I'm not emo. Ever since Penny kissed me, it's like the weight of the world has been lifted off my--
SELL-OUT!!!
EMO BOY IS A BIG, FAT PHONY!
EVERYONE STAY AWAY FROM THE PHONY!!
PHONY?

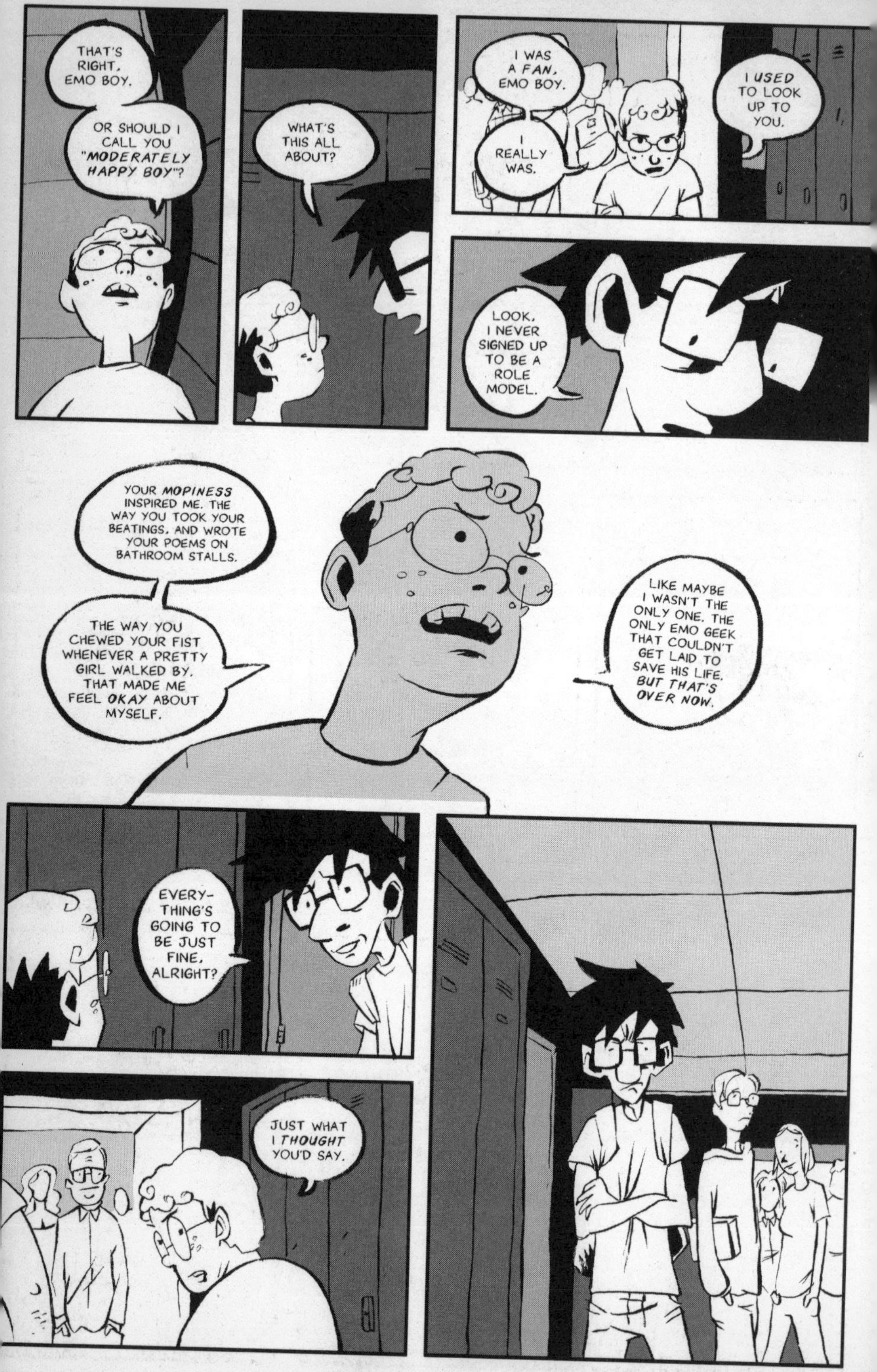
THAT'S RIGHT, EMO BOY.
OR SHOULD I CALL YOU "MODERATELY HAPPY BOY"?
WHAT'S THIS ALL ABOUT?
I WAS A FAN, EMO BOY.
I REALLY WAS.
I USED TO LOOK UP TO YOU.
LOOK, I NEVER SIGNED UP TO BE A ROLE MODEL.
YOUR MOPINESS INSPIRED ME. THE WAY YOU TOOK YOUR BEATINGS, AND WROTE YOUR POEMS ON BATHROOM STALLS.
THE WAY YOU CHEWED YOUR FIST WHENEVER A PRETTY GIRL WALKED BY, THAT MADE ME FEEL OKAY ABOUT MYSELF.
LIKE MAYBE I WASN'T THE ONLY ONE. THE ONLY EMO GEEK THAT COULDN'T GET LAID TO SAVE HIS LIFE. BUT THAT'S OVER NOW.
EVERY-THING'S GOING TO BE JUST FINE, ALRIGHT?
JUST WHAT I THOUGHT YOU'D SAY.

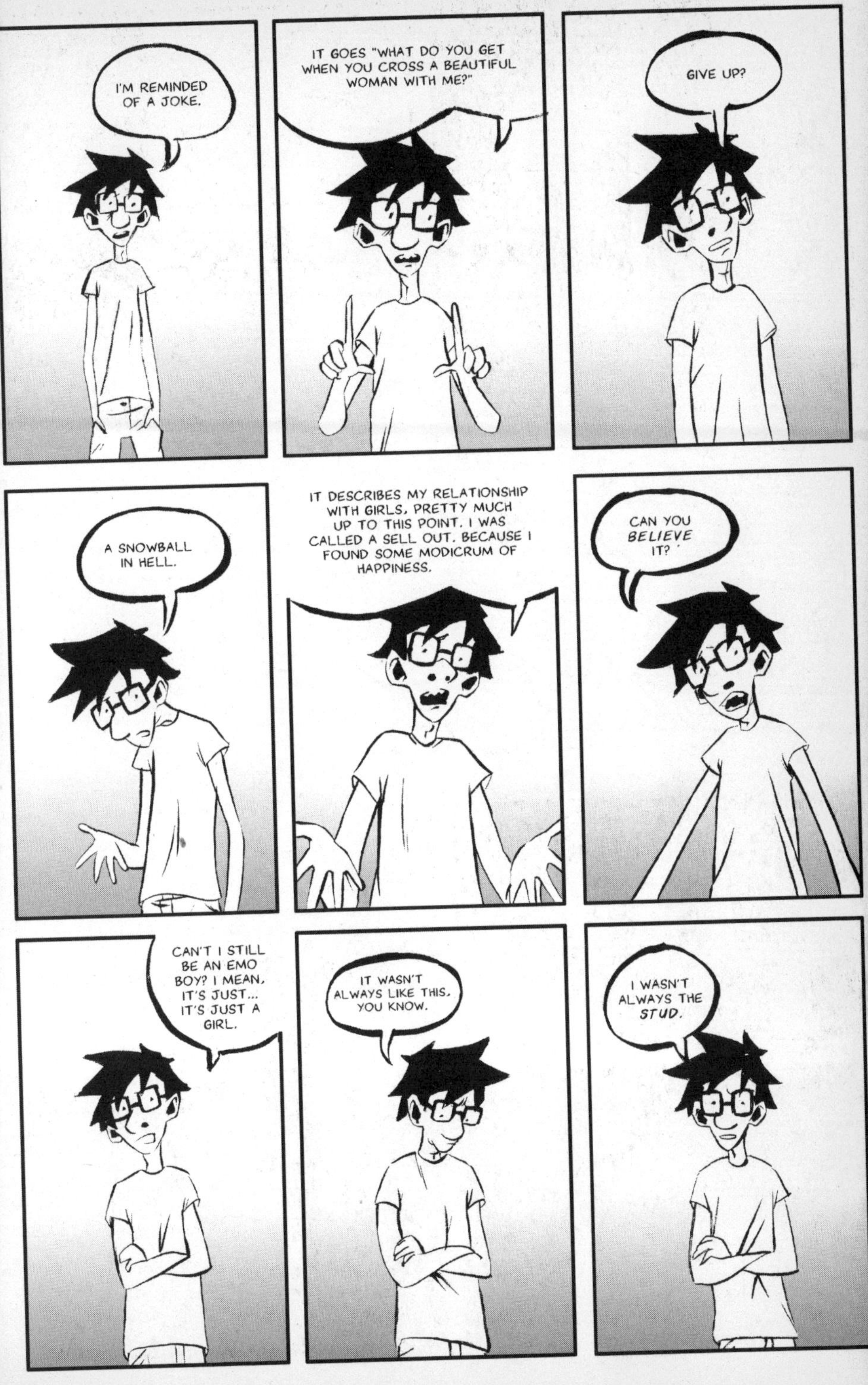
I'M REMINDED OF A JOKE.
IT GOES "WHAT DO YOU GET WHEN YOU CROSS A BEAUTIFUL WOMAN WITH ME?"
GIVE UP?
A SNOWBALL IN HELL.
IT DESCRIBES MY RELATIONSHIP WITH GIRLS, PRETTY MUCH UP TO THIS POINT. I WAS CALLED A SELL OUT. BECAUSE I FOUND SOME MODICRUM OF HAPPINESS.
CAN YOU *BELIEVE* IT?
CAN'T I STILL BE AN EMO BOY? I MEAN, IT'S JUST... IT'S JUST A GIRL.
IT WASN'T ALWAYS LIKE THIS, YOU KNOW.
I WASN'T ALWAYS THE *STUD*.

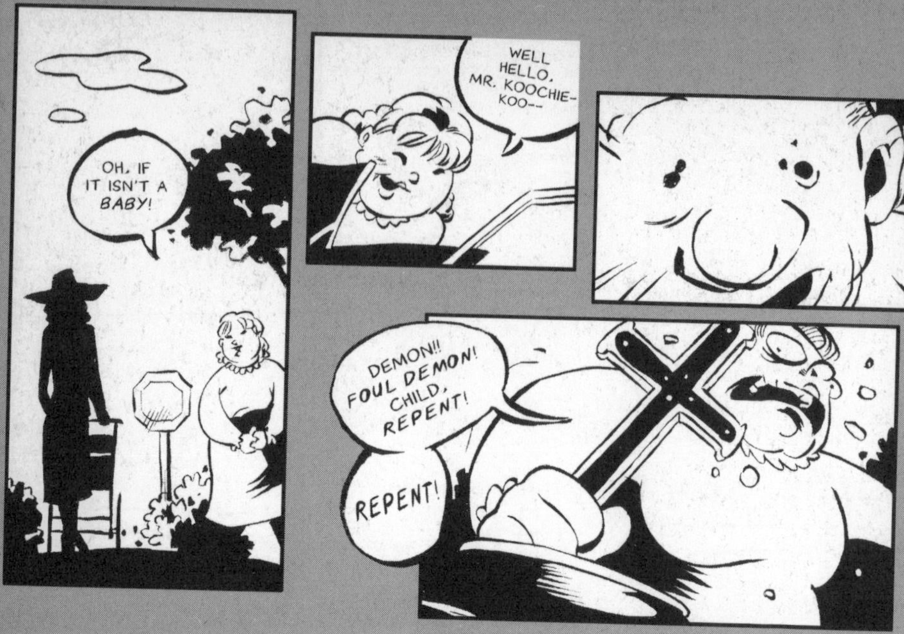
OH, IF IT ISN'T A BABY!
WELL HELLO, MR. KOOCHIE-KOO--
DEMON!! FOUL DEMON! CHILD, REPENT!
REPENT!

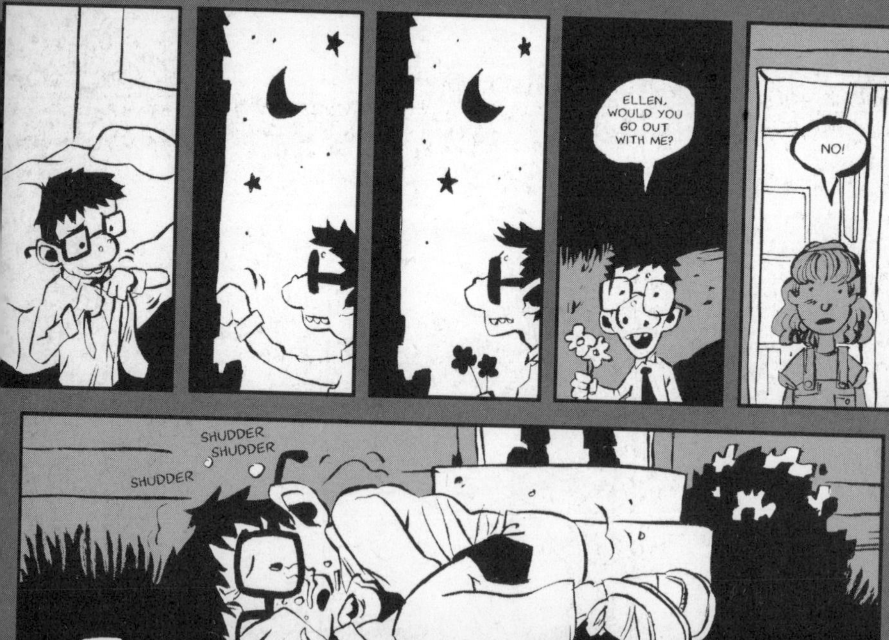
ELLEN, WOULD YOU GO OUT WITH ME?
NO!
SHUDDER
SHUDDER
SHUDDER

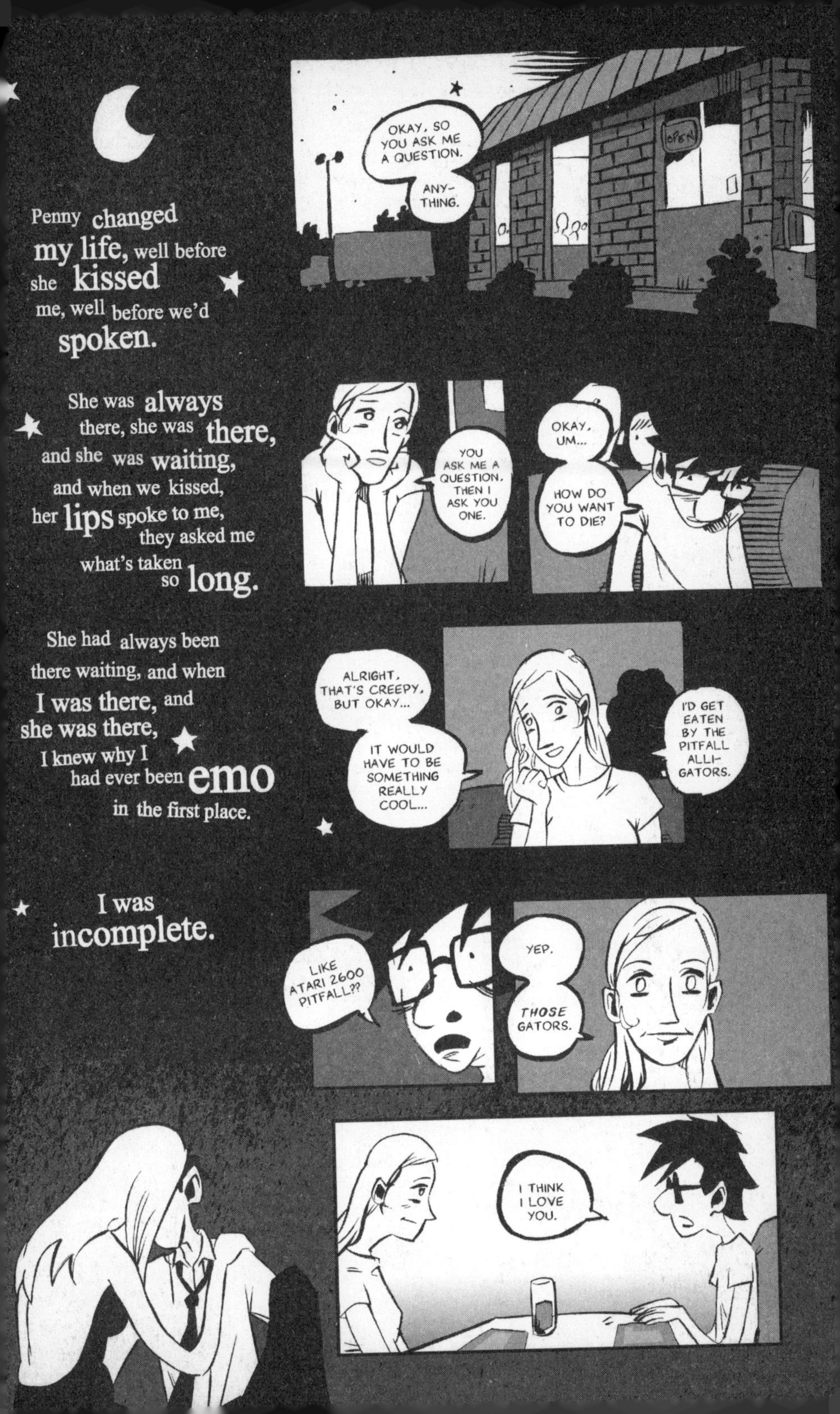
Penny changed my life, well before she kissed me, well before we'd spoken.
OKAY, SO YOU ASK ME A QUESTION.
ANY-THING.
OPEN
She was always there, she was there, and she was waiting, and when we kissed, her lips spoke to me, they asked me what's taken so long.
YOU ASK ME A QUESTION, THEN I ASK YOU ONE.
OKAY, UM...
HOW DO YOU WANT TO DIE?
She had always been there waiting, and when I was there, and she was there, I knew why I had ever been emo in the first place.
ALRIGHT, THAT'S CREEPY, BUT OKAY...
IT WOULD HAVE TO BE SOMETHING REALLY COOL...
I'D GET EATEN BY THE PITFALL ALLI-GATORS.
I was incomplete.
LIKE ATARI 2600 PITFALL??
YEP.
THOSE GATORS.
I THINK I LOVE YOU.

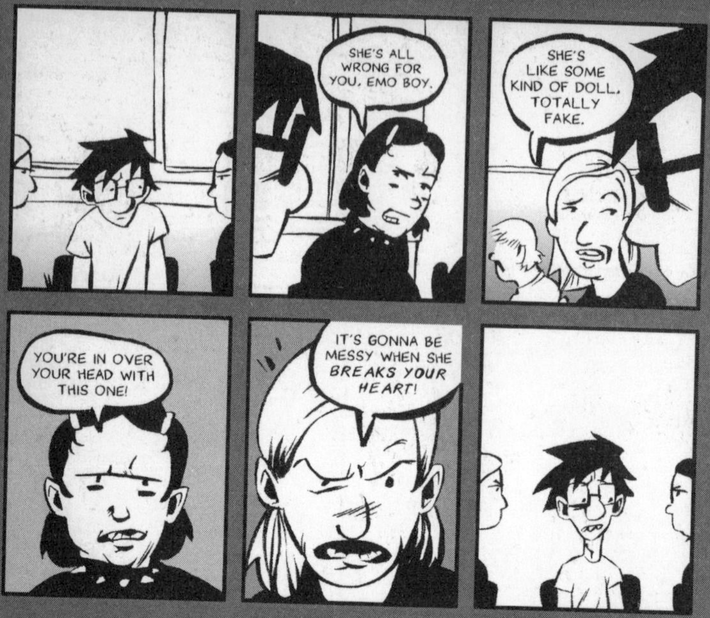
SHE'S ALL WRONG FOR YOU, EMO BOY.
SHE'S LIKE SOME KIND OF DOLL. TOTALLY FAKE.
YOU'RE IN OVER YOUR HEAD WITH THIS ONE!
IT'S GONNA BE MESSY WHEN SHE *BREAKS YOUR HEART!*

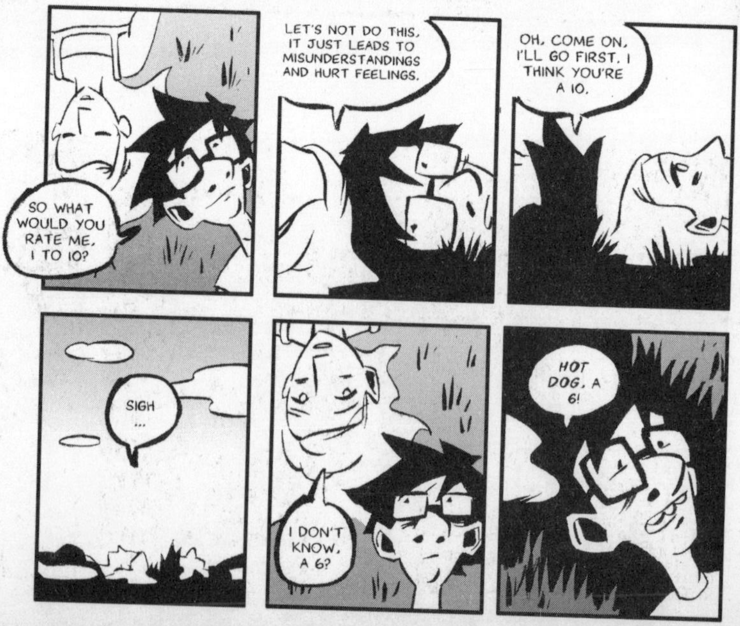
SO WHAT WOULD YOU RATE ME, 1 TO 10?
LET'S NOT DO THIS. IT JUST LEADS TO MISUNDERSTANDINGS AND HURT FEELINGS.
OH, COME ON, I'LL GO FIRST. I THINK YOU'RE A 10.
SIGH ...
I DON'T KNOW, A 6?
HOT DOG, A 6!

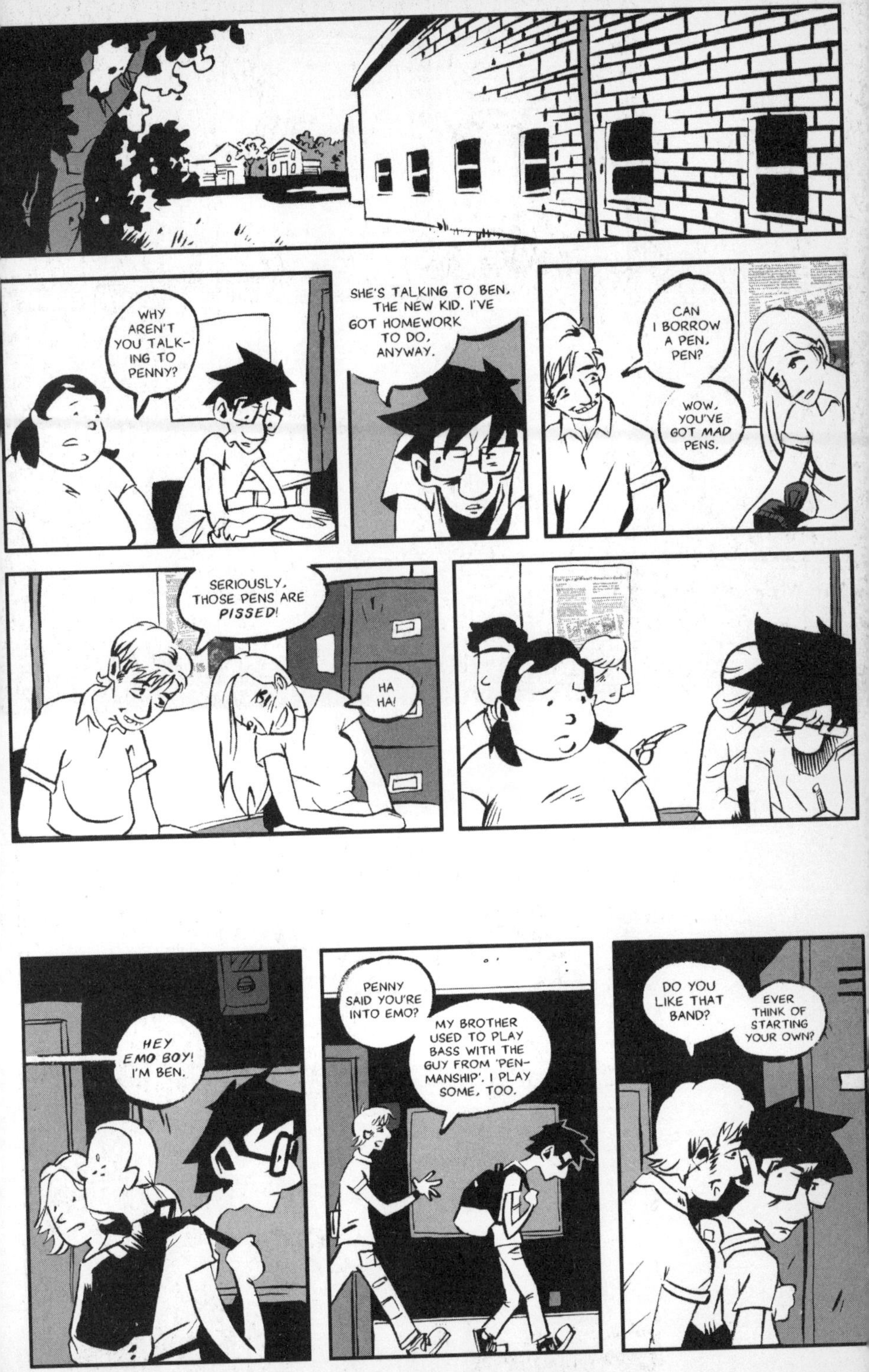
WHY AREN'T YOU TALK-ING TO PENNY?
SHE'S TALKING TO BEN, THE NEW KID. I'VE GOT HOMEWORK TO DO, ANYWAY.
CAN I BORROW A PEN, PEN?
WOW, YOU'VE GOT *MAD* PENS.
SERIOUSLY, THOSE PENS ARE ***PISSED***!
HA HA!
*HEY EMO BOY!* I'M BEN.
PENNY SAID YOU'RE INTO EMO?
MY BROTHER USED TO PLAY BASS WITH THE GUY FROM 'PEN-MANSHIP'. I PLAY SOME, TOO.
DO YOU LIKE THAT BAND?
EVER THINK OF STARTING YOUR OWN?

My love with Penny was not a slow climb, it was not an airplane lifting off, it skyrocketed.

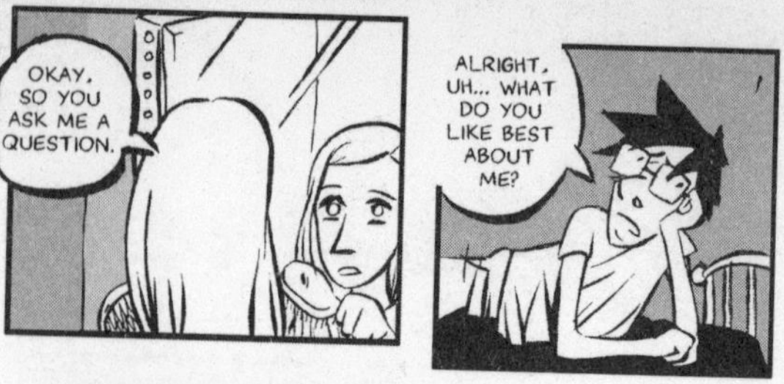
OKAY, SO YOU ASK ME A QUESTION.
ALRIGHT, UH... WHAT DO YOU LIKE BEST ABOUT ME?

It took off, it lept into the sky, spiraling and bursting out through the troposphere.

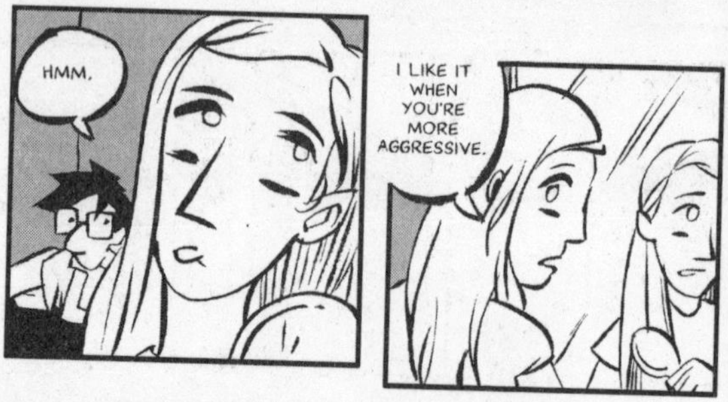
HMM.
I LIKE IT WHEN YOU'RE MORE AGGRESSIVE.

Beyond it.

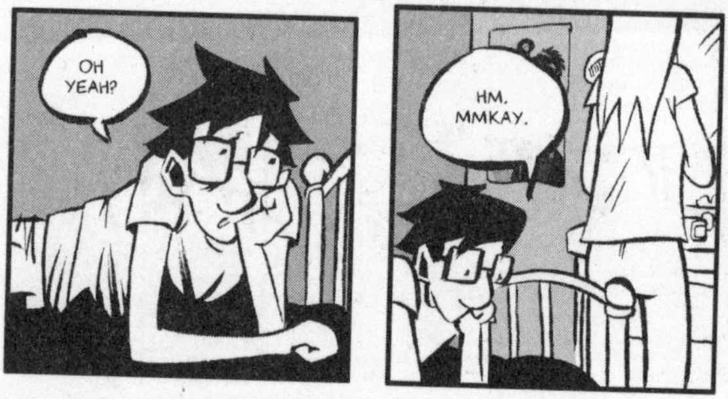
OH YEAH?
HM. MMKAY.

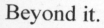

It reached out into the cosmos, dancing past the blue and through the stars.

Our love was intergalactic.

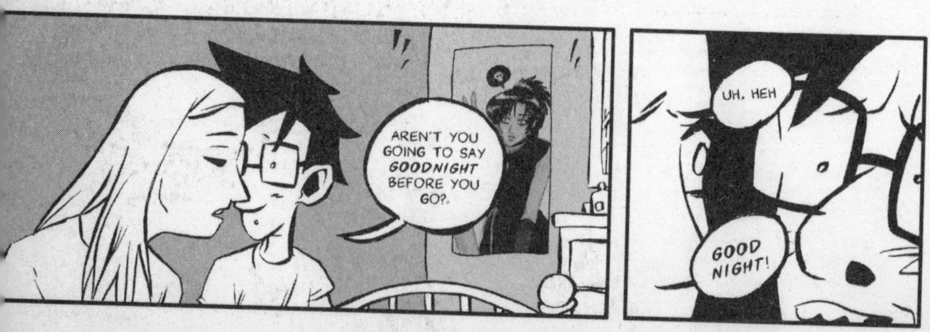
AREN'T YOU GOING TO SAY GOODNIGHT BEFORE YOU GO?
UH. HEH
GOOD NIGHT!

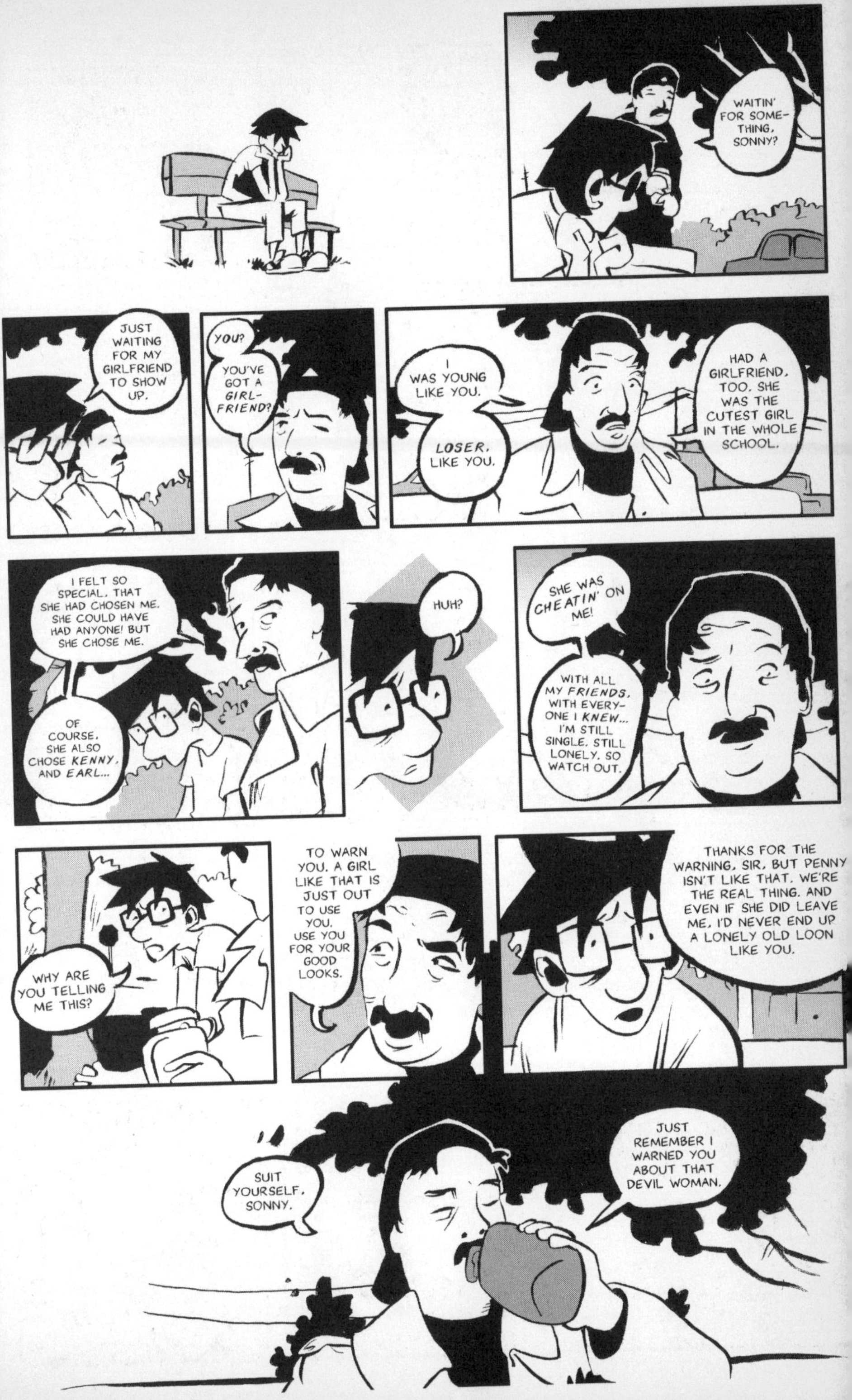

WAITIN' FOR SOME-THING, SONNY?
JUST WAITING FOR MY GIRLFRIEND TO SHOW UP.
YOU?
YOU'VE GOT A GIRL-FRIEND?
I WAS YOUNG LIKE YOU.
LOSER, LIKE YOU.
HAD A GIRLFRIEND, TOO. SHE WAS THE CUTEST GIRL IN THE WHOLE SCHOOL.
I FELT SO SPECIAL, THAT SHE HAD CHOSEN ME. SHE COULD HAVE HAD ANYONE! BUT SHE CHOSE ME.
OF COURSE, SHE ALSO CHOSE KENNY, AND EARL...
HUH?
SHE WAS CHEATIN' ON ME!
WITH ALL MY FRIENDS, WITH EVERY-ONE I KNEW... I'M STILL SINGLE, STILL LONELY. SO WATCH OUT.
WHY ARE YOU TELLING ME THIS?
TO WARN YOU. A GIRL LIKE THAT IS JUST OUT TO USE YOU. USE YOU FOR YOUR GOOD LOOKS.
THANKS FOR THE WARNING, SIR, BUT PENNY ISN'T LIKE THAT. WE'RE THE REAL THING. AND EVEN IF SHE DID LEAVE ME, I'D NEVER END UP A LONELY OLD LOON LIKE YOU.
SUIT YOURSELF, SONNY.
JUST REMEMBER I WARNED YOU ABOUT THAT DEVIL WOMAN.

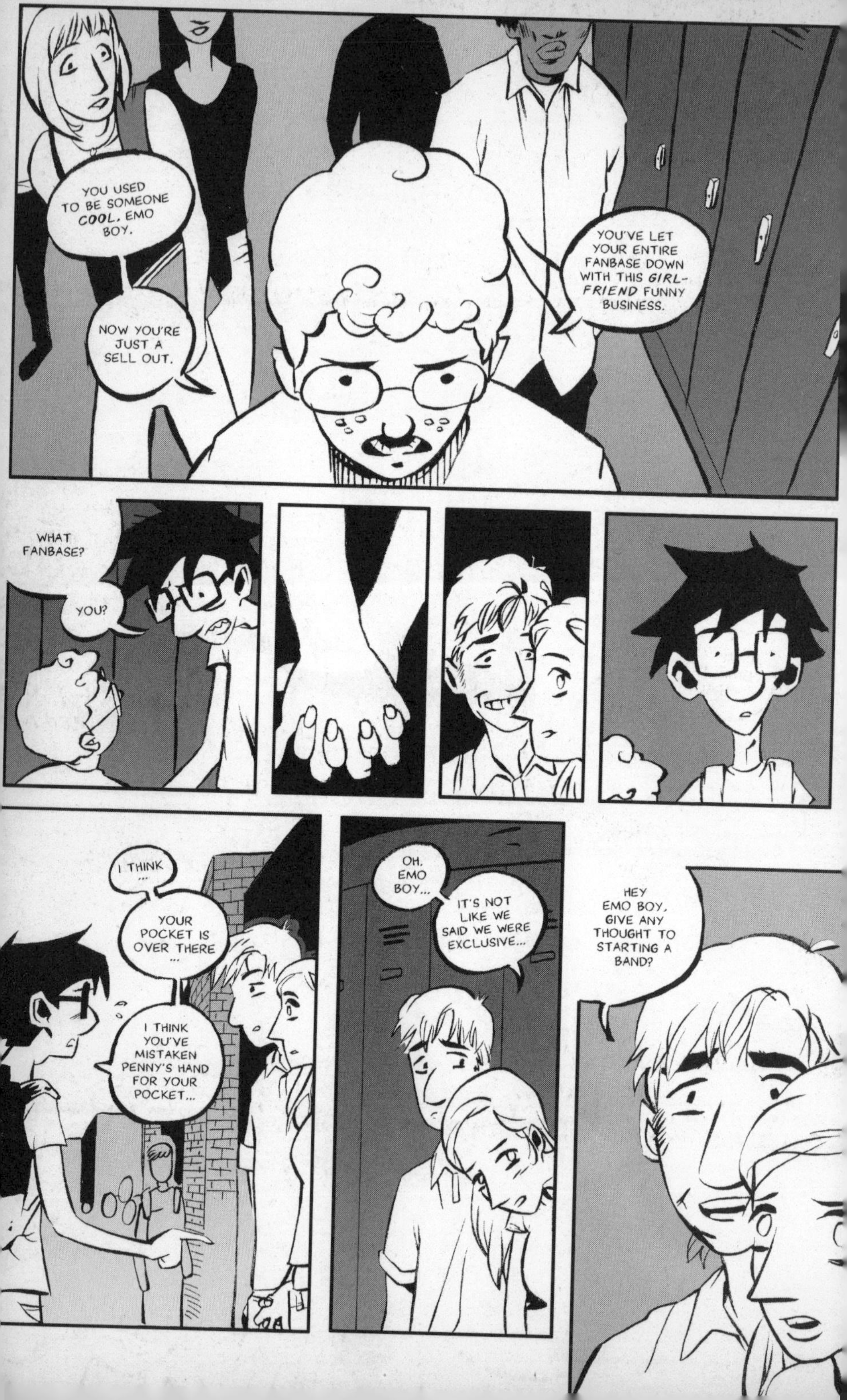
YOU USED TO BE SOMEONE COOL, EMO BOY.
NOW YOU'RE JUST A SELL OUT.
YOU'VE LET YOUR ENTIRE FANBASE DOWN WITH THIS GIRL-FRIEND FUNNY BUSINESS.
WHAT FANBASE?
YOU?
I THINK ...
YOUR POCKET IS OVER THERE ...
I THINK YOU'VE MISTAKEN PENNY'S HAND FOR YOUR POCKET...
OH, EMO BOY...
IT'S NOT LIKE WE SAID WE WERE EXCLUSIVE...
HEY EMO BOY, GIVE ANY THOUGHT TO STARTING A BAND?

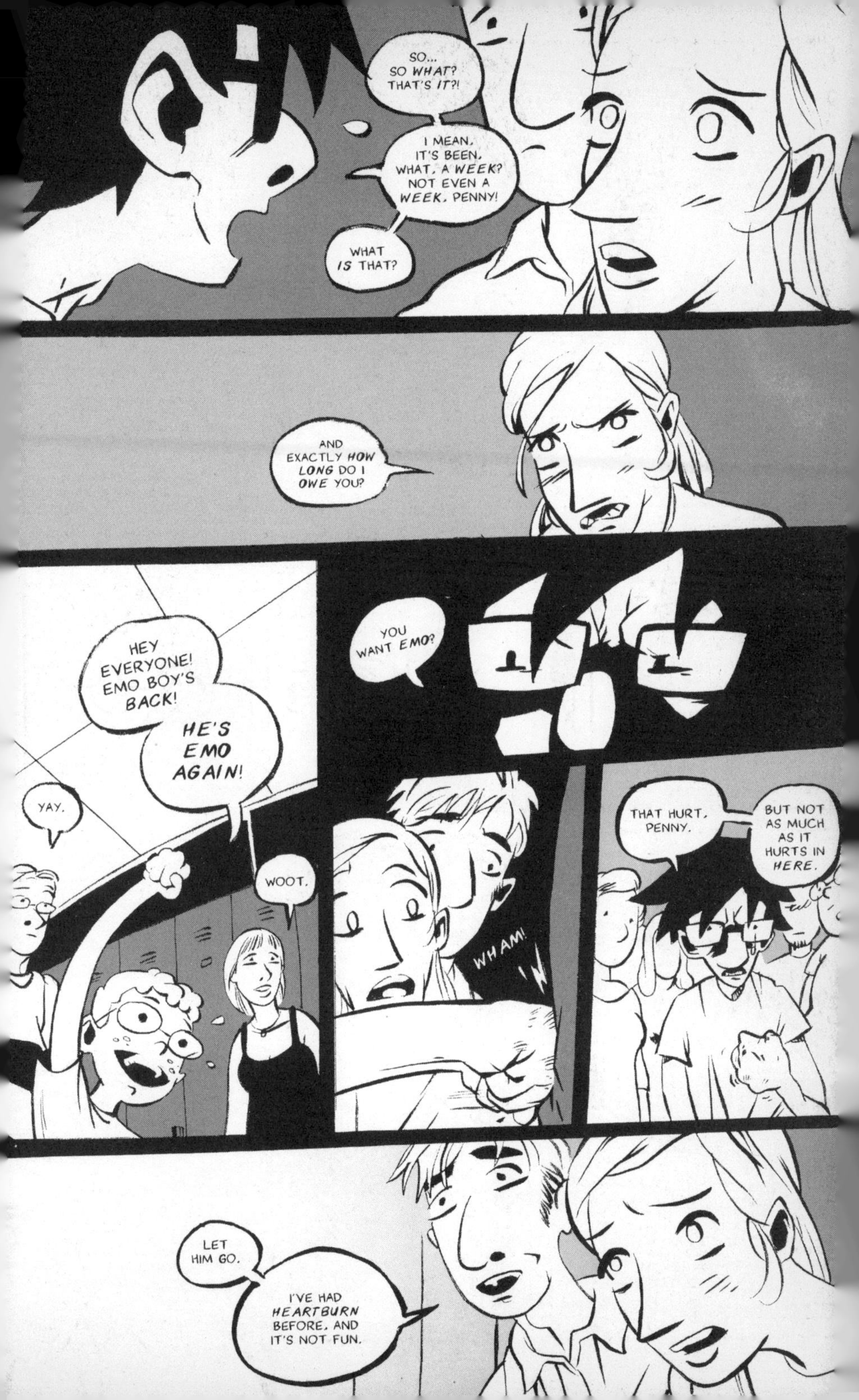
SO... SO WHAT? THAT'S IT?!
I MEAN, IT'S BEEN, WHAT, A WEEK? NOT EVEN A WEEK, PENNY!
WHAT IS THAT?
AND EXACTLY HOW LONG DO I OWE YOU?
HEY EVERYONE! EMO BOY'S BACK!
HE'S EMO AGAIN!
YAY.
WOOT.
YOU WANT EMO?
WHAM!
THAT HURT, PENNY.
BUT NOT AS MUCH AS IT HURTS IN HERE.
LET HIM GO.
I'VE HAD HEARTBURN BEFORE, AND IT'S NOT FUN.

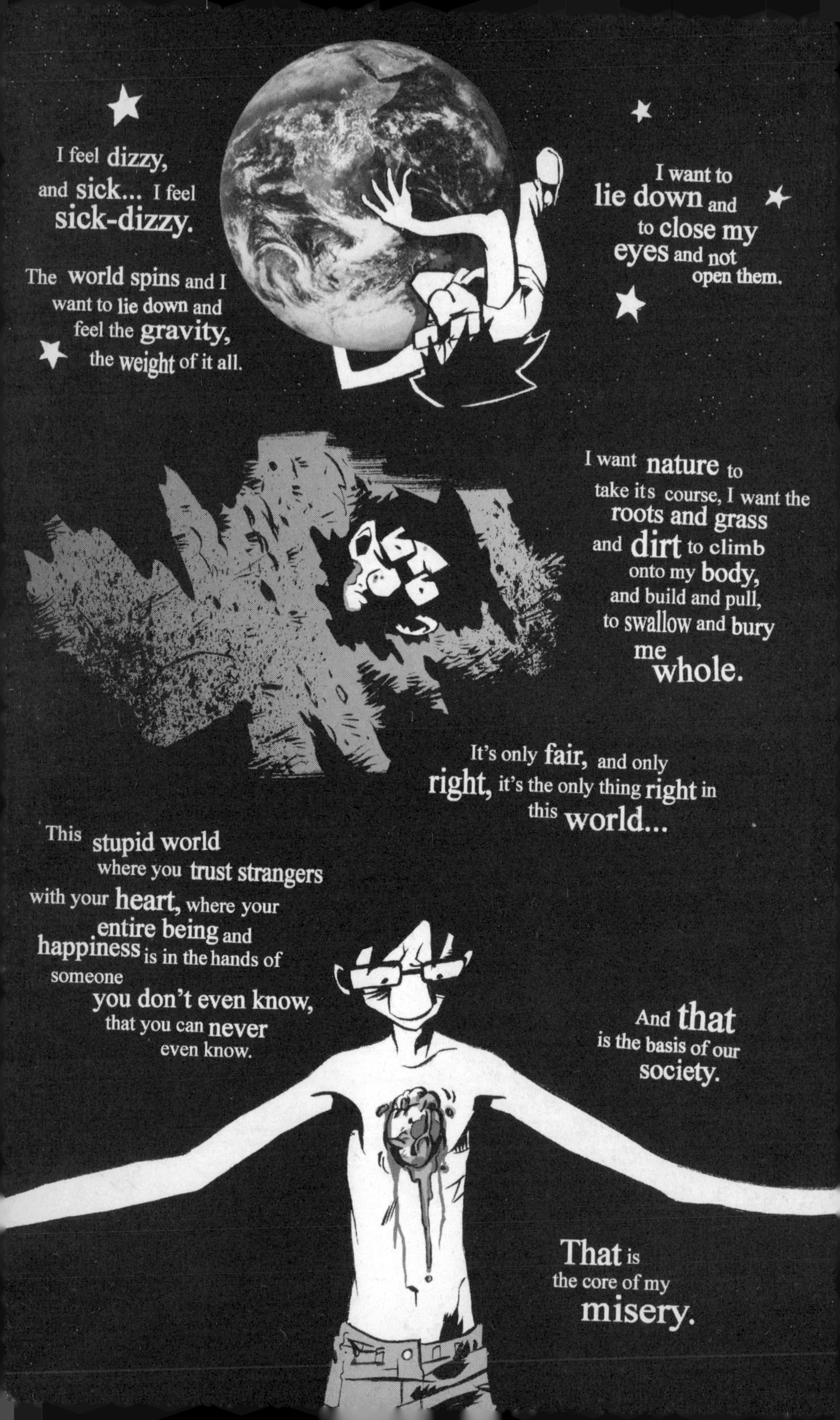
I feel dizzy, and sick... I feel sick-dizzy.
The world spins and I want to lie down and feel the gravity, the weight of it all.
I want to lie down and to close my eyes and not open them.
I want nature to take its course, I want the roots and grass and dirt to climb onto my body, and build and pull, to swallow and bury me whole.
It's only fair, and only right, it's the only thing right in this world...
This stupid world where you trust strangers with your heart, where your entire being and happiness is in the hands of someone you don't even know, that you can never even know.
And that is the basis of our society.
That is the core of my misery.

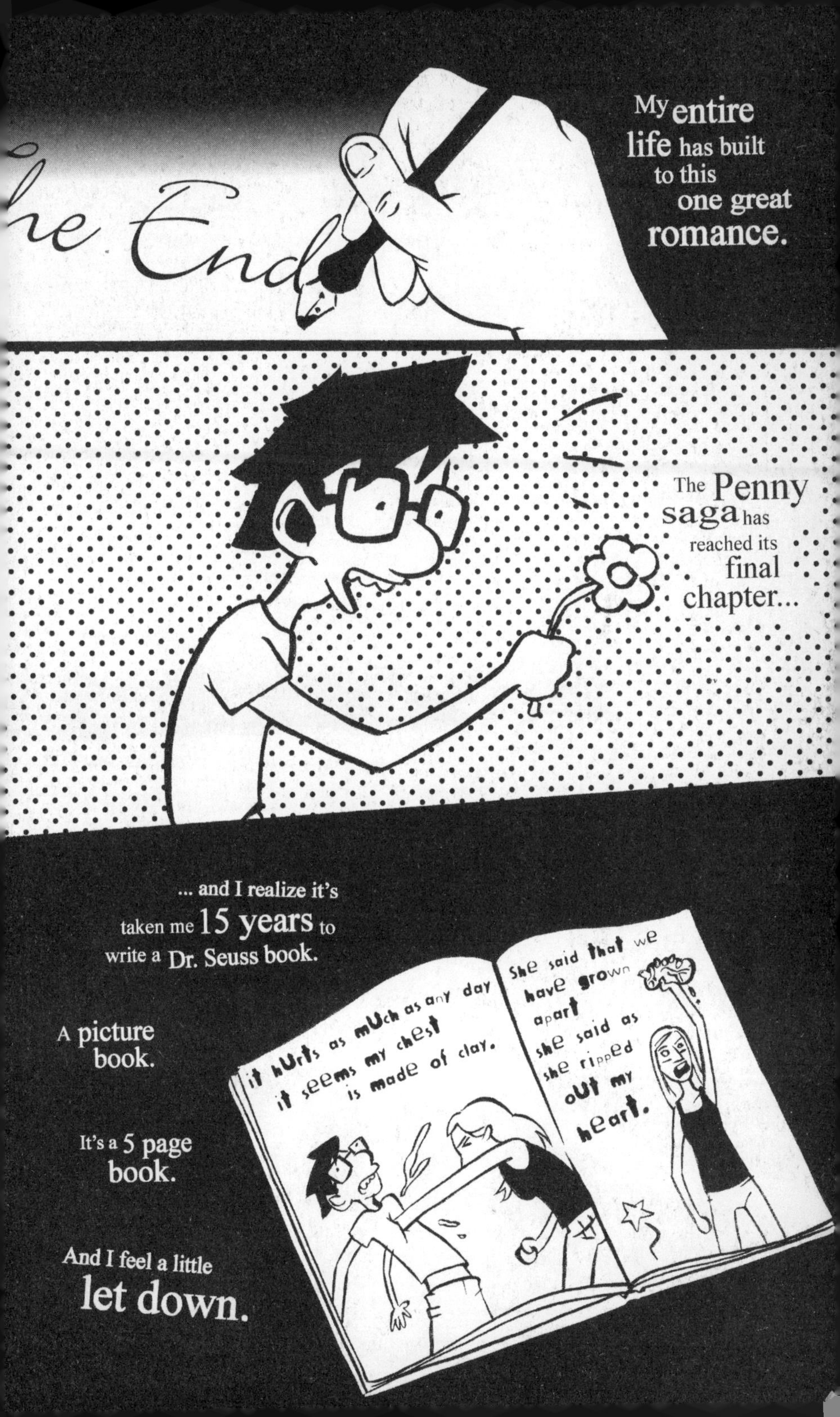

he End
My entire life has built to this one great romance.
The Penny saga has reached its final chapter...
... and I realize it's taken me 15 years to write a Dr. Seuss book.
A picture book.
It's a 5 page book.
And I feel a little let down.
it hurts as much as any day it seems my chest is made of clay.
She said that we have grown apart she said as she ripped out my heart.

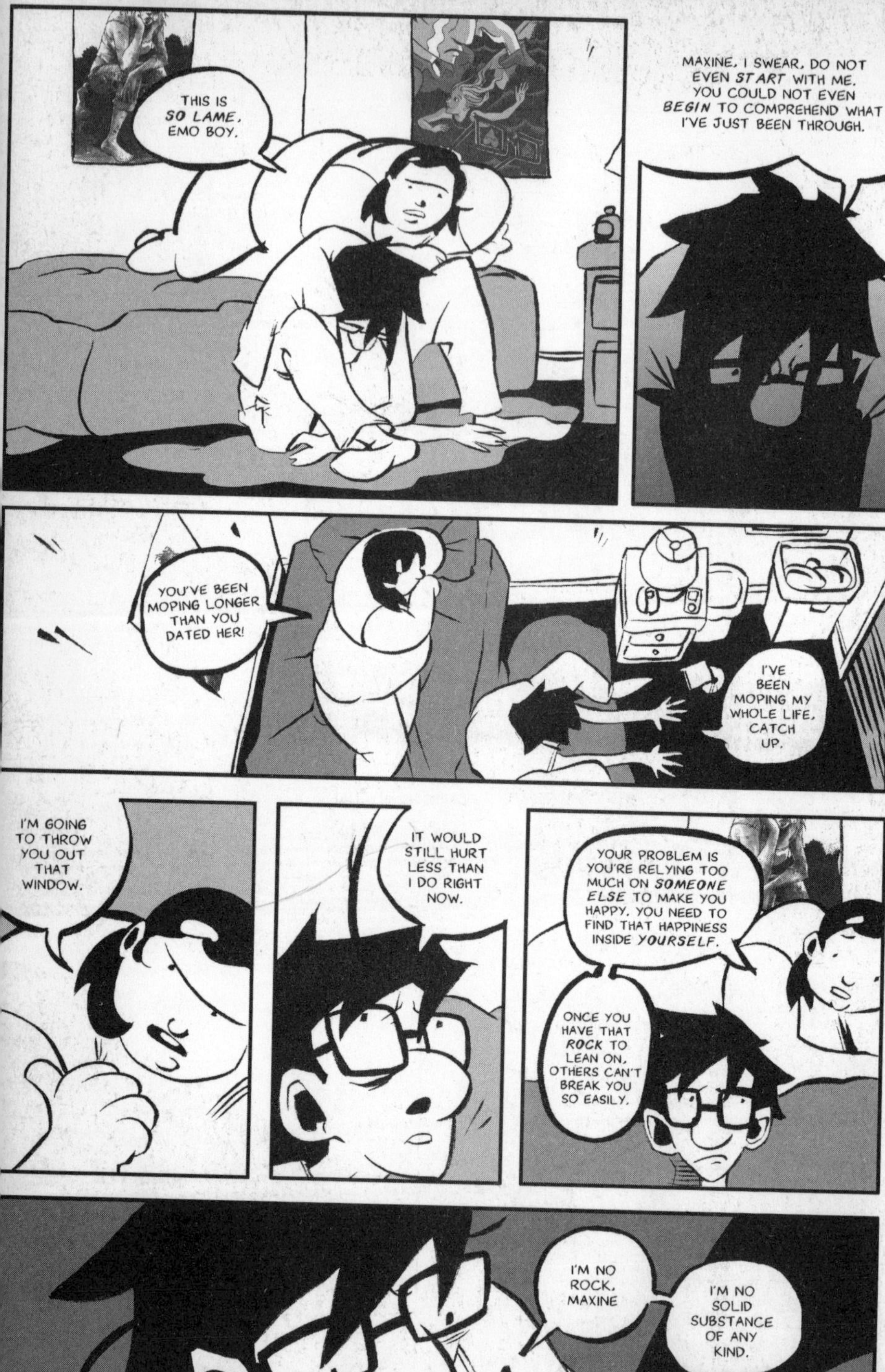
THIS IS SO LAME, EMO BOY.
MAXINE, I SWEAR, DO NOT EVEN START WITH ME. YOU COULD NOT EVEN BEGIN TO COMPREHEND WHAT I'VE JUST BEEN THROUGH.
YOU'VE BEEN MOPING LONGER THAN YOU DATED HER!
I'VE BEEN MOPING MY WHOLE LIFE, CATCH UP.
I'M GOING TO THROW YOU OUT THAT WINDOW.
IT WOULD STILL HURT LESS THAN I DO RIGHT NOW.
YOUR PROBLEM IS YOU'RE RELYING TOO MUCH ON SOMEONE ELSE TO MAKE YOU HAPPY. YOU NEED TO FIND THAT HAPPINESS INSIDE YOURSELF.
ONCE YOU HAVE THAT ROCK TO LEAN ON, OTHERS CAN'T BREAK YOU SO EASILY.
I'M NO ROCK, MAXINE
I'M NO SOLID SUBSTANCE OF ANY KIND.

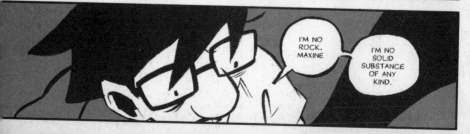

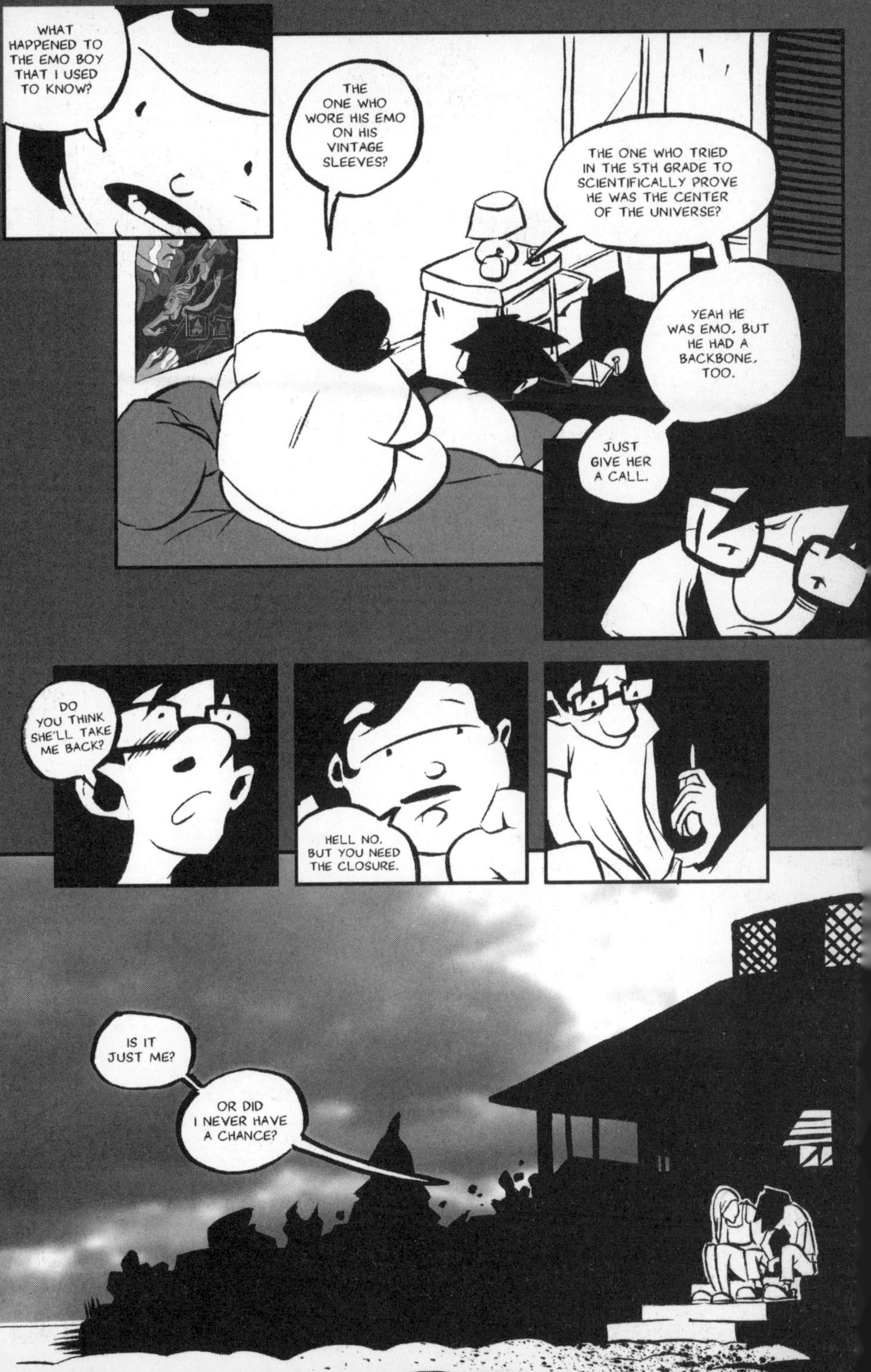
WHAT HAPPENED TO THE EMO BOY THAT I USED TO KNOW?
THE ONE WHO WORE HIS EMO ON HIS VINTAGE SLEEVES?
THE ONE WHO TRIED IN THE 5TH GRADE TO SCIENTIFICALLY PROVE HE WAS THE CENTER OF THE UNIVERSE?
YEAH HE WAS EMO, BUT HE HAD A BACKBONE, TOO.
JUST GIVE HER A CALL.
DO YOU THINK SHE'LL TAKE ME BACK?
HELL NO. BUT YOU NEED THE CLOSURE.
IS IT JUST ME?
OR DID I NEVER HAVE A CHANCE?

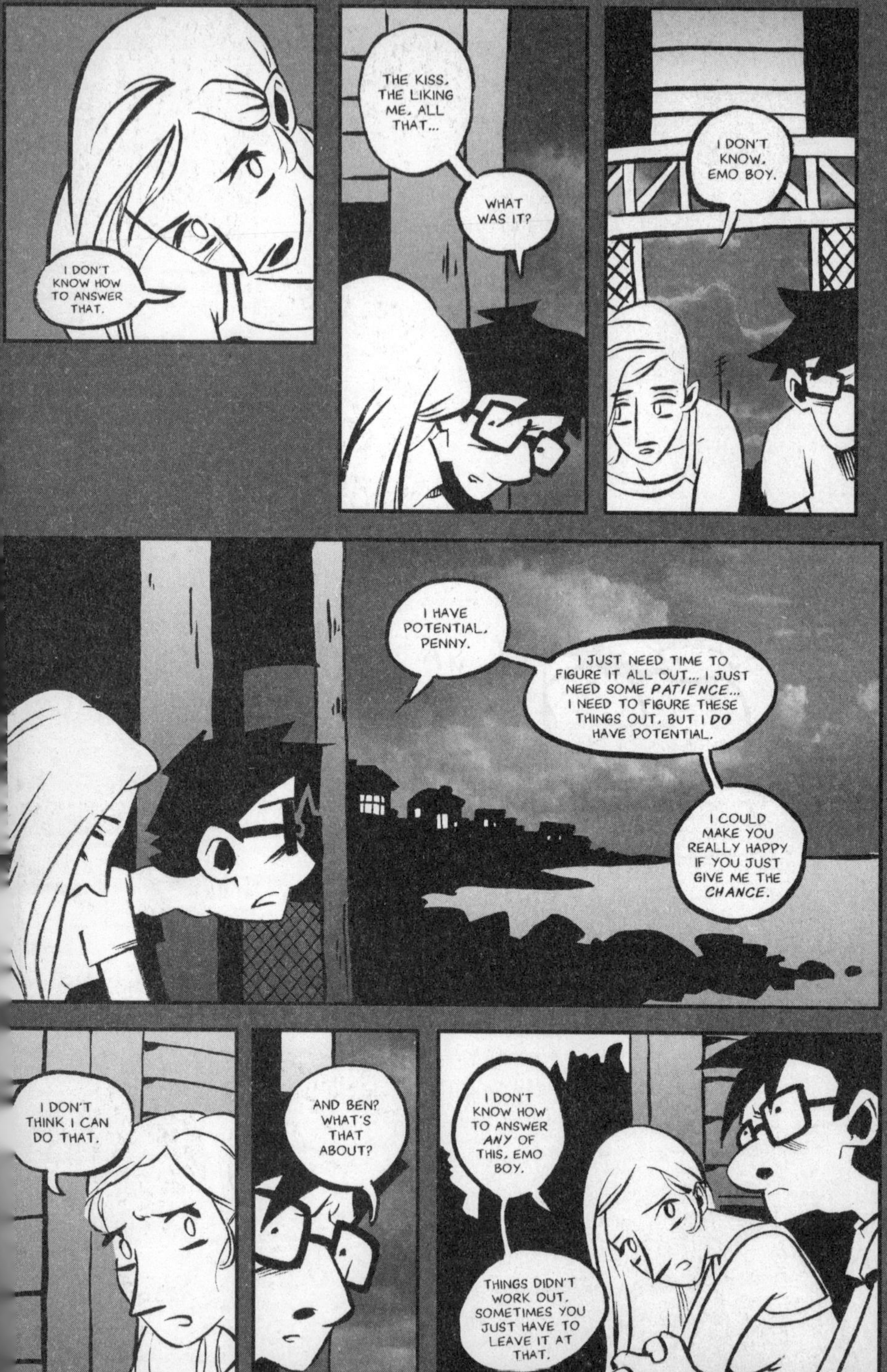
I DON'T KNOW HOW TO ANSWER THAT.
THE KISS, THE LIKING ME, ALL THAT...
WHAT WAS IT?
I DON'T KNOW, EMO BOY.
I HAVE POTENTIAL, PENNY.
I JUST NEED TIME TO FIGURE IT ALL OUT... I JUST NEED SOME PATIENCE... I NEED TO FIGURE THESE THINGS OUT. BUT I DO HAVE POTENTIAL.
I COULD MAKE YOU REALLY HAPPY IF YOU JUST GIVE ME THE CHANCE.
I DON'T THINK I CAN DO THAT.
AND BEN? WHAT'S THAT ABOUT?
I DON'T KNOW HOW TO ANSWER ANY OF THIS, EMO BOY.
THINGS DIDN'T WORK OUT. SOMETIMES YOU JUST HAVE TO LEAVE IT AT THAT.

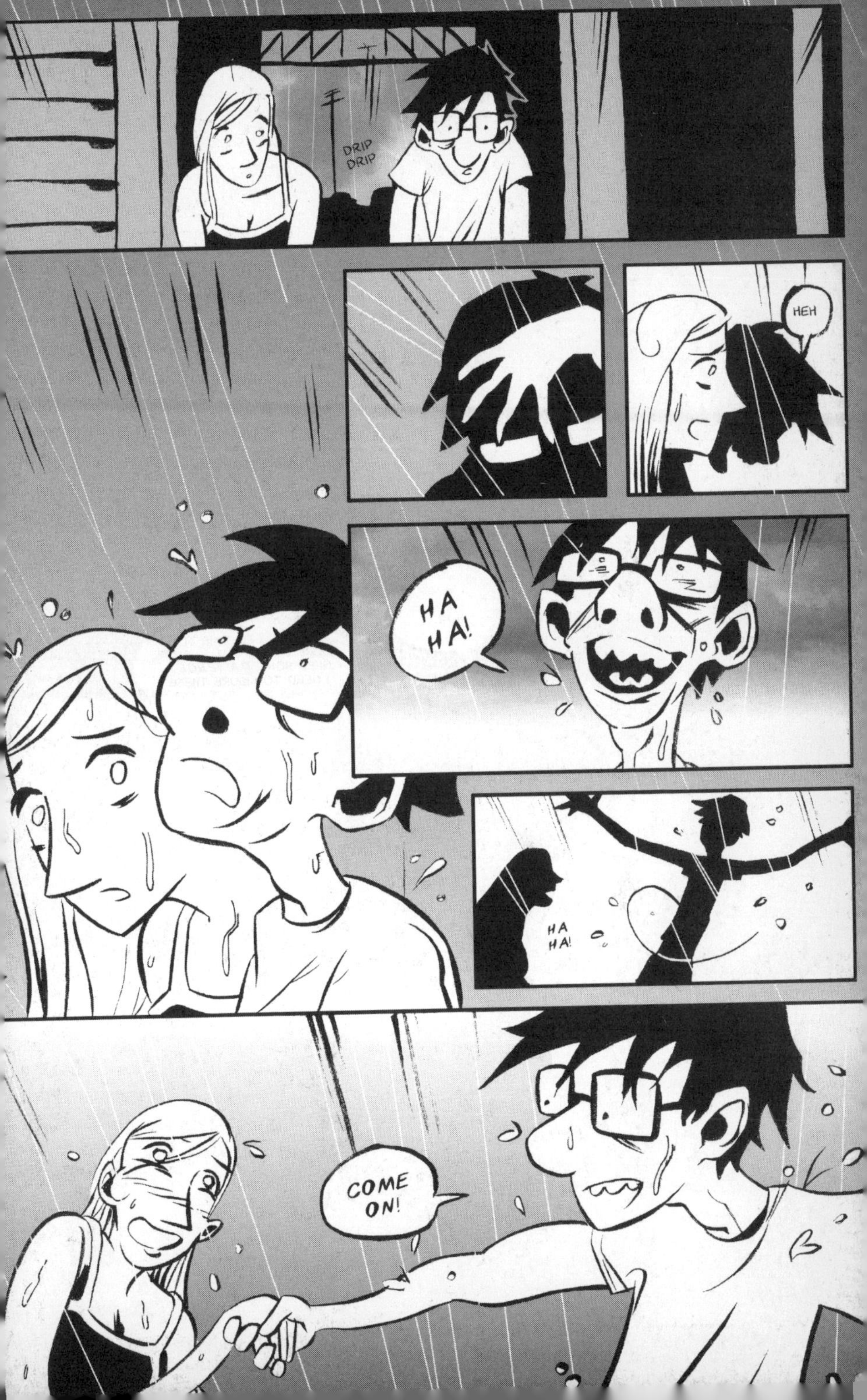
DRIP
DRIP
HEH
HA
HA!
HA
HA!
COME
ON!

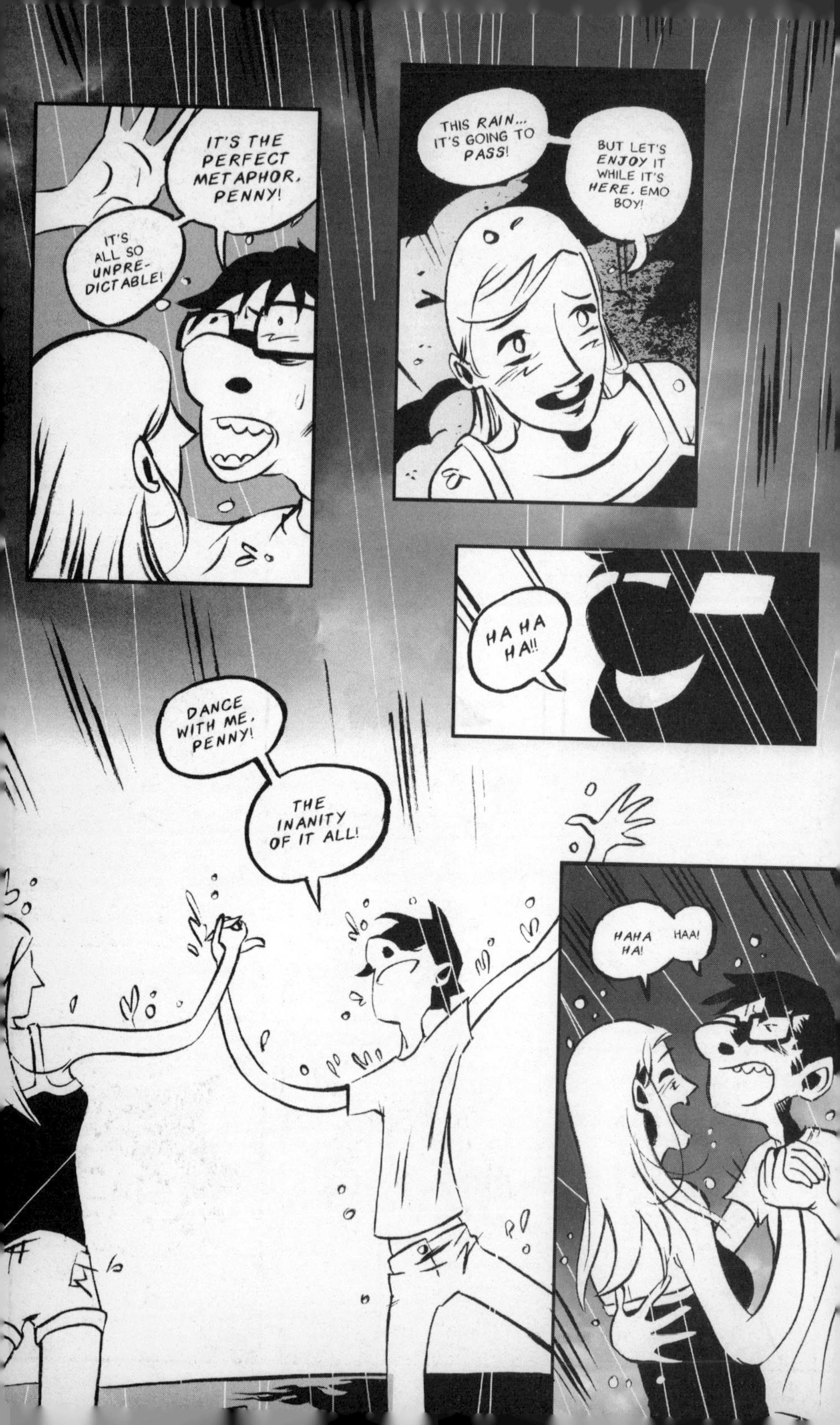

IT'S THE PERFECT METAPHOR, PENNY!
IT'S ALL SO UNPRE-DICTABLE!
THIS RAIN... IT'S GOING TO PASS!
BUT LET'S ENJOY IT WHILE IT'S HERE, EMO BOY!
HA HA HA!!
DANCE WITH ME, PENNY!
THE INANITY OF IT ALL!
HAHA HA!
HAA!

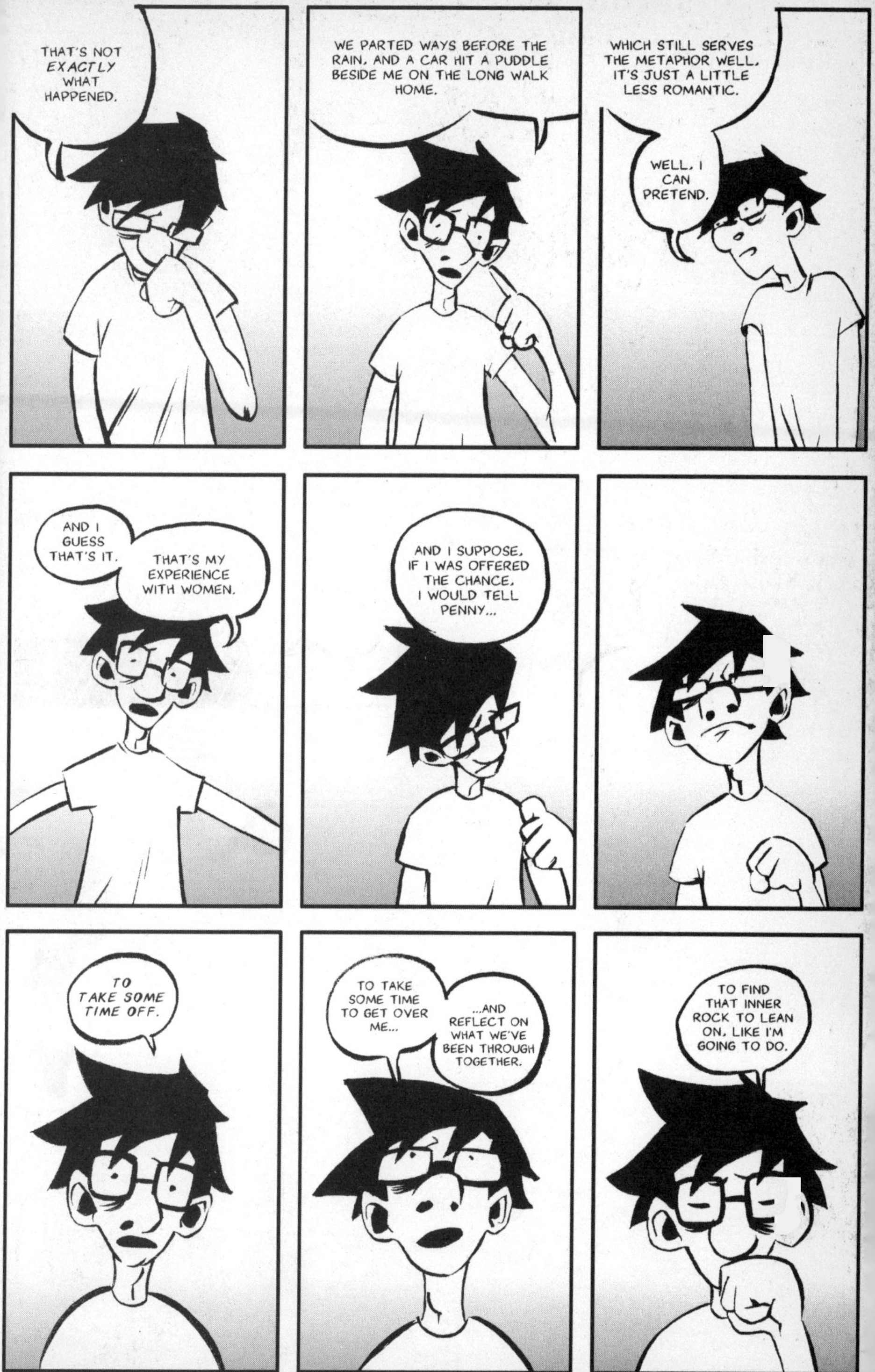
THAT'S NOT *EXACTLY* WHAT HAPPENED.
WE PARTED WAYS BEFORE THE RAIN, AND A CAR HIT A PUDDLE BESIDE ME ON THE LONG WALK HOME.
WHICH STILL SERVES THE METAPHOR WELL. IT'S JUST A LITTLE LESS ROMANTIC.
WELL, I CAN PRETEND.
AND I GUESS THAT'S IT.
THAT'S MY EXPERIENCE WITH WOMEN.
AND I SUPPOSE, IF I WAS OFFERED THE CHANCE, I WOULD TELL PENNY...
TO TAKE SOME TIME OFF.
TO TAKE SOME TIME TO GET OVER ME...
...AND REFLECT ON WHAT WE'VE BEEN THROUGH TOGETHER.
TO FIND THAT INNER ROCK TO LEAN ON, LIKE I'M GOING TO DO.

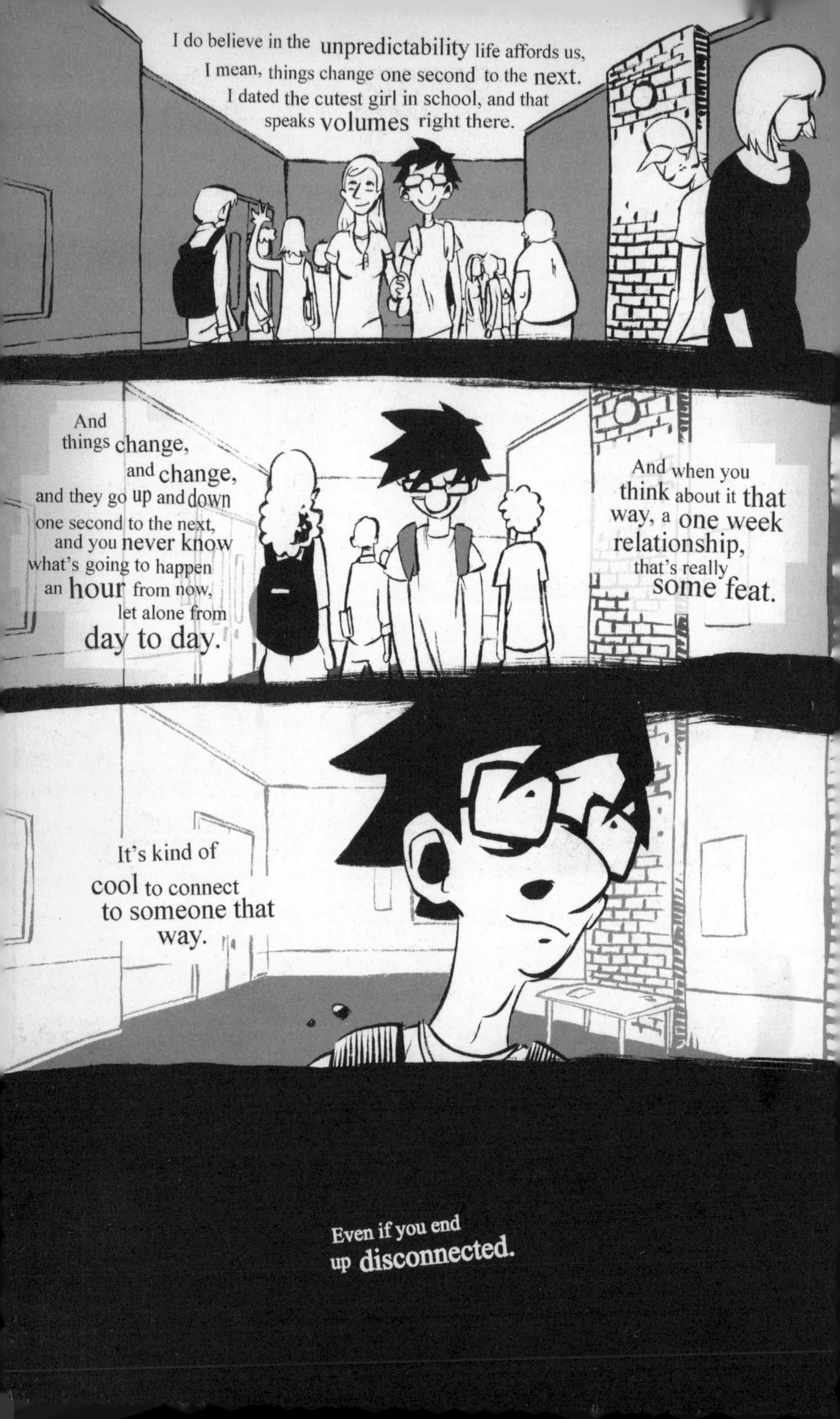
I do believe in the unpredictability life affords us, I mean, things change one second to the next. I dated the cutest girl in school, and that speaks volumes right there.
And things change, and change, and they go up and down one second to the next, and you never know what's going to happen an hour from now, let alone from day to day.
And when you think about it that way, a one week relationship, that's really some feat.
It's kind of cool to connect to someone that way.
Even if you end up disconnected.

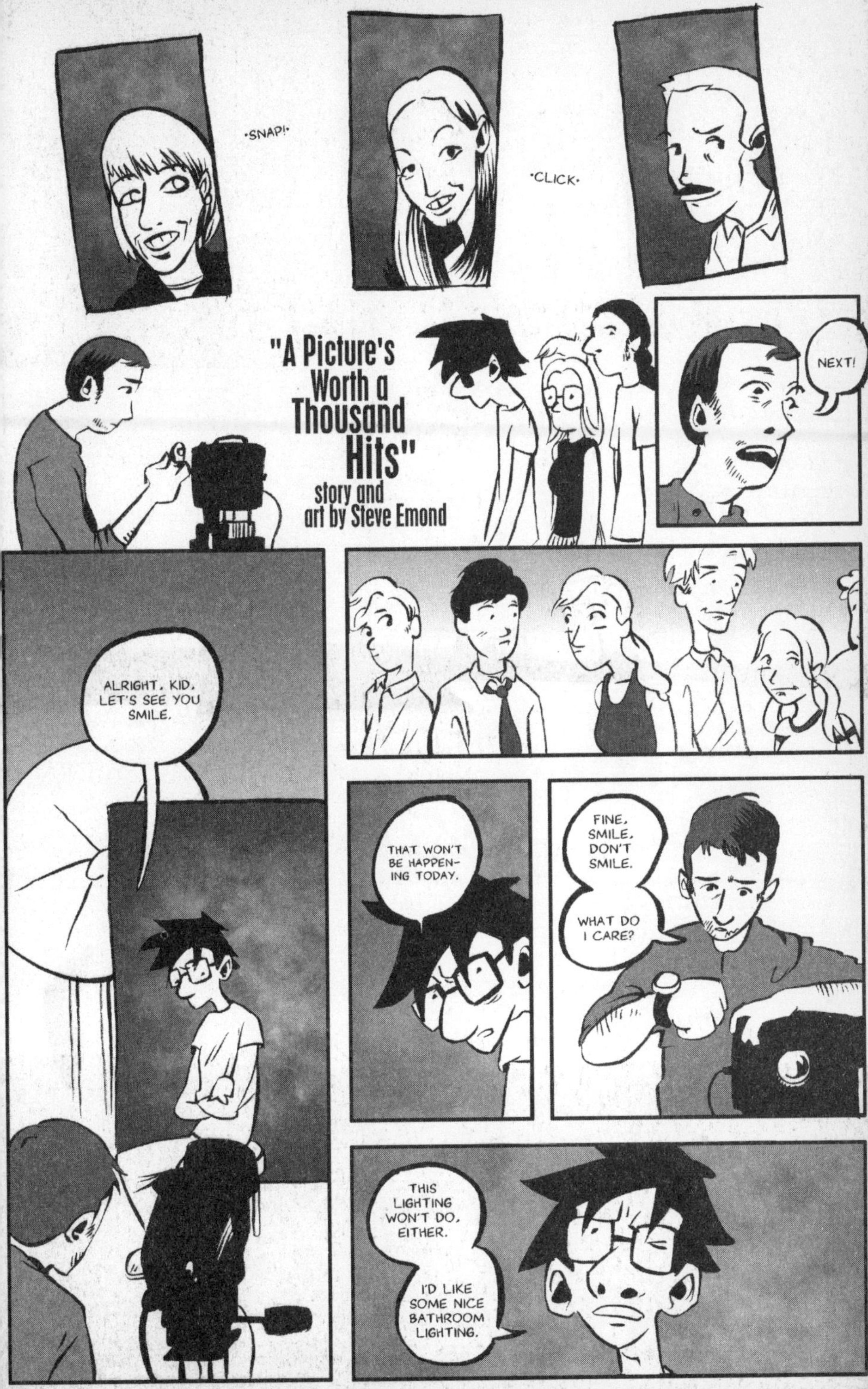
•SNAP!•
•CLICK•
"A Picture's Worth a Thousand Hits"
story and art by Steve Emond
NEXT!
ALRIGHT, KID, LET'S SEE YOU SMILE.
THAT WON'T BE HAPPEN-ING TODAY.
FINE, SMILE, DON'T SMILE.
WHAT DO I CARE?
THIS LIGHTING WON'T DO, EITHER.
I'D LIKE SOME NICE BATHROOM LIGHTING.

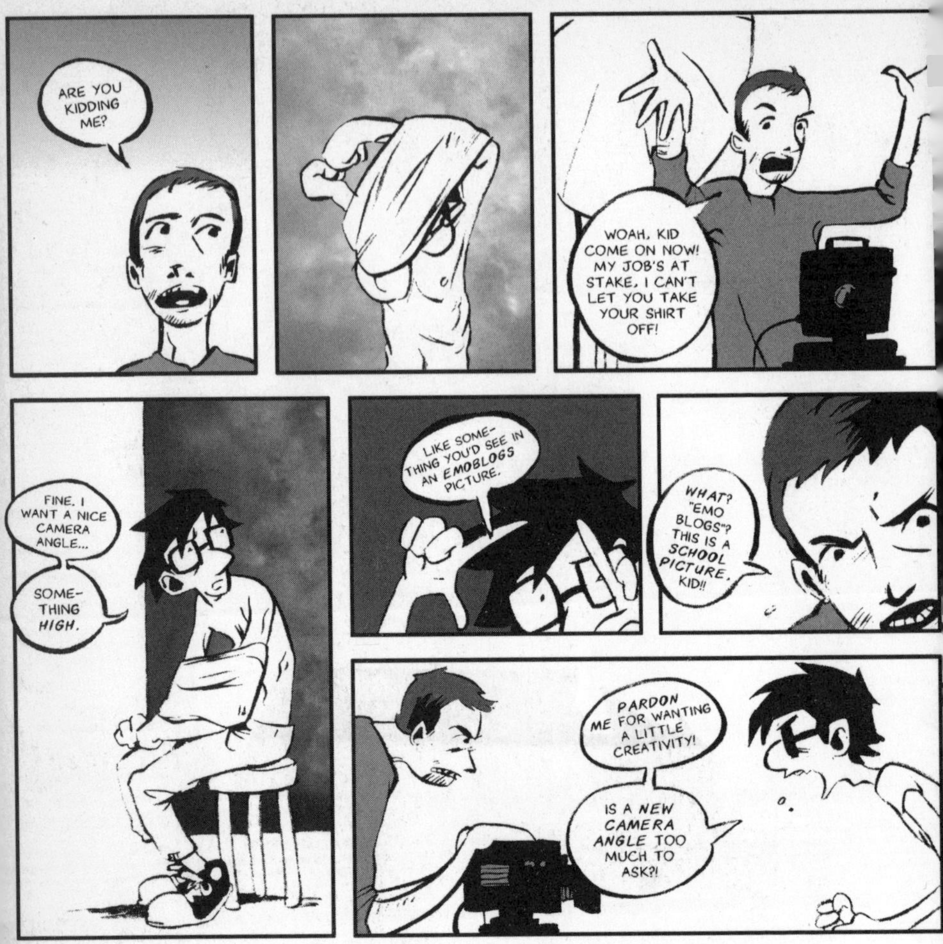
ARE YOU KIDDING ME?
WOAH, KID COME ON NOW! MY JOB'S AT STAKE, I CAN'T LET YOU TAKE YOUR SHIRT OFF!
FINE. I WANT A NICE CAMERA ANGLE...
SOMETHING HIGH.
LIKE SOMETHING YOU'D SEE IN AN EMOBLOGS PICTURE.
WHAT? "EMO BLOGS"? THIS IS A SCHOOL PICTURE, KID!!
PARDON ME FOR WANTING A LITTLE CREATIVITY!
IS A NEW CAMERA ANGLE TOO MUCH TO ASK?!

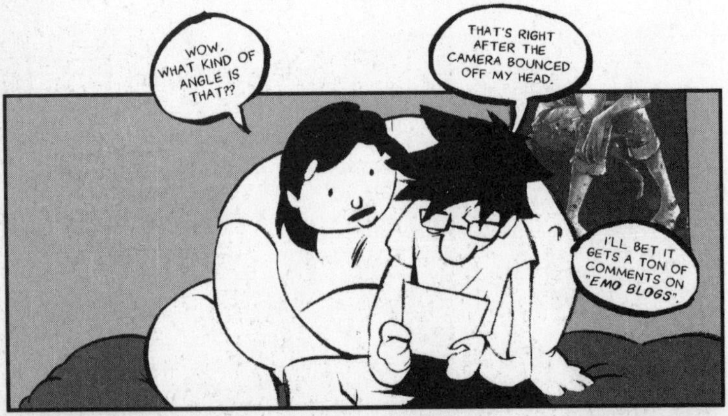
WOW, WHAT KIND OF ANGLE IS THAT??
THAT'S RIGHT AFTER THE CAMERA BOUNCED OFF MY HEAD.
I'LL BET IT GETS A TON OF COMMENTS ON "EMO BLOGS".

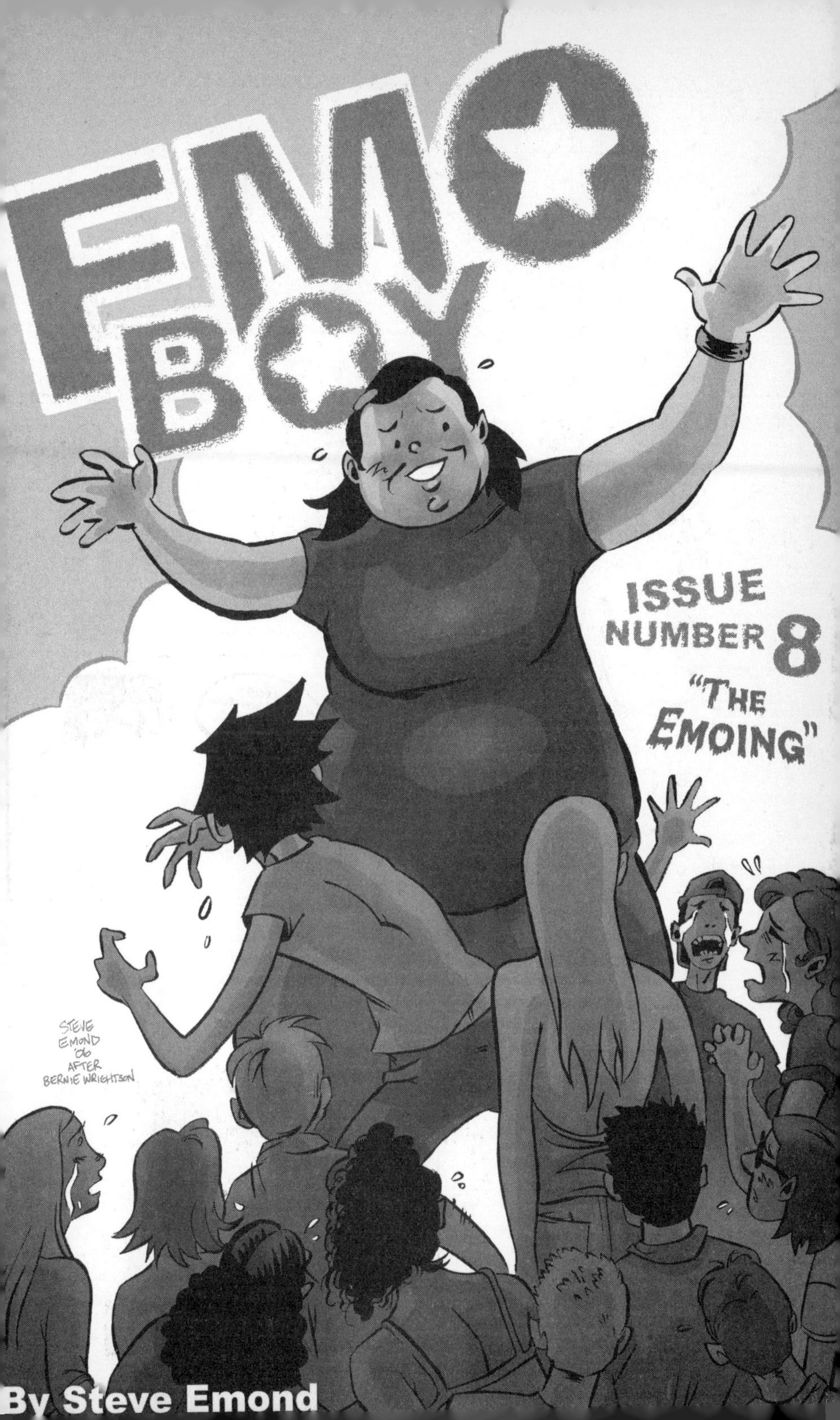
EMO BOY
ISSUE NUMBER 8
"THE EMOING"
STEVE EMOND '06 AFTER BERNIE WRIGHTSON
By Steve Emond

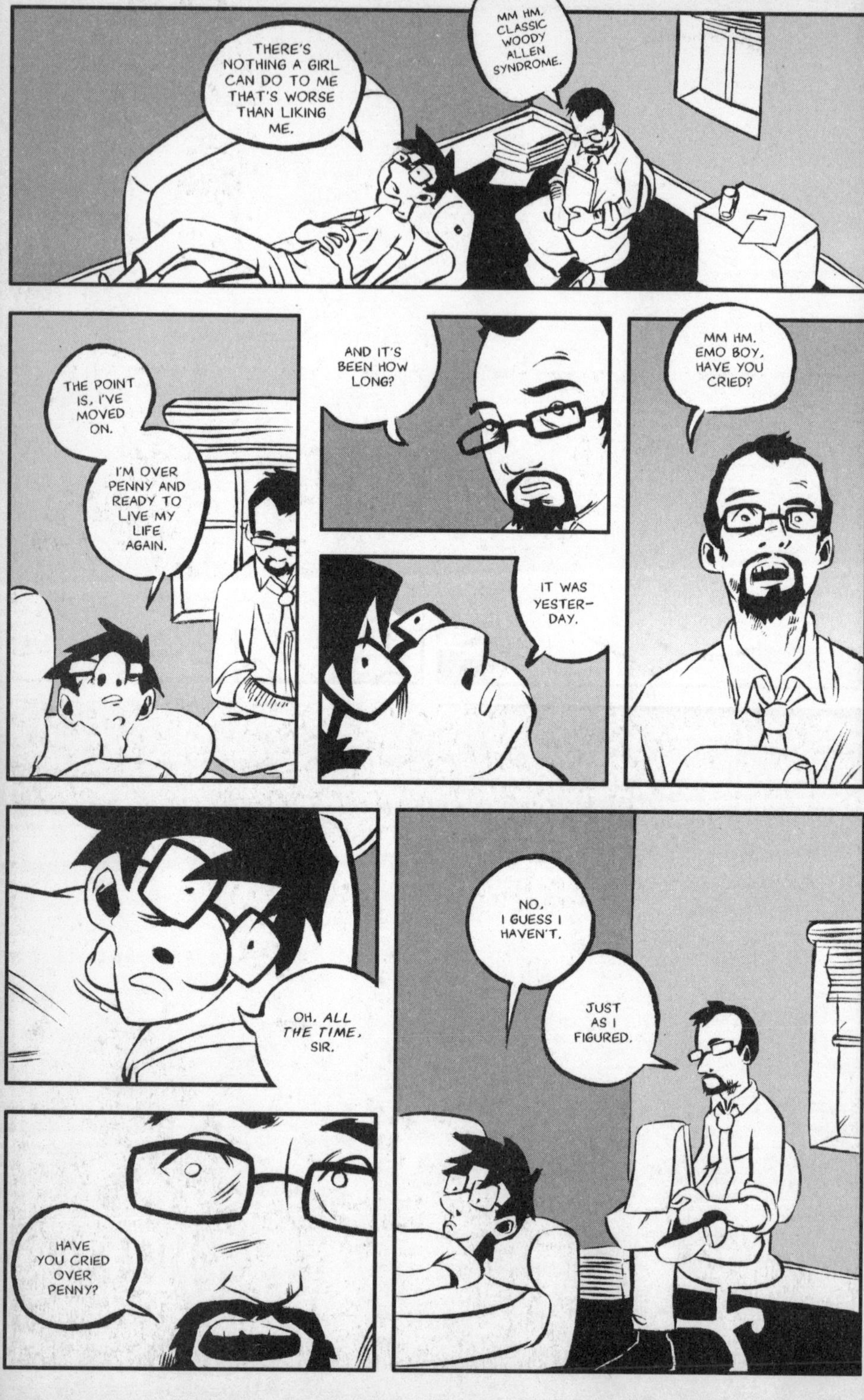
THERE'S NOTHING A GIRL CAN DO TO ME THAT'S WORSE THAN LIKING ME.
MM HM. CLASSIC WOODY ALLEN SYNDROME.
THE POINT IS, I'VE MOVED ON.
I'M OVER PENNY AND READY TO LIVE MY LIFE AGAIN.
AND IT'S BEEN HOW LONG?
IT WAS YESTER-DAY.
MM HM. EMO BOY, HAVE YOU CRIED?
OH, *ALL THE TIME*, SIR.
HAVE YOU CRIED OVER PENNY?
NO, I GUESS I HAVEN'T.
JUST AS I FIGURED.

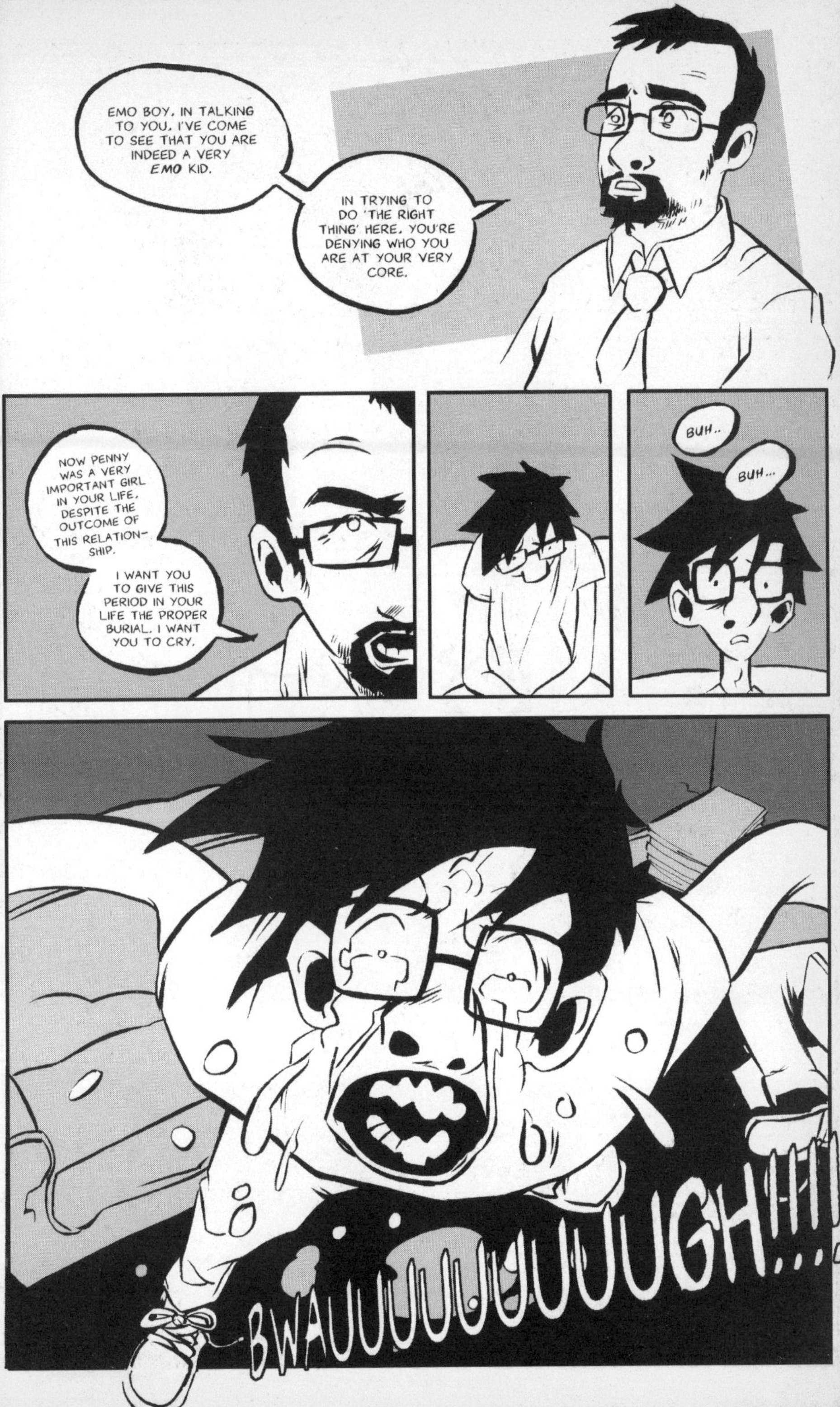
EMO BOY, IN TALKING TO YOU, I'VE COME TO SEE THAT YOU ARE INDEED A VERY *EMO* KID.
IN TRYING TO DO 'THE RIGHT THING' HERE, YOU'RE DENYING WHO YOU ARE AT YOUR VERY CORE.
NOW PENNY WAS A VERY IMPORTANT GIRL IN YOUR LIFE, DESPITE THE OUTCOME OF THIS RELATION-SHIP.
I WANT YOU TO GIVE THIS PERIOD IN YOUR LIFE THE PROPER BURIAL. I WANT YOU TO CRY.
BUH..
BUH...
BWAUUUUUUUUUUUGH!!!!

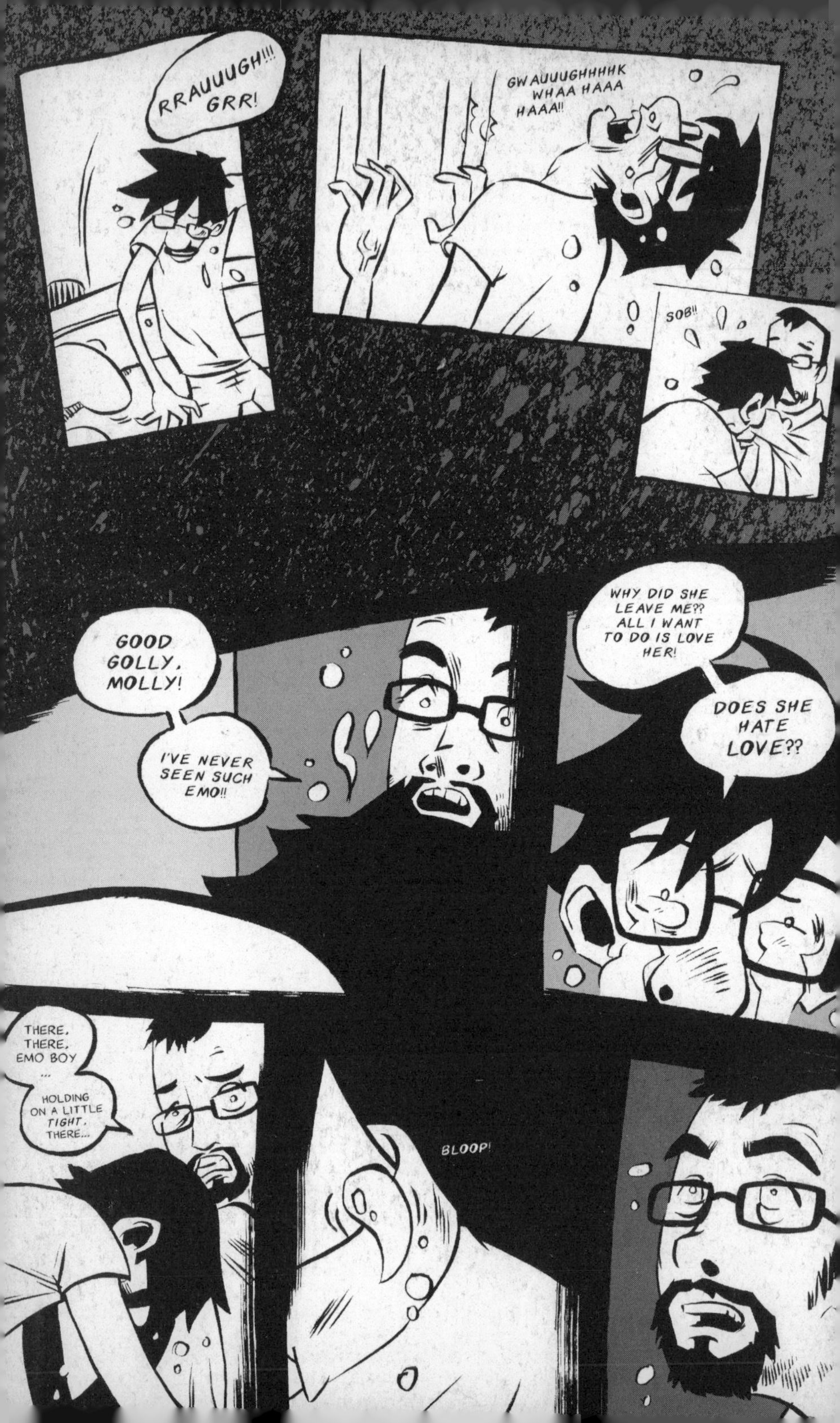
RRAUUUGH!!!
GRR!
GWAUUUGHHHHK
WHAA HAAA
HAAA!!
SOB!!
GOOD GOLLY, MOLLY!
I'VE NEVER SEEN SUCH EMO!!
WHY DID SHE LEAVE ME?? ALL I WANT TO DO IS LOVE HER!
DOES SHE HATE LOVE??
THERE, THERE, EMO BOY ...
HOLDING ON A LITTLE *TIGHT*, THERE...
BLOOP!

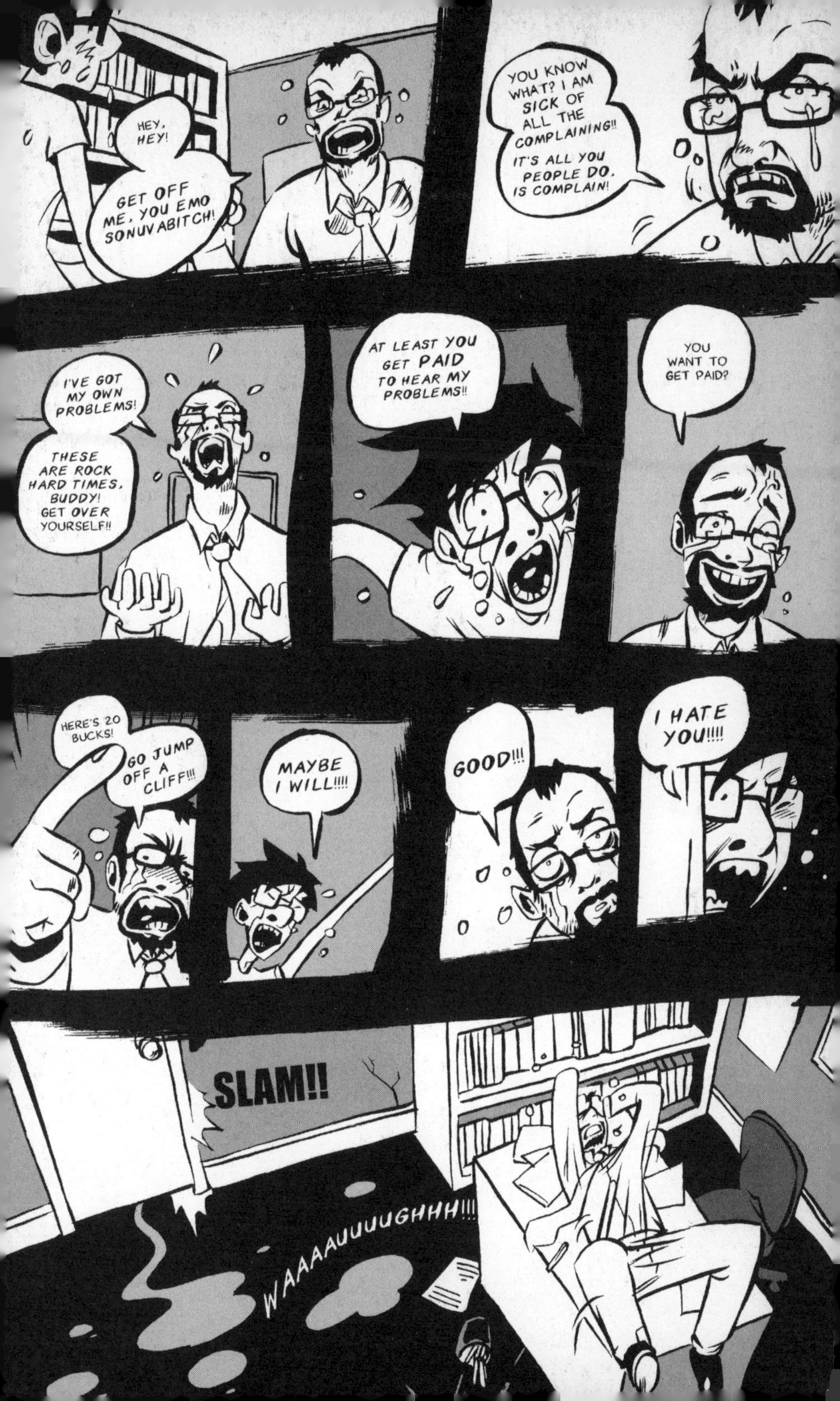

HEY, HEY!
GET OFF ME, YOU EMO SONUVABITCH!
YOU KNOW WHAT? I AM SICK OF ALL THE COMPLAINING!!
IT'S ALL YOU PEOPLE DO. IS COMPLAIN!
I'VE GOT MY OWN PROBLEMS!
THESE ARE ROCK HARD TIMES, BUDDY! GET OVER YOURSELF!!
AT LEAST YOU GET PAID TO HEAR MY PROBLEMS!!
YOU WANT TO GET PAID?
HERE'S 20 BUCKS!
GO JUMP OFF A CLIFF!!!
MAYBE I WILL!!!!
GOOD!!!
I HATE YOU!!!!
SLAM!!
WAAAAUUUUGHHH!!!!

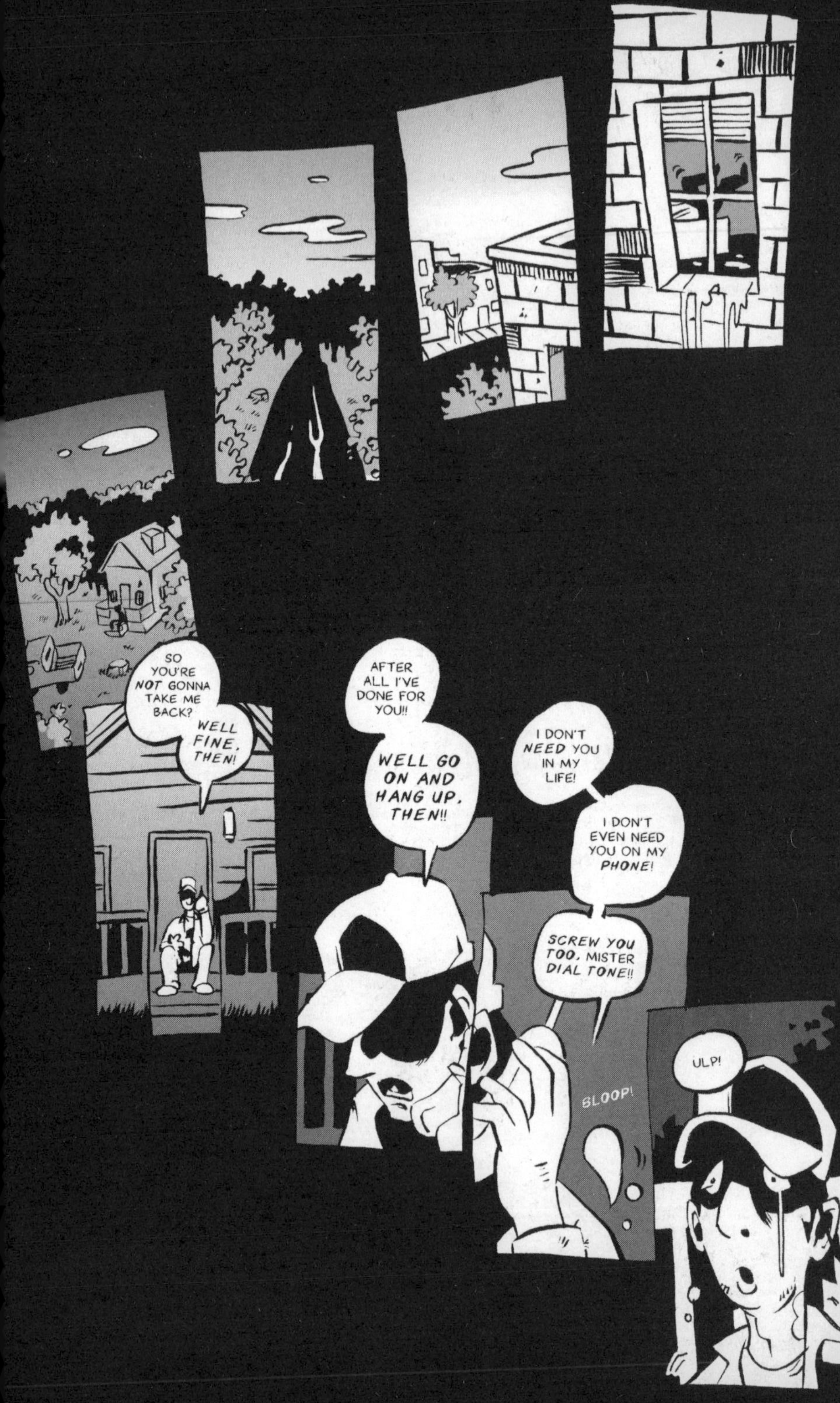
SO YOU'RE NOT GONNA TAKE ME BACK?
WELL FINE, THEN!
AFTER ALL I'VE DONE FOR YOU!!
WELL GO ON AND HANG UP, THEN!!
I DON'T NEED YOU IN MY LIFE!
I DON'T EVEN NEED YOU ON MY PHONE!
SCREW YOU TOO, MISTER DIAL TONE!!
BLOOP!
ULP!

Emo Boy #8

# "The Emoing"

Story and Art By Steve Emond

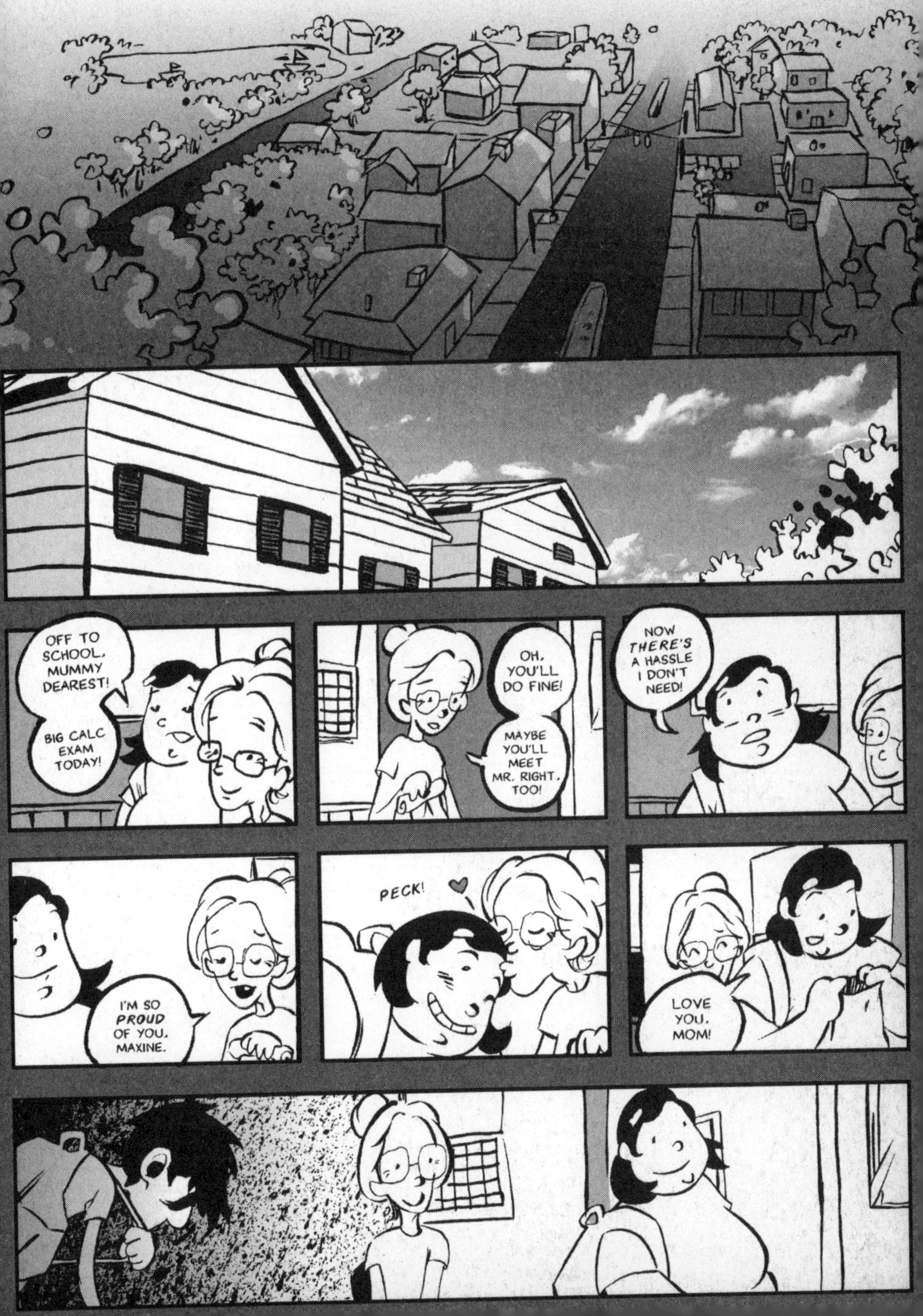
OFF TO SCHOOL, MUMMY DEAREST!
BIG CALC EXAM TODAY!
OH, YOU'LL DO FINE!
MAYBE YOU'LL MEET MR. RIGHT, TOO!
NOW *THERE'S* A HASSLE I DON'T NEED!
I'M SO *PROUD* OF YOU, MAXINE.
PECK!
LOVE YOU, MOM!

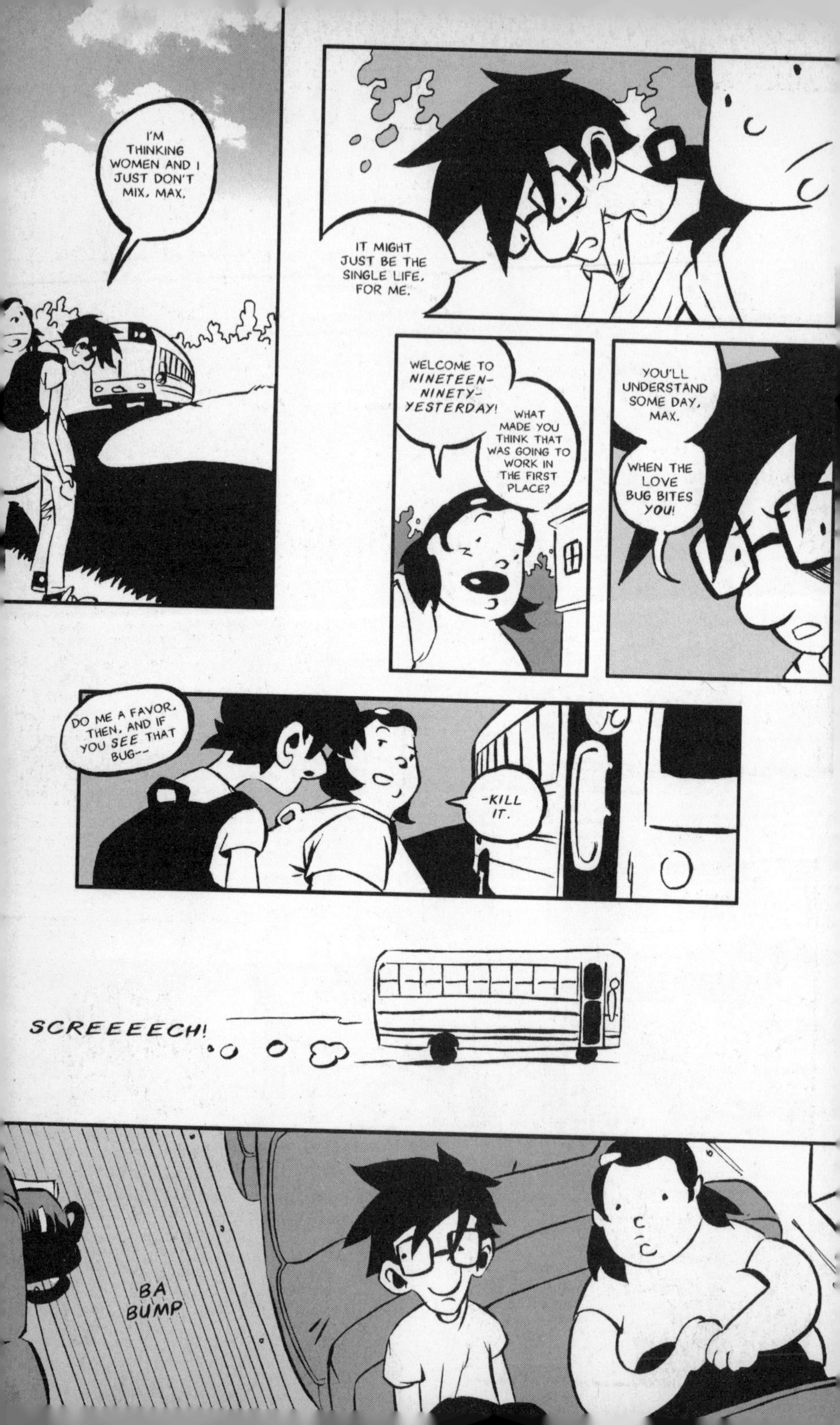

I'M THINKING WOMEN AND I JUST DON'T MIX, MAX.
IT MIGHT JUST BE THE SINGLE LIFE, FOR ME.
WELCOME TO NINETEEN-NINETY-YESTERDAY!
WHAT MADE YOU THINK THAT WAS GOING TO WORK IN THE FIRST PLACE?
YOU'LL UNDERSTAND SOME DAY, MAX.
WHEN THE LOVE BUG BITES YOU!
DO ME A FAVOR, THEN, AND IF YOU SEE THAT BUG--
-KILL IT.
SCREEEECH!
BA BUMP

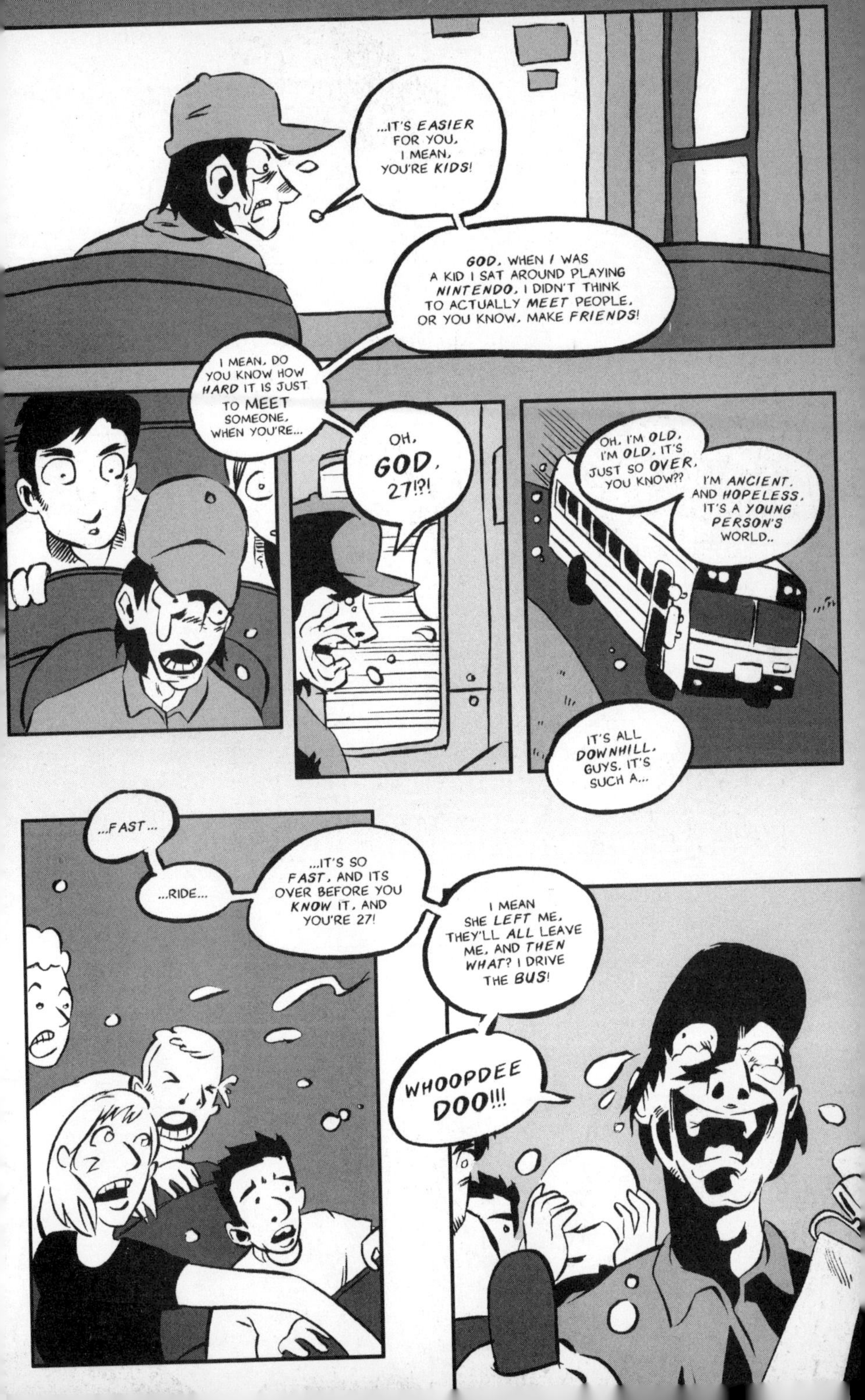
...IT'S EASIER FOR YOU, I MEAN, YOU'RE KIDS!
GOD. WHEN I WAS A KID I SAT AROUND PLAYING NINTENDO. I DIDN'T THINK TO ACTUALLY MEET PEOPLE, OR YOU KNOW, MAKE FRIENDS!
I MEAN, DO YOU KNOW HOW HARD IT IS JUST TO MEET SOMEONE, WHEN YOU'RE...
OH, GOD, 27!?!
OH, I'M OLD, I'M OLD, IT'S JUST SO OVER, YOU KNOW??
I'M ANCIENT, AND HOPELESS, IT'S A YOUNG PERSON'S WORLD..
IT'S ALL DOWNHILL, GUYS. IT'S SUCH A...
...FAST...
...RIDE...
...IT'S SO FAST, AND ITS OVER BEFORE YOU KNOW IT, AND YOU'RE 27!
I MEAN SHE LEFT ME, THEY'LL ALL LEAVE ME, AND THEN WHAT? I DRIVE THE BUS!
WHOOPDEE DOO!!!

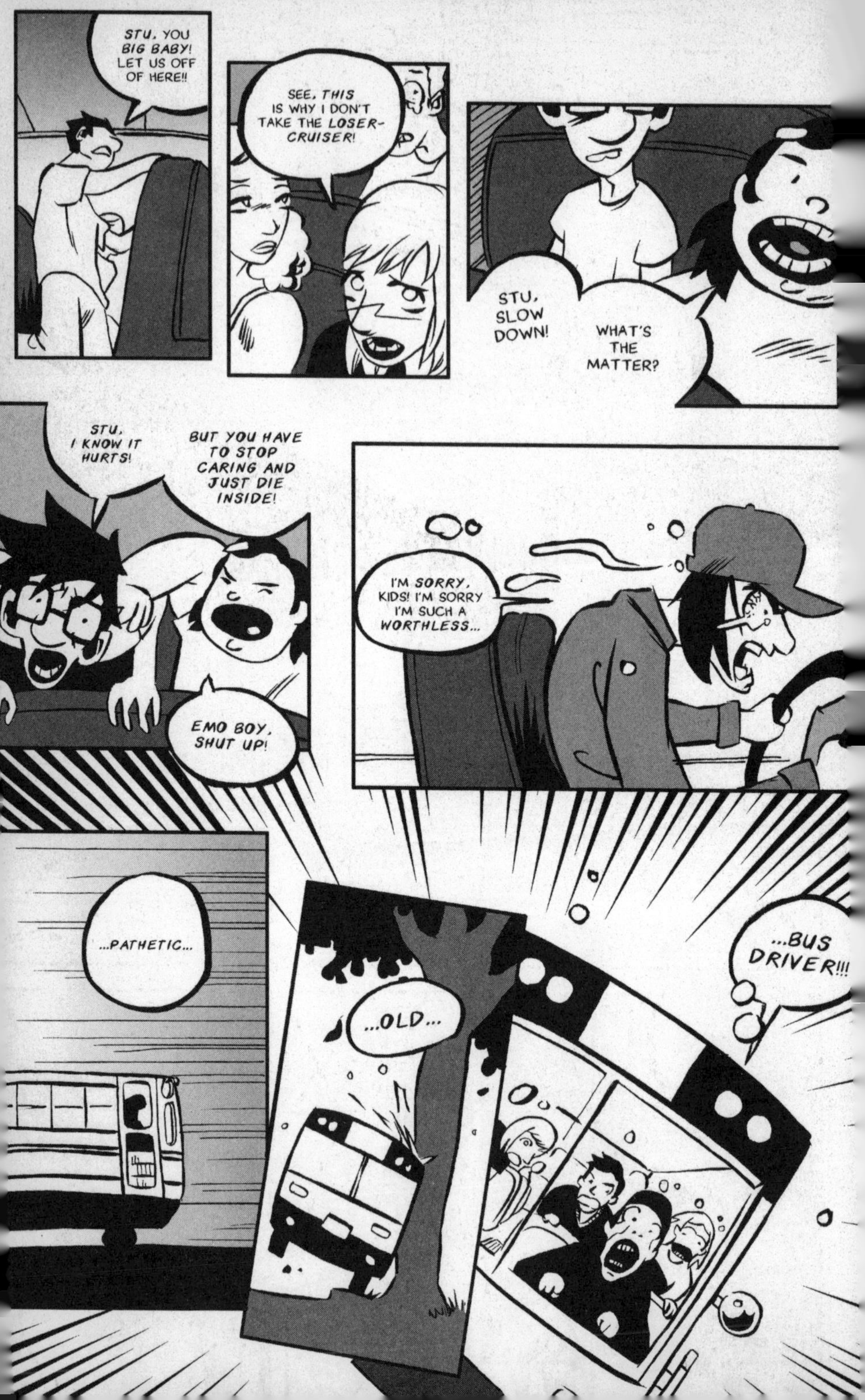
STU, YOU BIG BABY! LET US OFF OF HERE!!
SEE, THIS IS WHY I DON'T TAKE THE LOSER-CRUISER!
STU, SLOW DOWN!
WHAT'S THE MATTER?
STU, I KNOW IT HURTS!
BUT YOU HAVE TO STOP CARING AND JUST DIE INSIDE!
EMO BOY, SHUT UP!
I'M SORRY, KIDS! I'M SORRY I'M SUCH A WORTHLESS...
...PATHETIC...
...OLD...
...BUS DRIVER!!!

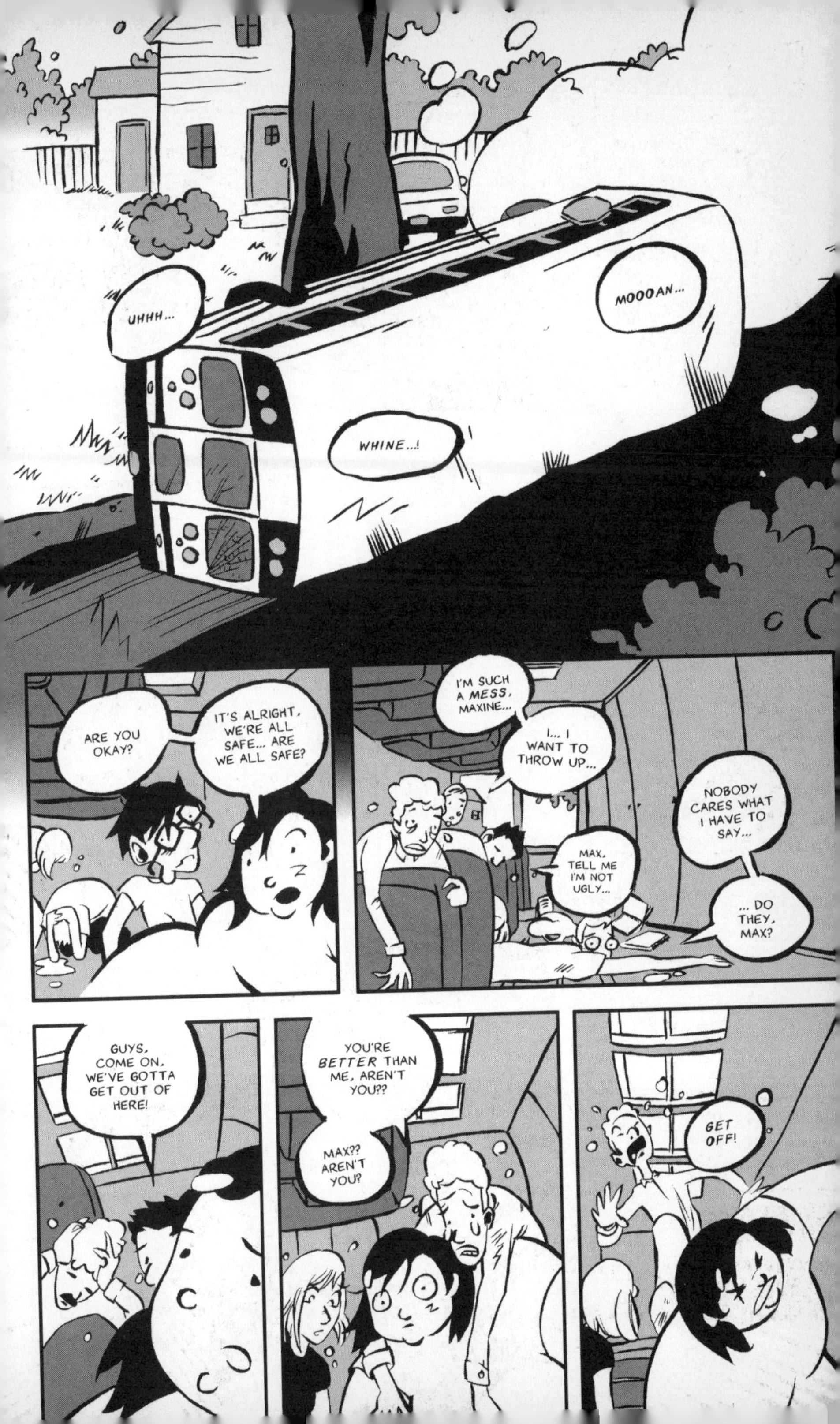
UHHH...
MOOOAN...
WHINE...!
ARE YOU OKAY?
IT'S ALRIGHT, WE'RE ALL SAFE... ARE WE ALL SAFE?
I'M SUCH A MESS, MAXINE...
I... I WANT TO THROW UP...
NOBODY CARES WHAT I HAVE TO SAY...
MAX, TELL ME I'M NOT UGLY...
... DO THEY, MAX?
GUYS, COME ON, WE'VE GOTTA GET OUT OF HERE!
YOU'RE BETTER THAN ME, AREN'T YOU??
MAX?? AREN'T YOU?
GET OFF!

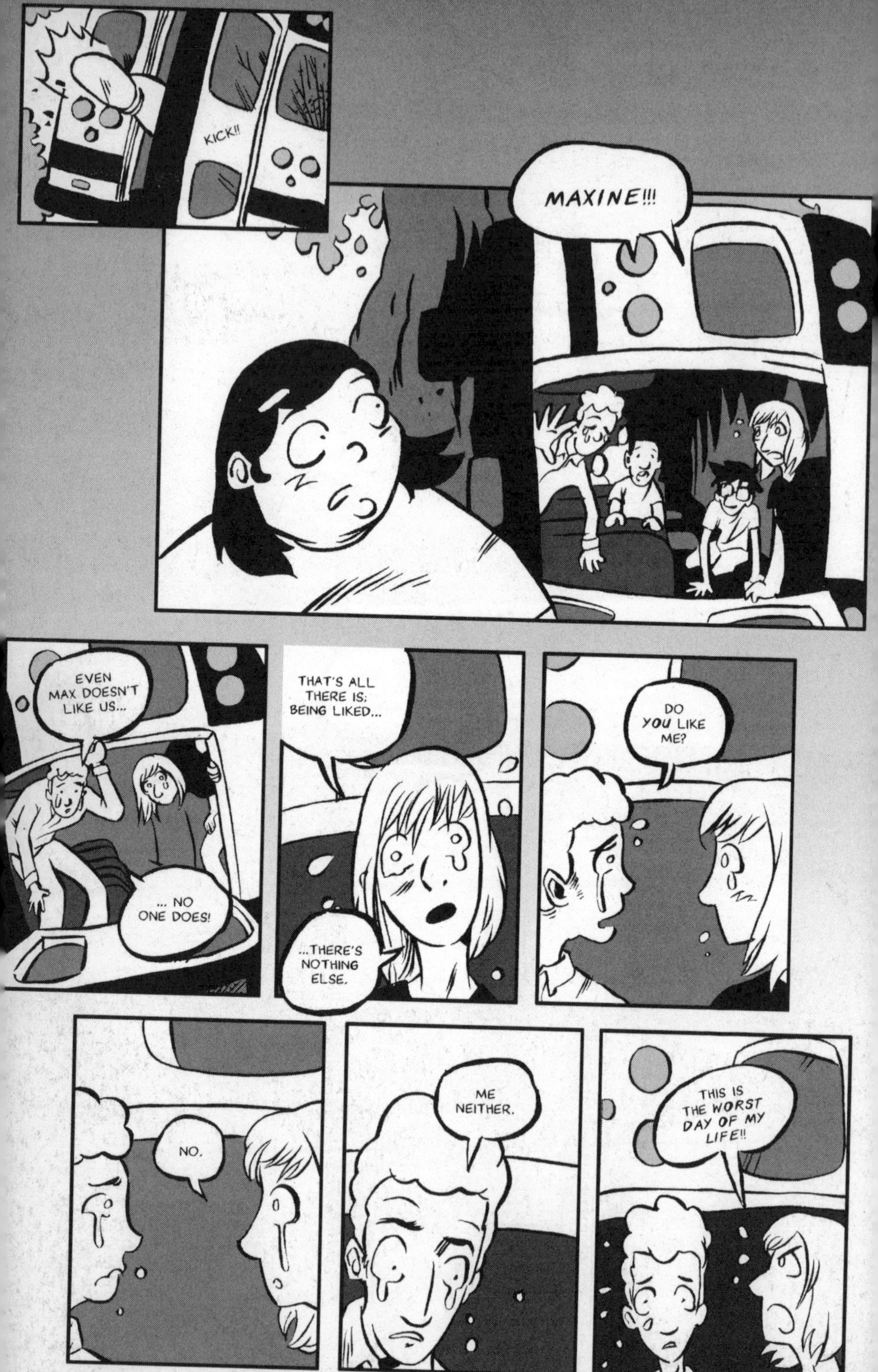
KICK!!
MAXINE!!!
EVEN MAX DOESN'T LIKE US...
... NO ONE DOES!
THAT'S ALL THERE IS; BEING LIKED...
...THERE'S NOTHING ELSE.
DO YOU LIKE ME?
NO.
ME NEITHER.
THIS IS THE WORST DAY OF MY LIFE!!

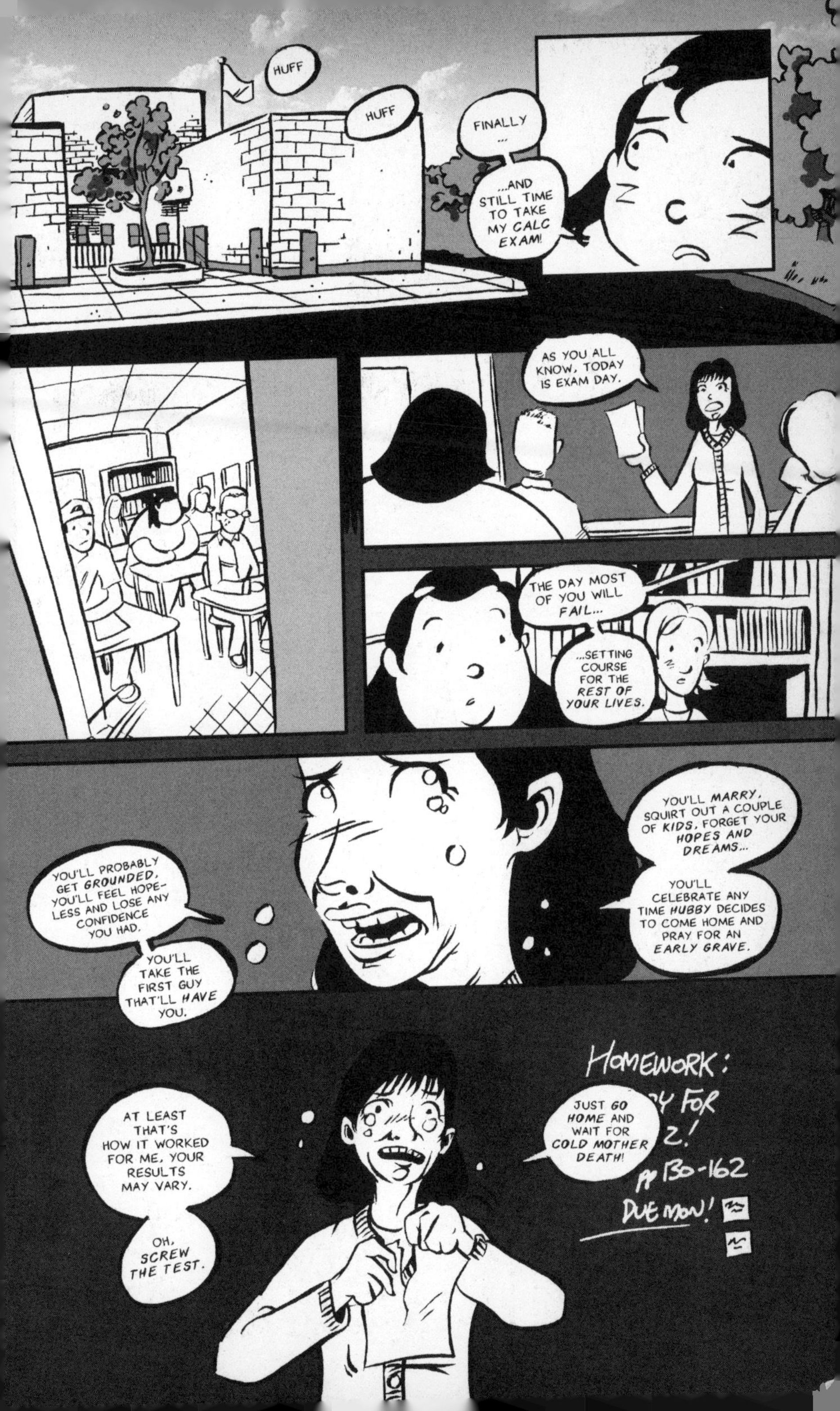
HUFF
HUFF
FINALLY ...
...AND STILL TIME TO TAKE MY CALC EXAM!
AS YOU ALL KNOW, TODAY IS EXAM DAY.
THE DAY MOST OF YOU WILL FAIL...
...SETTING COURSE FOR THE REST OF YOUR LIVES.
YOU'LL MARRY, SQUIRT OUT A COUPLE OF KIDS, FORGET YOUR HOPES AND DREAMS...
YOU'LL CELEBRATE ANY TIME HUBBY DECIDES TO COME HOME AND PRAY FOR AN EARLY GRAVE.
YOU'LL PROBABLY GET GROUNDED, YOU'LL FEEL HOPE-LESS AND LOSE ANY CONFIDENCE YOU HAD.
YOU'LL TAKE THE FIRST GUY THAT'LL HAVE YOU.
HOMEWORK:
pp 130-162
DUE MON!
JUST GO HOME AND WAIT FOR COLD MOTHER DEATH!
AT LEAST THAT'S HOW IT WORKED FOR ME. YOUR RESULTS MAY VARY.
OH, SCREW THE TEST.

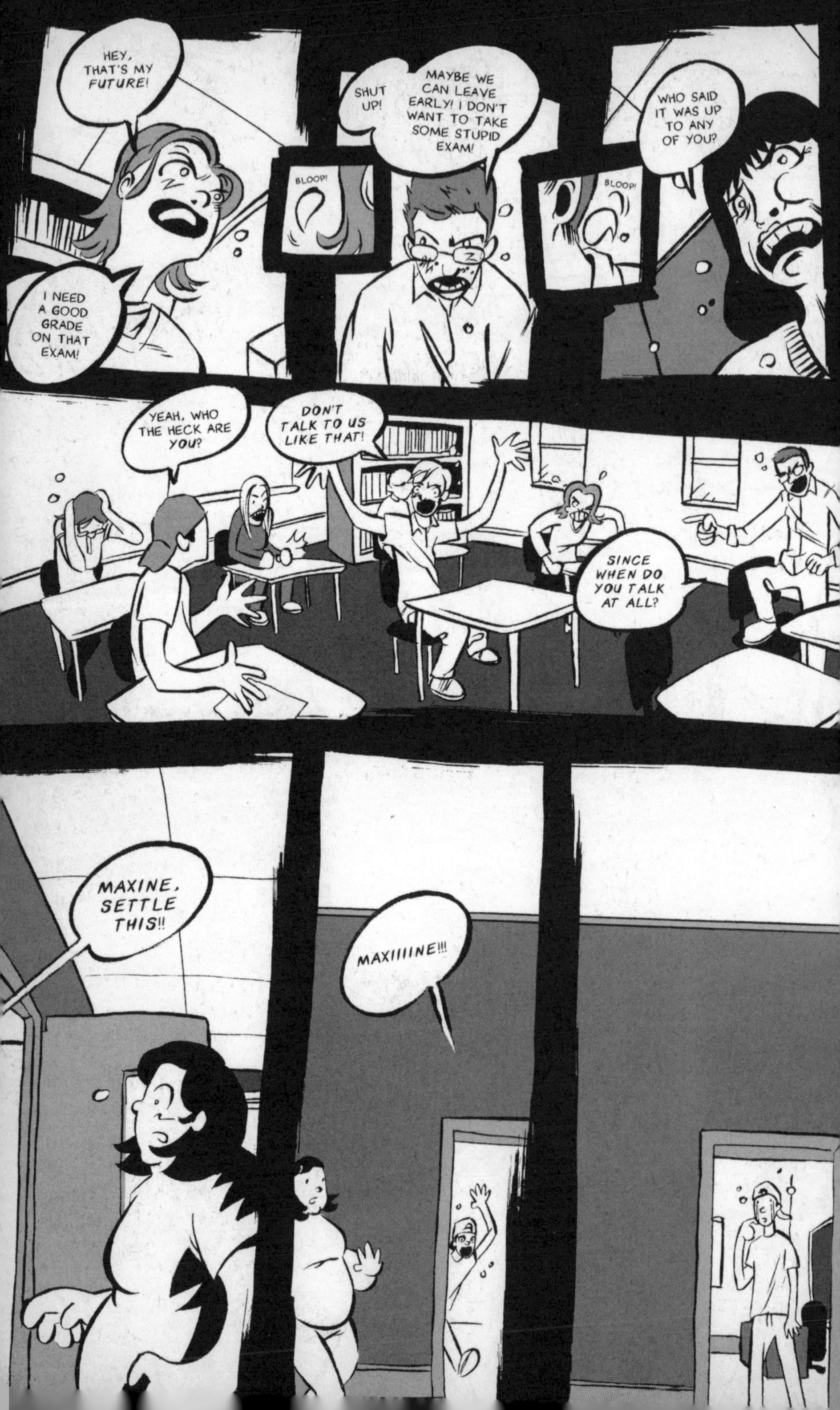
HEY, THAT'S MY FUTURE!
I NEED A GOOD GRADE ON THAT EXAM!
SHUT UP!
MAYBE WE CAN LEAVE EARLY! I DON'T WANT TO TAKE SOME STUPID EXAM!
BLOOP!
BLOOP!
WHO SAID IT WAS UP TO ANY OF YOU?
YEAH, WHO THE HECK ARE YOU?
DON'T TALK TO US LIKE THAT!
SINCE WHEN DO YOU TALK AT ALL?
MAXINE, SETTLE THIS!!
MAXIIIINE!!!

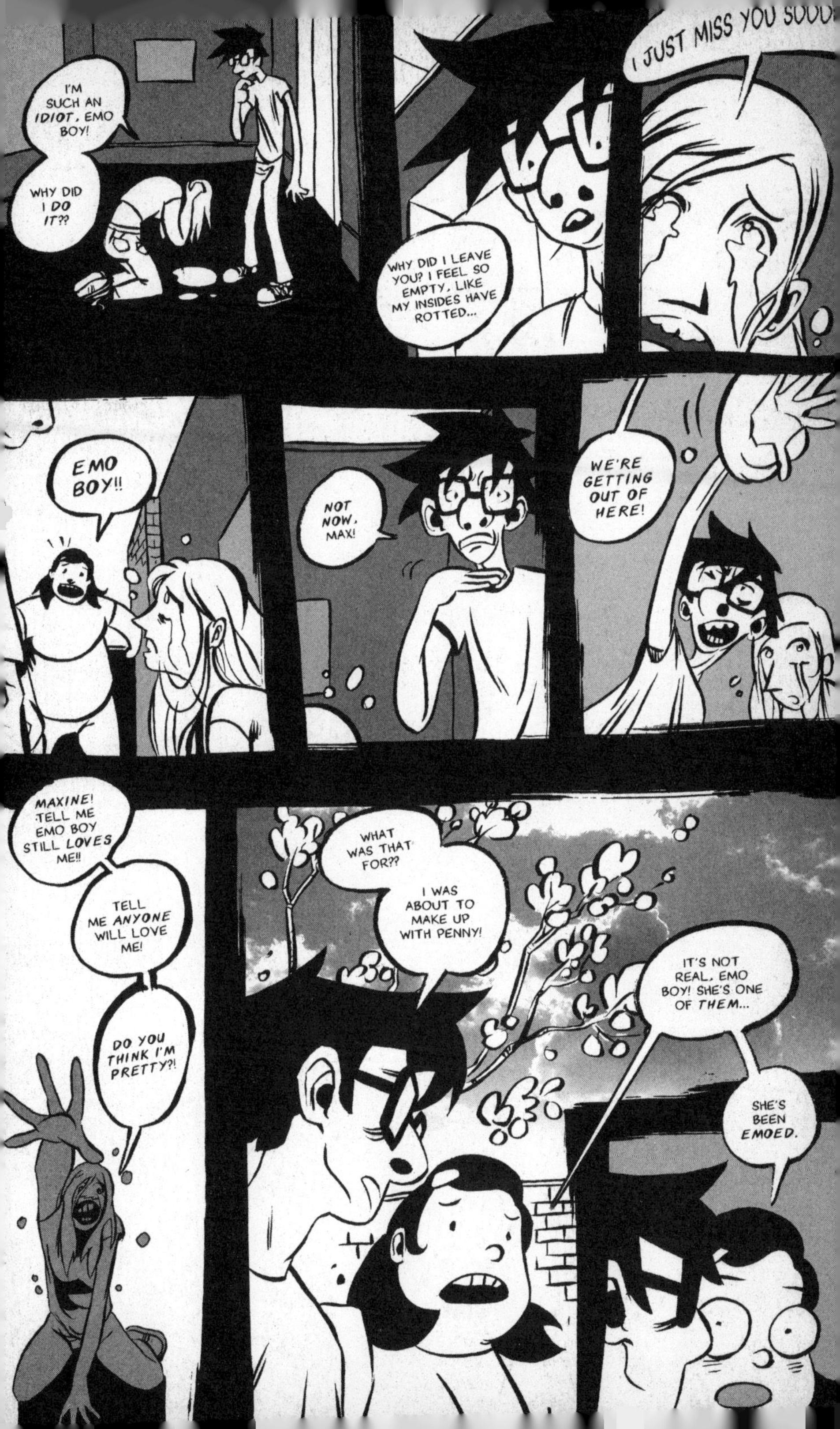

I'M SUCH AN IDIOT, EMO BOY!
WHY DID I DO IT??
WHY DID I LEAVE YOU? I FEEL SO EMPTY, LIKE MY INSIDES HAVE ROTTED...
I JUST MISS YOU SOOO
EMO BOY!!
NOT NOW, MAX!
WE'RE GETTING OUT OF HERE!
MAXINE! TELL ME EMO BOY STILL LOVES ME!!
TELL ME ANYONE WILL LOVE ME!
DO YOU THINK I'M PRETTY?!
WHAT WAS THAT FOR??
I WAS ABOUT TO MAKE UP WITH PENNY!
IT'S NOT REAL, EMO BOY! SHE'S ONE OF THEM...
SHE'S BEEN EMOED.

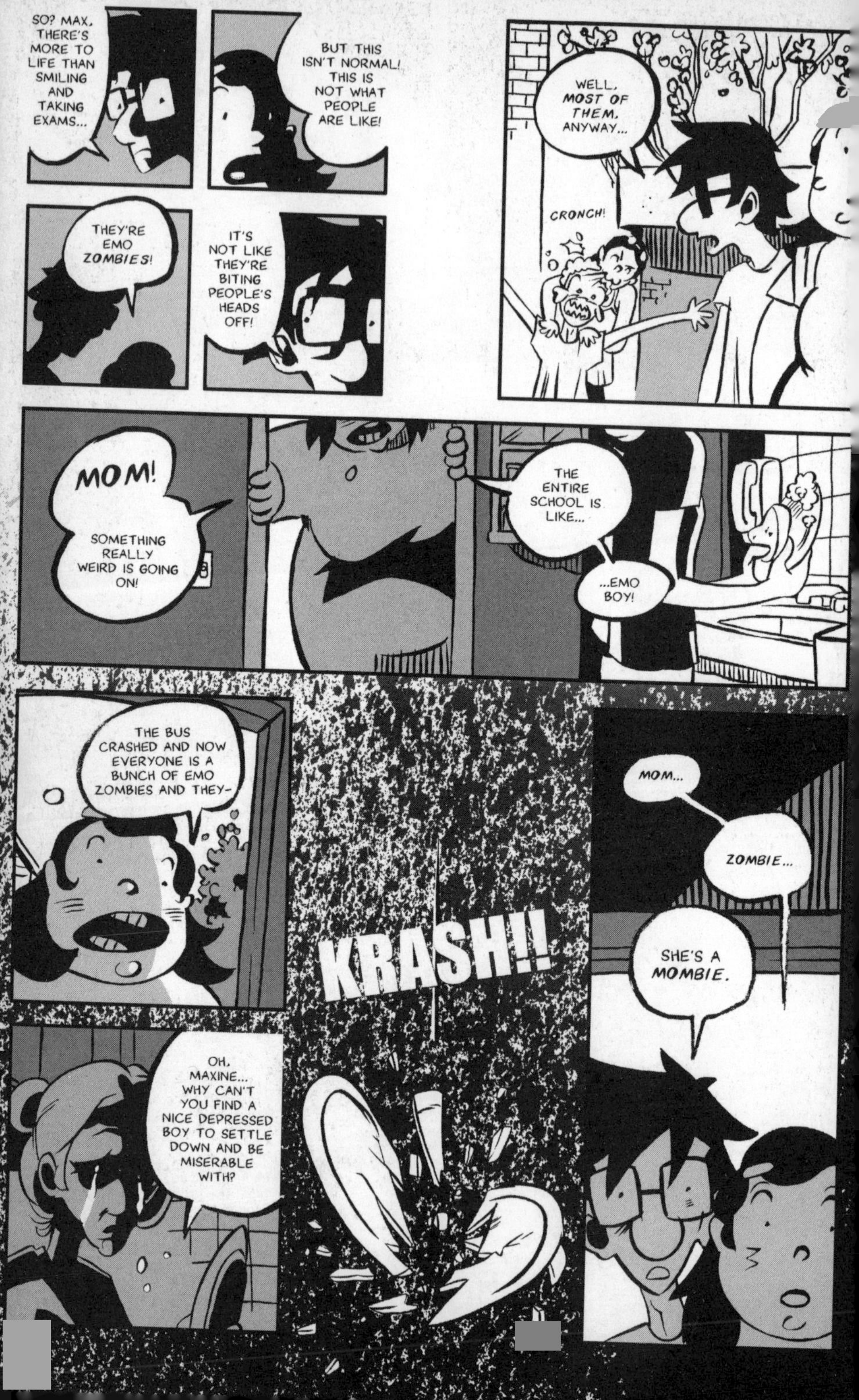
SO? MAX, THERE'S MORE TO LIFE THAN SMILING AND TAKING EXAMS...
BUT THIS ISN'T NORMAL! THIS IS NOT WHAT PEOPLE ARE LIKE!
THEY'RE EMO ZOMBIES!
IT'S NOT LIKE THEY'RE BITING PEOPLE'S HEADS OFF!
WELL, MOST OF THEM, ANYWAY...
CRONCH!
MOM!
SOMETHING REALLY WEIRD IS GOING ON!
THE ENTIRE SCHOOL IS LIKE...
...EMO BOY!
THE BUS CRASHED AND NOW EVERYONE IS A BUNCH OF EMO ZOMBIES AND THEY-
OH, MAXINE... WHY CAN'T YOU FIND A NICE DEPRESSED BOY TO SETTLE DOWN AND BE MISERABLE WITH?
KRASH!!
MOM...
ZOMBIE...
SHE'S A MOMBIE.

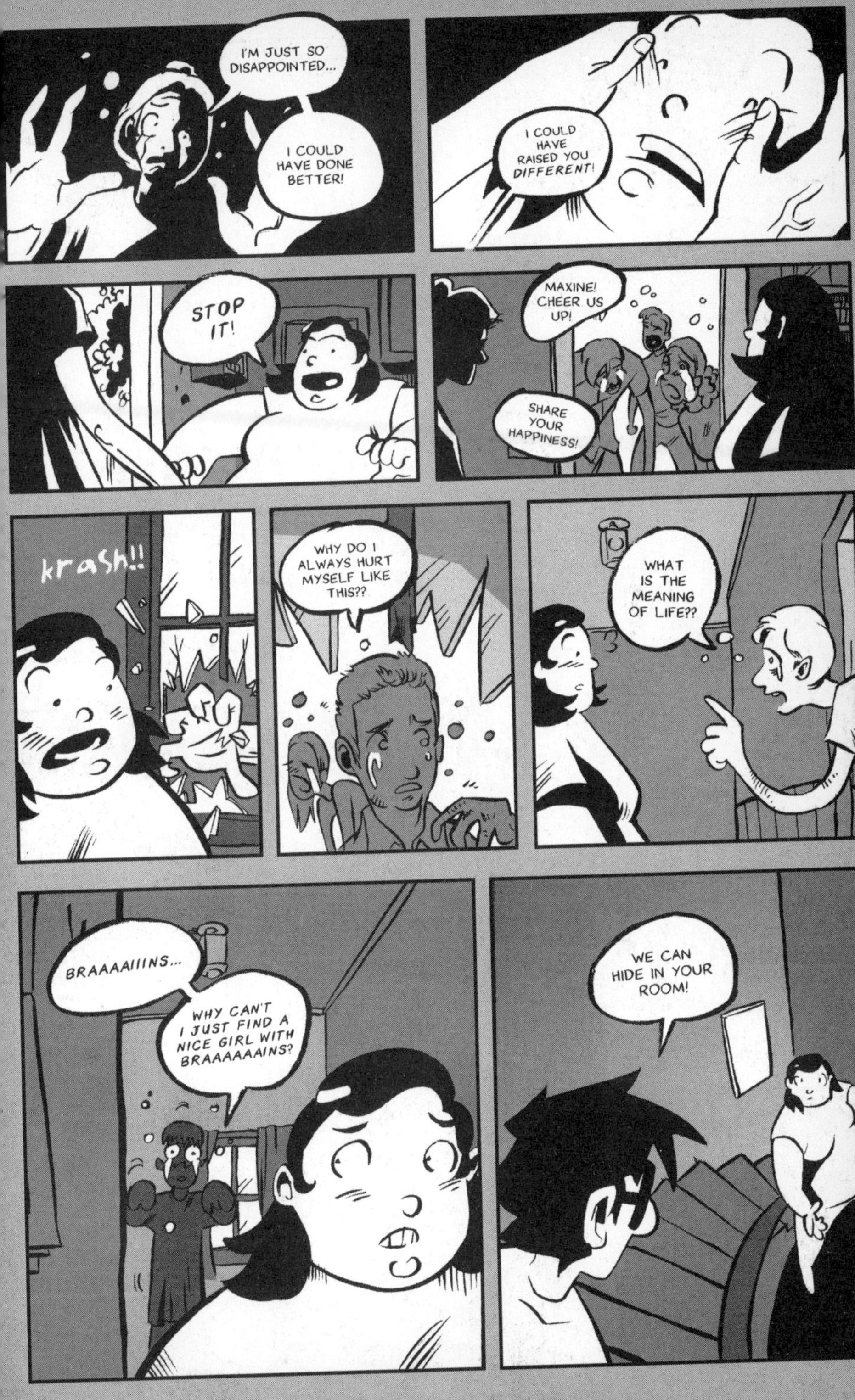

I'M JUST SO DISAPPOINTED...
I COULD HAVE DONE BETTER!
I COULD HAVE RAISED YOU DIFFERENT!
STOP IT!
MAXINE! CHEER US UP!
SHARE YOUR HAPPINESS!
krash!!
WHY DO I ALWAYS HURT MYSELF LIKE THIS??
WHAT IS THE MEANING OF LIFE??
BRAAAAIIINS...
WHY CAN'T I JUST FIND A NICE GIRL WITH BRAAAAAAINS?
WE CAN HIDE IN YOUR ROOM!

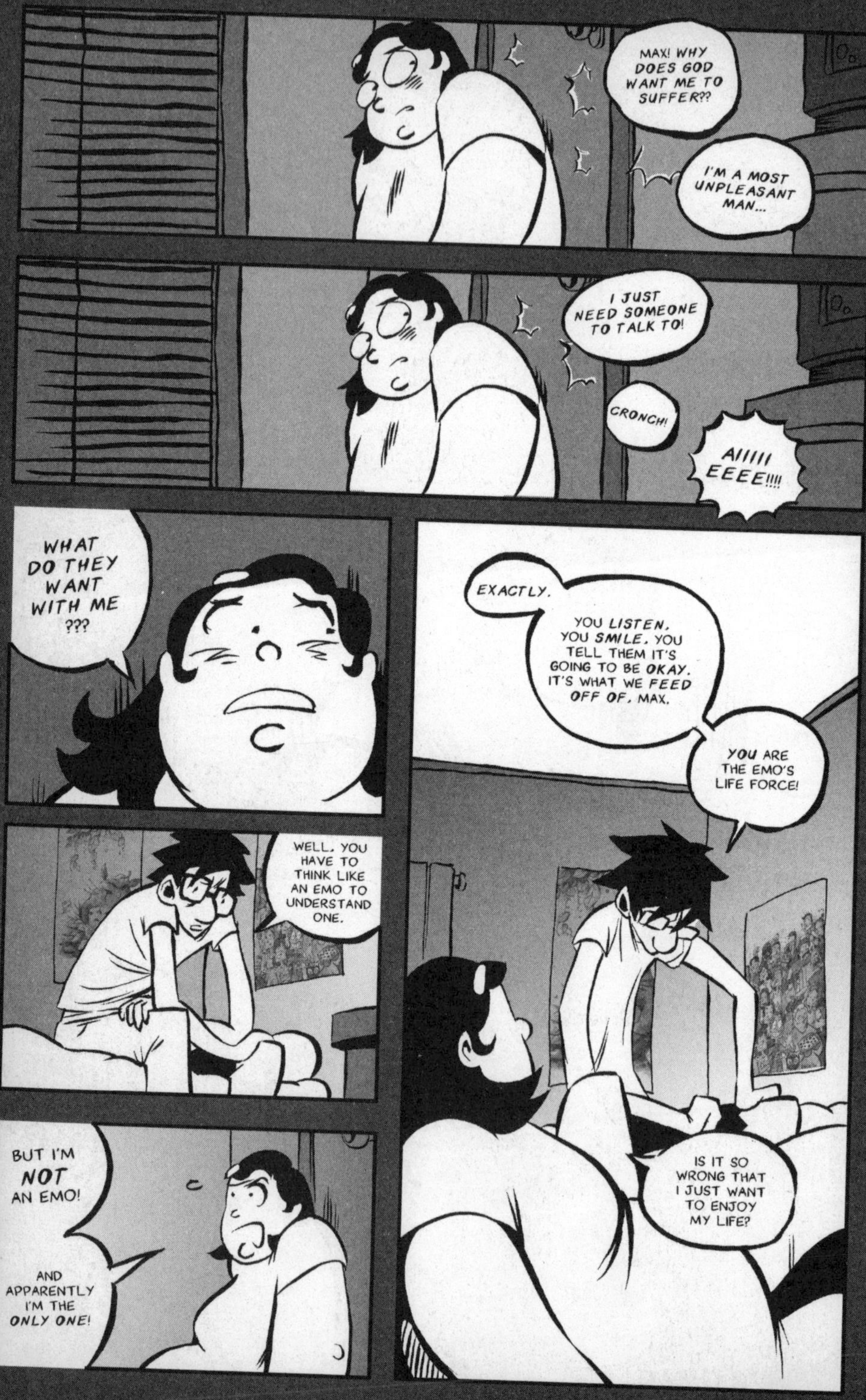
MAX! WHY DOES GOD WANT ME TO SUFFER??
I'M A MOST UNPLEASANT MAN...
I JUST NEED SOMEONE TO TALK TO!
CRONCH!
AIIIII EEEE!!!!
WHAT DO THEY WANT WITH ME ???
WELL, YOU HAVE TO THINK LIKE AN EMO TO UNDERSTAND ONE.
BUT I'M NOT AN EMO!
AND APPARENTLY I'M THE ONLY ONE!
EXACTLY.
YOU LISTEN, YOU SMILE, YOU TELL THEM IT'S GOING TO BE OKAY. IT'S WHAT WE FEED OFF OF, MAX.
YOU ARE THE EMO'S LIFE FORCE!
IS IT SO WRONG THAT I JUST WANT TO ENJOY MY LIFE?

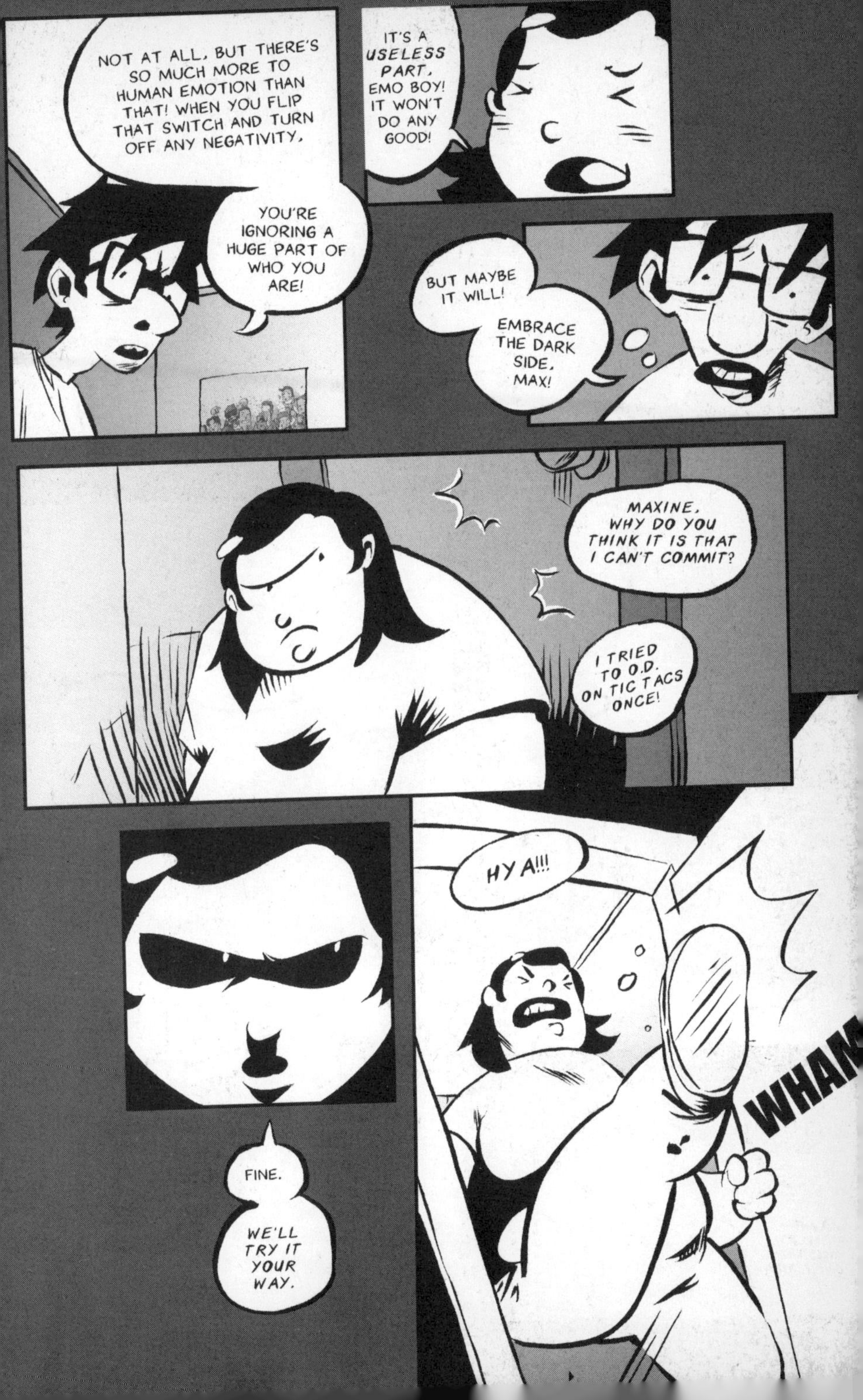
NOT AT ALL, BUT THERE'S SO MUCH MORE TO HUMAN EMOTION THAN THAT! WHEN YOU FLIP THAT SWITCH AND TURN OFF ANY NEGATIVITY,
YOU'RE IGNORING A HUGE PART OF WHO YOU ARE!
IT'S A USELESS PART, EMO BOY! IT WON'T DO ANY GOOD!
BUT MAYBE IT WILL!
EMBRACE THE DARK SIDE, MAX!
MAXINE, WHY DO YOU THINK IT IS THAT I CAN'T COMMIT?
I TRIED TO O.D. ON TIC TACS ONCE!
FINE.
WE'LL TRY IT YOUR WAY.
HYA!!!
WHAM

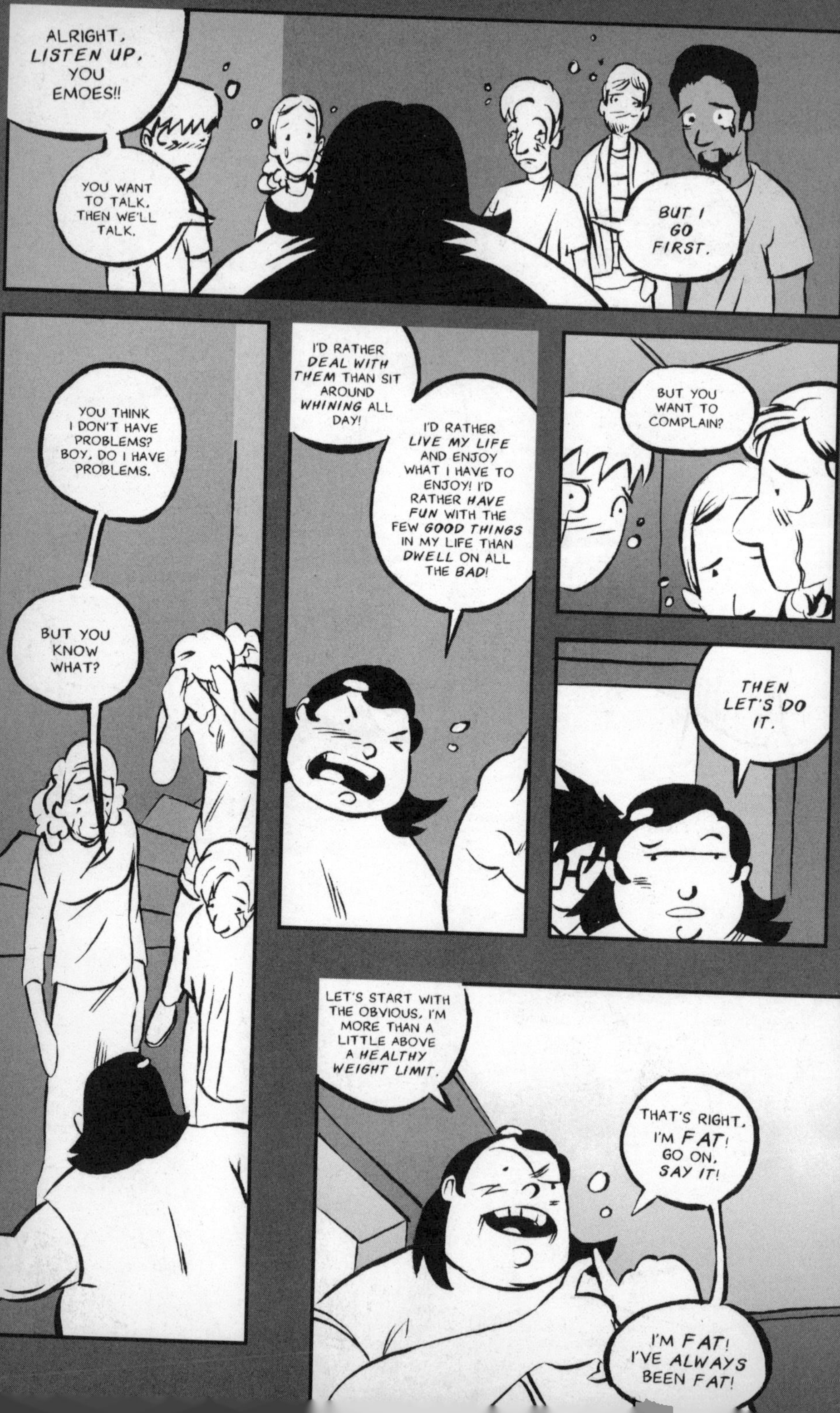
ALRIGHT, LISTEN UP, YOU EMOES!!
YOU WANT TO TALK, THEN WE'LL TALK.
BUT I GO FIRST.
YOU THINK I DON'T HAVE PROBLEMS? BOY, DO I HAVE PROBLEMS.
BUT YOU KNOW WHAT?
I'D RATHER DEAL WITH THEM THAN SIT AROUND WHINING ALL DAY!
I'D RATHER LIVE MY LIFE AND ENJOY WHAT I HAVE TO ENJOY! I'D RATHER HAVE FUN WITH THE FEW GOOD THINGS IN MY LIFE THAN DWELL ON ALL THE BAD!
BUT YOU WANT TO COMPLAIN?
THEN LET'S DO IT.
LET'S START WITH THE OBVIOUS. I'M MORE THAN A LITTLE ABOVE A HEALTHY WEIGHT LIMIT.
THAT'S RIGHT. I'M FAT! GO ON, SAY IT!
I'M FAT! I'VE ALWAYS BEEN FAT!

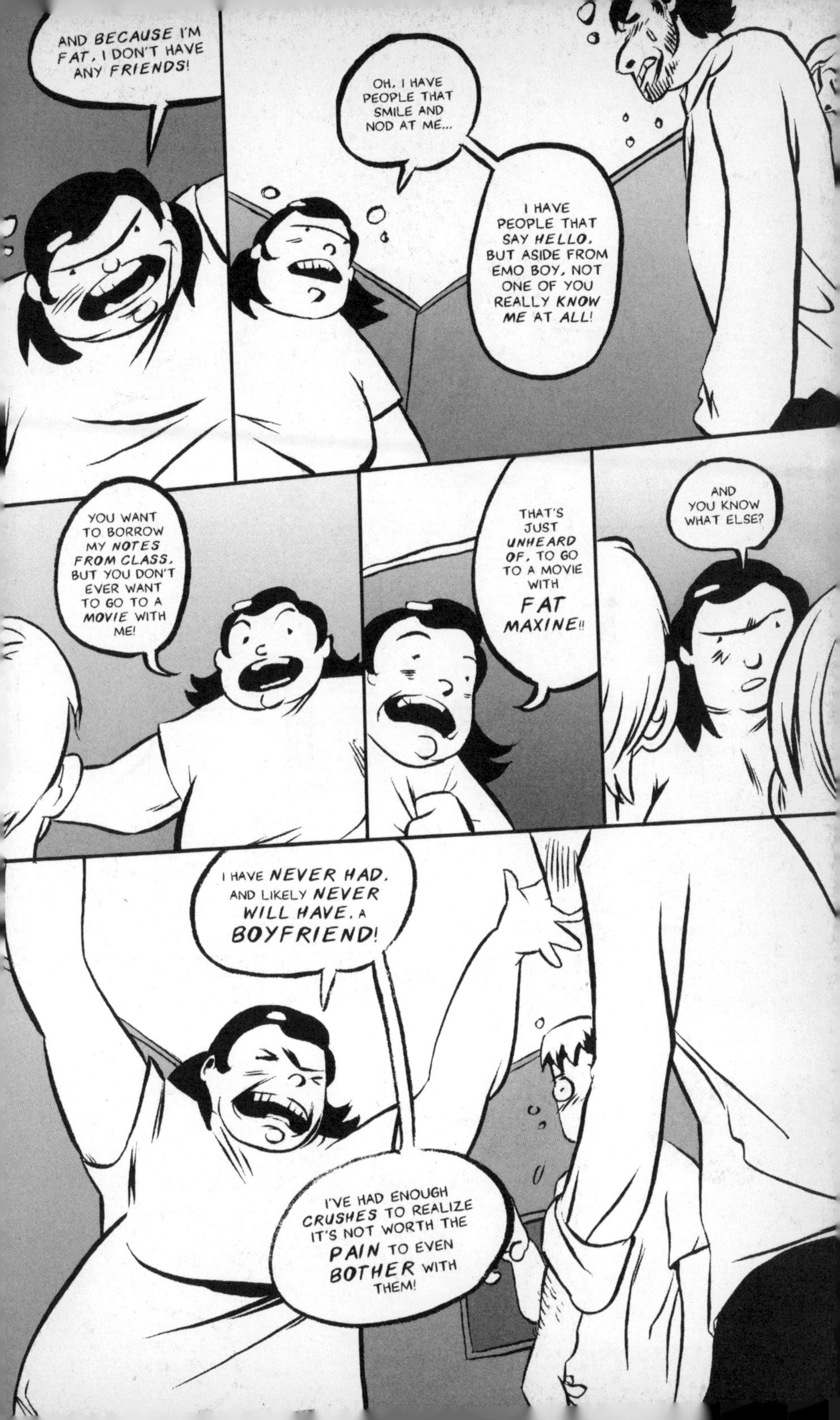
AND BECAUSE I'M FAT, I DON'T HAVE ANY FRIENDS!
OH, I HAVE PEOPLE THAT SMILE AND NOD AT ME...
I HAVE PEOPLE THAT SAY HELLO, BUT ASIDE FROM EMO BOY, NOT ONE OF YOU REALLY KNOW ME AT ALL!
YOU WANT TO BORROW MY NOTES FROM CLASS, BUT YOU DON'T EVER WANT TO GO TO A MOVIE WITH ME!
THAT'S JUST UNHEARD OF, TO GO TO A MOVIE WITH FAT MAXINE!!
AND YOU KNOW WHAT ELSE?
I HAVE NEVER HAD, AND LIKELY NEVER WILL HAVE, A BOYFRIEND!
I'VE HAD ENOUGH CRUSHES TO REALIZE IT'S NOT WORTH THE PAIN TO EVEN BOTHER WITH THEM!

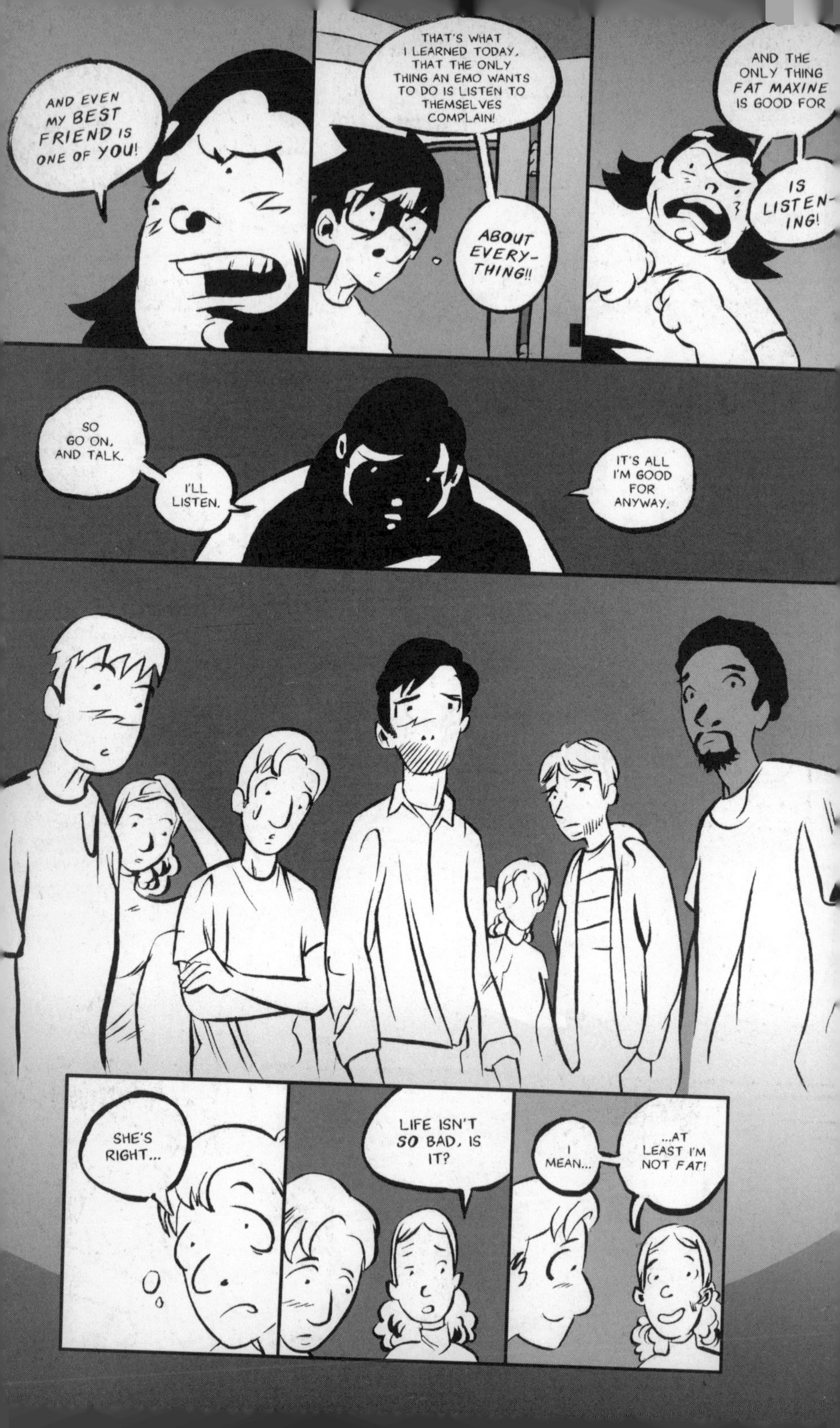
AND EVEN MY BEST FRIEND IS ONE OF YOU!
THAT'S WHAT I LEARNED TODAY, THAT THE ONLY THING AN EMO WANTS TO DO IS LISTEN TO THEMSELVES COMPLAIN!
ABOUT EVERY-THING!!
AND THE ONLY THING FAT MAXINE IS GOOD FOR
IS LISTEN-ING!
SO GO ON, AND TALK.
I'LL LISTEN.
IT'S ALL I'M GOOD FOR ANYWAY.
SHE'S RIGHT...
LIFE ISN'T SO BAD, IS IT?
I MEAN...
...AT LEAST I'M NOT FAT!

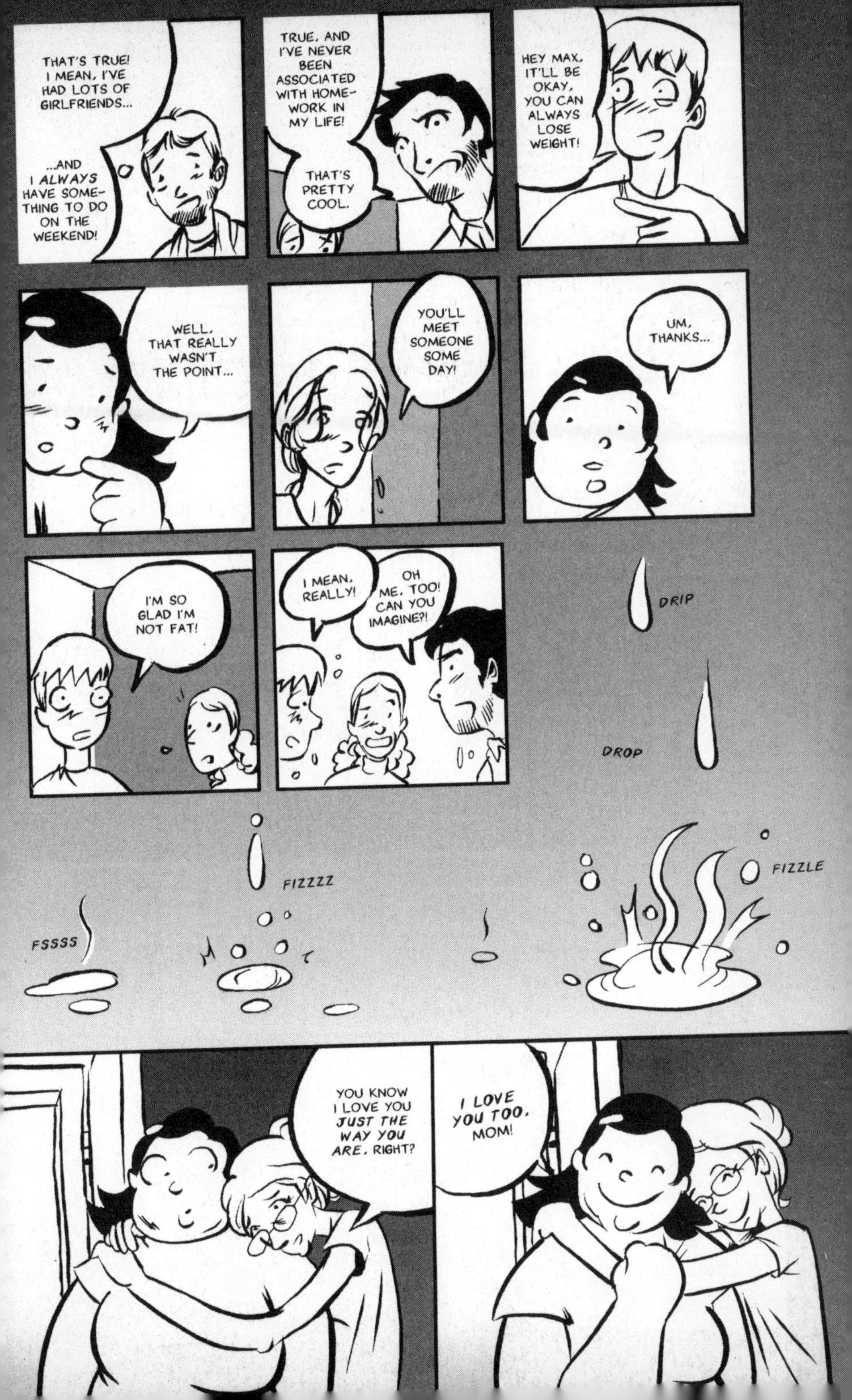
THAT'S TRUE! I MEAN, I'VE HAD LOTS OF GIRLFRIENDS...
...AND I ALWAYS HAVE SOMETHING TO DO ON THE WEEKEND!
TRUE, AND I'VE NEVER BEEN ASSOCIATED WITH HOMEWORK IN MY LIFE!
THAT'S PRETTY COOL.
HEY MAX, IT'LL BE OKAY, YOU CAN ALWAYS LOSE WEIGHT!
WELL, THAT REALLY WASN'T THE POINT...
YOU'LL MEET SOMEONE SOME DAY!
UM, THANKS...
I'M SO GLAD I'M NOT FAT!
I MEAN, REALLY!
OH ME, TOO! CAN YOU IMAGINE?!
DRIP
DROP
FSSSS
FIZZZZ
FIZZLE
YOU KNOW I LOVE YOU JUST THE WAY YOU ARE, RIGHT?
I LOVE YOU TOO, MOM!

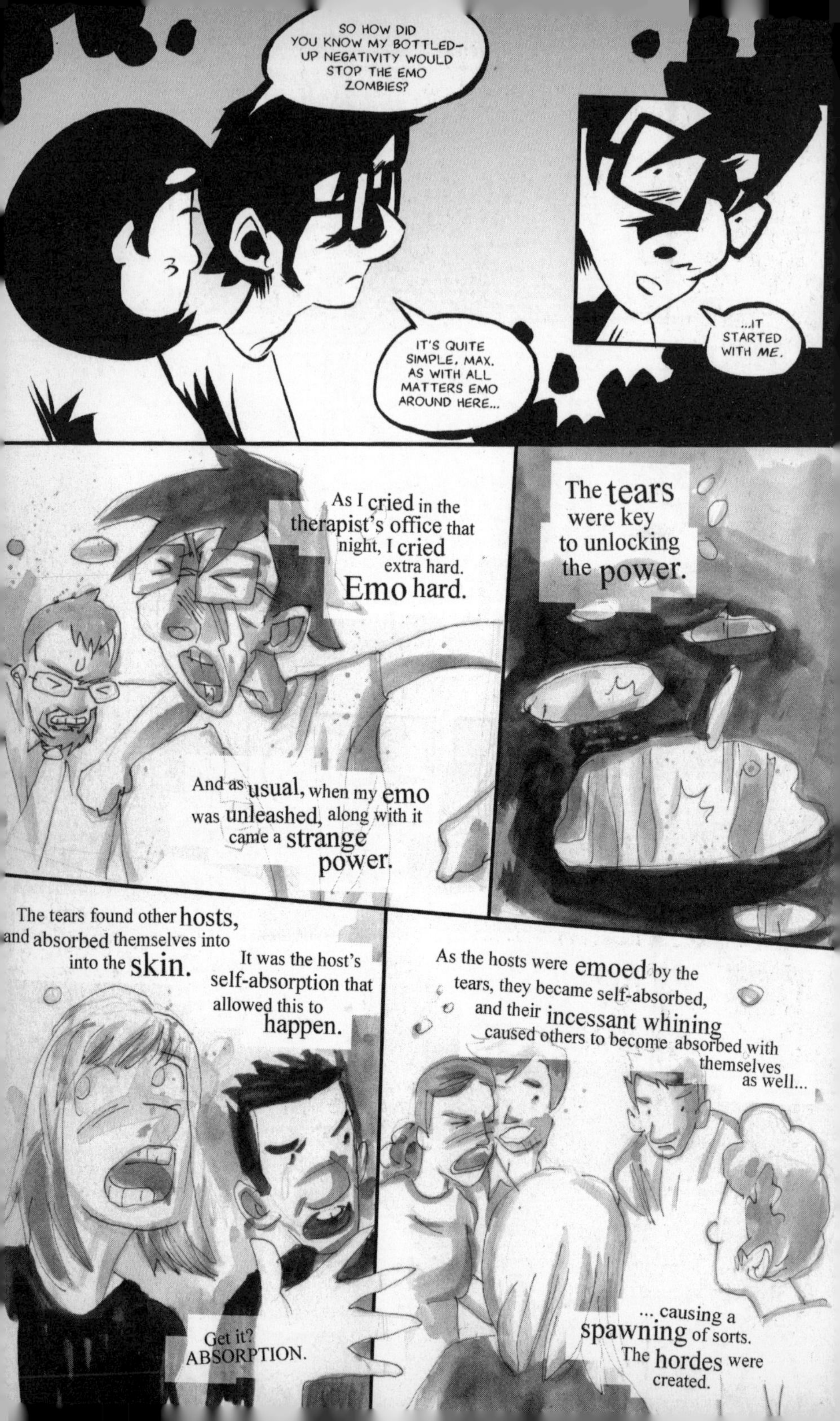
SO HOW DID YOU KNOW MY BOTTLED-UP NEGATIVITY WOULD STOP THE EMO ZOMBIES?
IT'S QUITE SIMPLE, MAX. AS WITH ALL MATTERS EMO AROUND HERE...
...IT STARTED WITH *ME*.
As I cried in the therapist's office that night, I cried extra hard. Emo hard.
And as usual, when my emo was unleashed, along with it came a strange power.
The tears were key to unlocking the power.
The tears found other hosts, and absorbed themselves into into the skin.
It was the host's self-absorption that allowed this to happen.
Get it? ABSORPTION.
As the hosts were emoed by the tears, they became self-absorbed, and their incessant whining caused others to become absorbed with themselves as well...
...causing a spawning of sorts. The hordes were created.

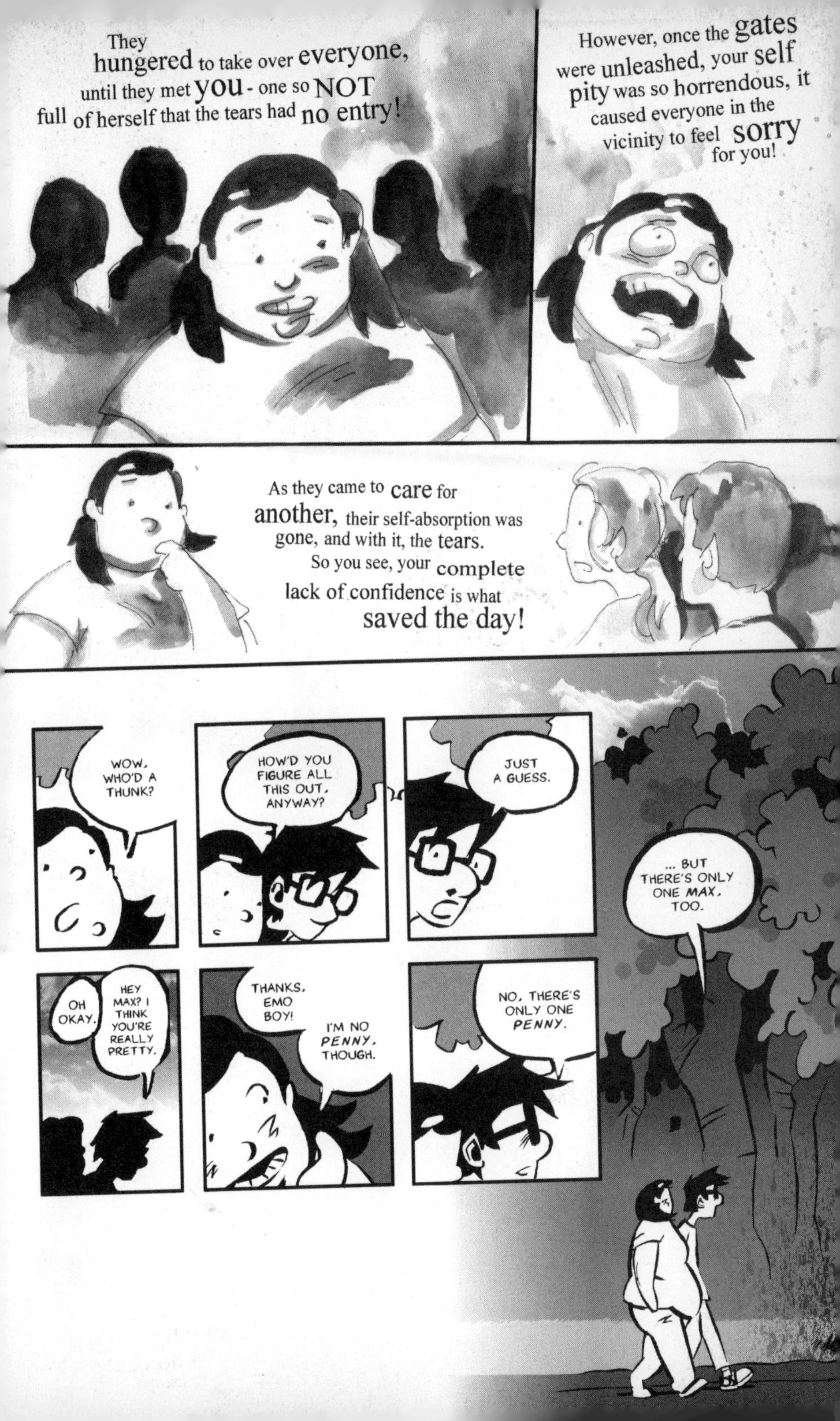
They hungered to take over everyone, until they met YOU - one so NOT full of herself that the tears had no entry!
However, once the gates were unleashed, your self pity was so horrendous, it caused everyone in the vicinity to feel sorry for you!
As they came to care for another, their self-absorption was gone, and with it, the tears.
So you see, your complete lack of confidence is what saved the day!
WOW, WHO'D A THUNK?
HOW'D YOU FIGURE ALL THIS OUT, ANYWAY?
JUST A GUESS.
... BUT THERE'S ONLY ONE MAX, TOO.
OH OKAY.
HEY MAX? I THINK YOU'RE REALLY PRETTY.
THANKS, EMO BOY!
I'M NO PENNY, THOUGH.
NO, THERE'S ONLY ONE PENNY.

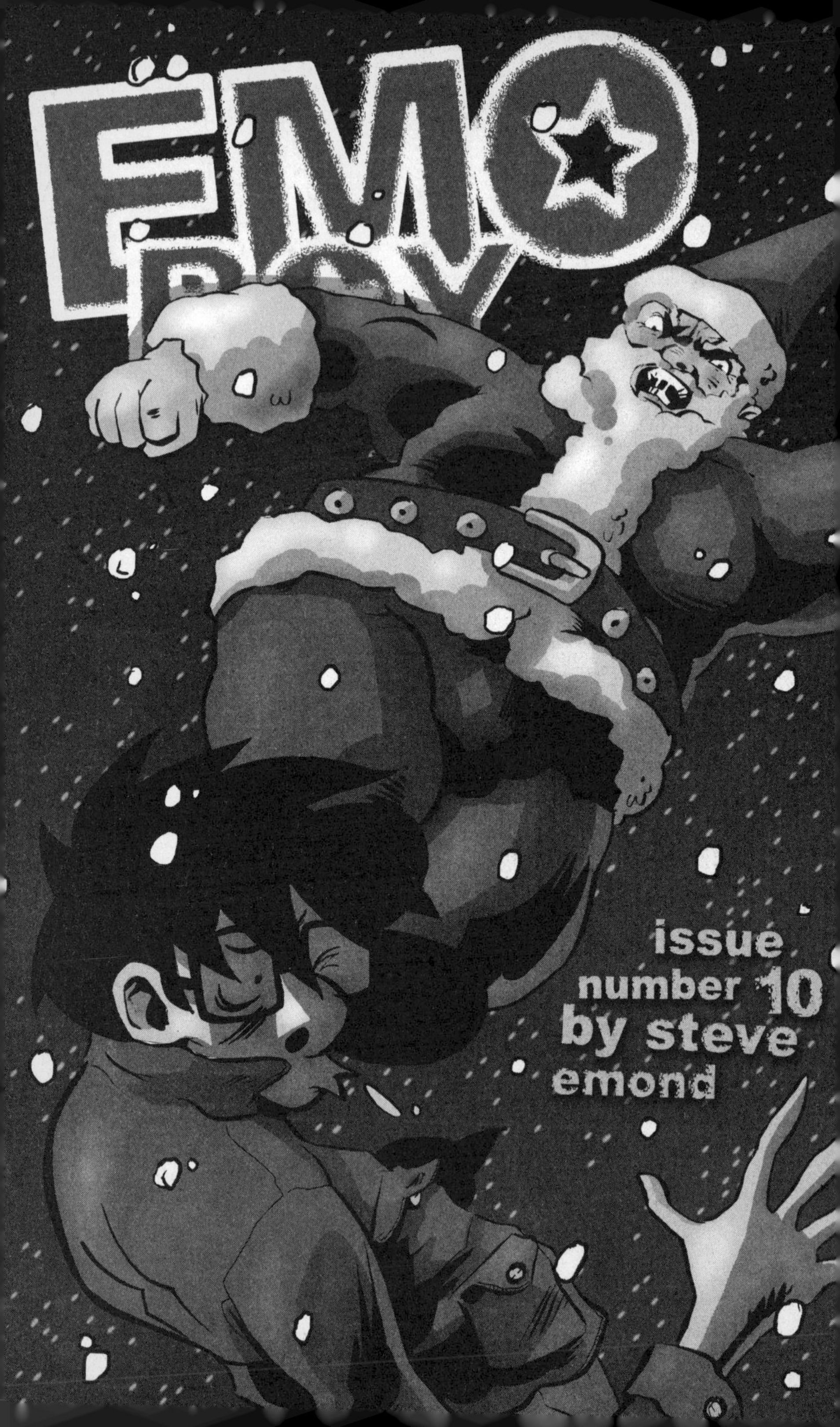
EMO BOY
issue number 10
by steve emond

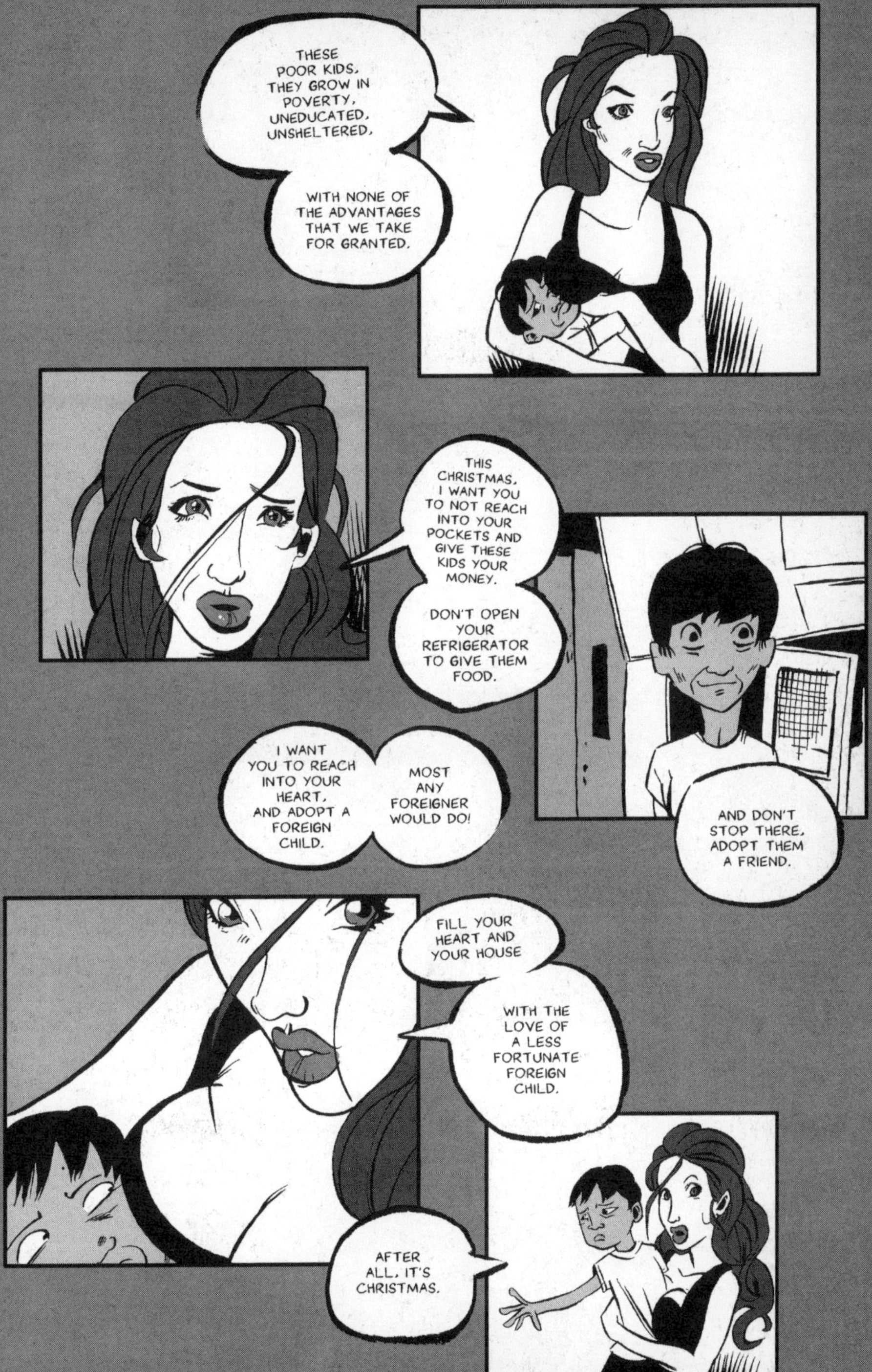
THESE POOR KIDS, THEY GROW IN POVERTY, UNEDUCATED, UNSHELTERED,
WITH NONE OF THE ADVANTAGES THAT WE TAKE FOR GRANTED.
THIS CHRISTMAS, I WANT YOU TO NOT REACH INTO YOUR POCKETS AND GIVE THESE KIDS YOUR MONEY.
DON'T OPEN YOUR REFRIGERATOR TO GIVE THEM FOOD.
I WANT YOU TO REACH INTO YOUR HEART, AND ADOPT A FOREIGN CHILD.
MOST ANY FOREIGNER WOULD DO!
AND DON'T STOP THERE, ADOPT THEM A FRIEND.
FILL YOUR HEART AND YOUR HOUSE
WITH THE LOVE OF A LESS FORTUNATE FOREIGN CHILD.
AFTER ALL, IT'S CHRISTMAS.

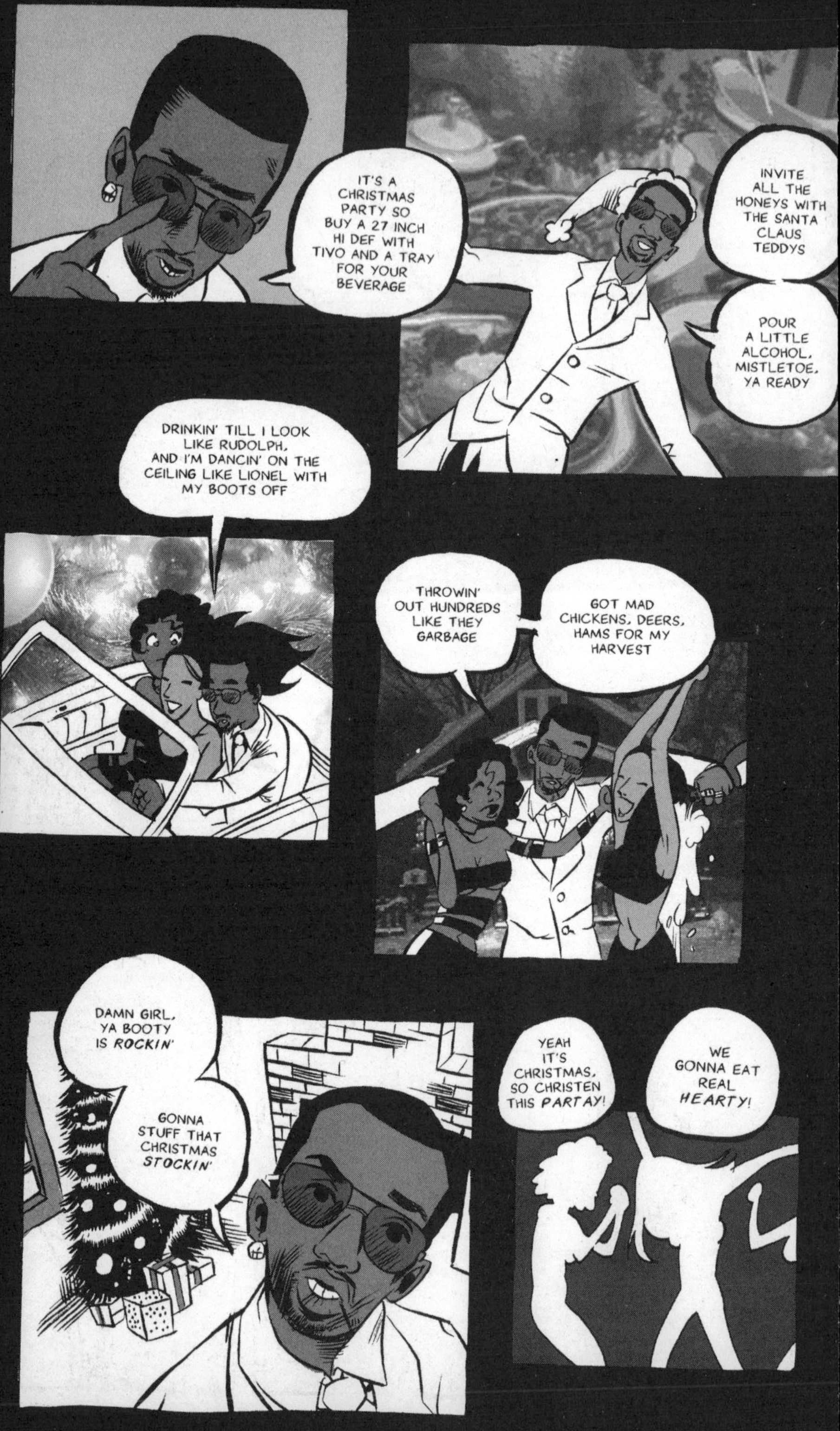
IT'S A CHRISTMAS PARTY SO BUY A 27 INCH HI DEF WITH TIVO AND A TRAY FOR YOUR BEVERAGE
INVITE ALL THE HONEYS WITH THE SANTA CLAUS TEDDYS
POUR A LITTLE ALCOHOL, MISTLETOE, YA READY
DRINKIN' TILL I LOOK LIKE RUDOLPH, AND I'M DANCIN' ON THE CEILING LIKE LIONEL WITH MY BOOTS OFF
THROWIN' OUT HUNDREDS LIKE THEY GARBAGE
GOT MAD CHICKENS, DEERS, HAMS FOR MY HARVEST
DAMN GIRL, YA BOOTY IS *ROCKIN'*
GONNA STUFF THAT CHRISTMAS *STOCKIN'*
YEAH IT'S CHRISTMAS, SO CHRISTEN THIS *PARTAY*!
WE GONNA EAT REAL *HEARTY*!

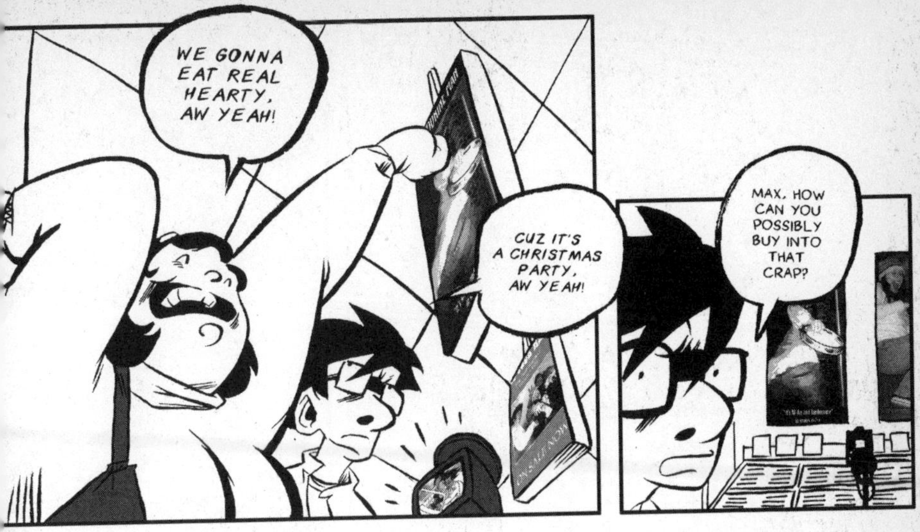
WE GONNA EAT REAL HEARTY, AW YEAH!
CUZ IT'S A CHRISTMAS PARTY, AW YEAH!
MAX, HOW CAN YOU POSSIBLY BUY INTO THAT CRAP?

# "A Very Emo Chrtistmas"
## written and drawn by steve emond

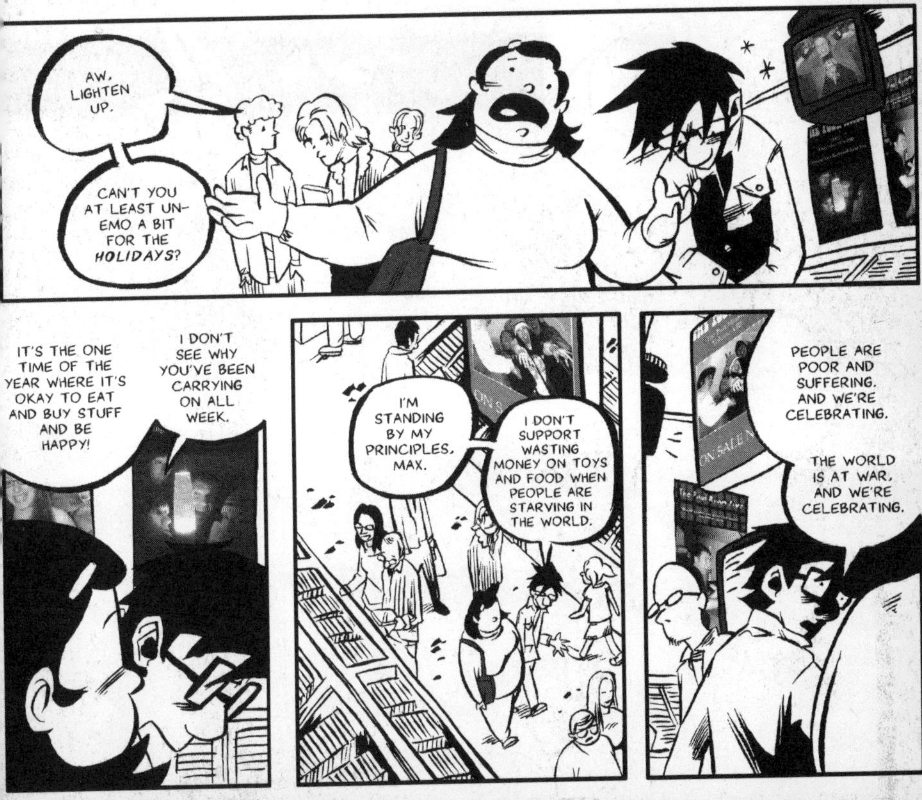
AW, LIGHTEN UP.
CAN'T YOU AT LEAST UN-EMO A BIT FOR THE *HOLIDAYS*?
IT'S THE ONE TIME OF THE YEAR WHERE IT'S OKAY TO EAT AND BUY STUFF AND BE HAPPY!
I DON'T SEE WHY YOU'VE BEEN CARRYING ON ALL WEEK.
I'M STANDING BY MY PRINCIPLES, MAX.
I DON'T SUPPORT WASTING MONEY ON TOYS AND FOOD WHEN PEOPLE ARE STARVING IN THE WORLD.
PEOPLE ARE POOR AND SUFFERING. AND WE'RE CELEBRATING.
THE WORLD IS AT WAR, AND WE'RE CELEBRATING.

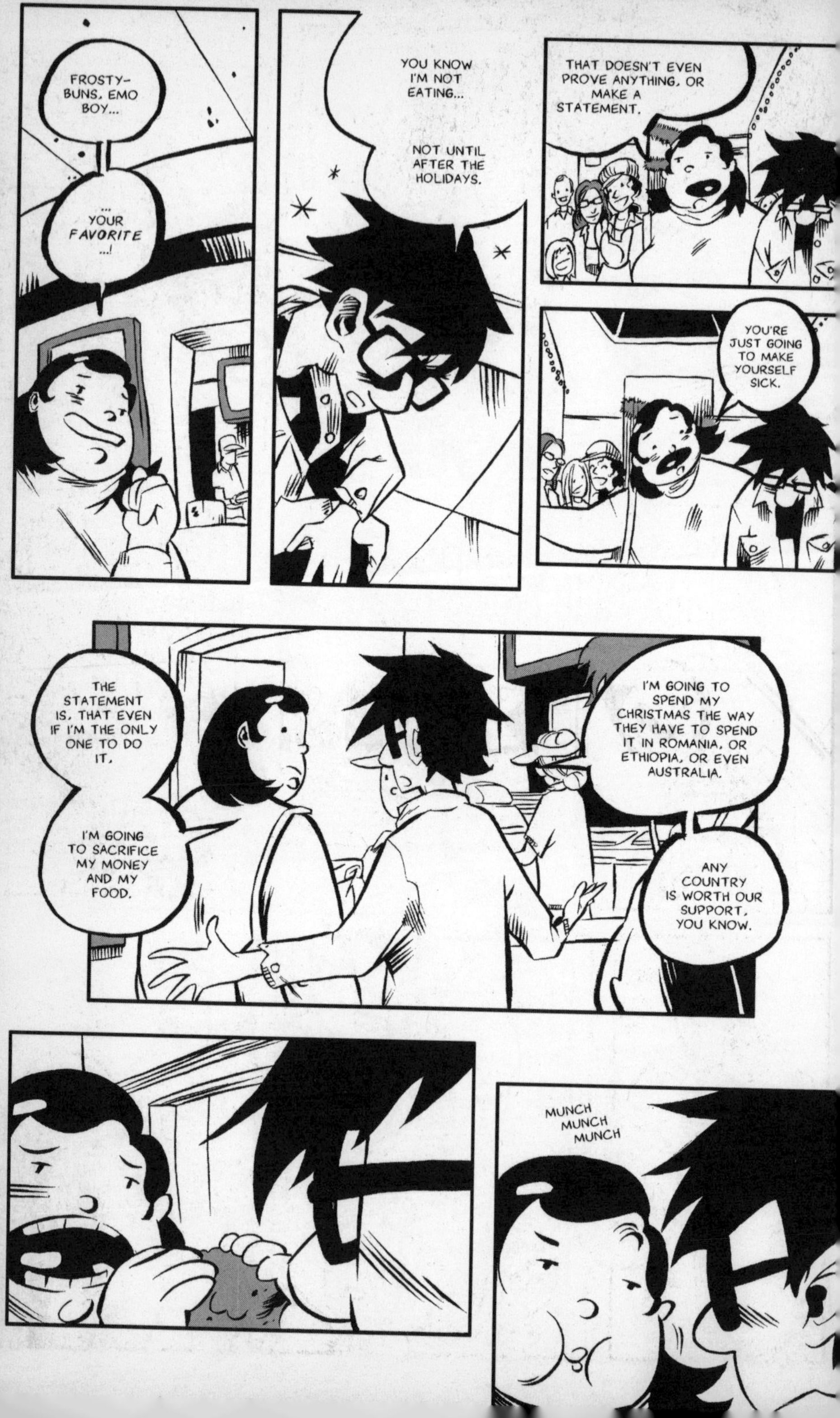
FROSTY-BUNS, EMO BOY...
... YOUR *FAVORITE* ...!
YOU KNOW I'M NOT EATING...
NOT UNTIL AFTER THE HOLIDAYS.
THAT DOESN'T EVEN PROVE ANYTHING, OR MAKE A STATEMENT.
YOU'RE JUST GOING TO MAKE YOURSELF SICK.
THE STATEMENT IS, THAT EVEN IF I'M THE ONLY ONE TO DO IT,
I'M GOING TO SACRIFICE MY MONEY AND MY FOOD.
I'M GOING TO SPEND MY CHRISTMAS THE WAY THEY HAVE TO SPEND IT IN ROMANIA, OR ETHIOPIA, OR EVEN AUSTRALIA.
ANY COUNTRY IS WORTH OUR SUPPORT, YOU KNOW.
MUNCH MUNCH MUNCH

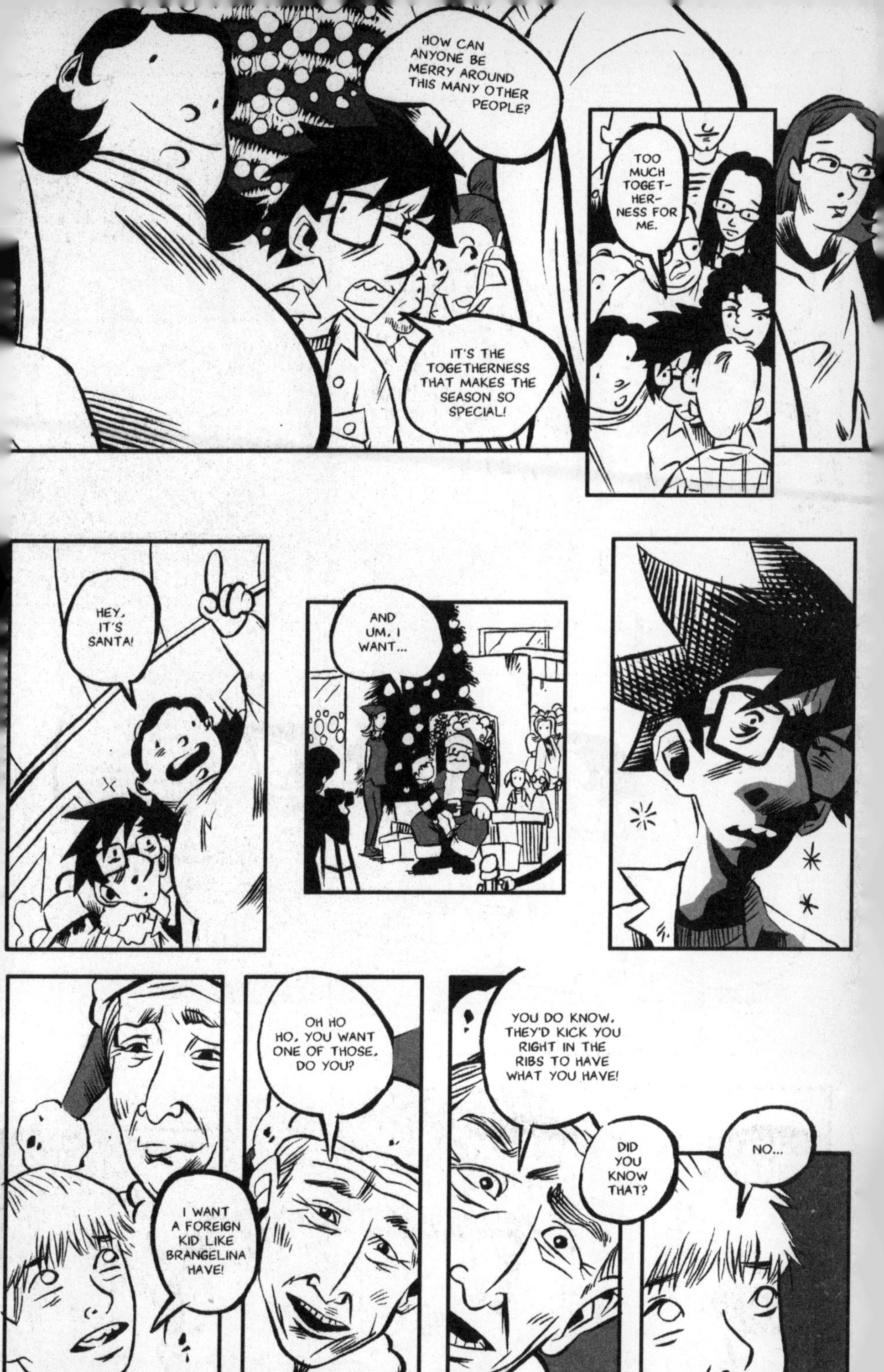
HOW CAN ANYONE BE MERRY AROUND THIS MANY OTHER PEOPLE?
IT'S THE TOGETHERNESS THAT MAKES THE SEASON SO SPECIAL!
TOO MUCH TOGETHERNESS FOR ME.
HEY, IT'S SANTA!
AND UM, I WANT...
I WANT A FOREIGN KID LIKE BRANGELINA HAVE!
OH HO HO, YOU WANT ONE OF THOSE, DO YOU?
YOU DO KNOW, THEY'D KICK YOU RIGHT IN THE RIBS TO HAVE WHAT YOU HAVE!
DID YOU KNOW THAT?
NO...

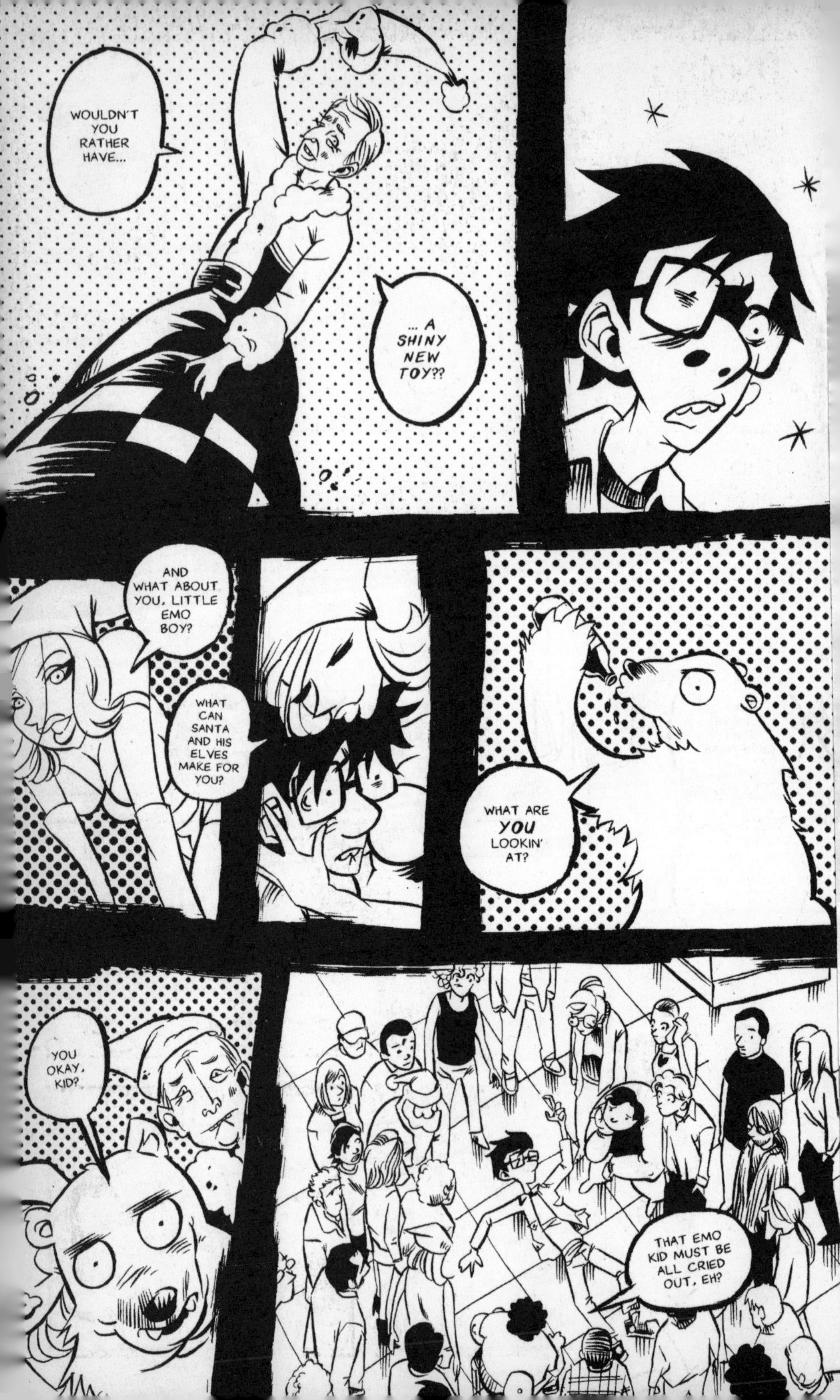
WOULDN'T YOU RATHER HAVE...
... A SHINY NEW TOY??
AND WHAT ABOUT YOU, LITTLE EMO BOY?
WHAT CAN SANTA AND HIS ELVES MAKE FOR YOU?
WHAT ARE *YOU* LOOKIN' AT?
YOU OKAY, KID?
THAT EMO KID MUST BE ALL CRIED OUT, EH?

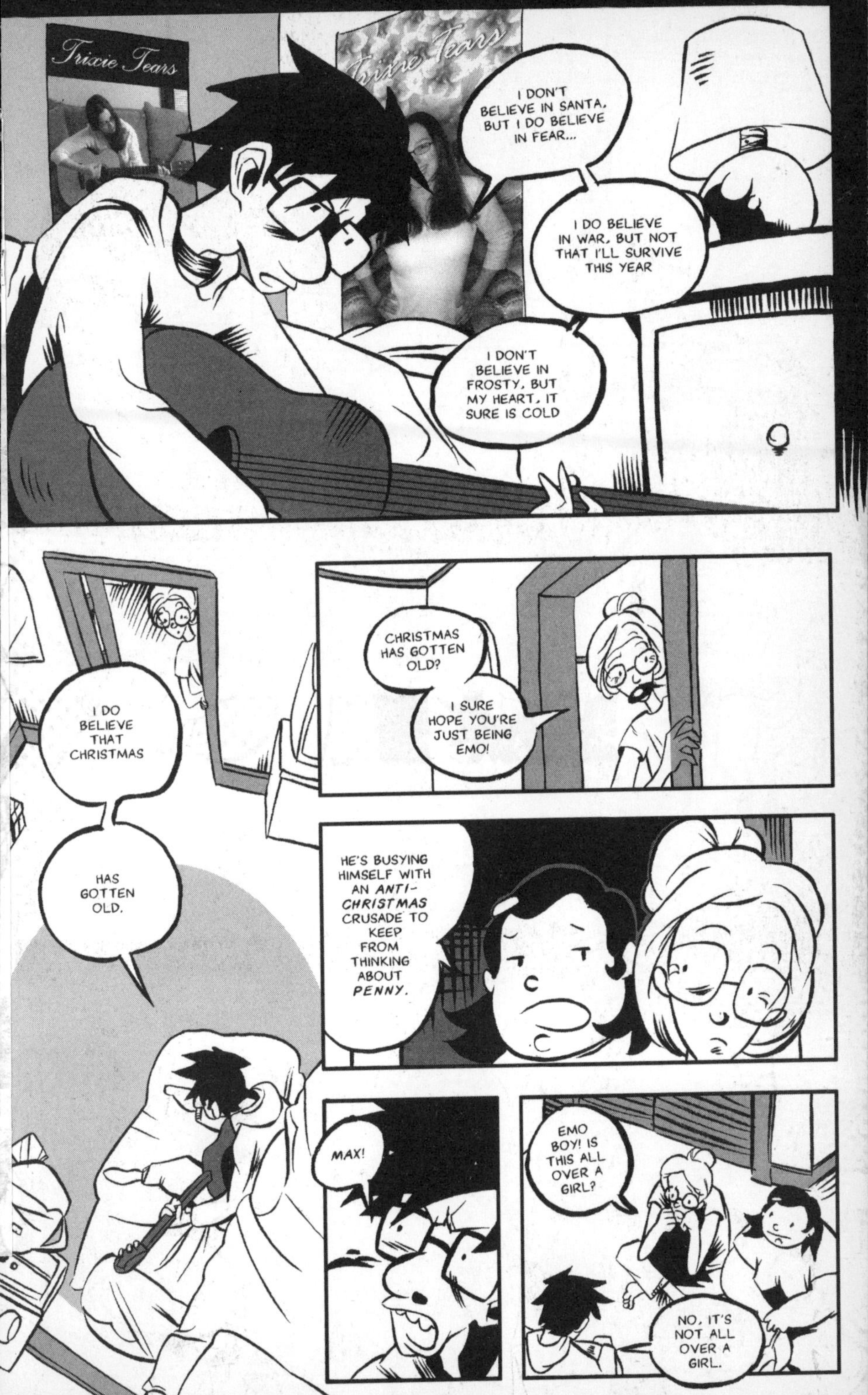
Trixie Tears
Trixie Tears
I DON'T BELIEVE IN SANTA, BUT I DO BELIEVE IN FEAR...
I DO BELIEVE IN WAR, BUT NOT THAT I'LL SURVIVE THIS YEAR
I DON'T BELIEVE IN FROSTY, BUT MY HEART, IT SURE IS COLD
I DO BELIEVE THAT CHRISTMAS
HAS GOTTEN OLD.
CHRISTMAS HAS GOTTEN OLD?
I SURE HOPE YOU'RE JUST BEING EMO!
HE'S BUSYING HIMSELF WITH AN *ANTI-CHRISTMAS* CRUSADE TO KEEP FROM THINKING ABOUT *PENNY*.
*MAX!*
EMO BOY! IS THIS ALL OVER A GIRL?
NO, IT'S NOT ALL OVER A GIRL.

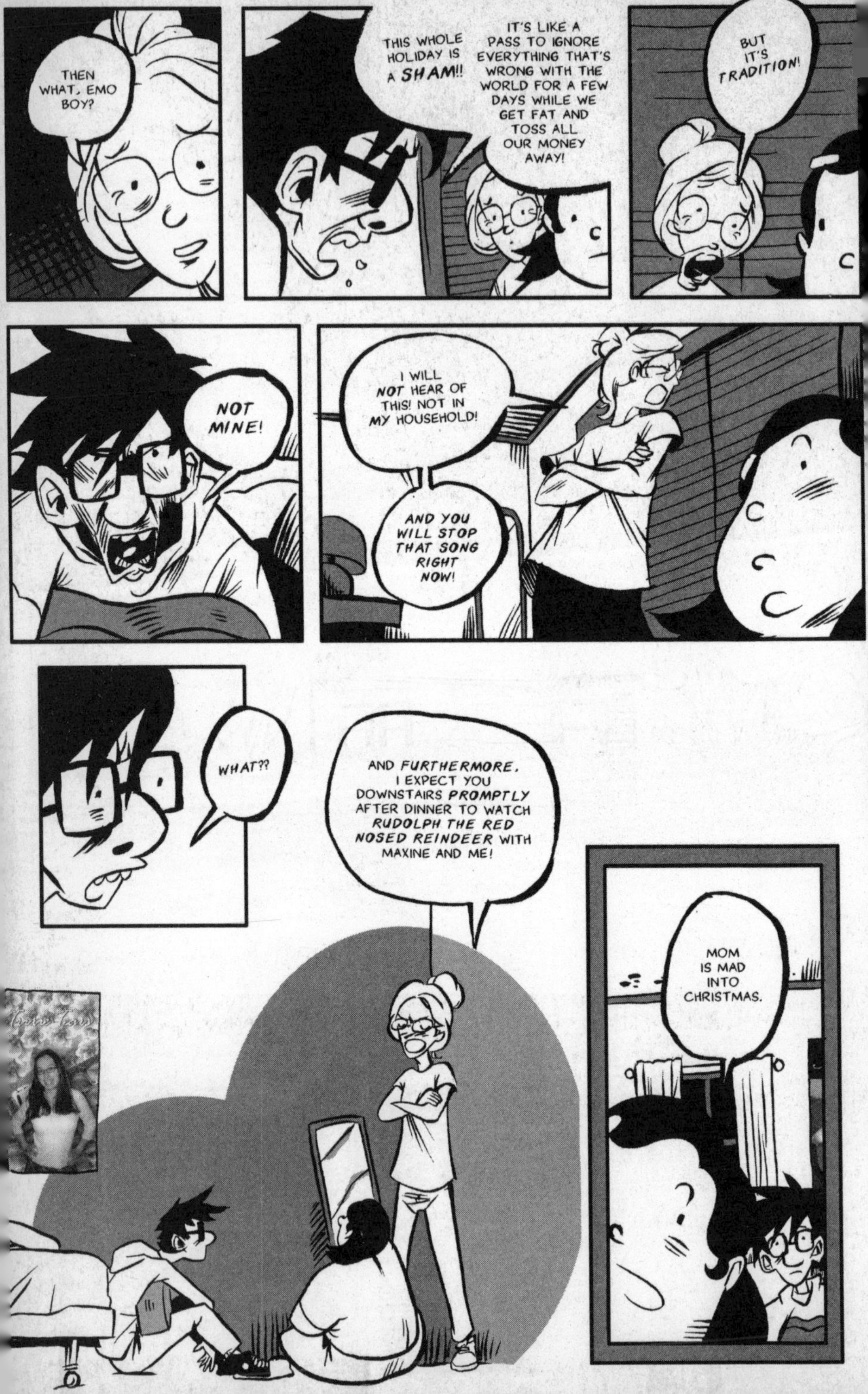
THEN WHAT, EMO BOY?
THIS WHOLE HOLIDAY IS A SHAM!!
IT'S LIKE A PASS TO IGNORE EVERYTHING THAT'S WRONG WITH THE WORLD FOR A FEW DAYS WHILE WE GET FAT AND TOSS ALL OUR MONEY AWAY!
BUT IT'S TRADITION!
NOT MINE!
I WILL NOT HEAR OF THIS! NOT IN MY HOUSEHOLD!
AND YOU WILL STOP THAT SONG RIGHT NOW!
WHAT??
AND FURTHERMORE, I EXPECT YOU DOWNSTAIRS PROMPTLY AFTER DINNER TO WATCH RUDOLPH THE RED NOSED REINDEER WITH MAXINE AND ME!
MOM IS MAD INTO CHRISTMAS.

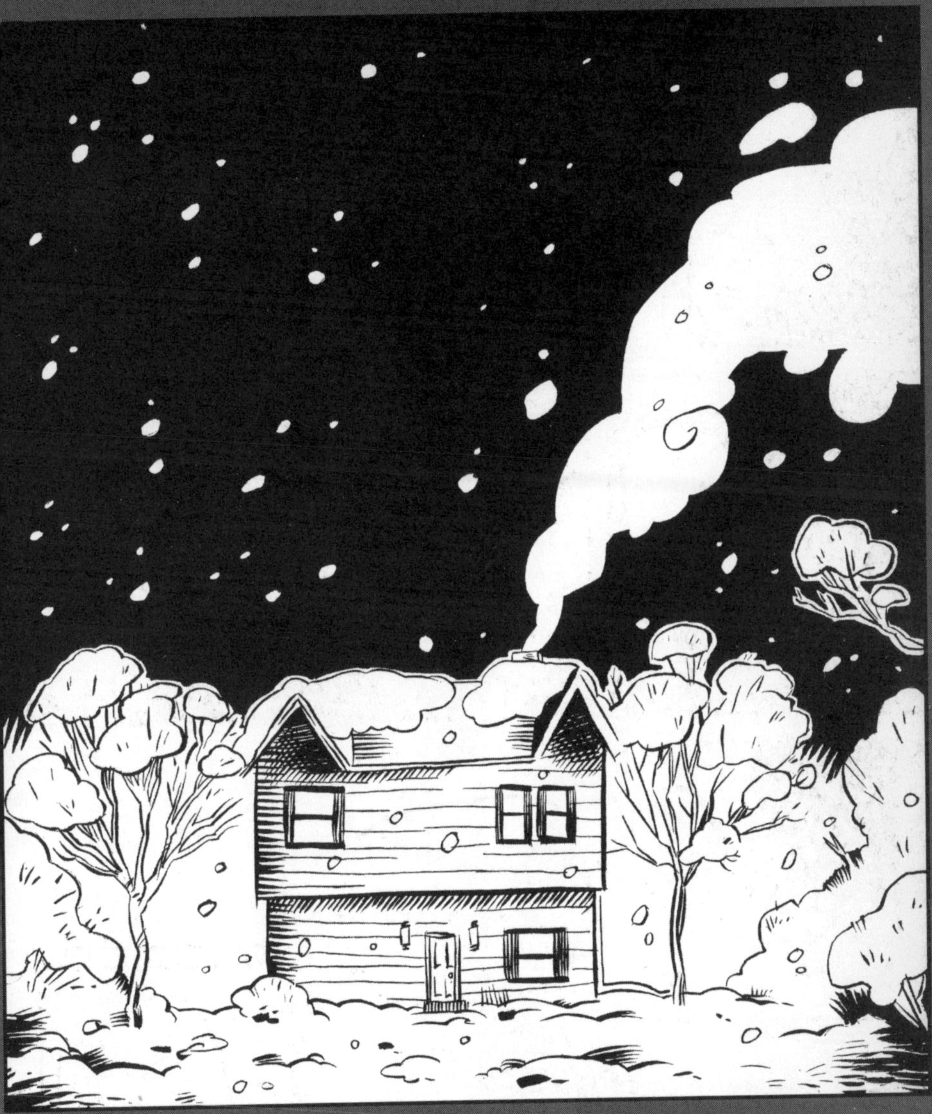
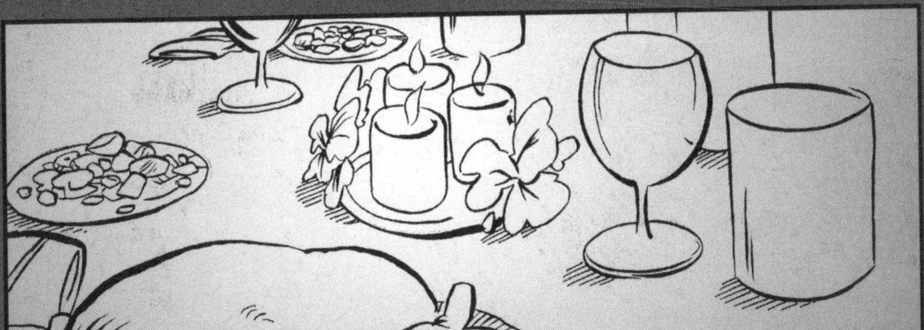

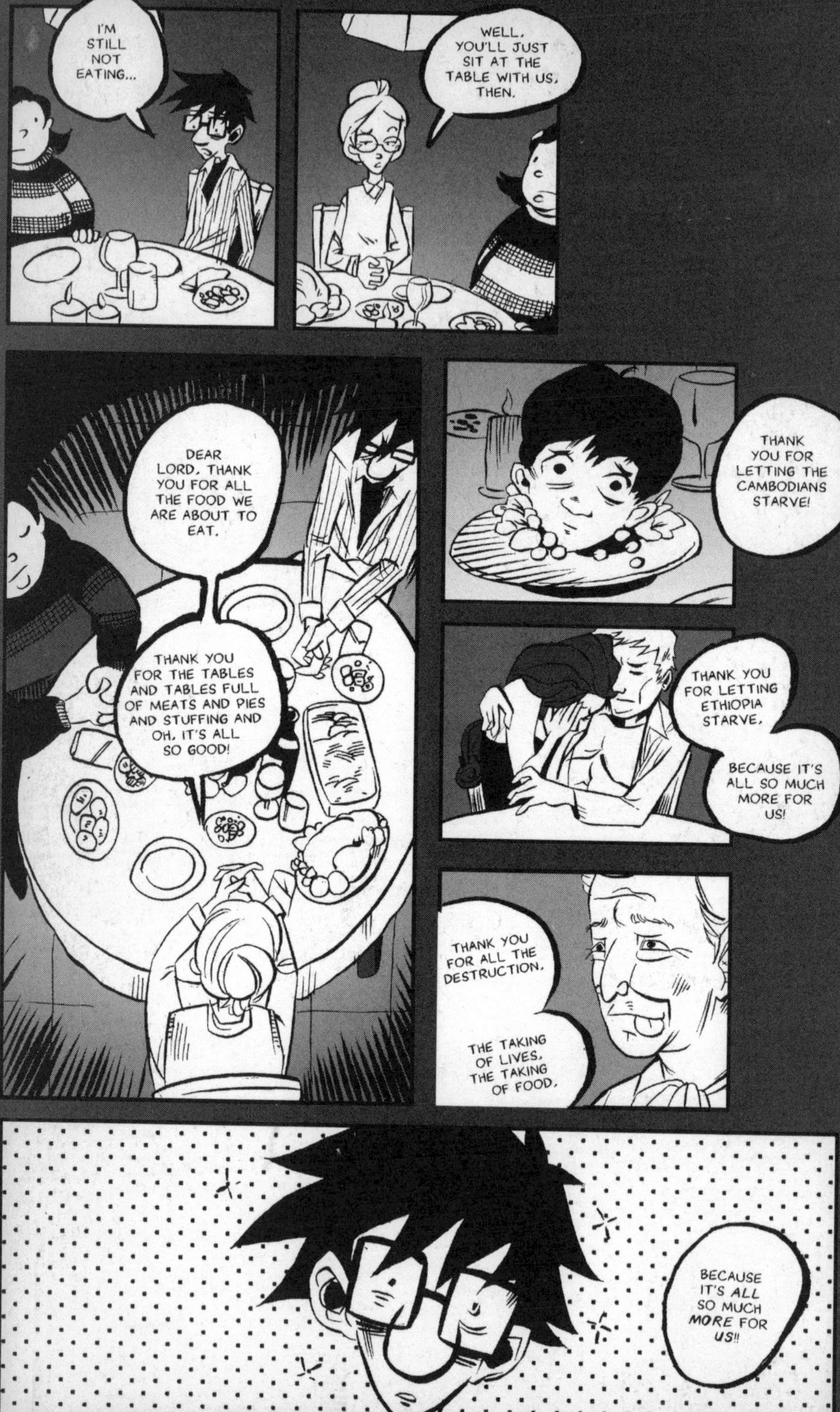
I'M STILL NOT EATING...
WELL, YOU'LL JUST SIT AT THE TABLE WITH US, THEN.
DEAR LORD, THANK YOU FOR ALL THE FOOD WE ARE ABOUT TO EAT.
THANK YOU FOR THE TABLES AND TABLES FULL OF MEATS AND PIES AND STUFFING AND OH, IT'S ALL SO GOOD!
THANK YOU FOR LETTING THE CAMBODIANS STARVE!
THANK YOU FOR LETTING ETHIOPIA STARVE,
BECAUSE IT'S ALL SO MUCH MORE FOR US!
THANK YOU FOR ALL THE DESTRUCTION,
THE TAKING OF LIVES, THE TAKING OF FOOD,
BECAUSE IT'S *ALL* SO MUCH *MORE* FOR *US*!!

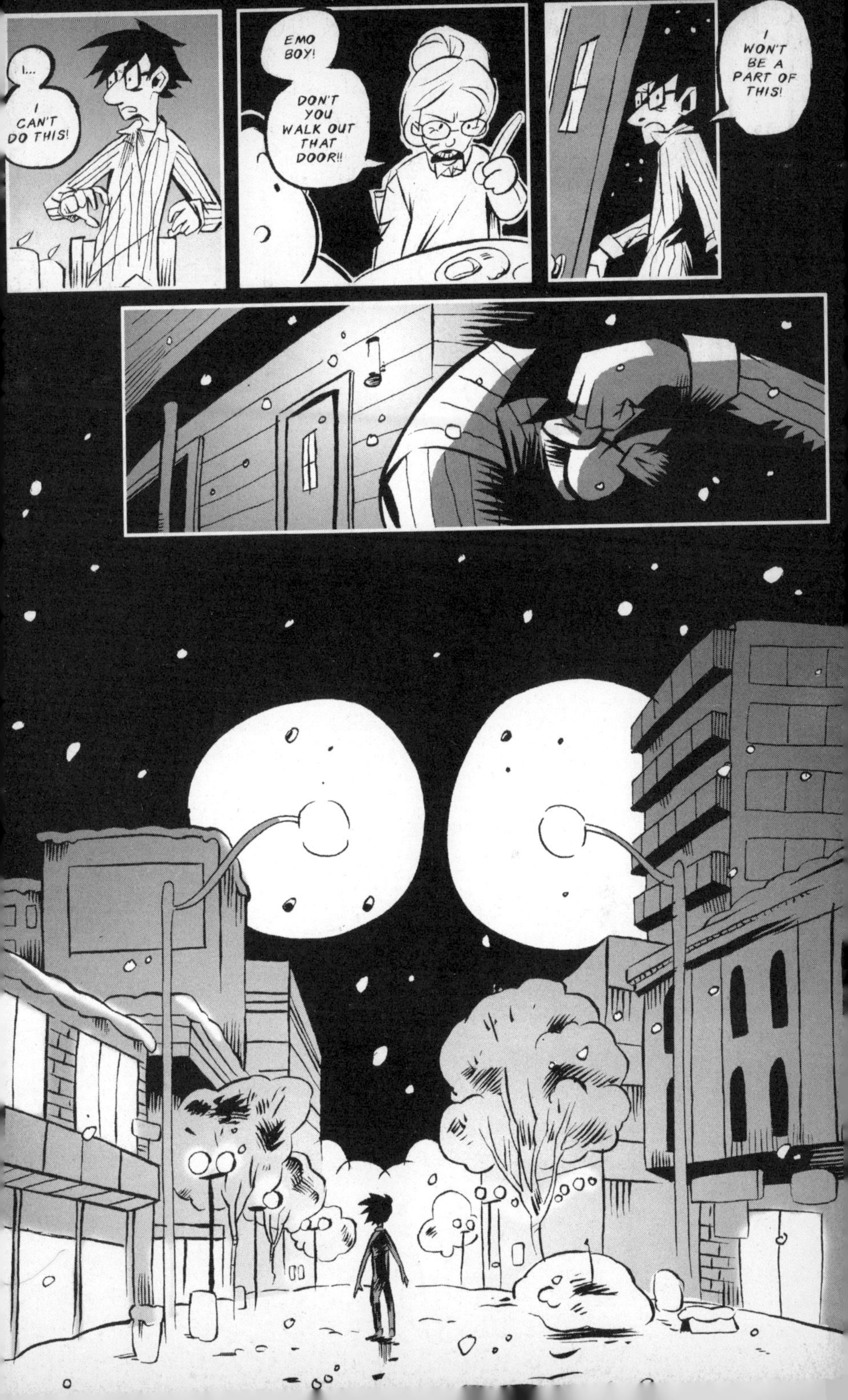
I...
I CAN'T DO THIS!
EMO BOY!
DON'T YOU WALK OUT THAT DOOR!!
I WON'T BE A PART OF THIS!

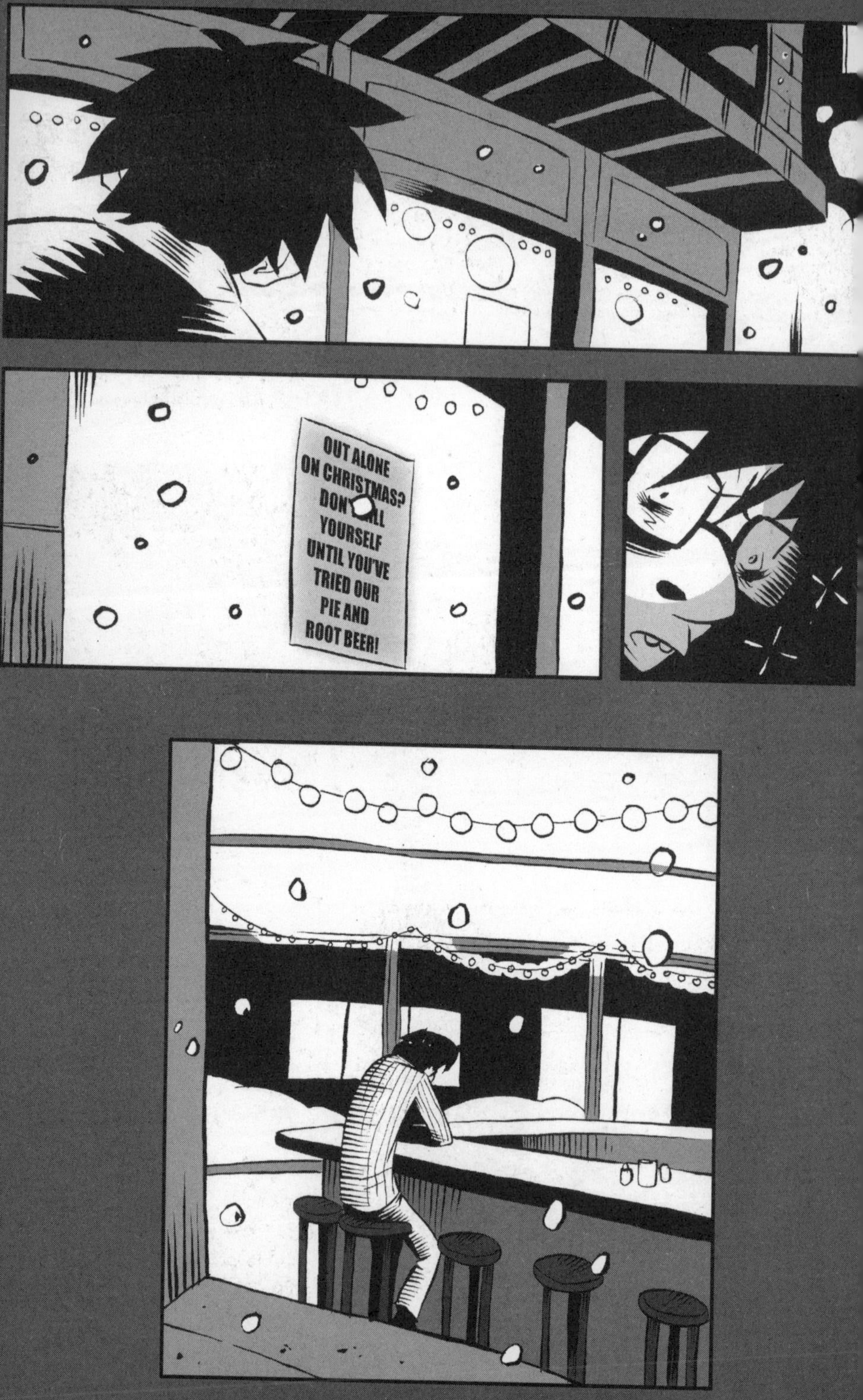
OUT ALONE
ON CHRISTMAS?
YOURSELF
UNTIL YOU'VE
TRIED OUR
PIE AND
ROOT BEER!

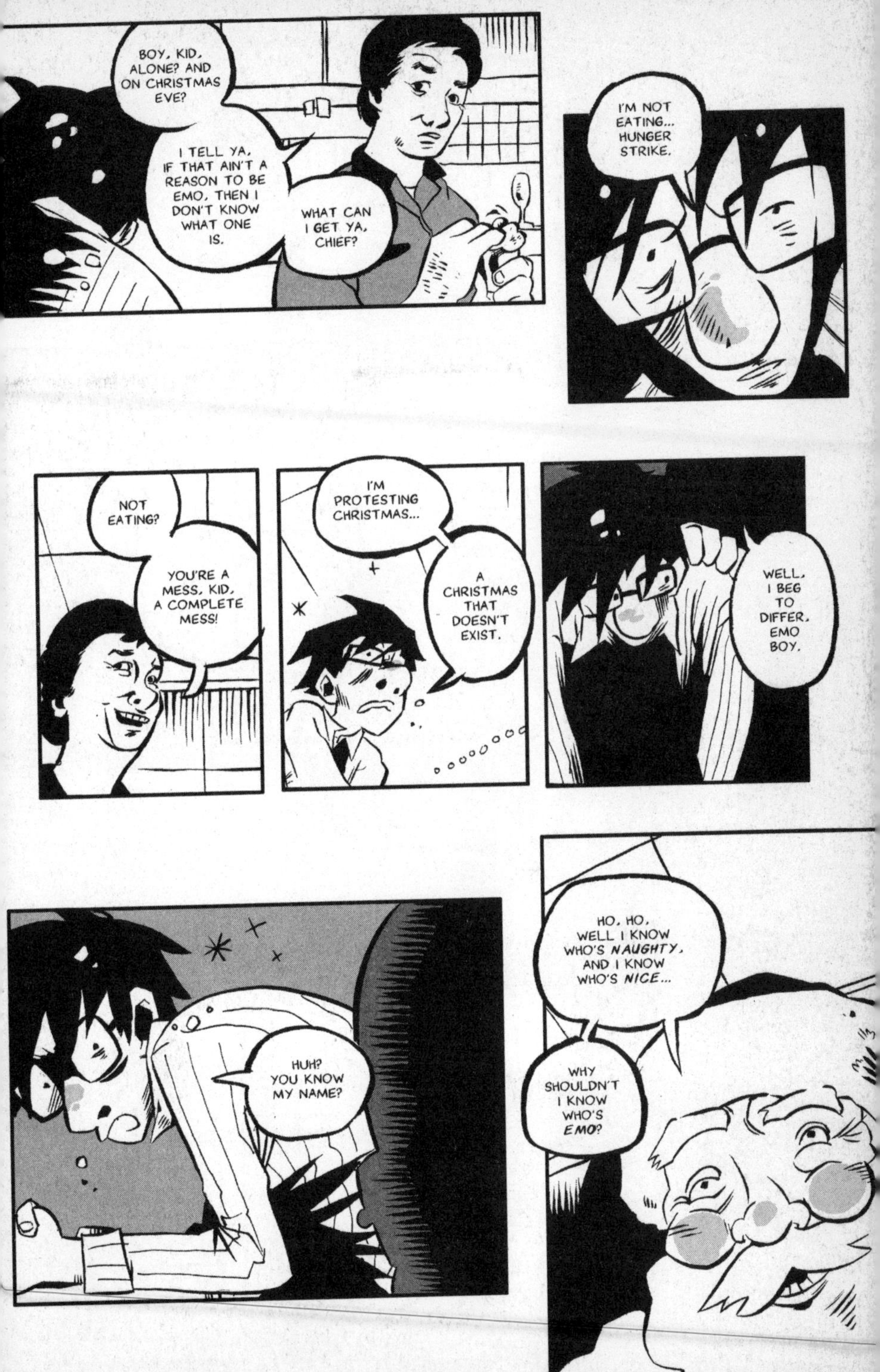
BOY, KID, ALONE? AND ON CHRISTMAS EVE?
I TELL YA, IF THAT AIN'T A REASON TO BE EMO, THEN I DON'T KNOW WHAT ONE IS.
WHAT CAN I GET YA, CHIEF?
I'M NOT EATING... HUNGER STRIKE.
NOT EATING?
YOU'RE A MESS, KID, A COMPLETE MESS!
I'M PROTESTING CHRISTMAS...
A CHRISTMAS THAT DOESN'T EXIST.
WELL, I BEG TO DIFFER, EMO BOY.
HUH? YOU KNOW MY NAME?
HO, HO, WELL I KNOW WHO'S *NAUGHTY*, AND I KNOW WHO'S *NICE*...
WHY SHOULDN'T I KNOW WHO'S *EMO*?

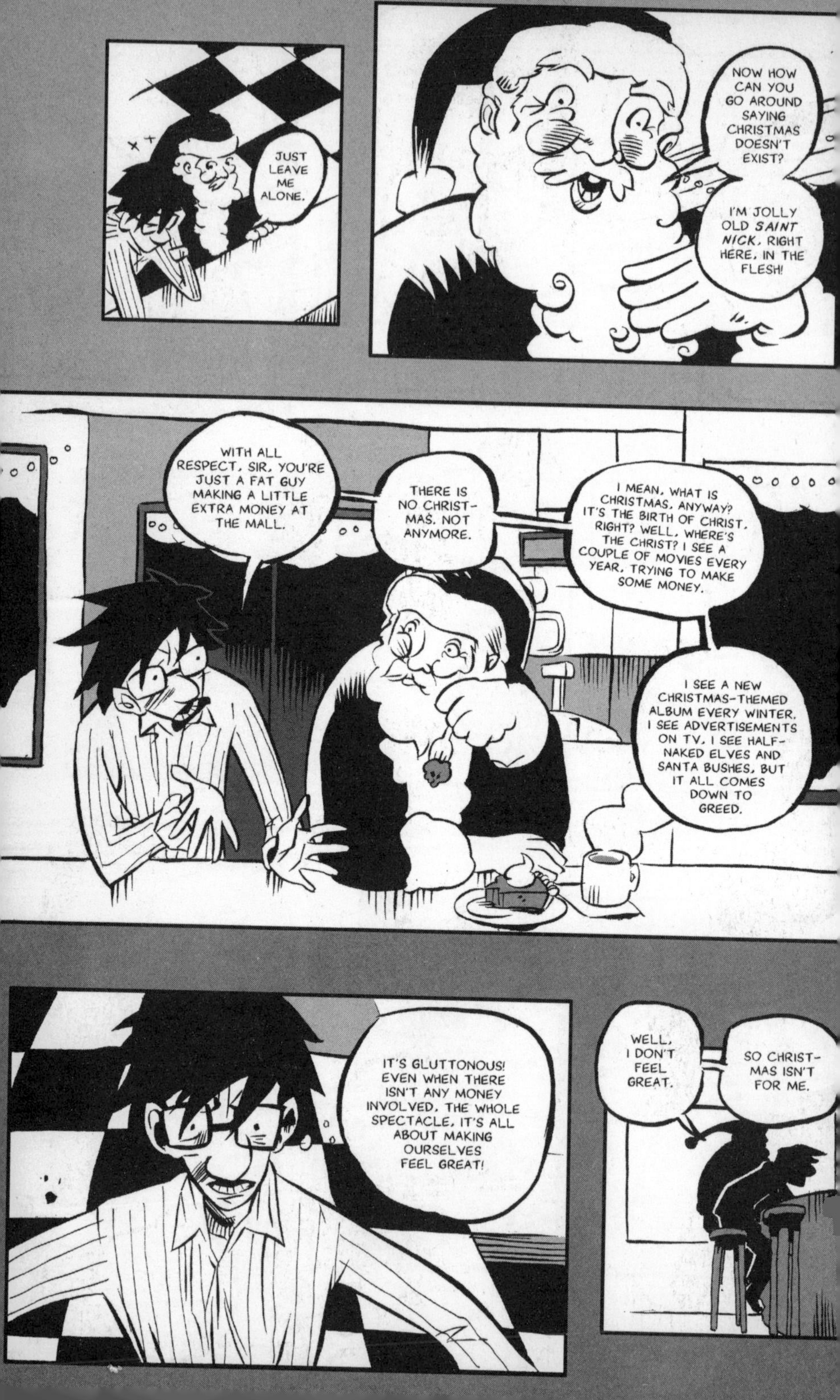
JUST LEAVE ME ALONE.
NOW HOW CAN YOU GO AROUND SAYING CHRISTMAS DOESN'T EXIST?
I'M JOLLY OLD SAINT NICK, RIGHT HERE, IN THE FLESH!
WITH ALL RESPECT, SIR, YOU'RE JUST A FAT GUY MAKING A LITTLE EXTRA MONEY AT THE MALL.
THERE IS NO CHRIST-MAS. NOT ANYMORE.
I MEAN, WHAT IS CHRISTMAS, ANYWAY? IT'S THE BIRTH OF CHRIST, RIGHT? WELL, WHERE'S THE CHRIST? I SEE A COUPLE OF MOVIES EVERY YEAR, TRYING TO MAKE SOME MONEY.
I SEE A NEW CHRISTMAS-THEMED ALBUM EVERY WINTER. I SEE ADVERTISEMENTS ON TV. I SEE HALF-NAKED ELVES AND SANTA BUSHES, BUT IT ALL COMES DOWN TO GREED.
IT'S GLUTTONOUS! EVEN WHEN THERE ISN'T ANY MONEY INVOLVED, THE WHOLE SPECTACLE, IT'S ALL ABOUT MAKING OURSELVES FEEL GREAT!
WELL, I DON'T FEEL GREAT.
SO CHRIST-MAS ISN'T FOR ME.

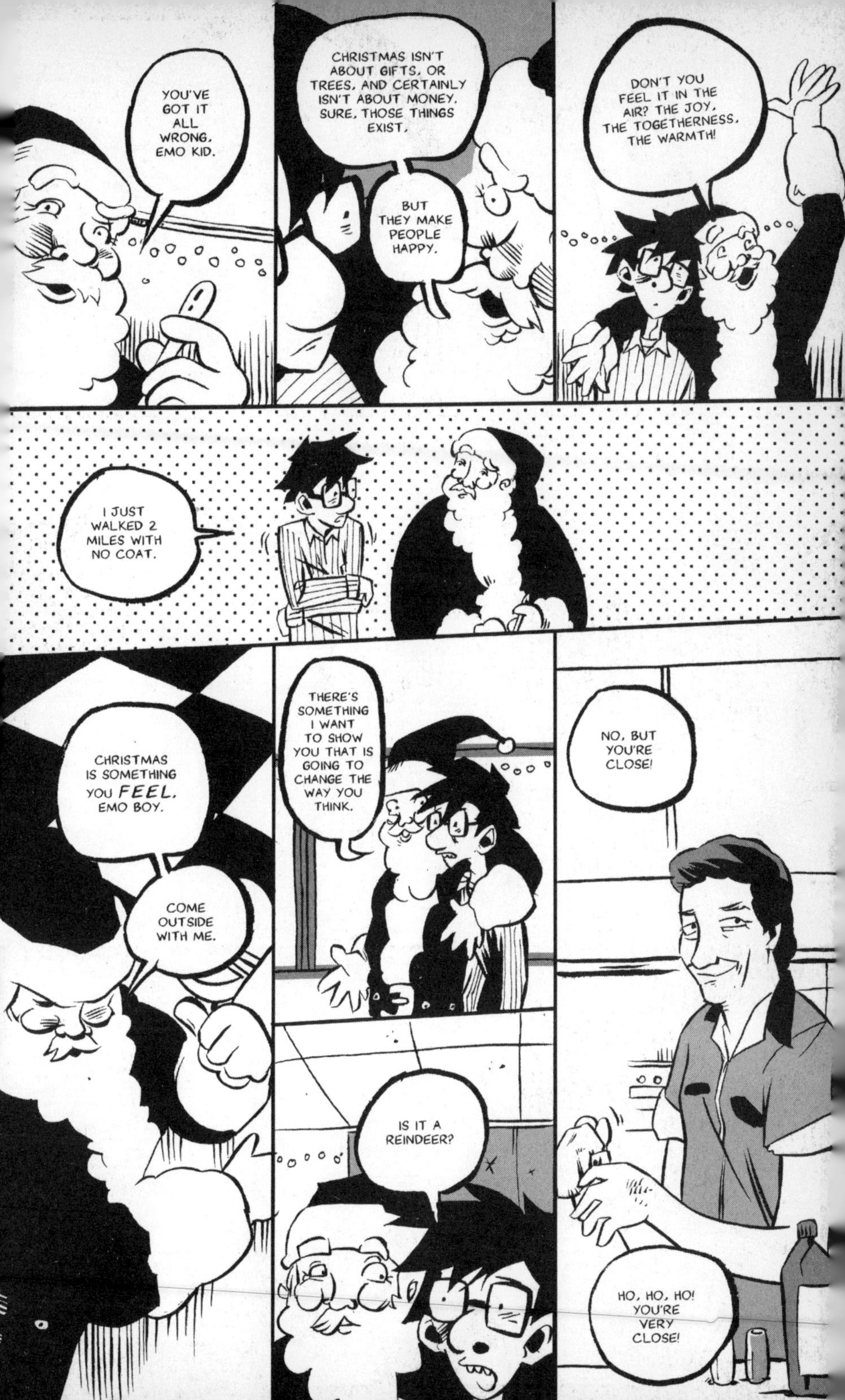
YOU'VE GOT IT ALL WRONG, EMO KID.
CHRISTMAS ISN'T ABOUT GIFTS, OR TREES, AND CERTAINLY ISN'T ABOUT MONEY. SURE, THOSE THINGS EXIST.
BUT THEY MAKE PEOPLE HAPPY.
DON'T YOU FEEL IT IN THE AIR? THE JOY, THE TOGETHERNESS, THE WARMTH!
I JUST WALKED 2 MILES WITH NO COAT.
CHRISTMAS IS SOMETHING YOU FEEL, EMO BOY.
COME OUTSIDE WITH ME.
THERE'S SOMETHING I WANT TO SHOW YOU THAT IS GOING TO CHANGE THE WAY YOU THINK.
IS IT A REINDEER?
NO, BUT YOU'RE CLOSE!
HO, HO, HO! YOU'RE VERY CLOSE!

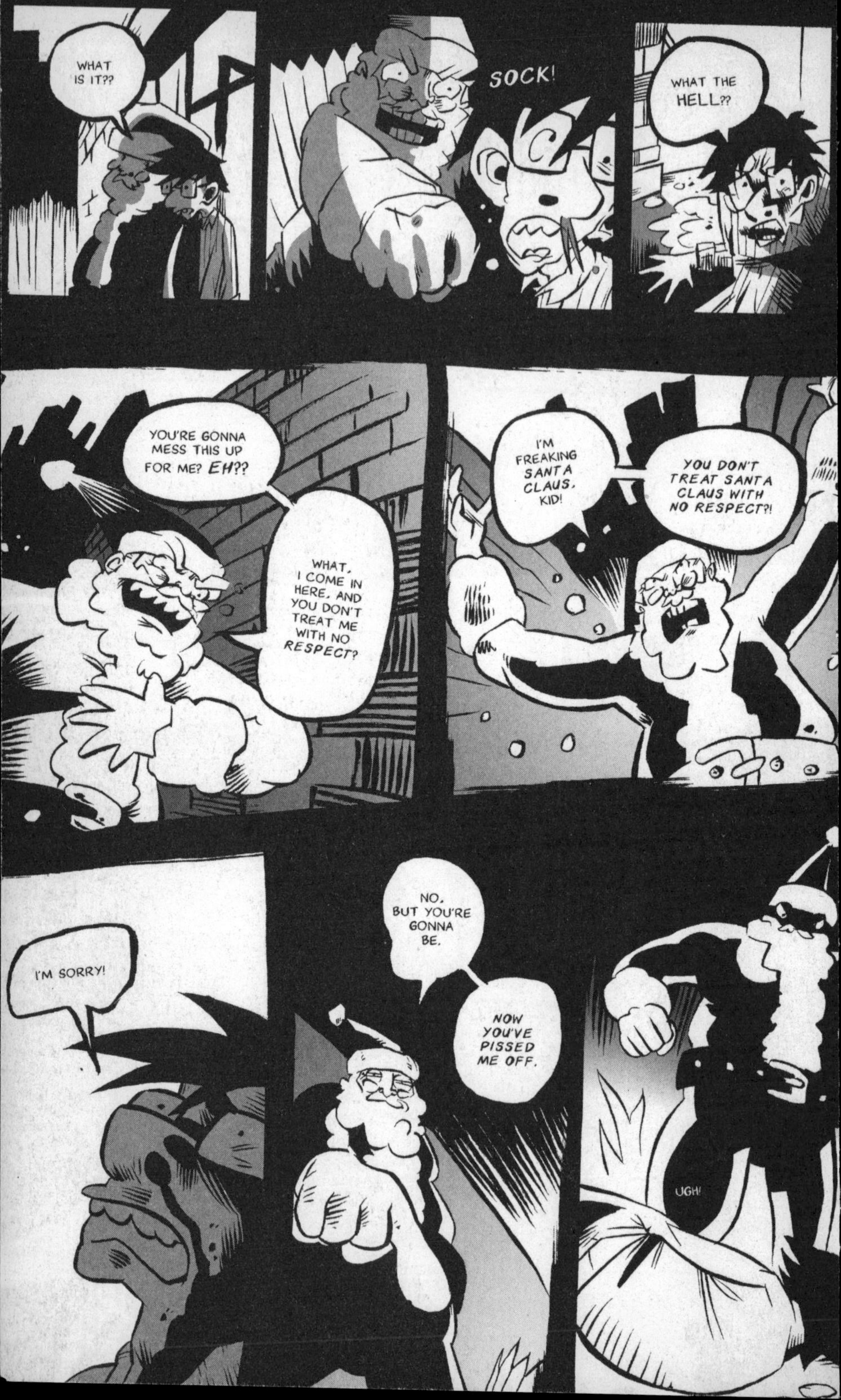
WHAT IS IT??
SOCK!
WHAT THE HELL??
YOU'RE GONNA MESS THIS UP FOR ME? EH??
WHAT, I COME IN HERE, AND YOU DON'T TREAT ME WITH NO RESPECT?
I'M FREAKING SANTA CLAUS, KID!
YOU DON'T TREAT SANTA CLAUS WITH NO RESPECT?!
I'M SORRY!
NO. BUT YOU'RE GONNA BE.
NOW YOU'VE PISSED ME OFF.
UGH!

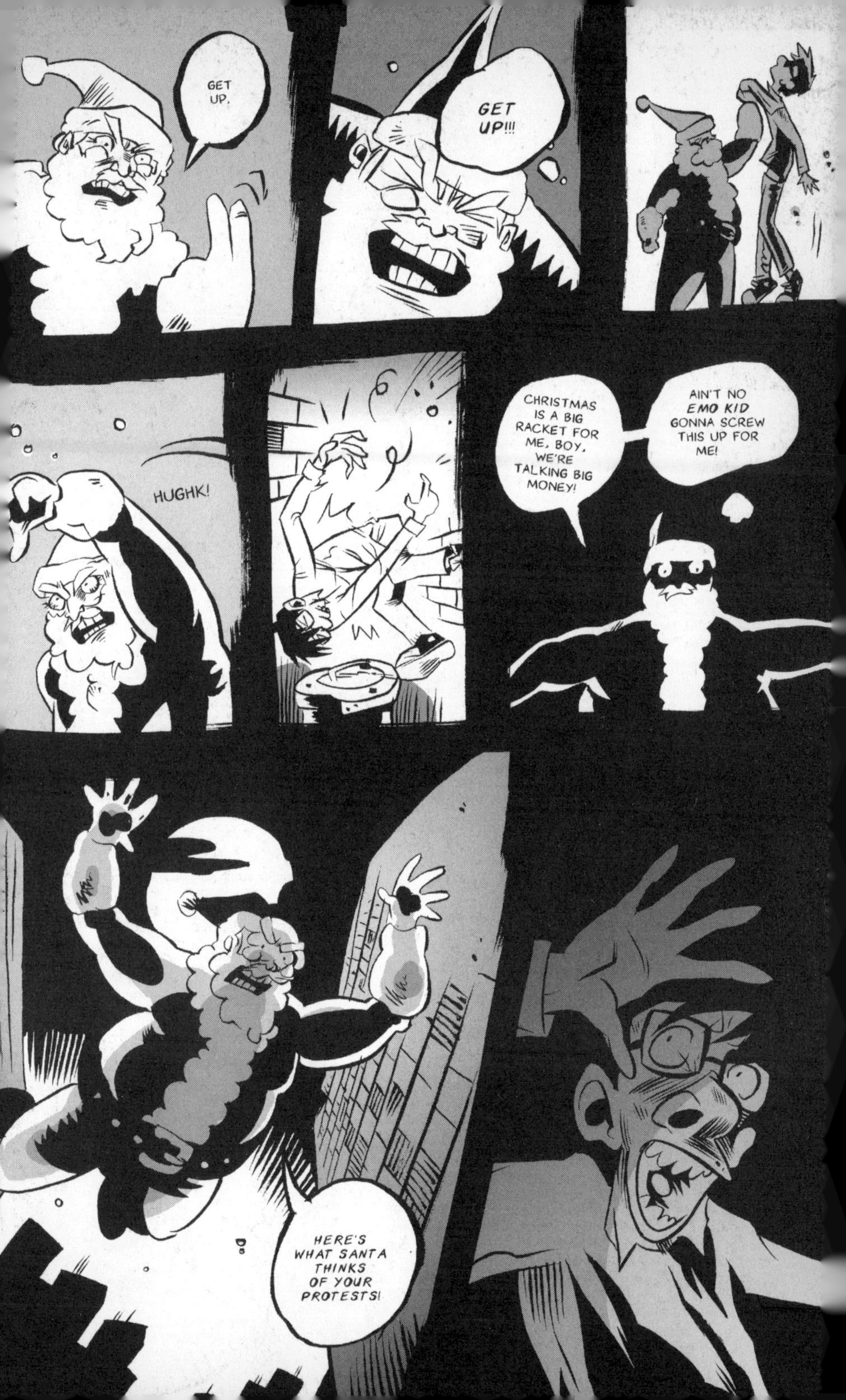
GET UP.
GET UP!!!
HUGHK!
CHRISTMAS IS A BIG RACKET FOR ME, BOY. WE'RE TALKING BIG MONEY!
AIN'T NO EMO KID GONNA SCREW THIS UP FOR ME!
HERE'S WHAT SANTA THINKS OF YOUR PROTESTS!

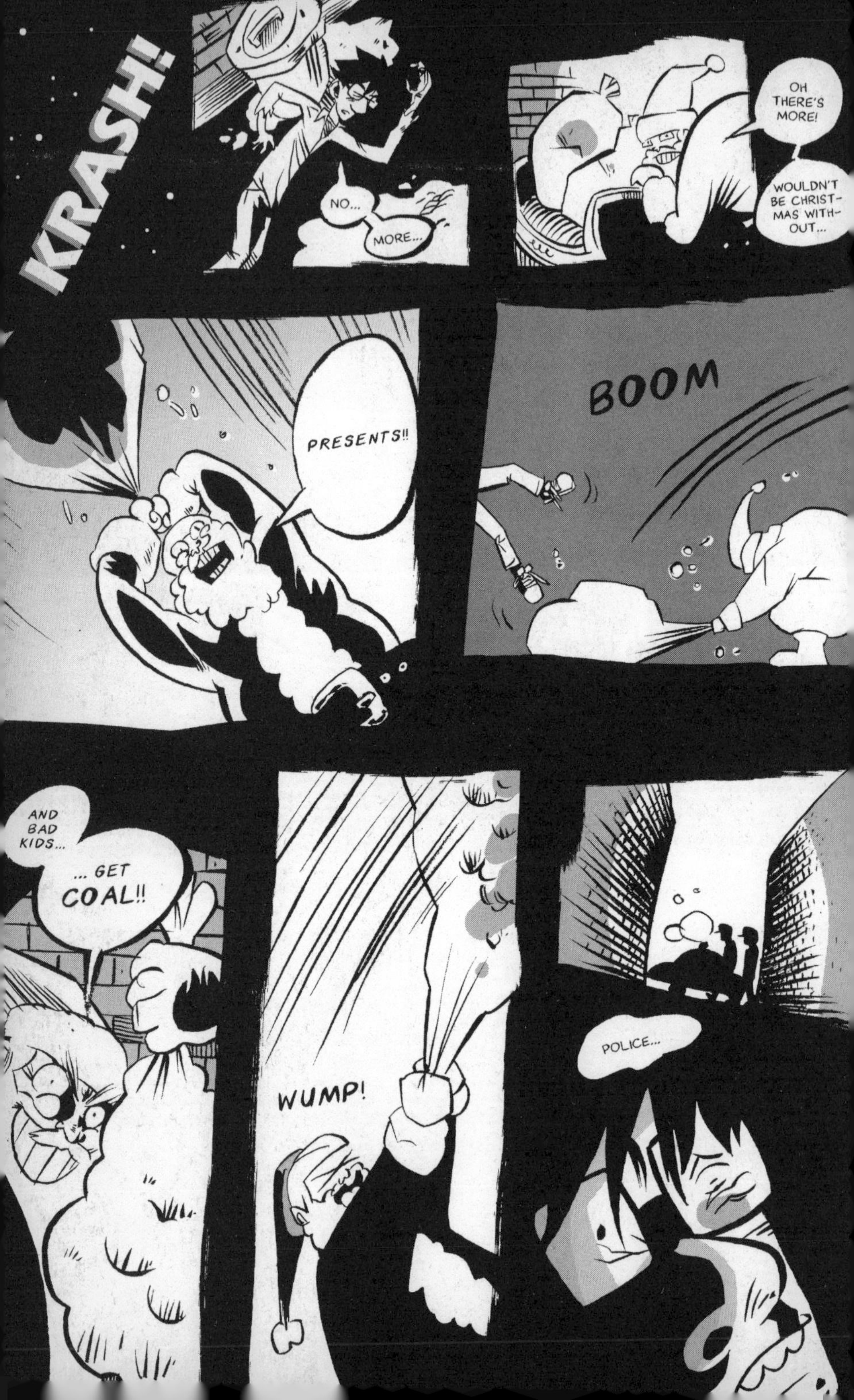
KRASH!
NO...
MORE...
OH THERE'S MORE!
WOULDN'T BE CHRISTMAS WITHOUT...
PRESENTS!!
BOOM
AND BAD KIDS...
... GET COAL!!
WUMP!
POLICE...

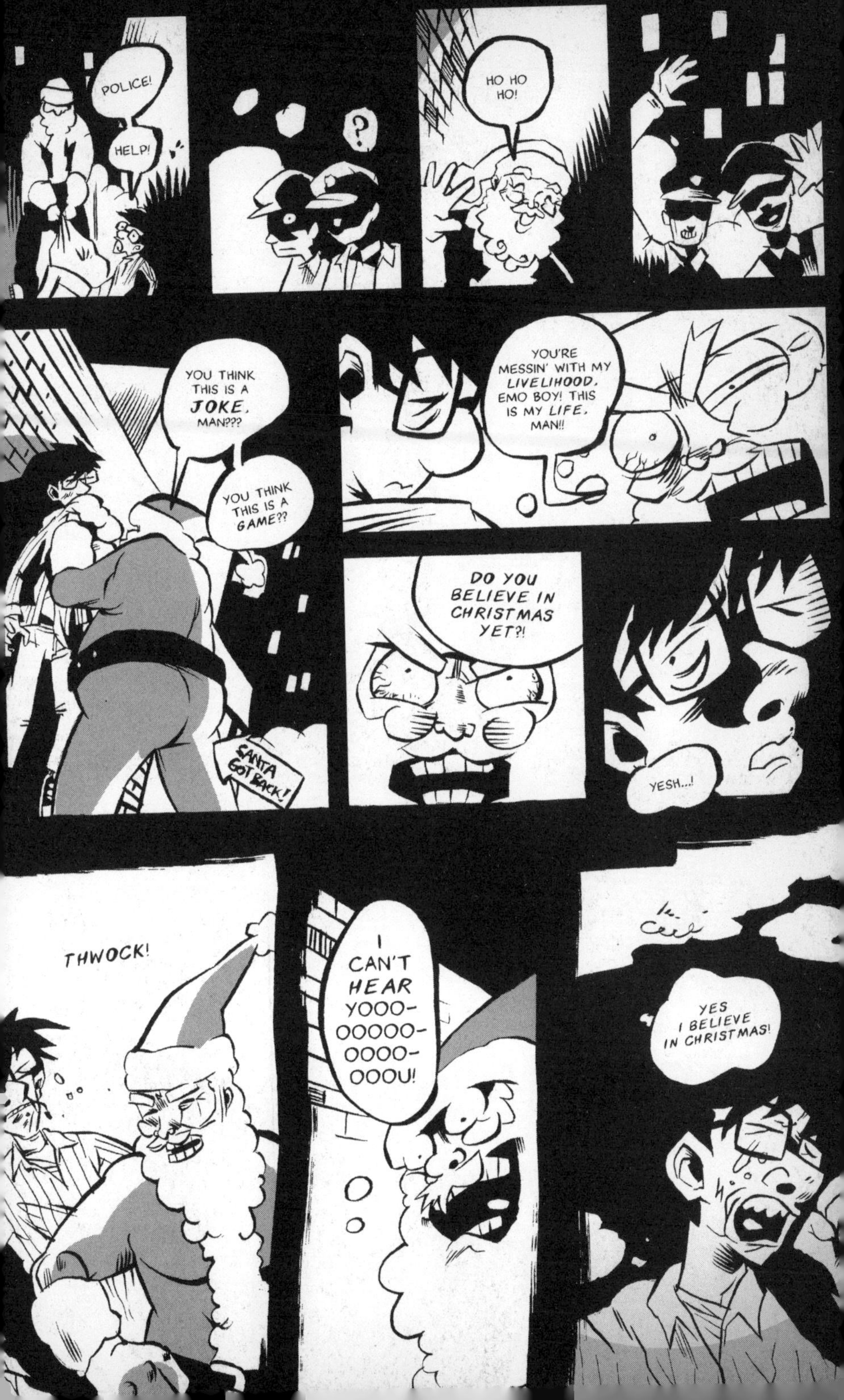
POLICE!
HELP!
?
HO HO HO!
YOU THINK THIS IS A JOKE, MAN???
YOU THINK THIS IS A GAME??
SANTA GOT BACK!
YOU'RE MESSIN' WITH MY LIVELIHOOD, EMO BOY! THIS IS MY LIFE, MAN!!
DO YOU BELIEVE IN CHRISTMAS YET?!
YESH...!
THWOCK!
I CAN'T HEAR YOOO-OOOOO-OOOO-OOOU!
YES I BELIEVE IN CHRISTMAS!

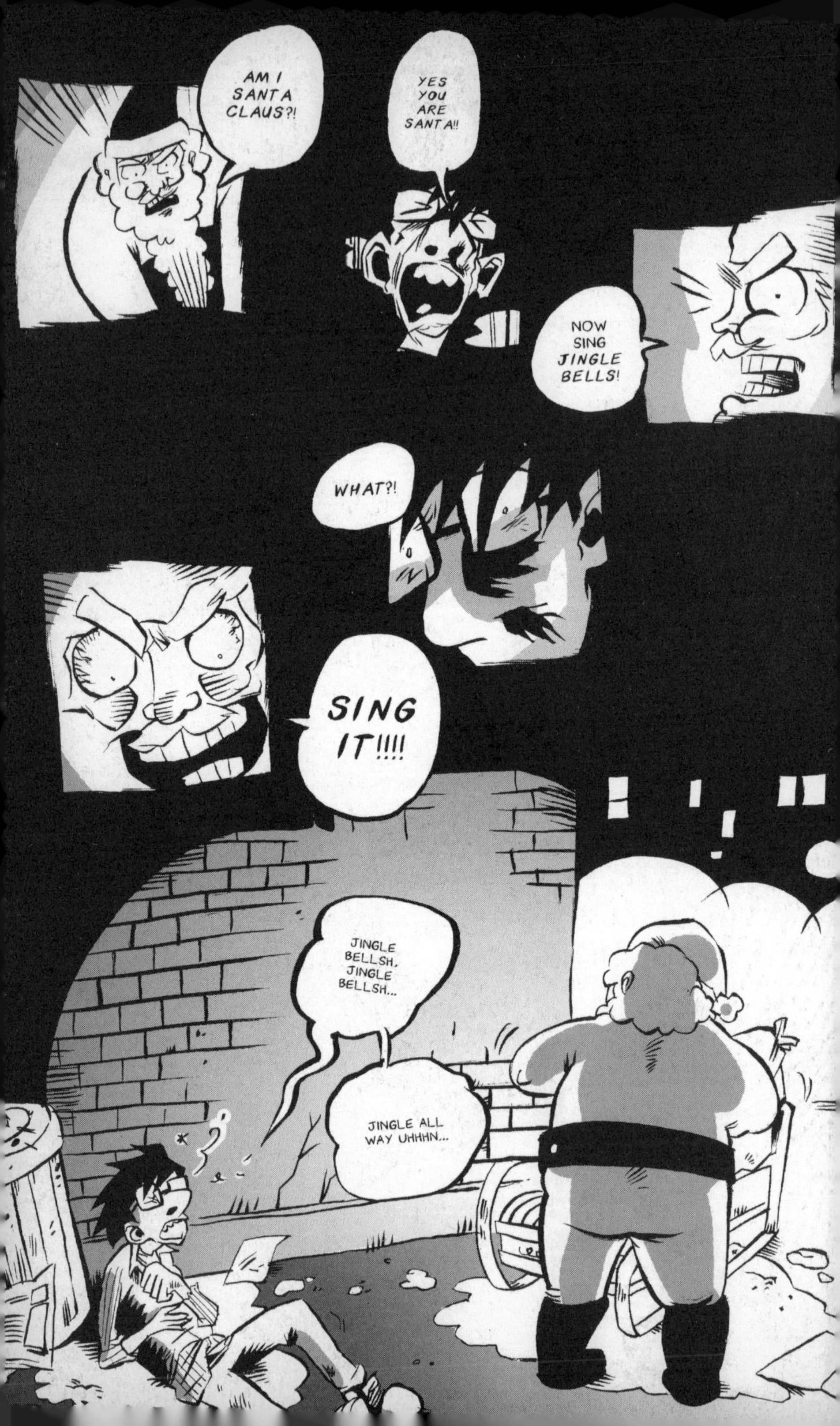
AM I SANTA CLAUS?!
YES YOU ARE SANTA!!
NOW SING JINGLE BELLS!
WHAT?!
SING IT!!!!
JINGLE BELLSH, JINGLE BELLSH...
JINGLE ALL WAY UHHHN...

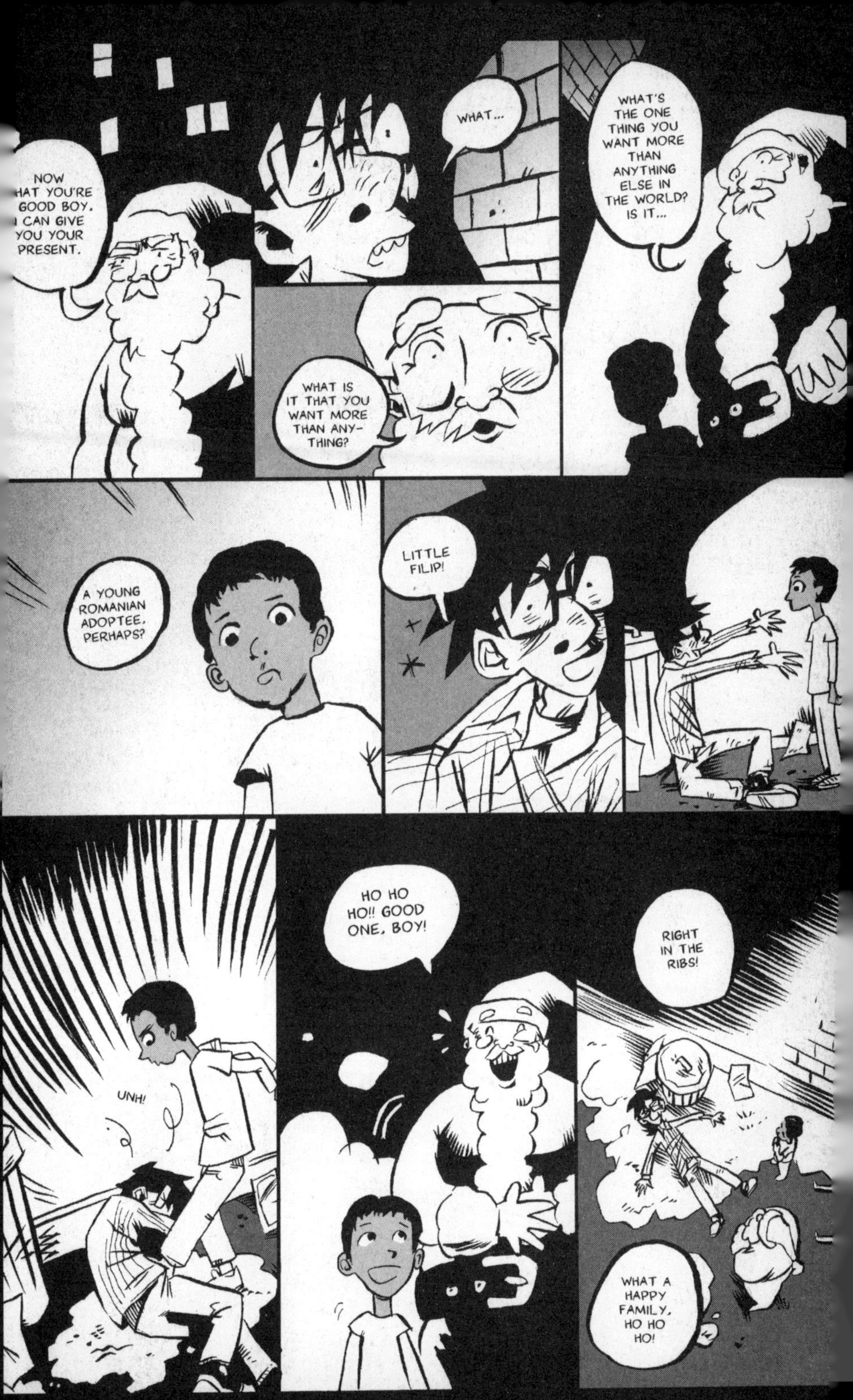
NOW
HAT YOU'RE
GOOD BOY,
CAN GIVE
YOU YOUR
PRESENT.
WHAT...
WHAT IS
IT THAT YOU
WANT MORE
THAN ANY-
THING?
WHAT'S
THE ONE
THING YOU
WANT MORE
THAN
ANYTHING
ELSE IN
THE WORLD?
IS IT...
A YOUNG
ROMANIAN
ADOPTEE,
PERHAPS?
LITTLE
FILIP!
UNH!
HO HO
HO!! GOOD
ONE, BOY!
RIGHT
IN THE
RIBS!
WHAT A
HAPPY
FAMILY,
HO HO
HO!

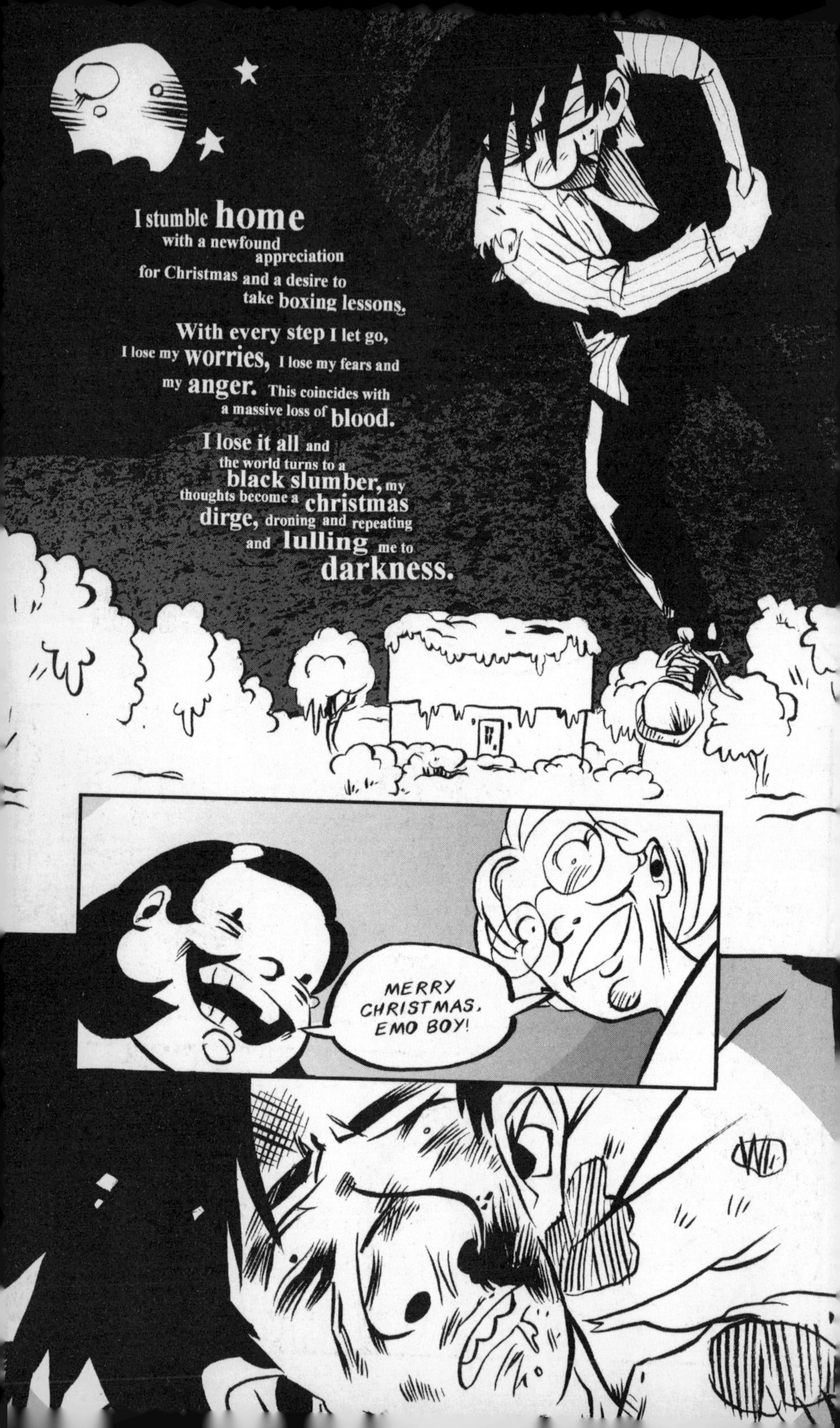
I stumble home with a newfound appreciation for Christmas and a desire to take boxing lessons.
With every step I let go, I lose my worries, I lose my fears and my anger. This coincides with a massive loss of blood.
I lose it all and the world turns to a black slumber, my thoughts become a christmas dirge, droning and repeating and lulling me to darkness.
MERRY CHRISTMAS, EMO BOY!

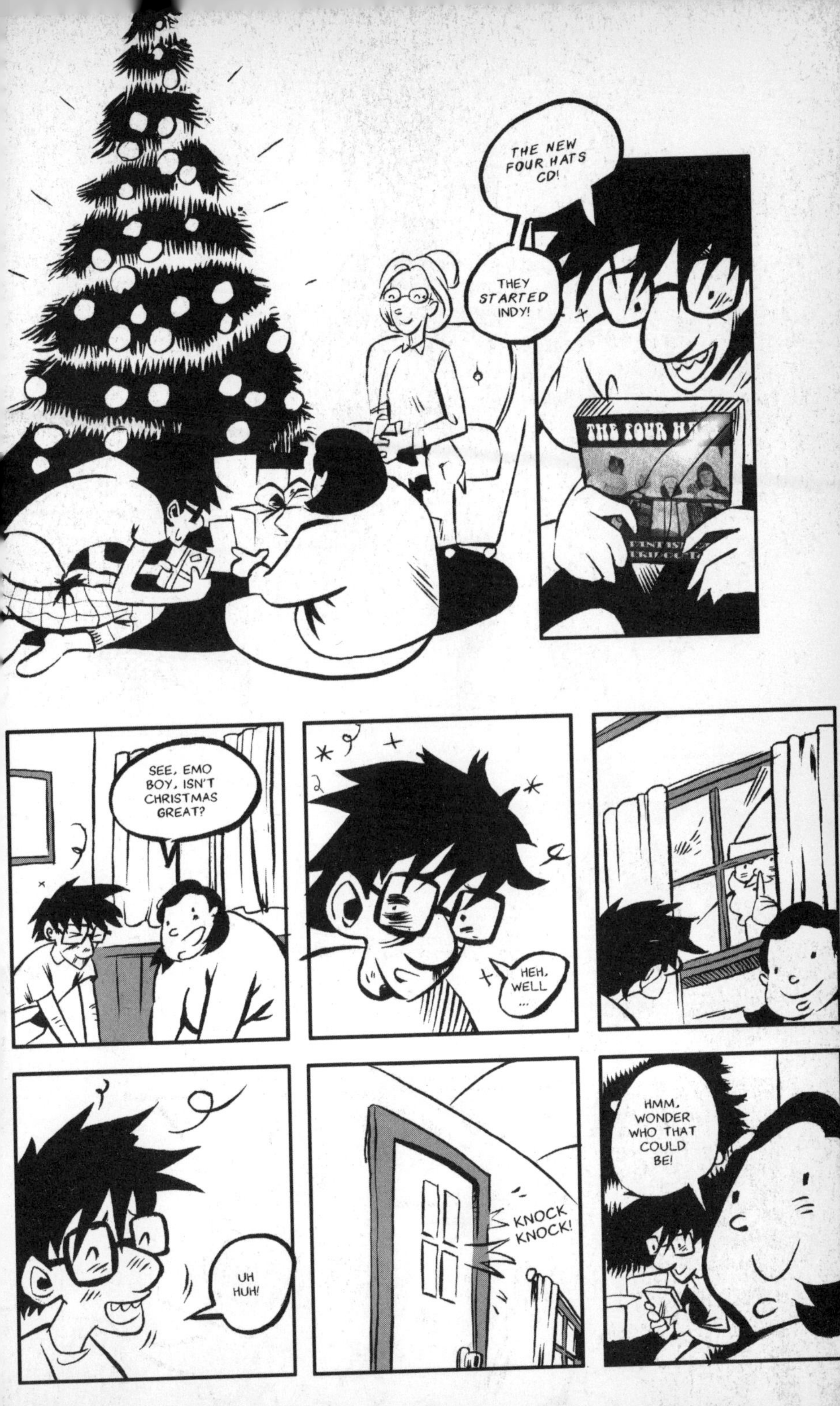
THE NEW FOUR HATS CD!
THEY STARTED INDY!
THE FOUR H
SEE, EMO BOY, ISN'T CHRISTMAS GREAT?
HEH, WELL ...
UH HUH!
KNOCK KNOCK!
HMM, WONDER WHO THAT COULD BE!

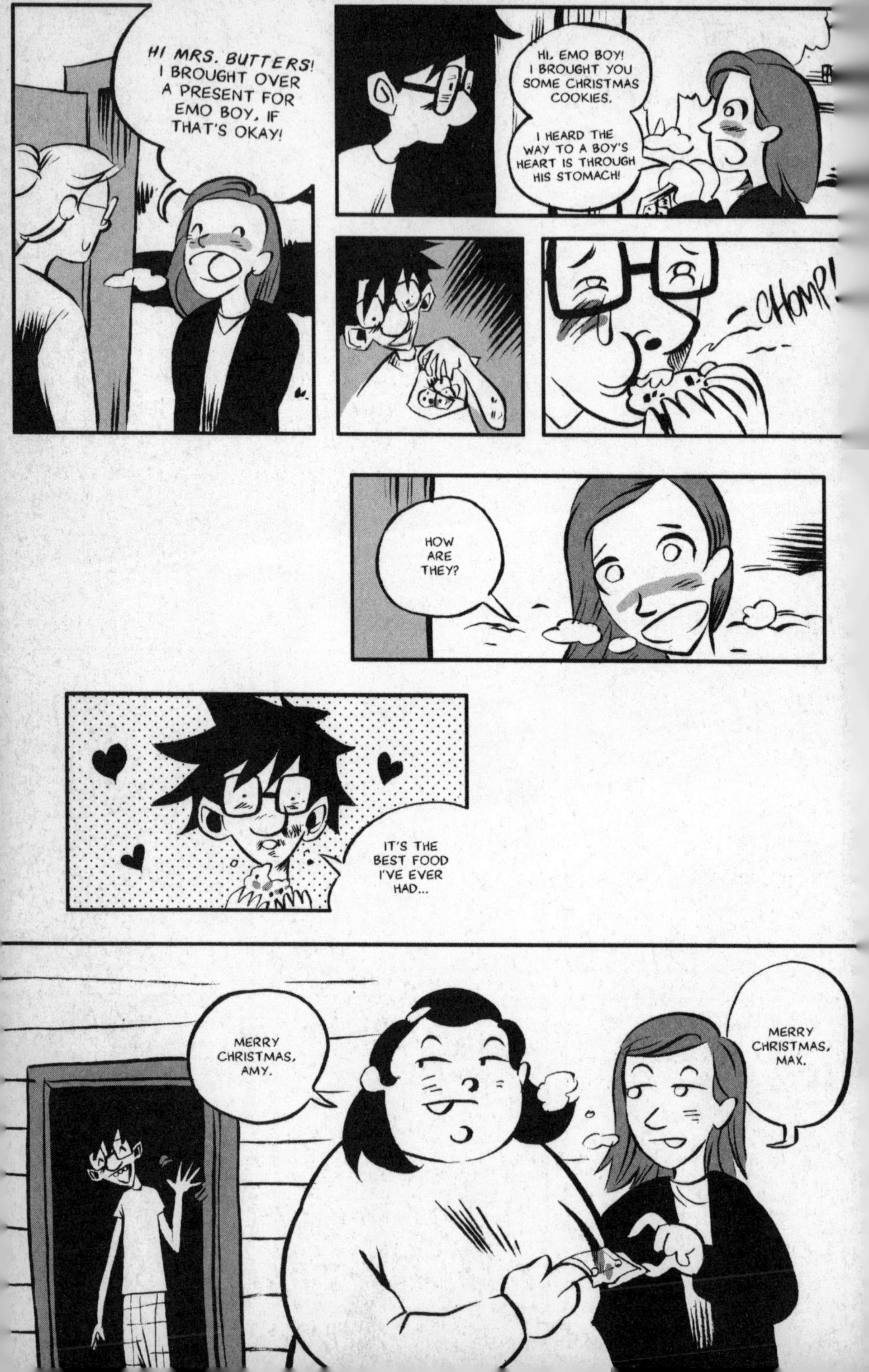
HI MRS. BUTTERS! I BROUGHT OVER A PRESENT FOR EMO BOY, IF THAT'S OKAY!
HI, EMO BOY! I BROUGHT YOU SOME CHRISTMAS COOKIES.
I HEARD THE WAY TO A BOY'S HEART IS THROUGH HIS STOMACH!
CHOMP!
HOW ARE THEY?
IT'S THE BEST FOOD I'VE EVER HAD...
MERRY CHRISTMAS, AMY.
MERRY CHRISTMAS, MAX.

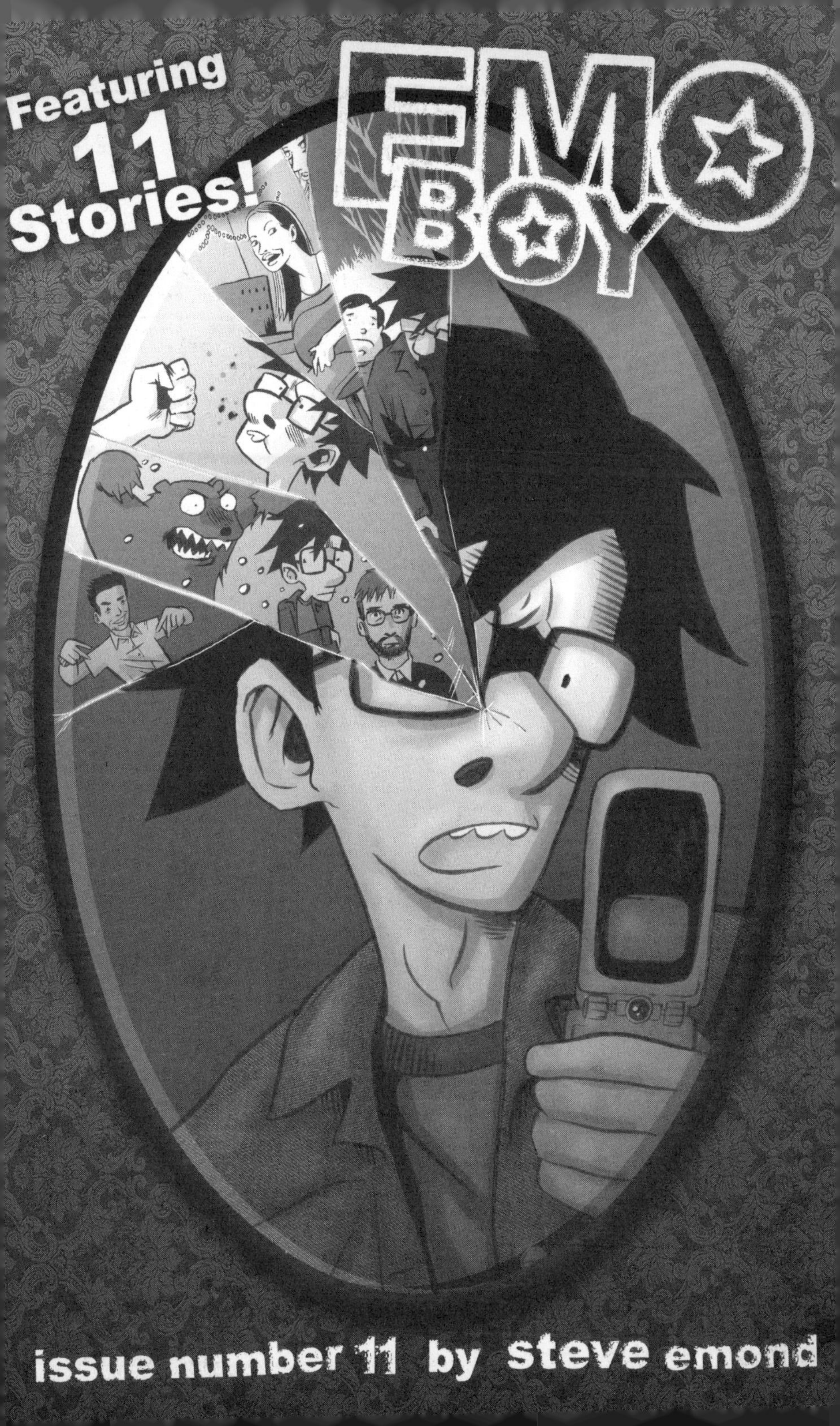

Featuring 11 Stories!
EMO BOY
issue number 11 by steve emond

# BI POLAR BEAR - By STEVE EMOND

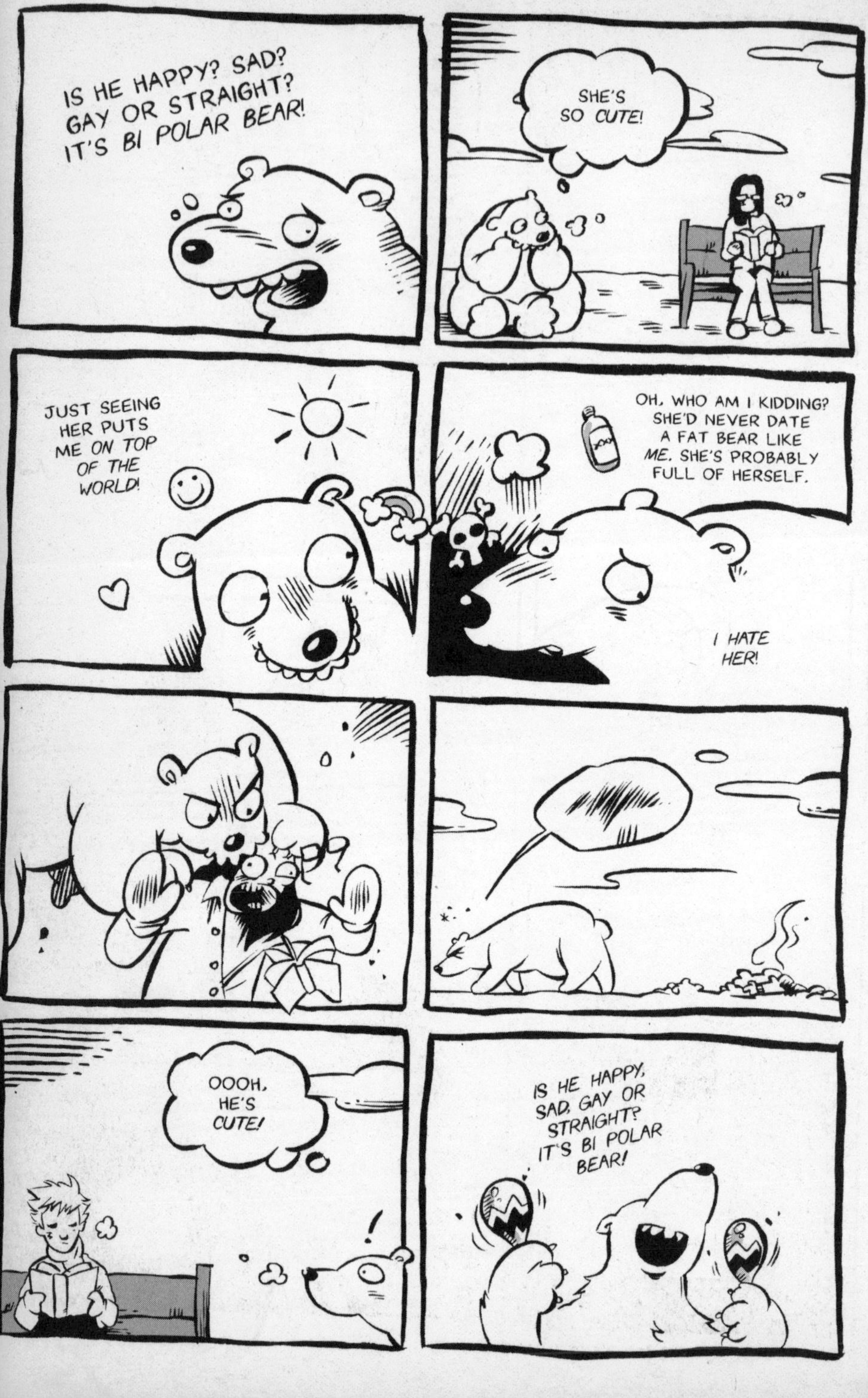

IS HE HAPPY? SAD? GAY OR STRAIGHT? IT'S BI POLAR BEAR!
SHE'S SO CUTE!
JUST SEEING HER PUTS ME ON TOP OF THE WORLD!
OH, WHO AM I KIDDING? SHE'D NEVER DATE A FAT BEAR LIKE ME. SHE'S PROBABLY FULL OF HERSELF.
I HATE HER!
OOOH, HE'S CUTE!
IS HE HAPPY, SAD, GAY OR STRAIGHT? IT'S BI POLAR BEAR!

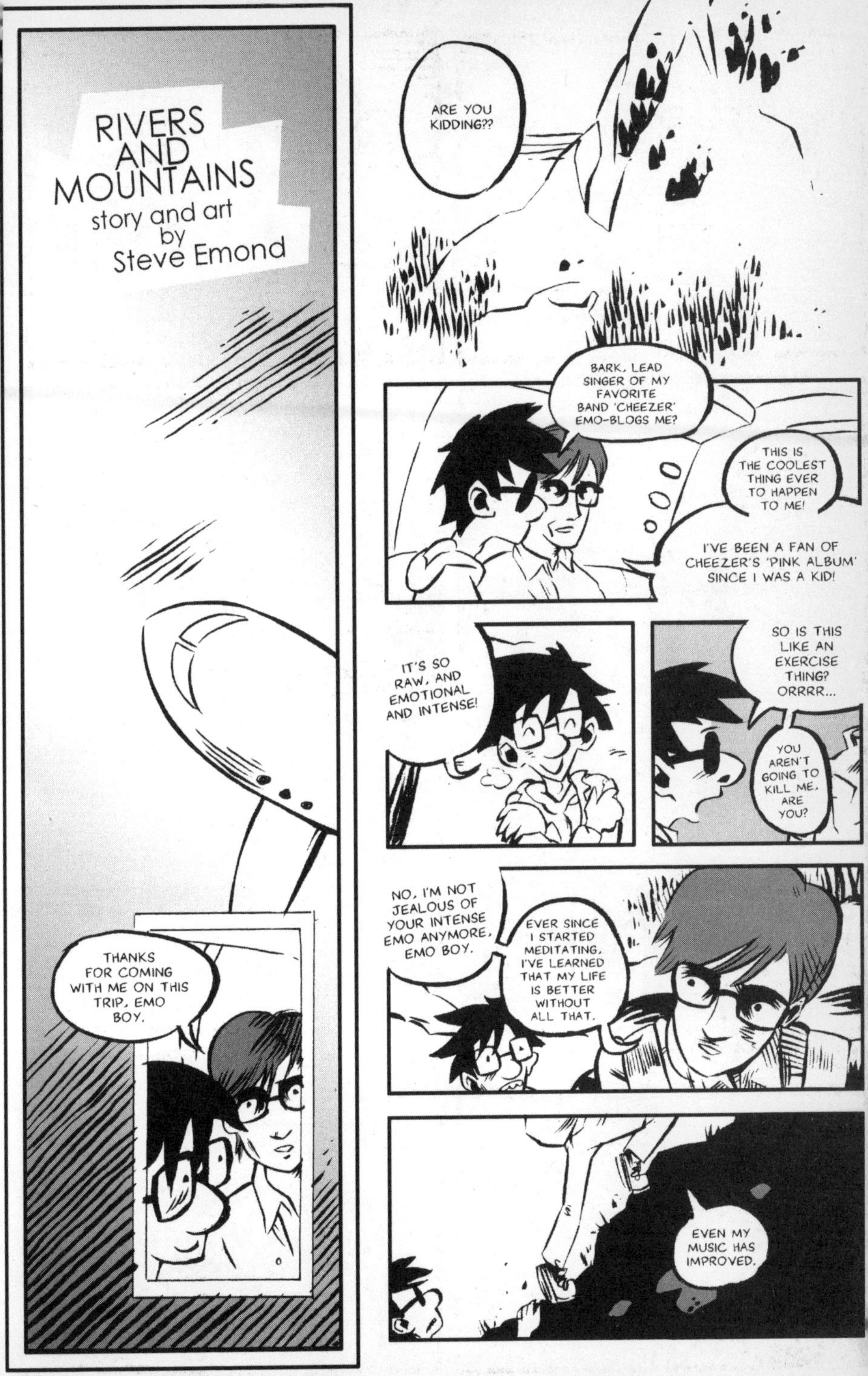
RIVERS AND MOUNTAINS
story and art by Steve Emond
THANKS FOR COMING WITH ME ON THIS TRIP, EMO BOY.
ARE YOU KIDDING??
BARK, LEAD SINGER OF MY FAVORITE BAND 'CHEEZER' EMO-BLOGS ME?
THIS IS THE COOLEST THING EVER TO HAPPEN TO ME!
I'VE BEEN A FAN OF CHEEZER'S 'PINK ALBUM' SINCE I WAS A KID!
IT'S SO RAW, AND EMOTIONAL AND INTENSE!
SO IS THIS LIKE AN EXERCISE THING? ORRRR...
YOU AREN'T GOING TO KILL ME, ARE YOU?
NO, I'M NOT JEALOUS OF YOUR INTENSE EMO ANYMORE, EMO BOY.
EVER SINCE I STARTED MEDITATING, I'VE LEARNED THAT MY LIFE IS BETTER WITHOUT ALL THAT.
EVEN MY MUSIC HAS IMPROVED.

THIS IS THE SPOT.

NOW JUST LET IT ALL GO. CLOSE YOUR EYES AND THINK, UNTIL YOU CAN THINK NO MORE.

SEE YOU TO-MORROW!

WELL, WHAT IF—

THUMP

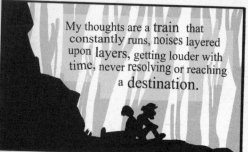

My thoughts are a **train** that constantly runs, noises layered upon layers, getting louder with time, never resolving or reaching **a destination.**

And so it begins, as I think about the noises around me. Some **distant**, some **close.**

Noises and fears that feel like they are **watching** me, waiting for a moment of **weakness.**

Noises that come out to greet me. To **devour** me whole.

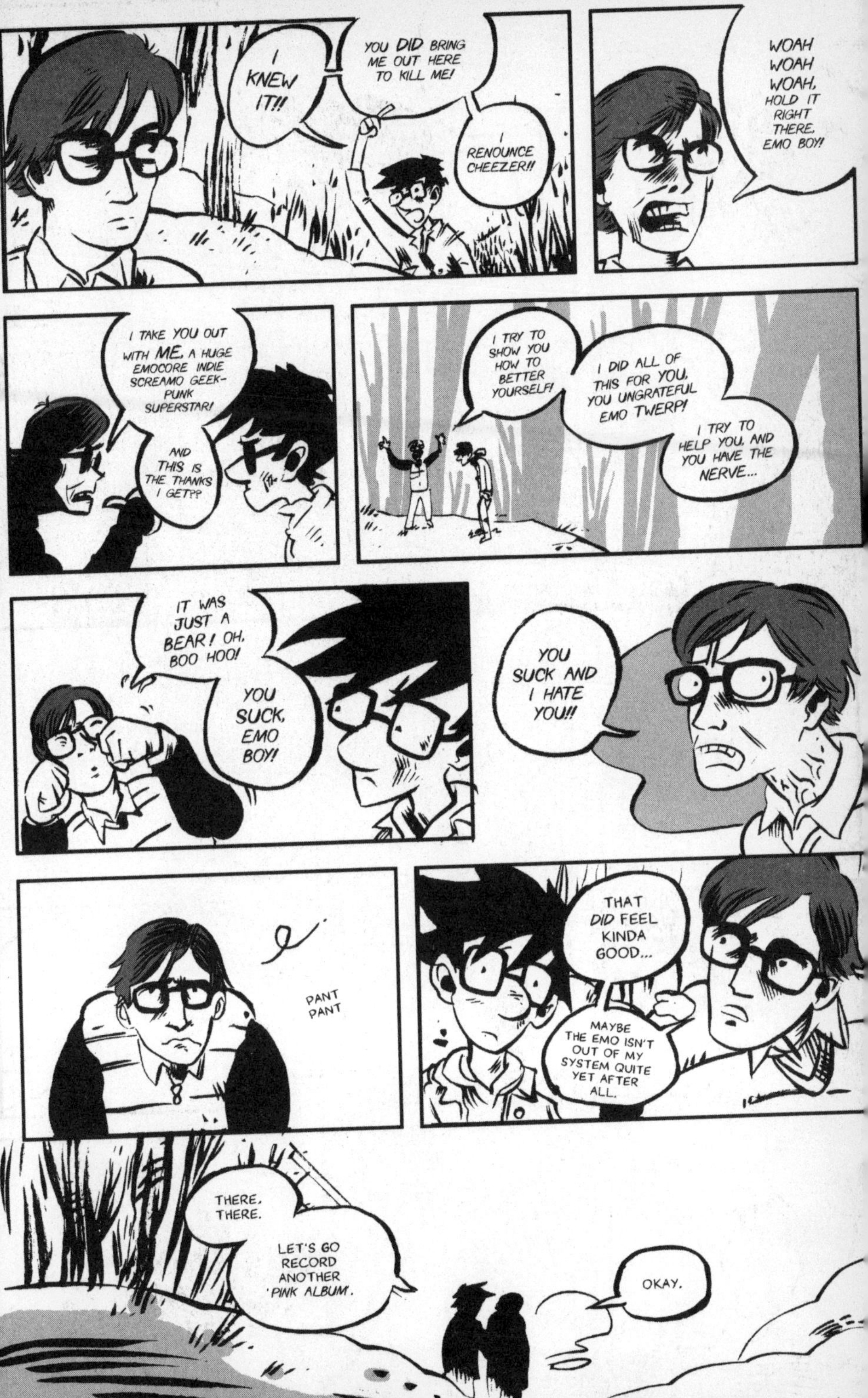
I KNEW IT!!
YOU DID BRING ME OUT HERE TO KILL ME!
I RENOUNCE CHEEZER!!
WOAH WOAH WOAH, HOLD IT RIGHT THERE, EMO BOY!
I TAKE YOU OUT WITH ME, A HUGE EMOCORE INDIE SCREAMO GEEK-PUNK SUPERSTAR!
AND THIS IS THE THANKS I GET??
I TRY TO SHOW YOU HOW TO BETTER YOURSELF!
I DID ALL OF THIS FOR YOU, YOU UNGRATEFUL EMO TWERP!
I TRY TO HELP YOU, AND YOU HAVE THE NERVE...
IT WAS JUST A BEAR! OH, BOO HOO!
YOU SUCK, EMO BOY!
YOU SUCK AND I HATE YOU!!
PANT PANT
THAT DID FEEL KINDA GOOD...
MAYBE THE EMO ISN'T OUT OF MY SYSTEM QUITE YET AFTER ALL.
THERE, THERE.
LET'S GO RECORD ANOTHER 'PINK ALBUM'.
OKAY.

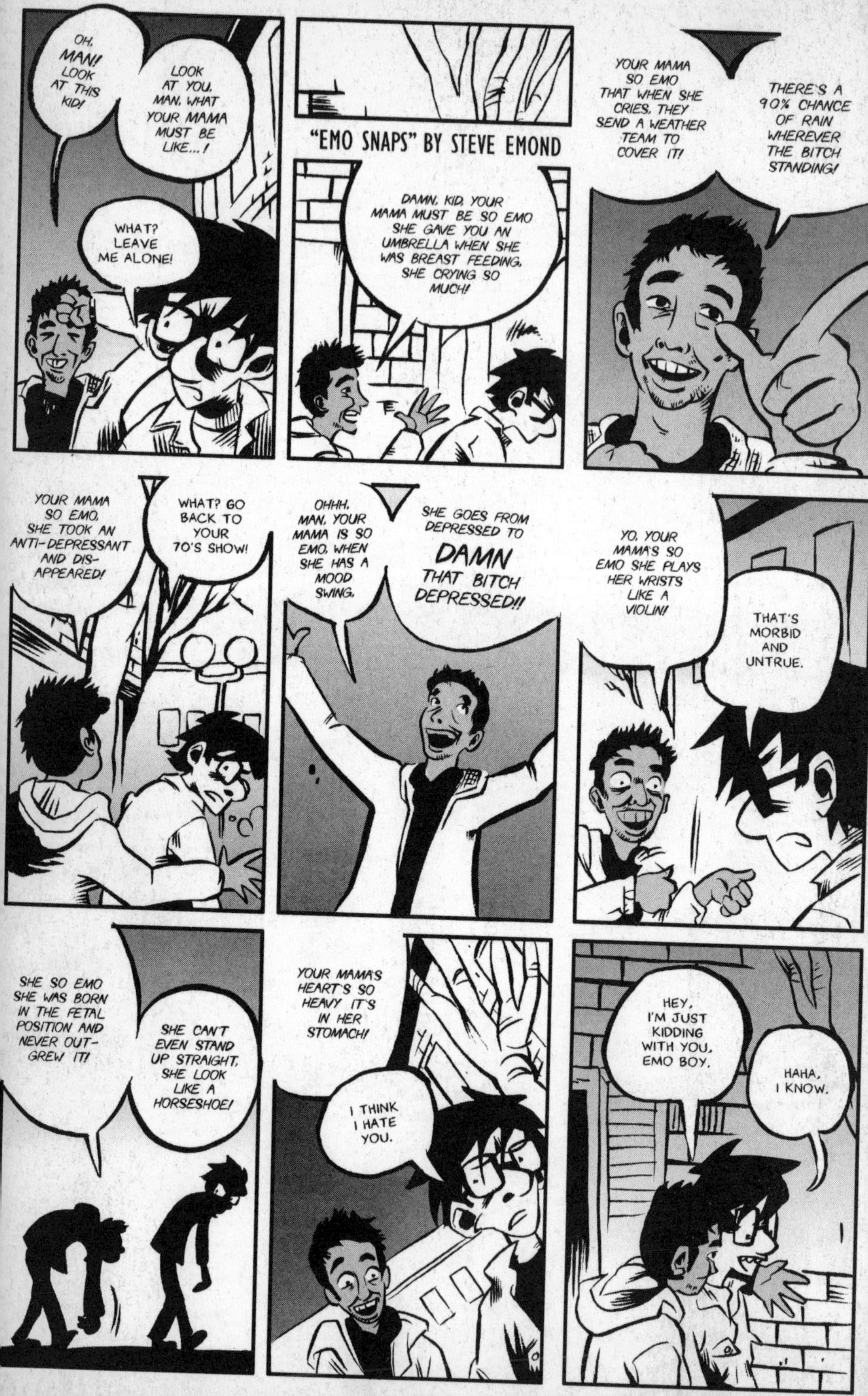
OH, MAN! LOOK AT THIS KID!
LOOK AT YOU, MAN, WHAT YOUR MAMA MUST BE LIKE...!
WHAT? LEAVE ME ALONE!
"EMO SNAPS" BY STEVE EMOND
DAMN, KID, YOUR MAMA MUST BE SO EMO SHE GAVE YOU AN UMBRELLA WHEN SHE WAS BREAST FEEDING, SHE CRYING SO MUCH!
YOUR MAMA SO EMO THAT WHEN SHE CRIES, THEY SEND A WEATHER TEAM TO COVER IT!
THERE'S A 90% CHANCE OF RAIN WHEREVER THE BITCH STANDING!
YOUR MAMA SO EMO, SHE TOOK AN ANTI-DEPRESSANT AND DIS-APPEARED!
WHAT? GO BACK TO YOUR 70'S SHOW!
OHHH, MAN, YOUR MAMA IS SO EMO, WHEN SHE HAS A MOOD SWING,
SHE GOES FROM DEPRESSED TO DAMN THAT BITCH DEPRESSED!!
YO, YOUR MAMA'S SO EMO SHE PLAYS HER WRISTS LIKE A VIOLIN!
THAT'S MORBID AND UNTRUE.
SHE SO EMO SHE WAS BORN IN THE FETAL POSITION AND NEVER OUT-GREW IT!
SHE CAN'T EVEN STAND UP STRAIGHT, SHE LOOK LIKE A HORSESHOE!
YOUR MAMA'S HEART'S SO HEAVY IT'S IN HER STOMACH!
I THINK I HATE YOU.
HEY, I'M JUST KIDDING WITH YOU, EMO BOY.
HAHA, I KNOW.

I am an emo vampire. I slip into darkness and feel nothing. I feel numbness, and bitterness, and nothing more. I am an emo vampire, and when night falls, I exit my coffin and search for prey. The lonely, the hurt, the broken. I feed off their misery and it makes me strong. They aren't hard to find; they're everywhere I look.

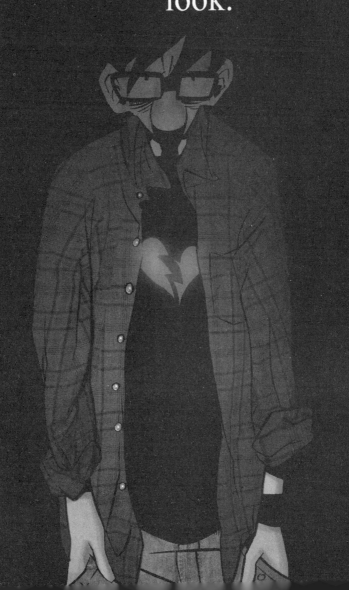

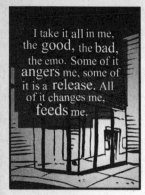

I take it all in me, the good, the bad, the emo. Some of it angers me, some of it is a release. All of it changes me, feeds me.

I pity him and his American dream. Too busy, too active, too full of himself to have any meaning or self actualization in his life.

I pity the whole lot of them.

She jumps from man to man; she lives for everyone but herself. She isn't even a character in her own life.

She's someone else's fantasy and beyond that she doesn't exist at all.

He's broken and pathetic. If anyone here, I identify with him. I pity him most of all.

But tonight I am cool and aloof, I live in the shadows, because I am--

WHAT ARE YOU LOOKING AT??

I'M A VAMPIRE!!

I look at the stars when I can. I stare until they blur. Slowly, I look ahead and the stars turn into headlights, forming a long bracelet, a shiny golden bracelet and I want to share it with someone. I want to place it on Penny's wrist but she's gone now and I'm alone and miserable.

"I Could Dance If You'd Just Stop Watching" by Steve Emond

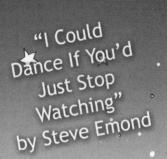

With no company but my broken heart,

the stars, a golden bracelet and

a car full of guys that insist I have a good time.

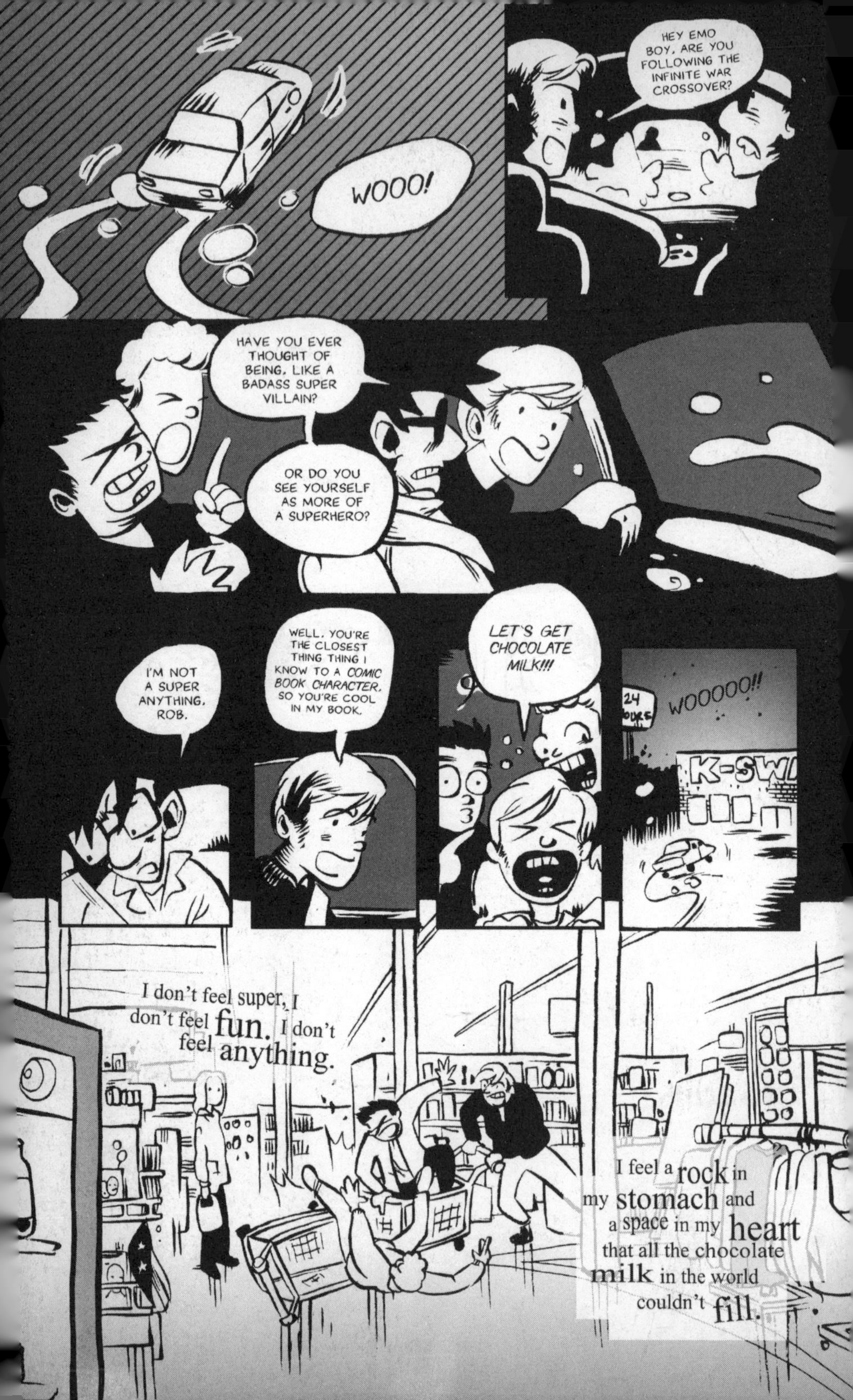
WOOO!
HEY EMO BOY, ARE YOU FOLLOWING THE INFINITE WAR CROSSOVER?
HAVE YOU EVER THOUGHT OF BEING, LIKE A BADASS SUPER VILLAIN?
OR DO YOU SEE YOURSELF AS MORE OF A SUPERHERO?
I'M NOT A SUPER ANYTHING, ROB.
WELL, YOU'RE THE CLOSEST THING THING I KNOW TO A COMIC BOOK CHARACTER, SO YOU'RE COOL IN MY BOOK.
LET'S GET CHOCOLATE MILK!!!
24
WOOOOO!!
K-SW
I don't feel super, I don't feel fun. I don't feel anything.
I feel a rock in my stomach and a space in my heart that all the chocolate milk in the world couldn't fill.

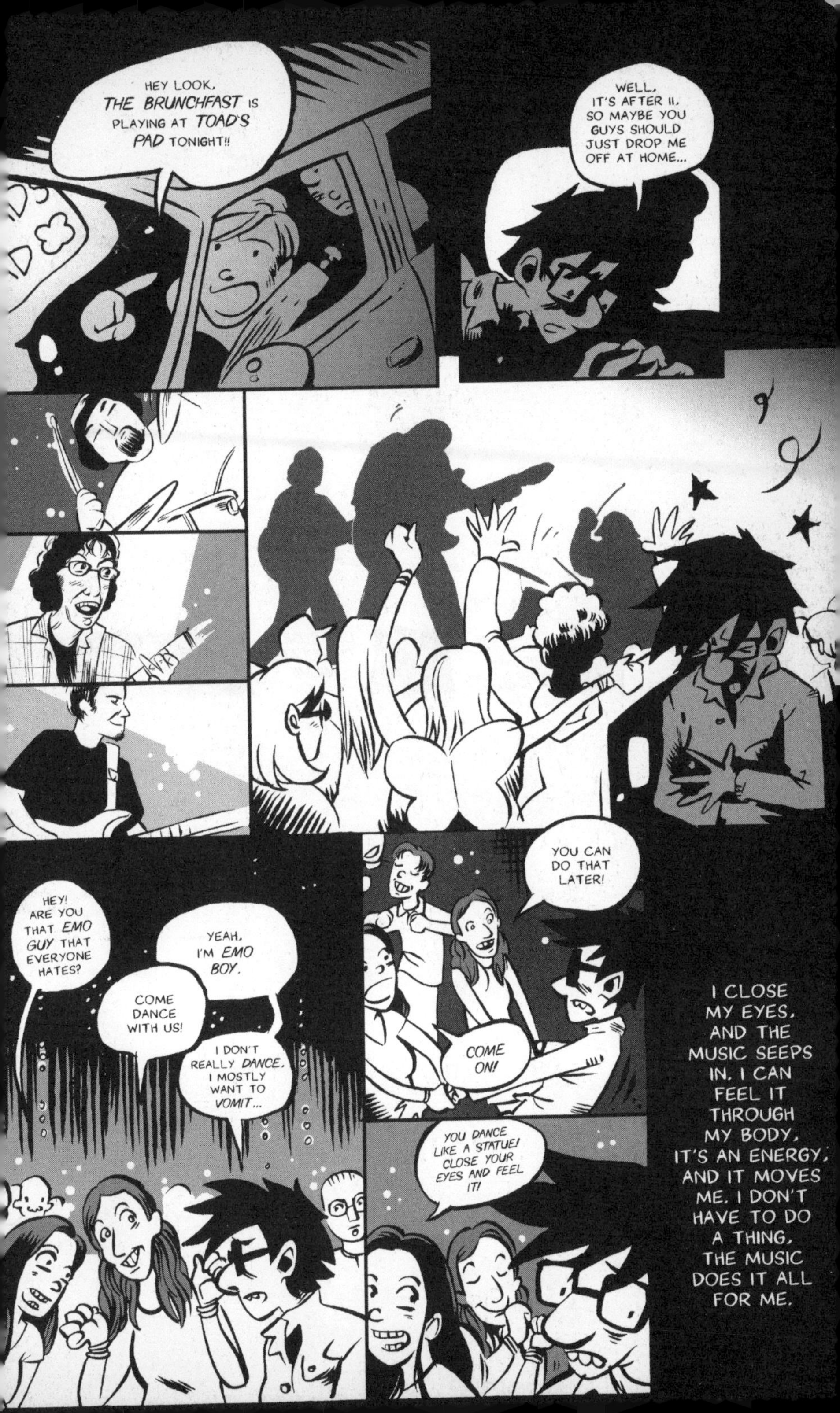

HEY LOOK, THE BRUNCHFAST IS PLAYING AT TOAD'S PAD TONIGHT!!
WELL, IT'S AFTER 11, SO MAYBE YOU GUYS SHOULD JUST DROP ME OFF AT HOME...
HEY! ARE YOU THAT EMO GUY THAT EVERYONE HATES?
YEAH, I'M EMO BOY.
COME DANCE WITH US!
I DON'T REALLY DANCE, I MOSTLY WANT TO VOMIT...
YOU CAN DO THAT LATER!
COME ON!
YOU DANCE LIKE A STATUE! CLOSE YOUR EYES AND FEEL IT!
I CLOSE MY EYES, AND THE MUSIC SEEPS IN. I CAN FEEL IT THROUGH MY BODY, IT'S AN ENERGY, AND IT MOVES ME. I DON'T HAVE TO DO A THING, THE MUSIC DOES IT ALL FOR ME.

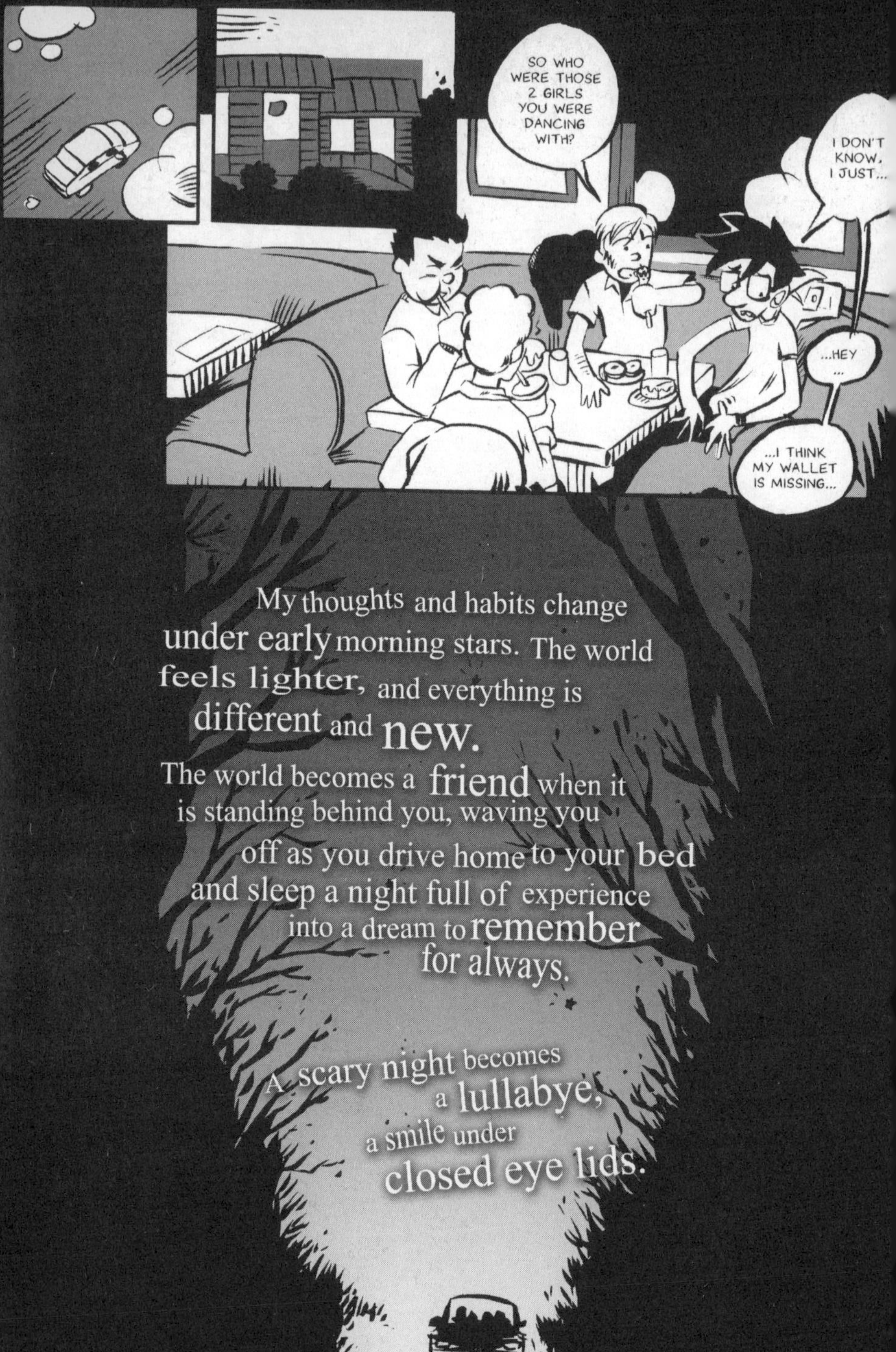
SO WHO WERE THOSE 2 GIRLS YOU WERE DANCING WITH?
I DON'T KNOW, I JUST...
...HEY ...
...I THINK MY WALLET IS MISSING...
My thoughts and habits change under early morning stars. The world feels lighter, and everything is different and new.
The world becomes a friend when it is standing behind you, waving you off as you drive home to your bed and sleep a night full of experience into a dream to remember for always.
A scary night becomes a lullabye, a smile under closed eye lids.

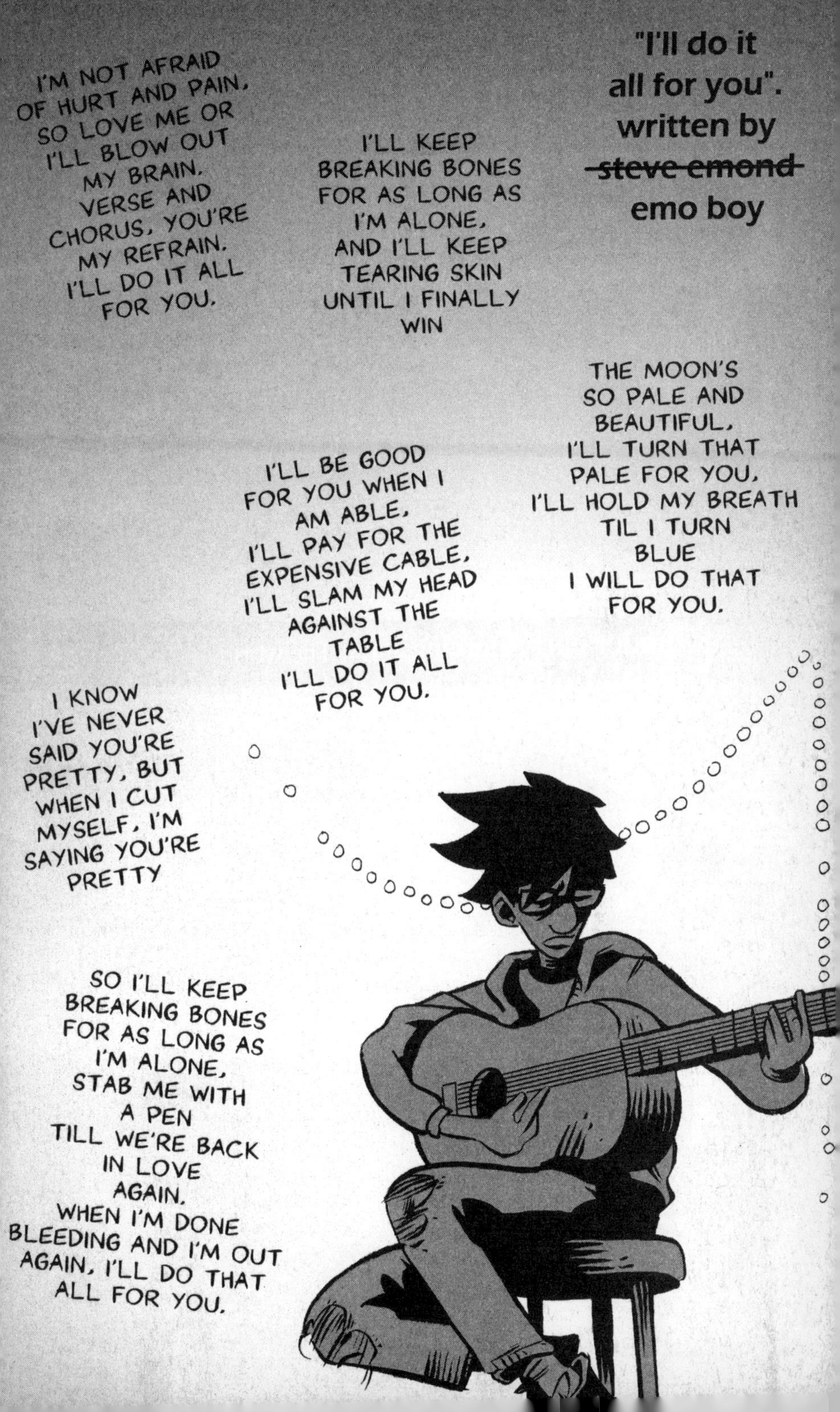
"I'll do it all for you". written by ~~steve emond~~ emo boy
I'M NOT AFRAID OF HURT AND PAIN, SO LOVE ME OR I'LL BLOW OUT MY BRAIN. VERSE AND CHORUS, YOU'RE MY REFRAIN. I'LL DO IT ALL FOR YOU.
I'LL KEEP BREAKING BONES FOR AS LONG AS I'M ALONE, AND I'LL KEEP TEARING SKIN UNTIL I FINALLY WIN
THE MOON'S SO PALE AND BEAUTIFUL, I'LL TURN THAT PALE FOR YOU, I'LL HOLD MY BREATH TIL I TURN BLUE I WILL DO THAT FOR YOU.
I'LL BE GOOD FOR YOU WHEN I AM ABLE, I'LL PAY FOR THE EXPENSIVE CABLE, I'LL SLAM MY HEAD AGAINST THE TABLE I'LL DO IT ALL FOR YOU.
I KNOW I'VE NEVER SAID YOU'RE PRETTY, BUT WHEN I CUT MYSELF, I'M SAYING YOU'RE PRETTY
SO I'LL KEEP BREAKING BONES FOR AS LONG AS I'M ALONE, STAB ME WITH A PEN TILL WE'RE BACK IN LOVE AGAIN. WHEN I'M DONE BLEEDING AND I'M OUT AGAIN, I'LL DO THAT ALL FOR YOU.

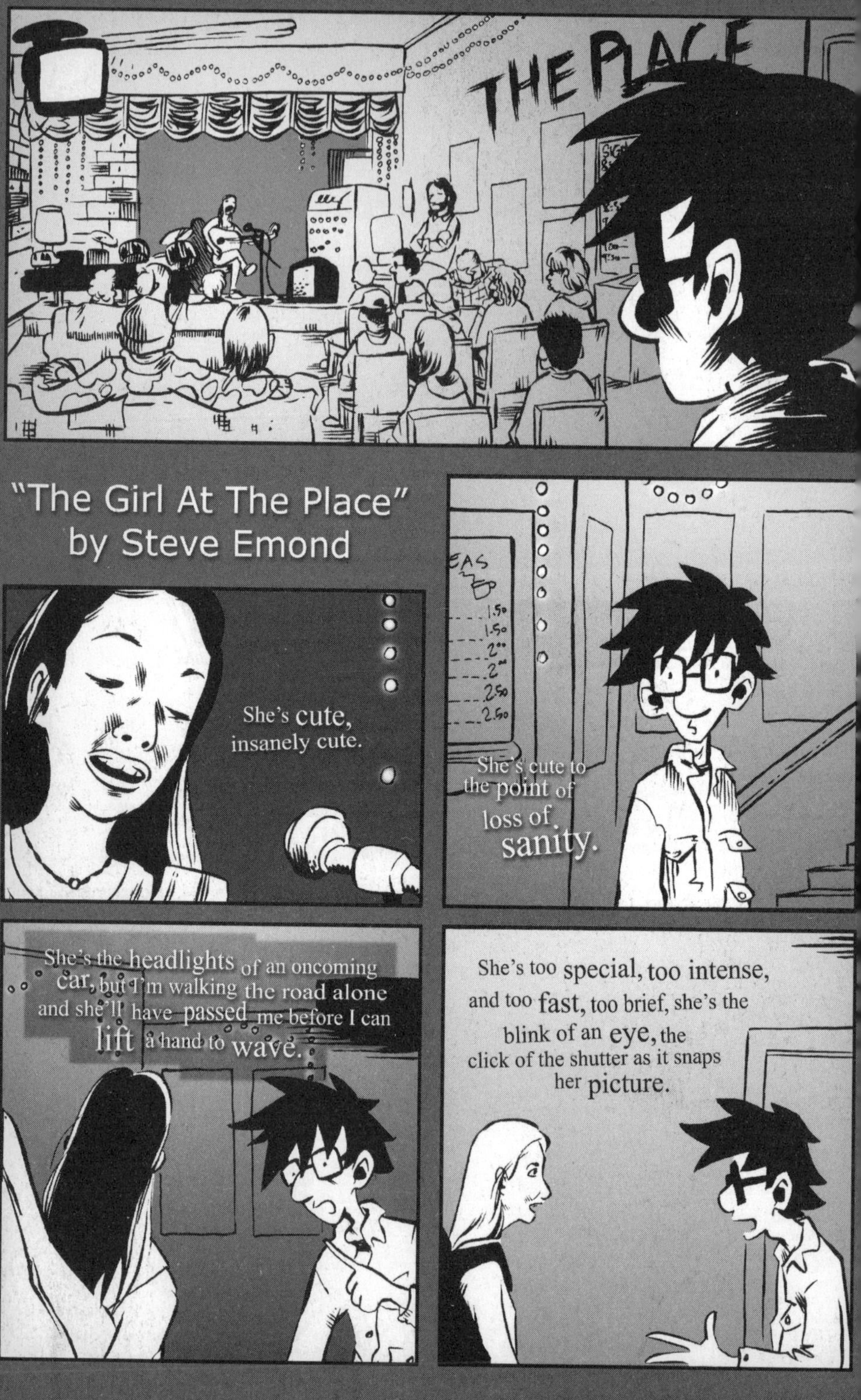
THE PLACE
"The Girl At The Place"
by Steve Emond
She's cute, insanely cute.
She's cute to the point of loss of sanity.
She's the headlights of an oncoming car, but I'm walking the road alone and she'll have passed me before I can lift a hand to wave.
She's too special, too intense, and too fast, too brief, she's the blink of an eye, the click of the shutter as it snaps her picture.

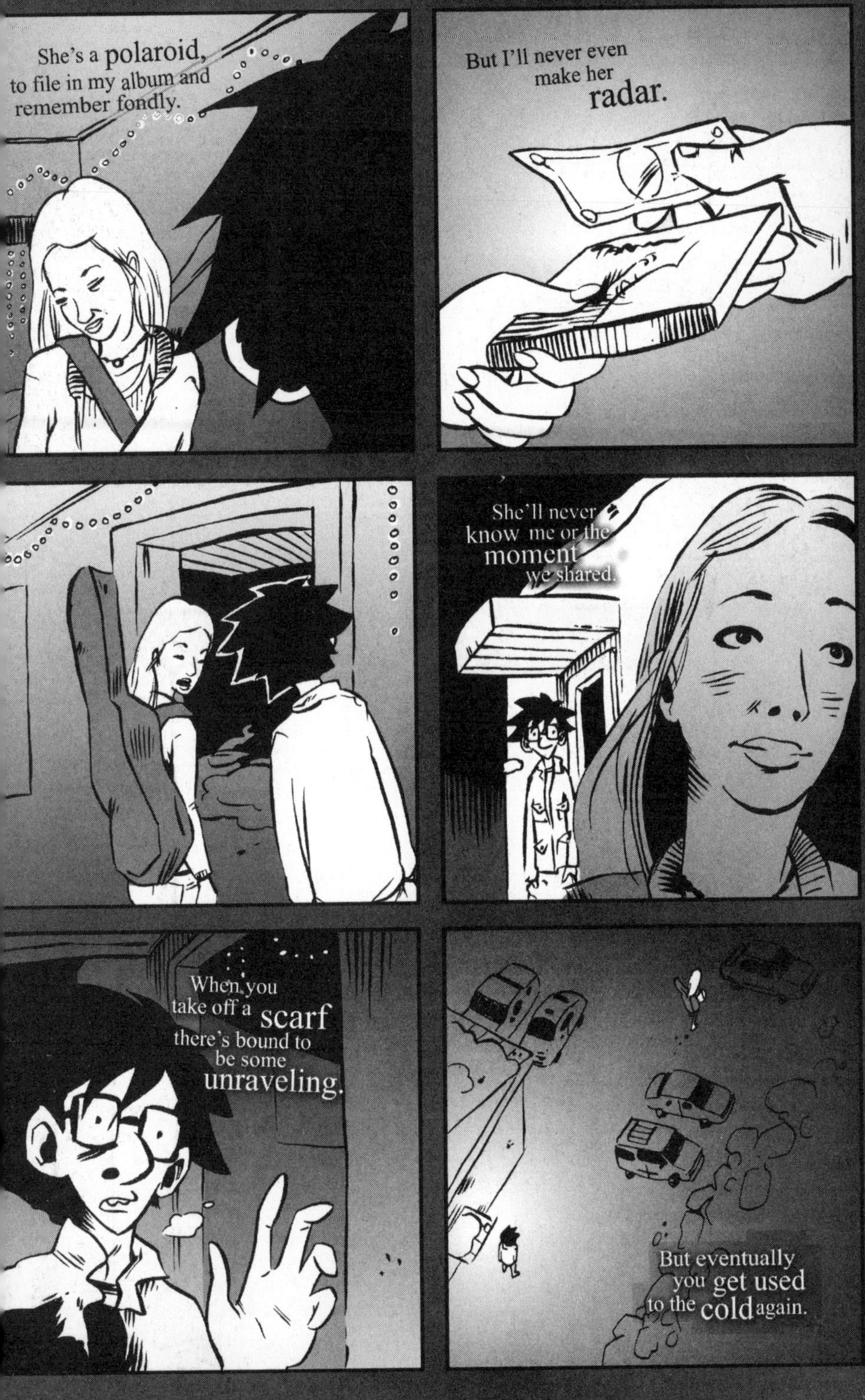
She's a polaroid, to file in my album and remember fondly.
But I'll never even make her radar.
She'll never know me or the moment we shared.
When you take off a scarf there's bound to be some unraveling.
But eventually you get used to the cold again.

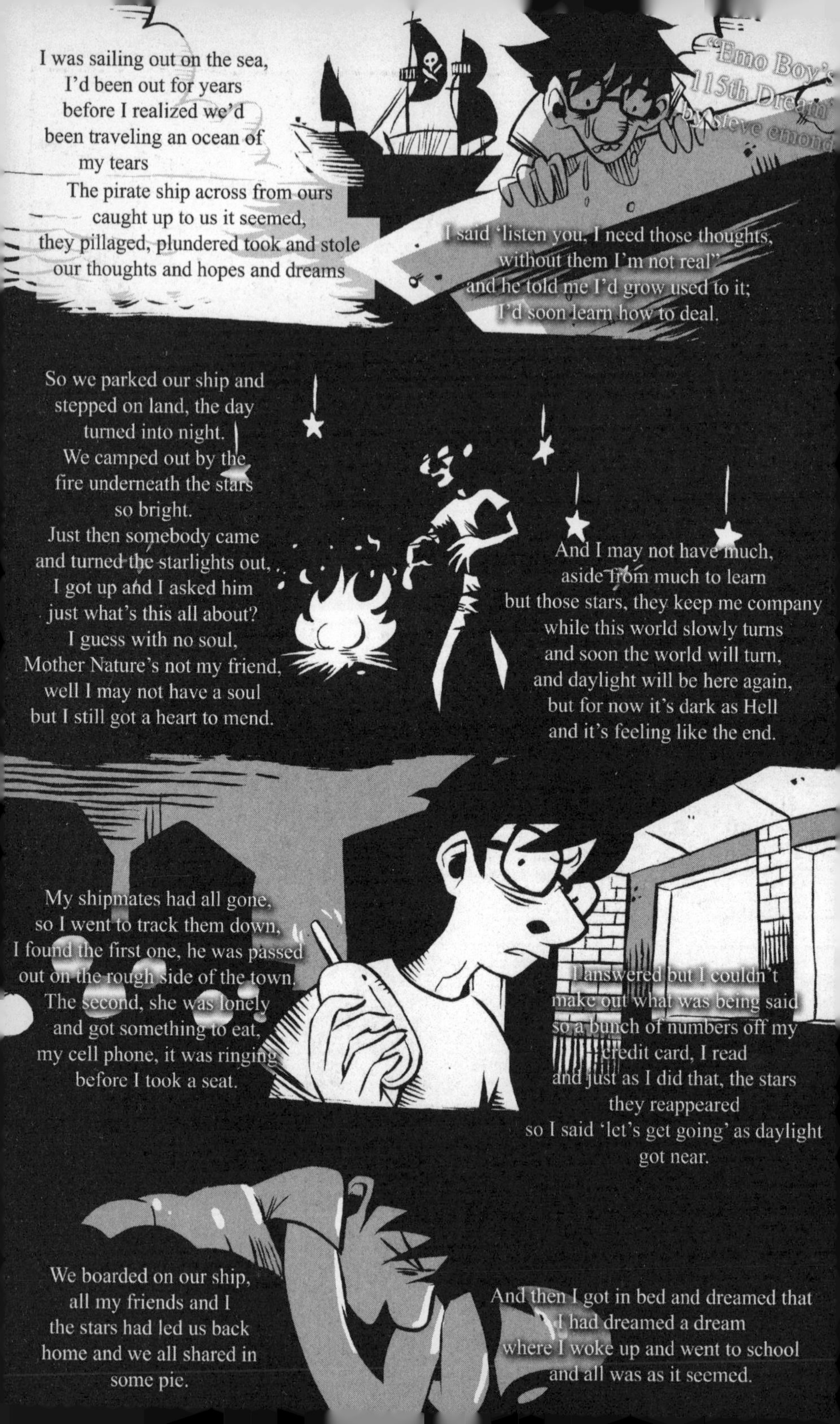
"Emo Boy's 115th Dream" by steve emond
I was sailing out on the sea,
I'd been out for years
before I realized we'd
been traveling an ocean of
my tears
The pirate ship across from ours
caught up to us it seemed,
they pillaged, plundered took and stole
our thoughts and hopes and dreams
I said 'listen you, I need those thoughts,
without them I'm not real"
and he told me I'd grow used to it;
I'd soon learn how to deal.
So we parked our ship and
stepped on land, the day
turned into night.
We camped out by the
fire underneath the stars
so bright.
Just then somebody came
and turned the starlights out,
I got up and I asked him
just what's this all about?
I guess with no soul,
Mother Nature's not my friend,
well I may not have a soul
but I still got a heart to mend.
And I may not have much,
aside from much to learn
but those stars, they keep me company
while this world slowly turns
and soon the world will turn,
and daylight will be here again,
but for now it's dark as Hell
and it's feeling like the end.
My shipmates had all gone,
so I went to track them down,
I found the first one, he was passed
out on the rough side of the town.
The second, she was lonely
and got something to eat,
my cell phone, it was ringing
before I took a seat.
I answered but I couldn't
make out what was being said
so a bunch of numbers off my
credit card, I read
and just as I did that, the stars
they reappeared
so I said 'let's get going' as daylight
got near.
We boarded on our ship,
all my friends and I
the stars had led us back
home and we all shared in
some pie.
And then I got in bed and dreamed that
I had dreamed a dream
where I woke up and went to school
and all was as it seemed.

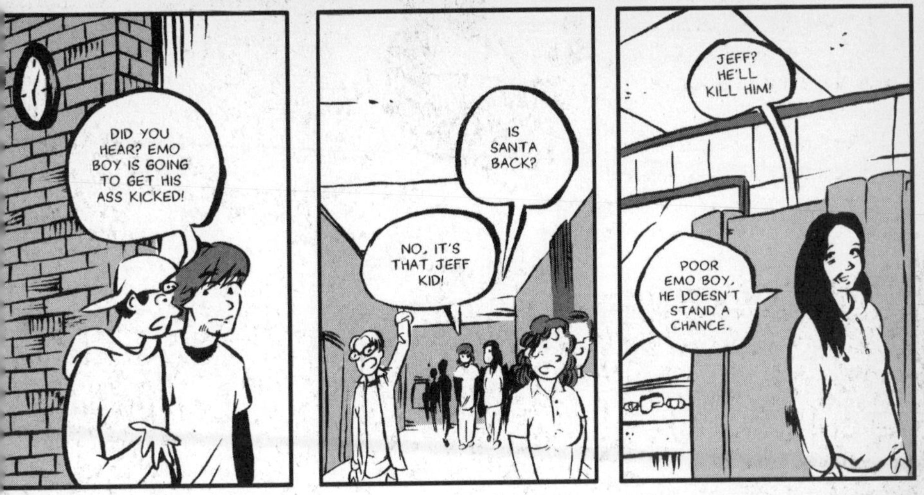
DID YOU HEAR? EMO BOY IS GOING TO GET HIS ASS KICKED!
IS SANTA BACK?
NO, IT'S THAT JEFF KID!
JEFF? HE'LL KILL HIM!
POOR EMO BOY, HE DOESN'T STAND A CHANCE.

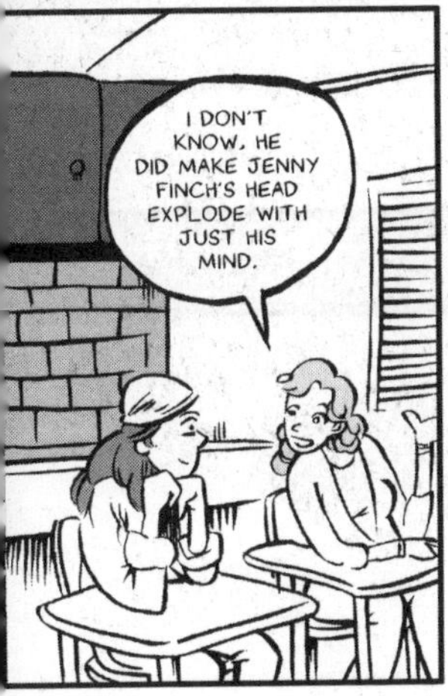
I DON'T KNOW, HE DID MAKE JENNY FINCH'S HEAD EXPLODE WITH JUST HIS MIND.

*Story number 9, in which our hero unleashes the power of the cosmos.*

*written and illustrated by Steve Emond*

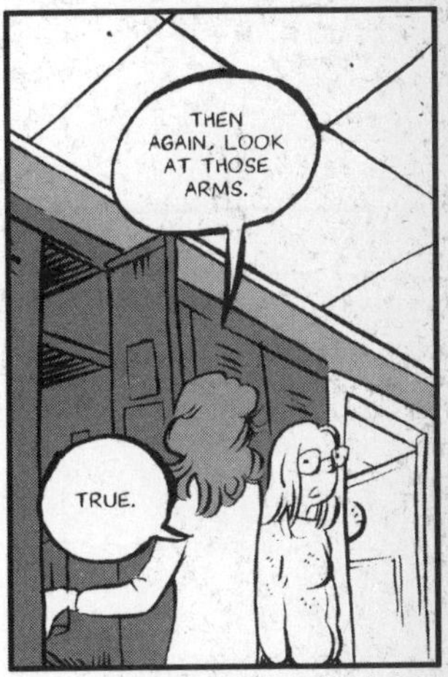
THEN AGAIN, LOOK AT THOSE ARMS.
TRUE.

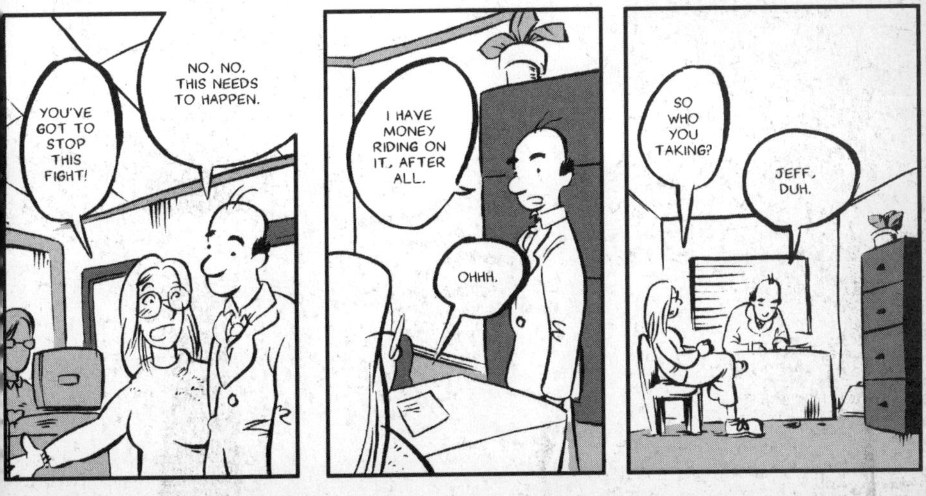
YOU'VE GOT TO STOP THIS FIGHT!
NO, NO. THIS NEEDS TO HAPPEN.
I HAVE MONEY RIDING ON IT, AFTER ALL.
OHHH.
SO WHO YOU TAKING?
JEFF, DUH.

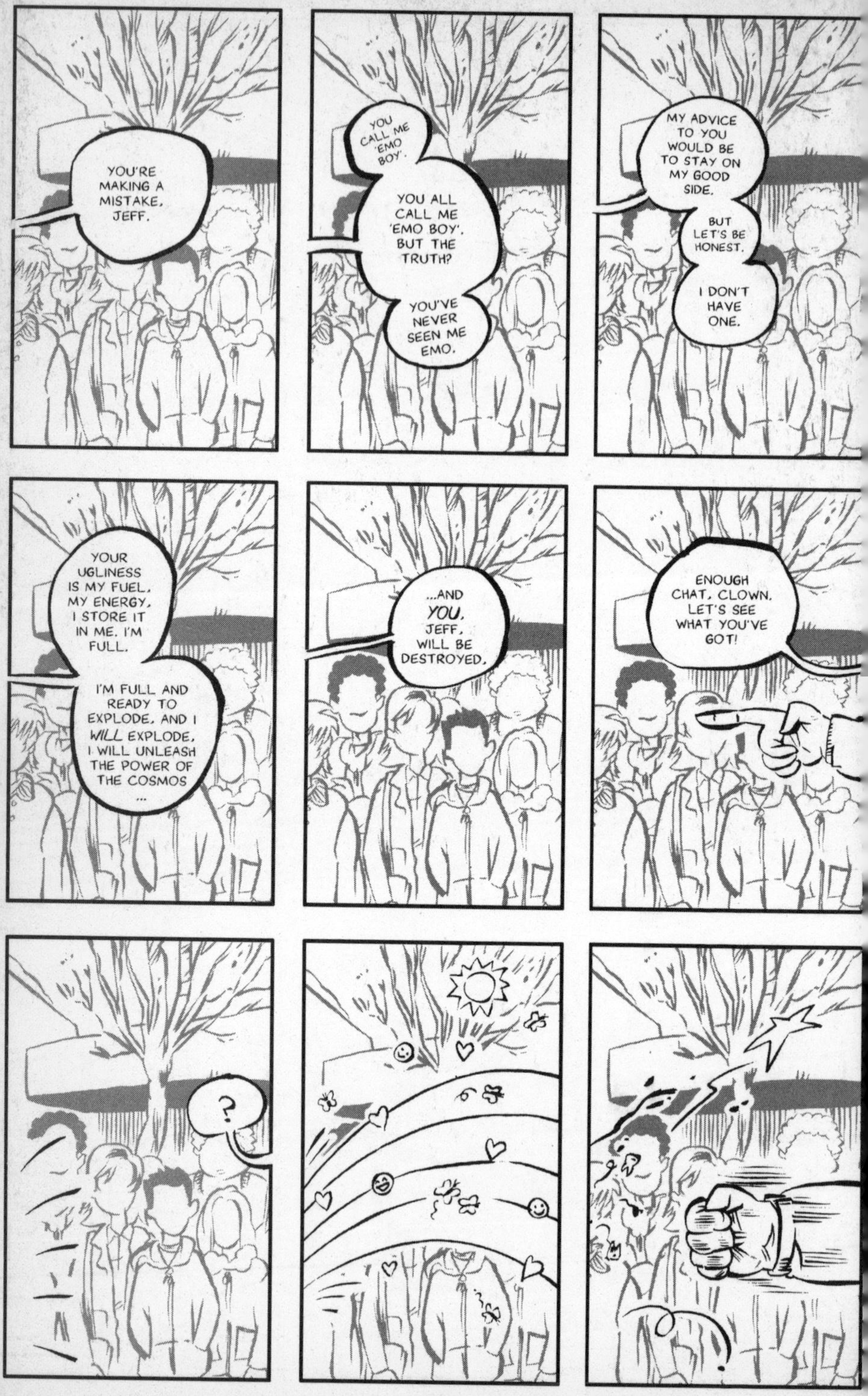
YOU'RE MAKING A MISTAKE, JEFF.
YOU CALL ME 'EMO BOY'.
YOU ALL CALL ME 'EMO BOY'. BUT THE TRUTH?
YOU'VE NEVER SEEN ME EMO.
MY ADVICE TO YOU WOULD BE TO STAY ON MY GOOD SIDE.
BUT LET'S BE HONEST.
I DON'T HAVE ONE.
YOUR UGLINESS IS MY FUEL, MY ENERGY, I STORE IT IN ME. I'M FULL.
I'M FULL AND READY TO EXPLODE, AND I WILL EXPLODE, I WILL UNLEASH THE POWER OF THE COSMOS ...
...AND YOU, JEFF, WILL BE DESTROYED.
ENOUGH CHAT, CLOWN. LET'S SEE WHAT YOU'VE GOT!
?

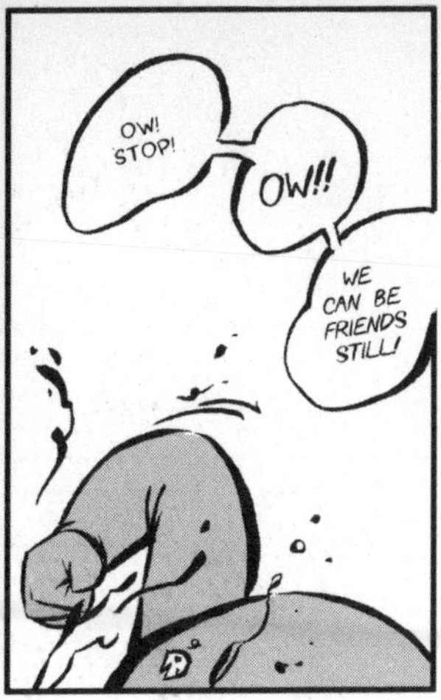
OW! STOP!
OW!!
WE CAN BE FRIENDS STILL!

The colors diluted, the sound muffled. The hi def world had gone 8mm.

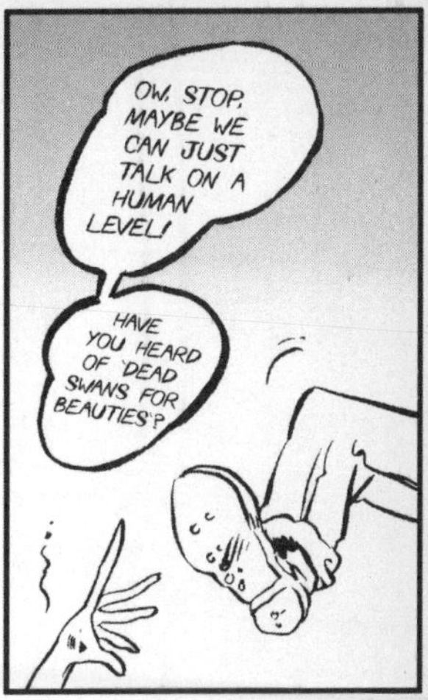
OW. STOP. MAYBE WE CAN JUST TALK ON A HUMAN LEVEL!
HAVE YOU HEARD OF 'DEAD SWANS FOR BEAUTIES'?

Time seemed to stop and go. The animation was choppy, frames were missing.

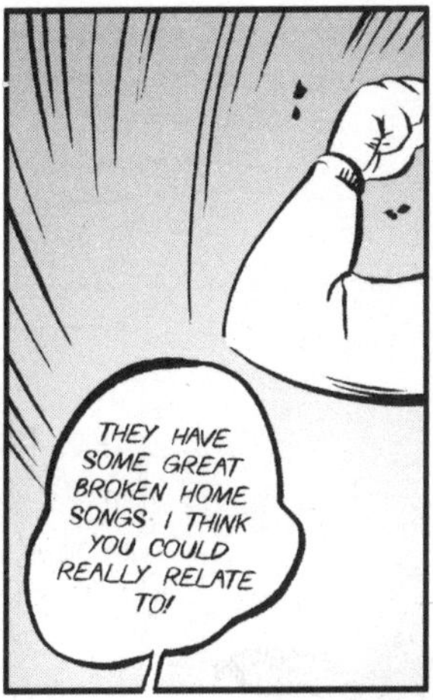
THEY HAVE SOME GREAT BROKEN HOME SONGS I THINK YOU COULD REALLY RELATE TO!

The reel spun and spun but the filmstrip was cut.

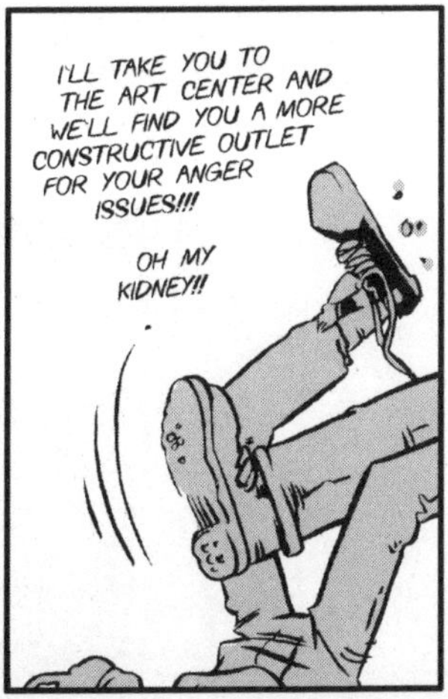
I'LL TAKE YOU TO THE ART CENTER AND WE'LL FIND YOU A MORE CONSTRUCTIVE OUTLET FOR YOUR ANGER ISSUES!!!
OH MY KIDNEY!!

The cosmos had let me down.

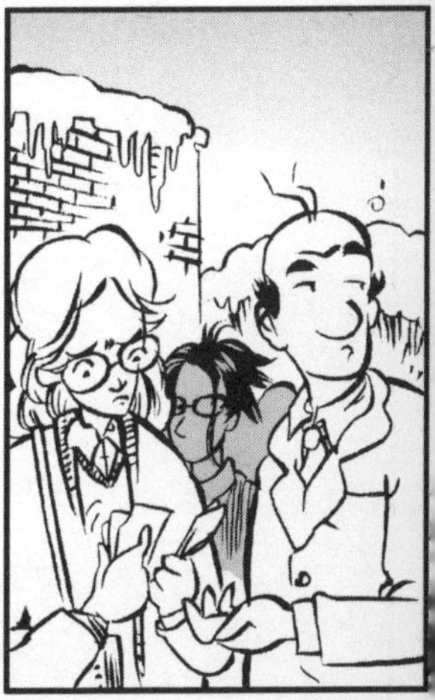

"Penny Goes Home"

Story and art by Steve Emond

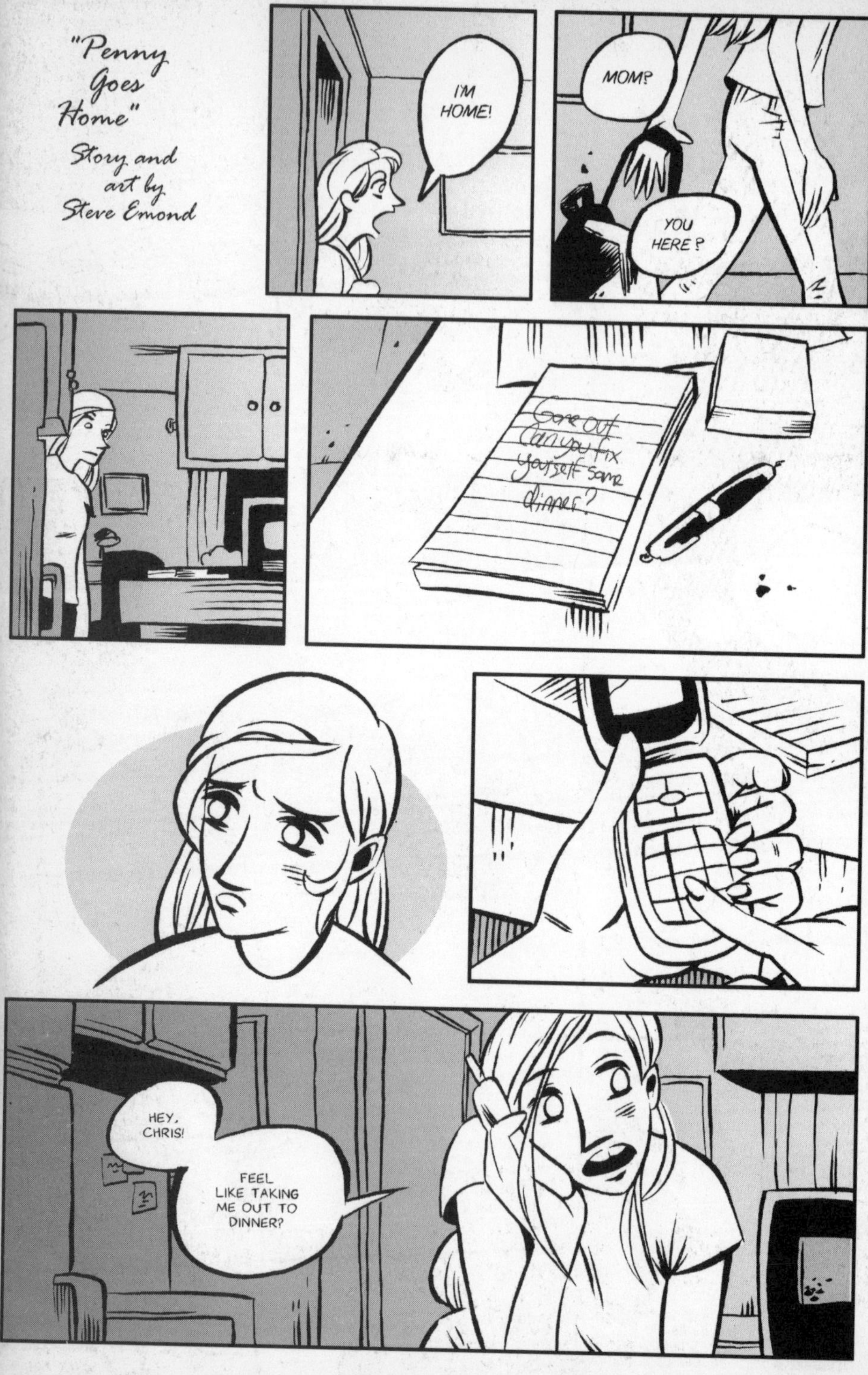
I'M HOME!
MOM?
YOU HERE?
Gone out Can you fix yourself some dinner?
HEY, CHRIS!
FEEL LIKE TAKING ME OUT TO DINNER?

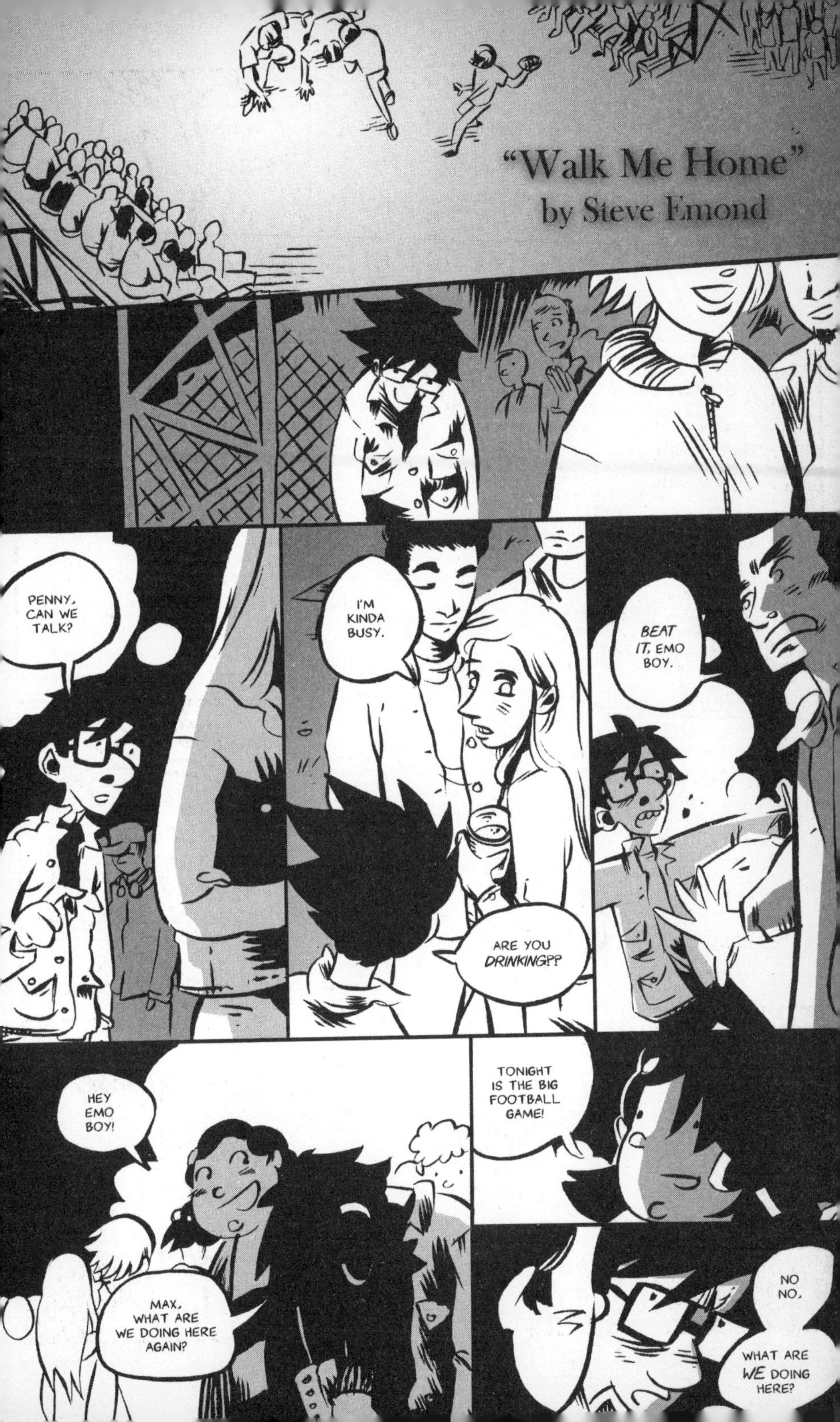

"Walk Me Home"
by Steve Emond
PENNY, CAN WE TALK?
I'M KINDA BUSY.
ARE YOU DRINKING?!?
BEAT IT, EMO BOY.
HEY EMO BOY!
MAX, WHAT ARE WE DOING HERE AGAIN?
TONIGHT IS THE BIG FOOTBALL GAME!
NO NO.
WHAT ARE WE DOING HERE?

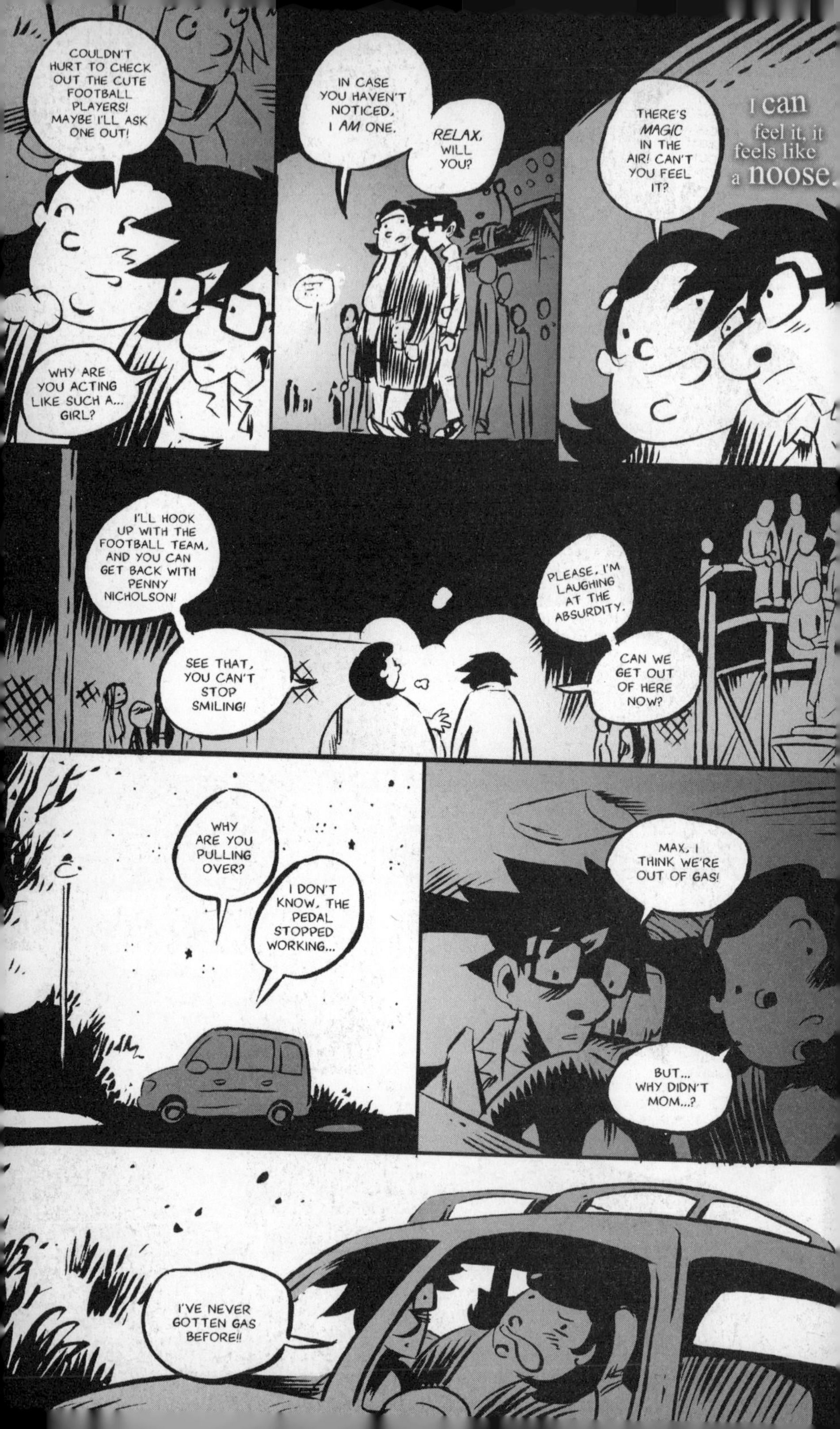
COULDN'T HURT TO CHECK OUT THE CUTE FOOTBALL PLAYERS! MAYBE I'LL ASK ONE OUT!
WHY ARE YOU ACTING LIKE SUCH A... GIRL?
IN CASE YOU HAVEN'T NOTICED, I AM ONE.
RELAX, WILL YOU?
THERE'S MAGIC IN THE AIR! CAN'T YOU FEEL IT?
I can feel it, it feels like a noose.
I'LL HOOK UP WITH THE FOOTBALL TEAM, AND YOU CAN GET BACK WITH PENNY NICHOLSON!
SEE THAT, YOU CAN'T STOP SMILING!
PLEASE, I'M LAUGHING AT THE ABSURDITY.
CAN WE GET OUT OF HERE NOW?
WHY ARE YOU PULLING OVER?
I DON'T KNOW, THE PEDAL STOPPED WORKING...
MAX, I THINK WE'RE OUT OF GAS!
BUT... WHY DIDN'T MOM...?
I'VE NEVER GOTTEN GAS BEFORE!!

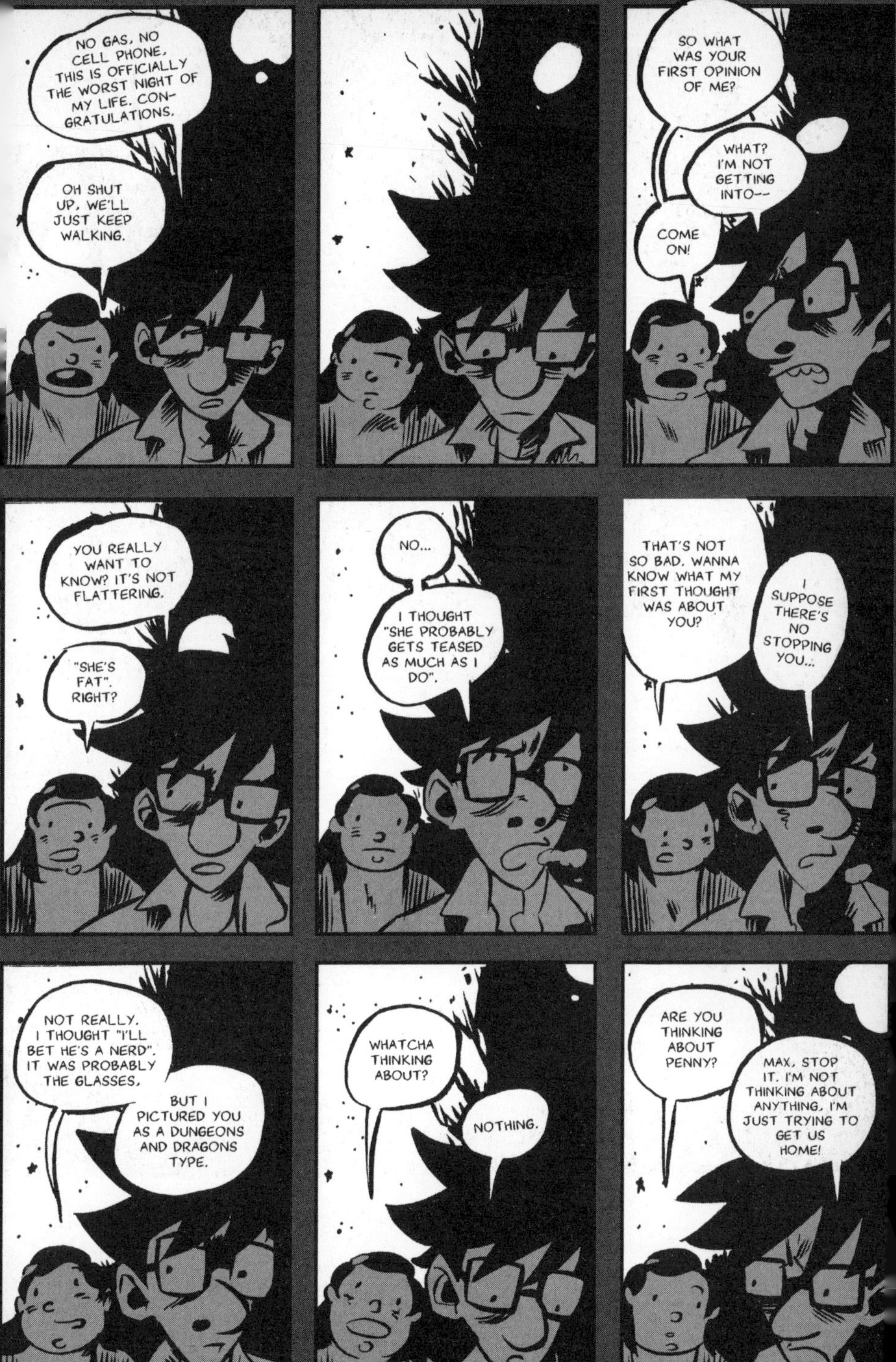
NO GAS, NO CELL PHONE, THIS IS OFFICIALLY THE WORST NIGHT OF MY LIFE. CONGRATULATIONS.
OH SHUT UP, WE'LL JUST KEEP WALKING.
SO WHAT WAS YOUR FIRST OPINION OF ME?
WHAT? I'M NOT GETTING INTO--
COME ON!
YOU REALLY WANT TO KNOW? IT'S NOT FLATTERING.
"SHE'S FAT". RIGHT?
NO...
I THOUGHT "SHE PROBABLY GETS TEASED AS MUCH AS I DO".
THAT'S NOT SO BAD. WANNA KNOW WHAT MY FIRST THOUGHT WAS ABOUT YOU?
I SUPPOSE THERE'S NO STOPPING YOU...
NOT REALLY. I THOUGHT "I'LL BET HE'S A NERD". IT WAS PROBABLY THE GLASSES.
BUT I PICTURED YOU AS A DUNGEONS AND DRAGONS TYPE.
WHATCHA THINKING ABOUT?
NOTHING.
ARE YOU THINKING ABOUT PENNY?
MAX, STOP IT. I'M NOT THINKING ABOUT ANYTHING. I'M JUST TRYING TO GET US HOME!

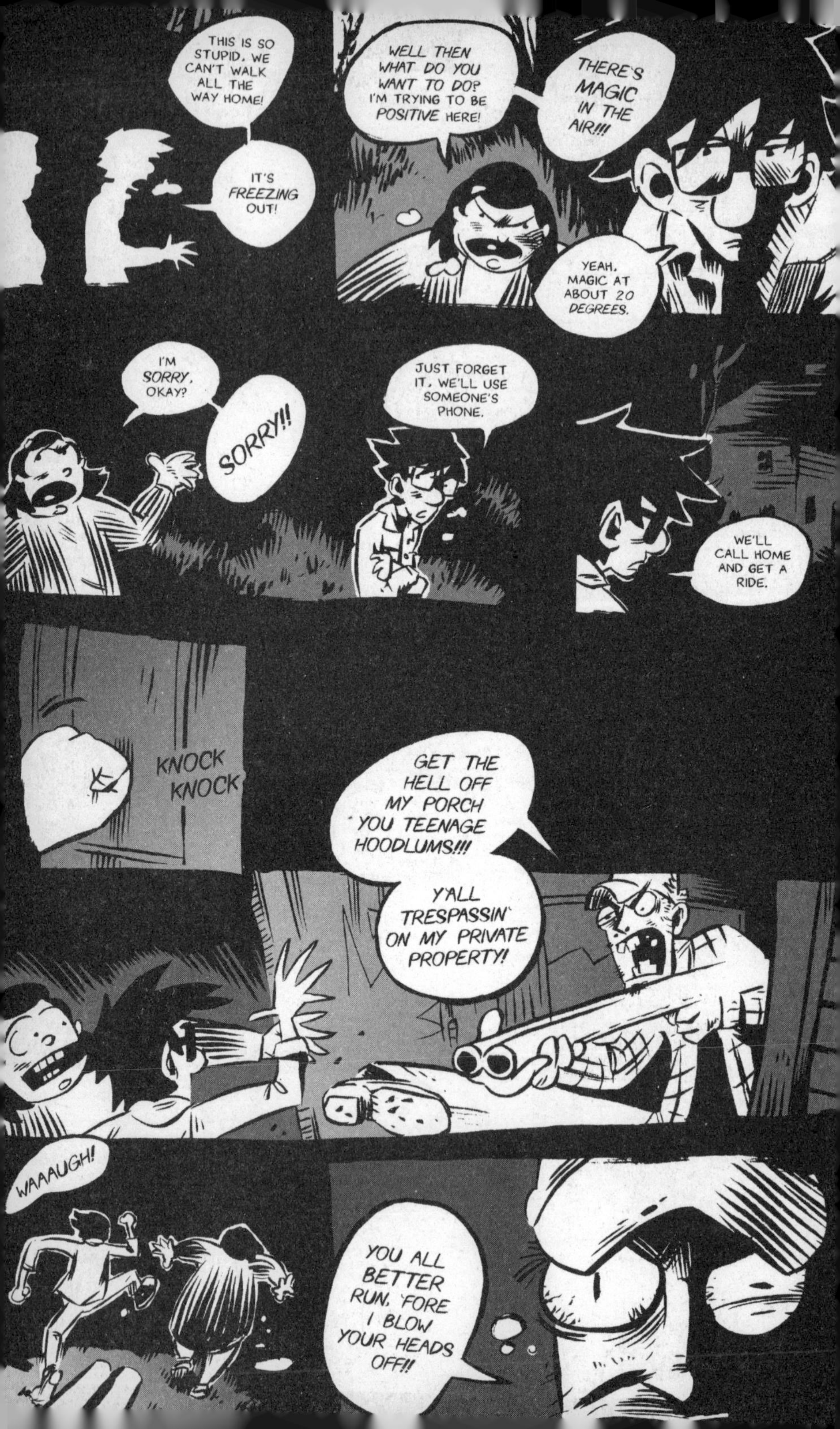
THIS IS SO STUPID. WE CAN'T WALK ALL THE WAY HOME!
IT'S FREEZING OUT!
WELL THEN WHAT DO YOU WANT TO DO? I'M TRYING TO BE POSITIVE HERE!
THERE'S MAGIC IN THE AIR!!!
YEAH. MAGIC AT ABOUT 20 DEGREES.
I'M SORRY. OKAY?
SORRY!!
JUST FORGET IT. WE'LL USE SOMEONE'S PHONE.
WE'LL CALL HOME AND GET A RIDE.
KNOCK KNOCK
GET THE HELL OFF MY PORCH YOU TEENAGE HOODLUMS!!!
Y'ALL TRESPASSIN' ON MY PRIVATE PROPERTY!
WAAAUGH!
YOU ALL BETTER RUN, 'FORE I BLOW YOUR HEADS OFF!!

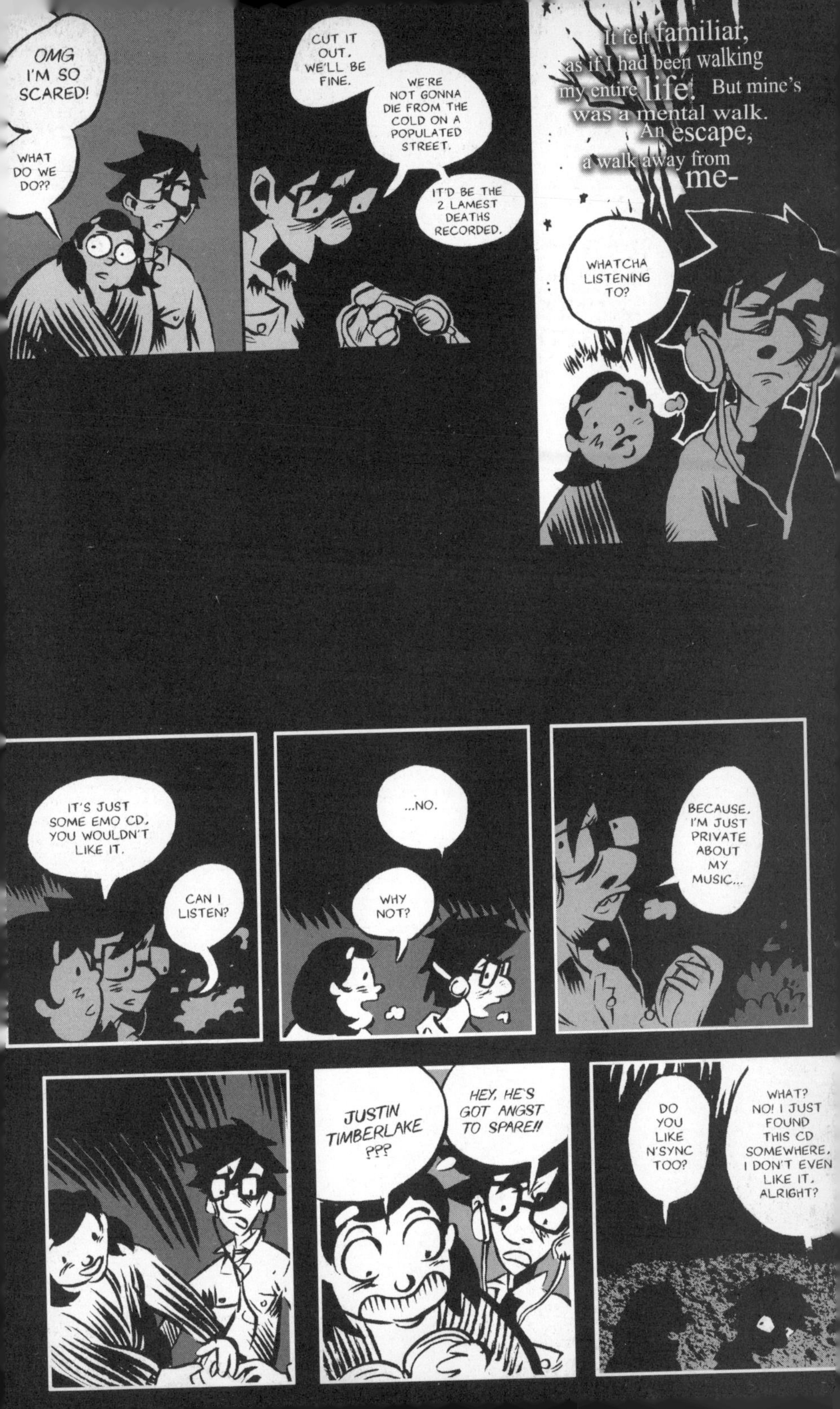
OMG I'M SO SCARED!
WHAT DO WE DO??
CUT IT OUT. WE'LL BE FINE.
WE'RE NOT GONNA DIE FROM THE COLD ON A POPULATED STREET.
IT'D BE THE 2 LAMEST DEATHS RECORDED.
It felt familiar, as if I had been walking my entire life! But mine's was a mental walk. An escape, a walk away from me-
WHATCHA LISTENING TO?
IT'S JUST SOME EMO CD, YOU WOULDN'T LIKE IT.
CAN I LISTEN?
...NO.
WHY NOT?
BECAUSE, I'M JUST PRIVATE ABOUT MY MUSIC...
JUSTIN TIMBERLAKE ???
HEY, HE'S GOT ANGST TO SPARE!!
DO YOU LIKE N'SYNC TOO?
WHAT? NO! I JUST FOUND THIS CD SOMEWHERE. I DON'T EVEN LIKE IT. ALRIGHT?

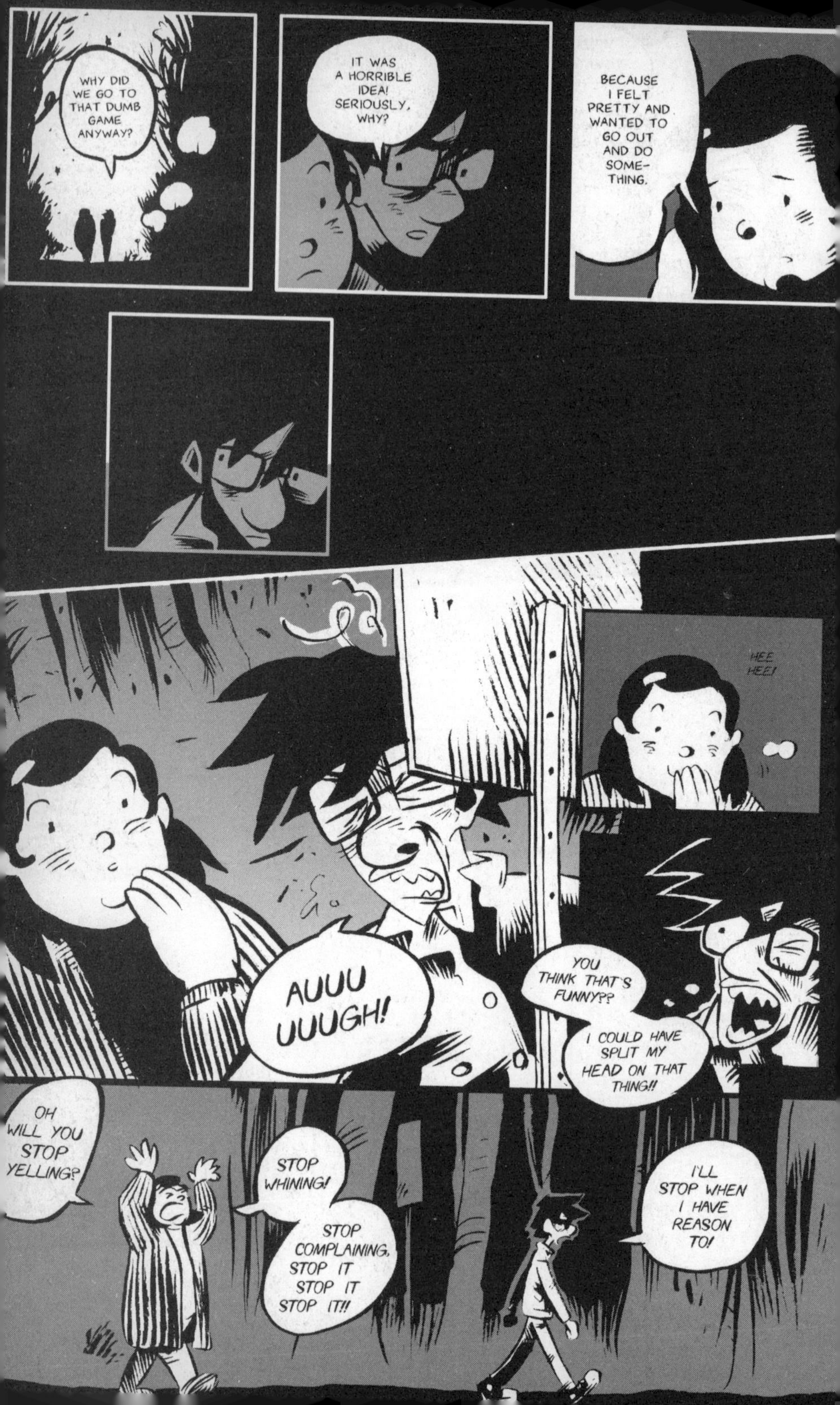
WHY DID WE GO TO THAT DUMB GAME ANYWAY?
IT WAS A HORRIBLE IDEA! SERIOUSLY, WHY?
BECAUSE I FELT PRETTY AND WANTED TO GO OUT AND DO SOME-THING.
HEE HEE!
AUUU UUUGH!
YOU THINK THAT'S FUNNY??
I COULD HAVE SPLIT MY HEAD ON THAT THING!!
OH WILL YOU STOP YELLING?
STOP WHINING!
STOP COMPLAINING, STOP IT STOP IT STOP IT!!
I'LL STOP WHEN I HAVE REASON TO!

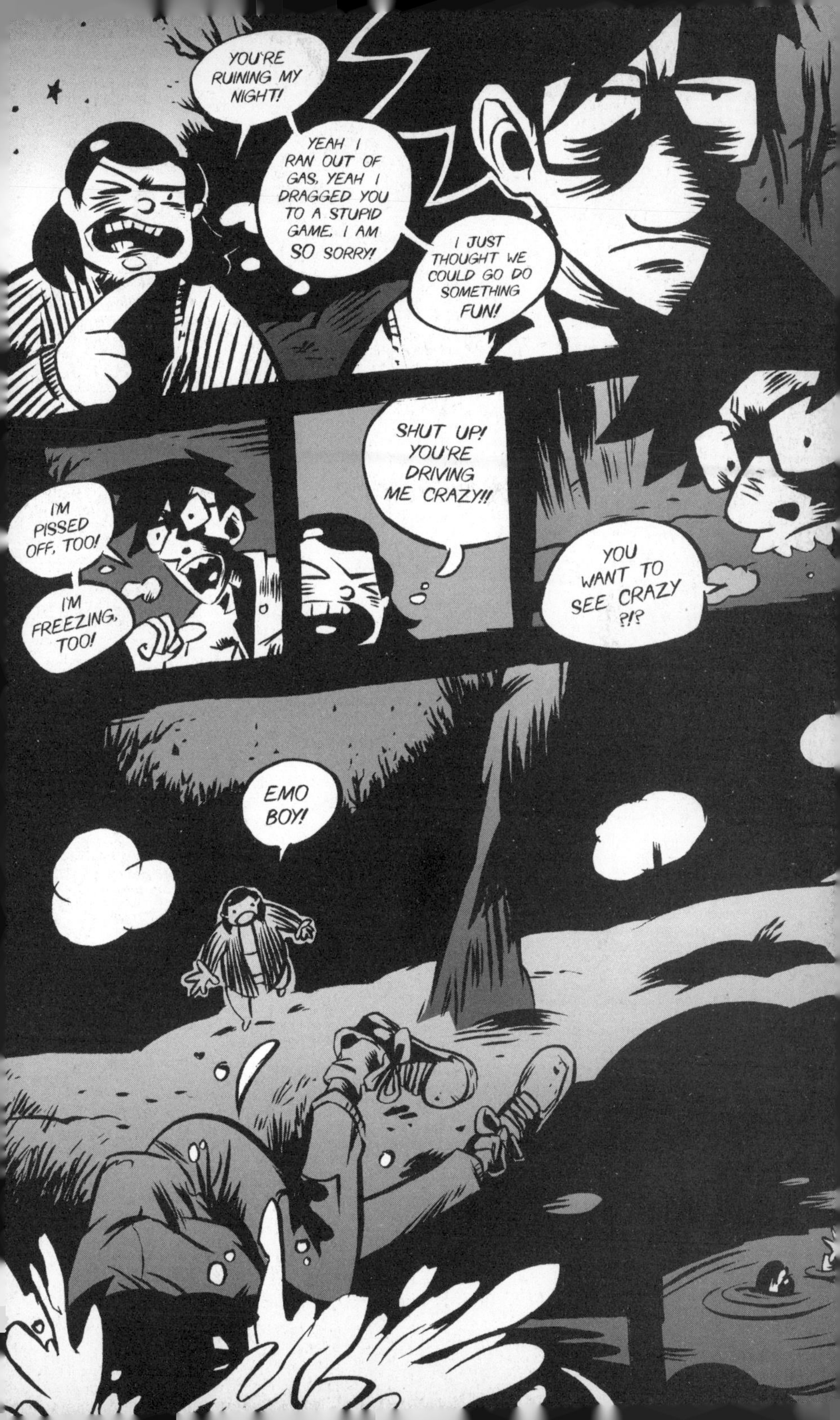
YOU'RE RUINING MY NIGHT!
YEAH I RAN OUT OF GAS, YEAH I DRAGGED YOU TO A STUPID GAME, I AM SO SORRY!
I JUST THOUGHT WE COULD GO DO SOMETHING FUN!
I'M PISSED OFF, TOO!
I'M FREEZING, TOO!
SHUT UP! YOU'RE DRIVING ME CRAZY!!
YOU WANT TO SEE CRAZY ?!?
EMO BOY!

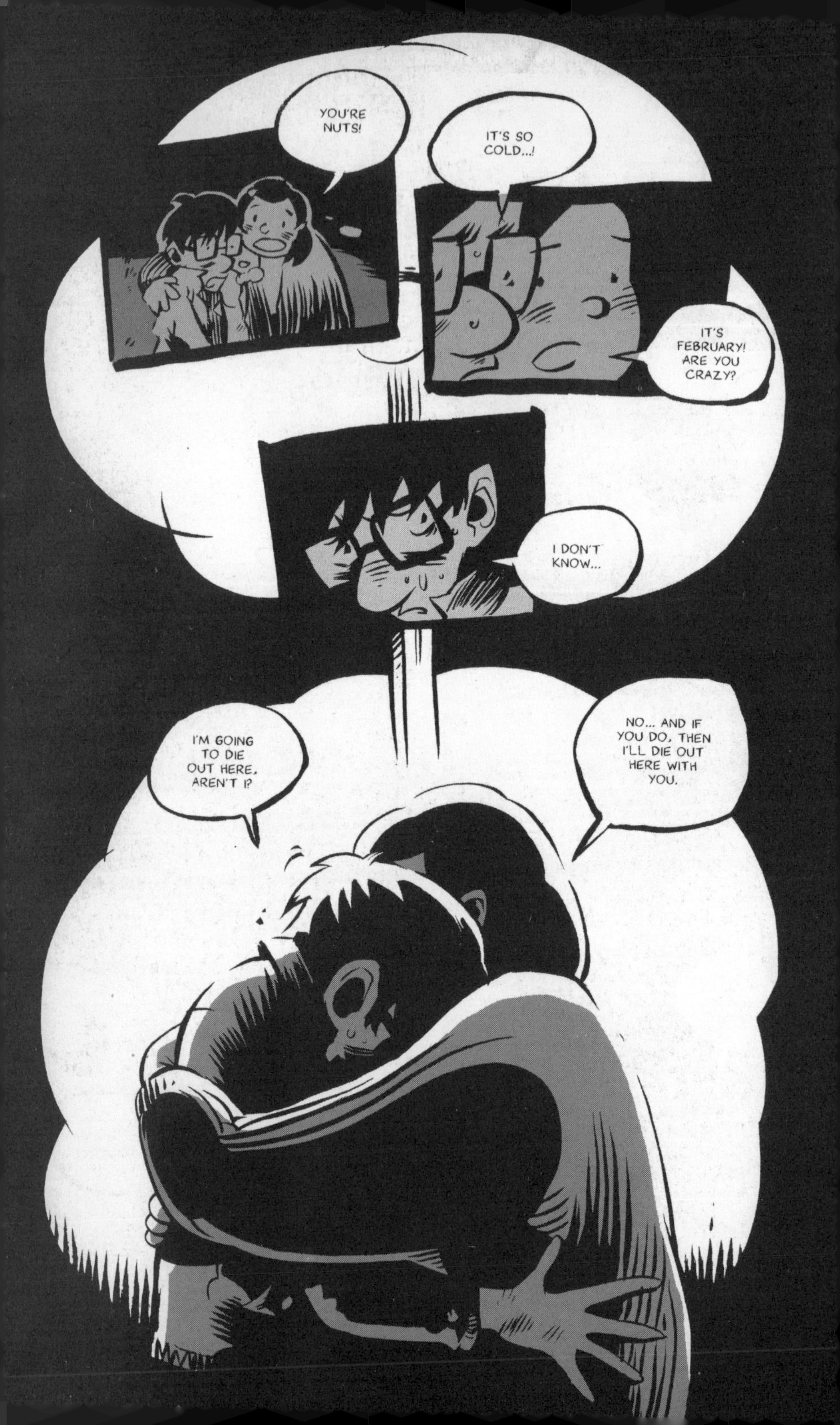

YOU'RE NUTS!
IT'S SO COLD...!
IT'S FEBRUARY! ARE YOU CRAZY?
I DON'T KNOW...
I'M GOING TO DIE OUT HERE, AREN'T I?
NO... AND IF YOU DO, THEN I'LL DIE OUT HERE WITH YOU.

MAXINE... ALL THAT STUFF YOU WERE TALKING ABOUT...

MY ATTENTION FOR YOU... MY FRIENDSHIP, MY DEDICATION TO YOU... THAT SHOULD NEVER BE AN ISSUE.

IT SHOULD BE IMPLIED. BECAUSE IT'S ALWAYS THERE. AND I'M SORRY IF I HAVEN'T COMMUNICATED THAT TO YOU.

YOU'RE MY BEST FRIEND.

FOR ALWAYS, OKAY?

HEY, WHO'S OUT THERE??

YOU GOT A *DEATH WISH*, KID? IT'S FREEZING OUT HERE!

WE'RE GOING TO LIVE!!

I HAD A ROUGH DAY, MAX.

AND A ROUGH NIGHT?

NO... THE NIGHT'S NOT SO BAD.

*TOLD YA* THERE WAS MAGIC IN THE AIR.

# EMO BOY

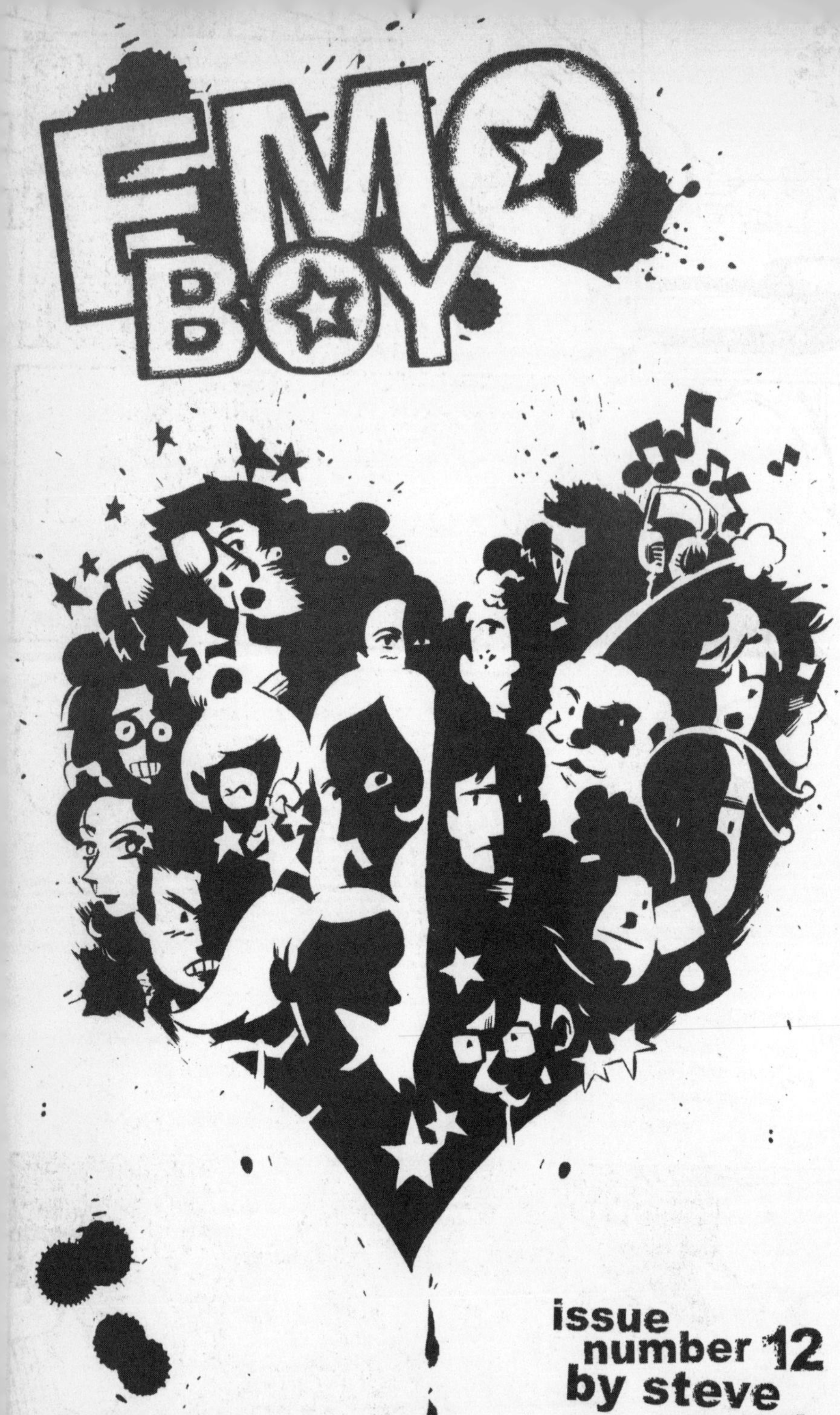

issue
number 12
by steve
emond

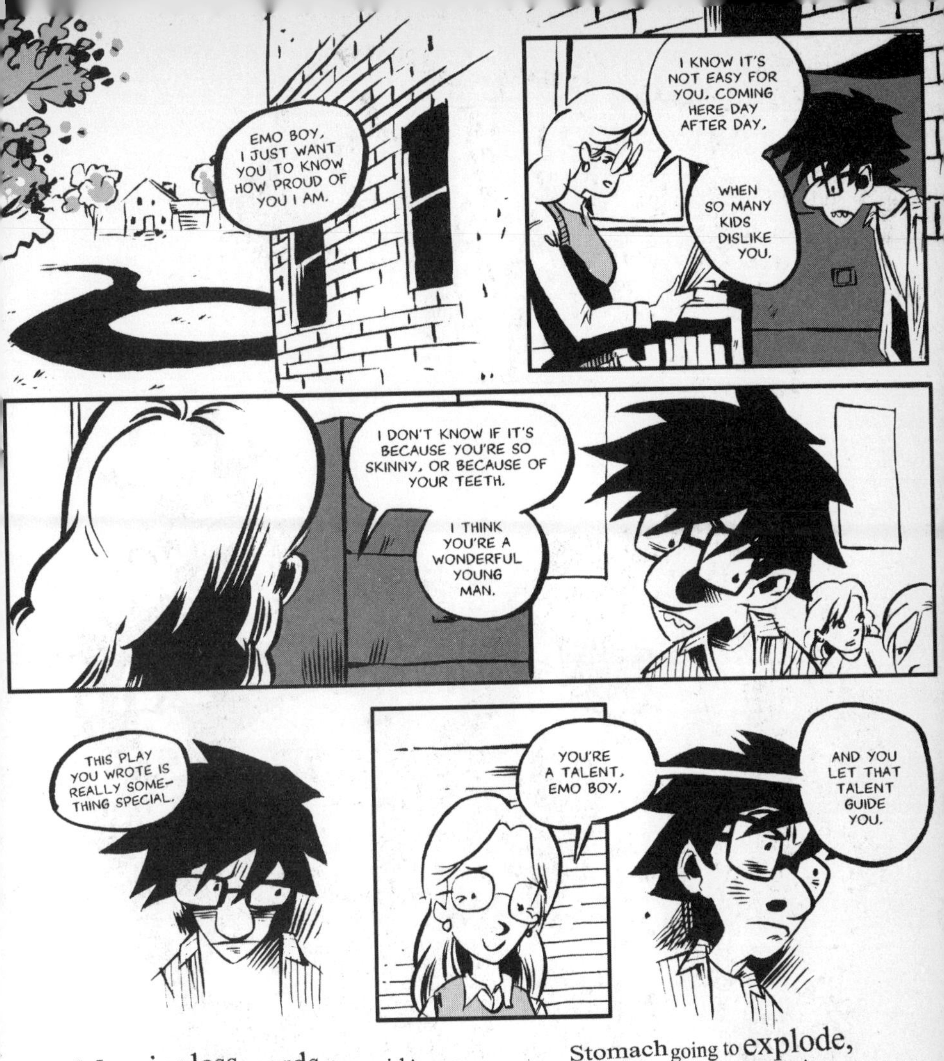
EMO BOY, I JUST WANT YOU TO KNOW HOW PROUD OF YOU I AM.
I KNOW IT'S NOT EASY FOR YOU, COMING HERE DAY AFTER DAY,
WHEN SO MANY KIDS DISLIKE YOU.
I DON'T KNOW IF IT'S BECAUSE YOU'RE SO SKINNY, OR BECAUSE OF YOUR TEETH.
I THINK YOU'RE A WONDERFUL YOUNG MAN.
THIS PLAY YOU WROTE IS REALLY SOMETHING SPECIAL.
YOU'RE A TALENT, EMO BOY.
AND YOU LET THAT TALENT GUIDE YOU.

Meaningless words that swirl in my mind like toilet water being flushed. Forgotten quickly, encouragement disappears, gone into some sub-surface world to sink and rot in feces and piss.

Stomach going to explode, I feel sick. I want to vomit at her feet, pass out on the floor and let the world do with me what it will. I want to act out how I feel. Let them all see it, feel it.

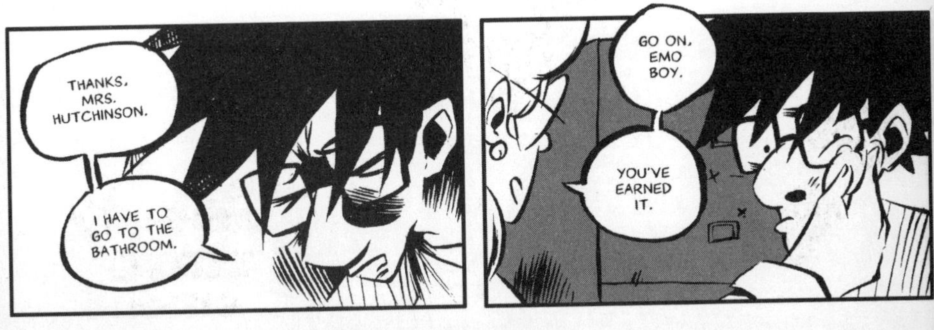
THANKS, MRS. HUTCHINSON.
I HAVE TO GO TO THE BATHROOM.
GO ON, EMO BOY.
YOU'VE EARNED IT.

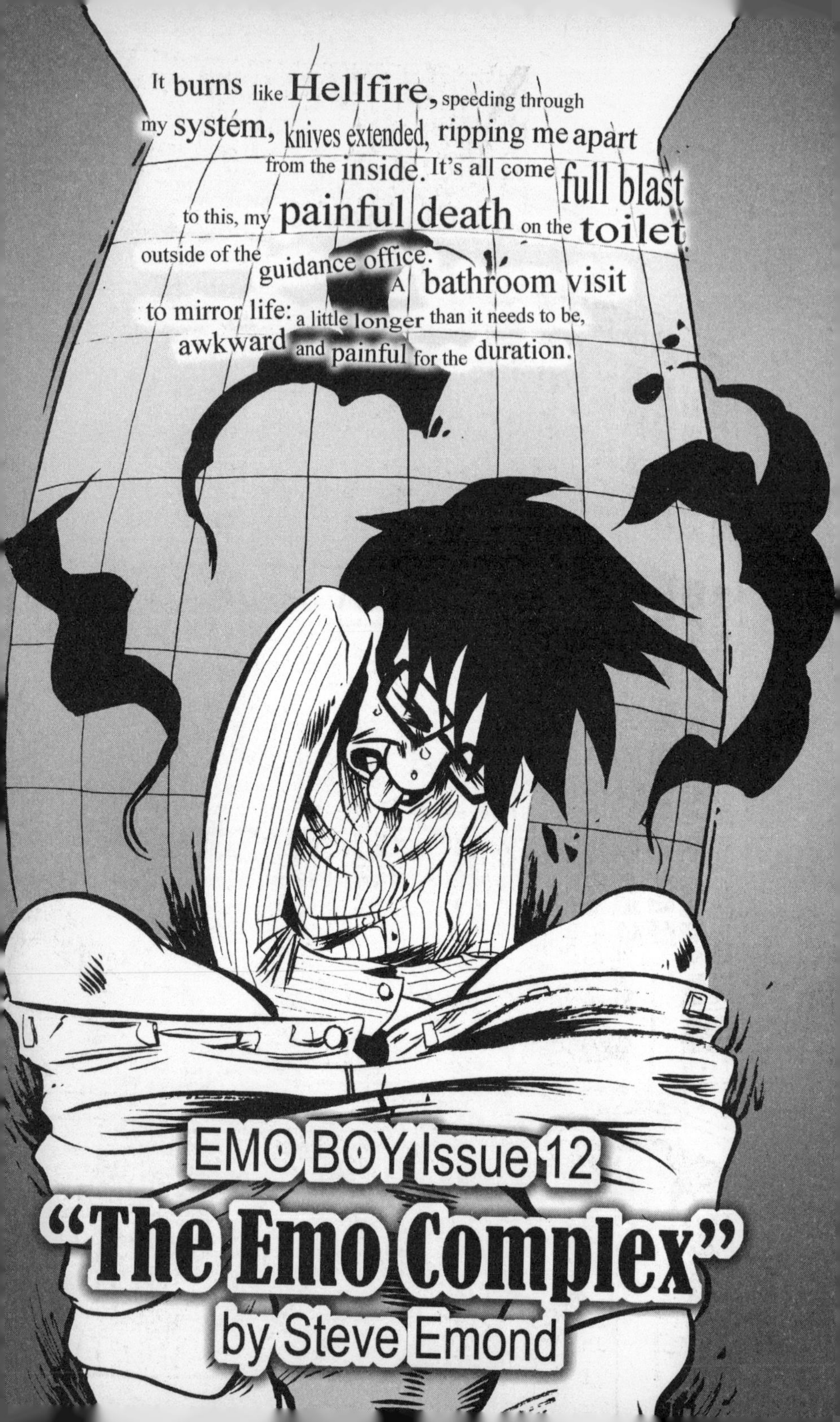
It burns like Hellfire, speeding through my system, knives extended, ripping me apart from the inside. It's all come full blast to this, my painful death on the toilet outside of the guidance office. A bathroom visit to mirror life: a little longer than it needs to be, awkward and painful for the duration.
EMO BOY Issue 12
"The Emo Complex"
by Steve Emond

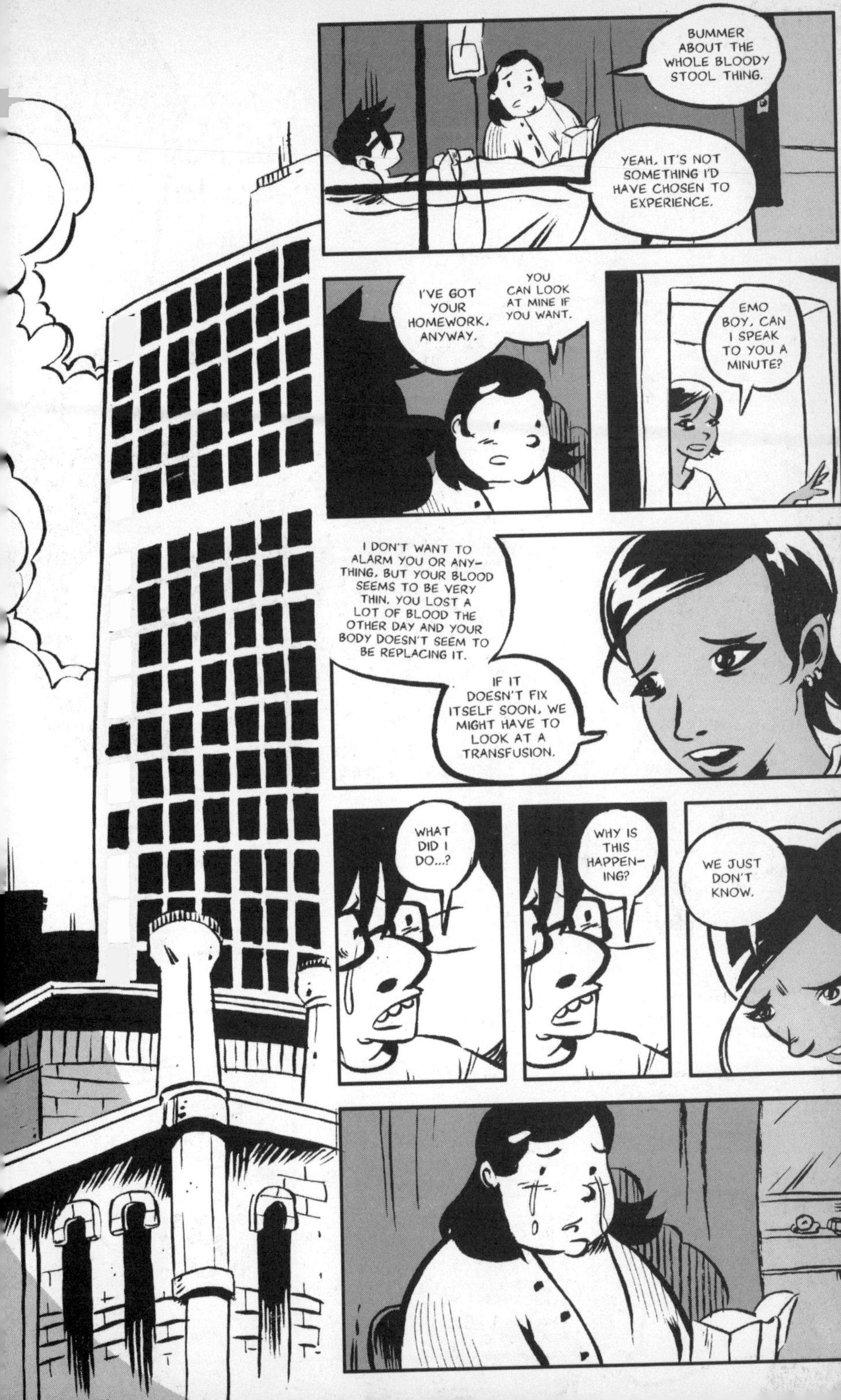

BUMMER ABOUT THE WHOLE BLOODY STOOL THING.
YEAH, IT'S NOT SOMETHING I'D HAVE CHOSEN TO EXPERIENCE.
I'VE GOT YOUR HOMEWORK, ANYWAY.
YOU CAN LOOK AT MINE IF YOU WANT.
EMO BOY, CAN I SPEAK TO YOU A MINUTE?
I DON'T WANT TO ALARM YOU OR ANY-THING, BUT YOUR BLOOD SEEMS TO BE VERY THIN. YOU LOST A LOT OF BLOOD THE OTHER DAY AND YOUR BODY DOESN'T SEEM TO BE REPLACING IT.
IF IT DOESN'T FIX ITSELF SOON, WE MIGHT HAVE TO LOOK AT A TRANSFUSION.
WHAT DID I DO...?
WHY IS THIS HAPPEN-ING?
WE JUST DON'T KNOW.

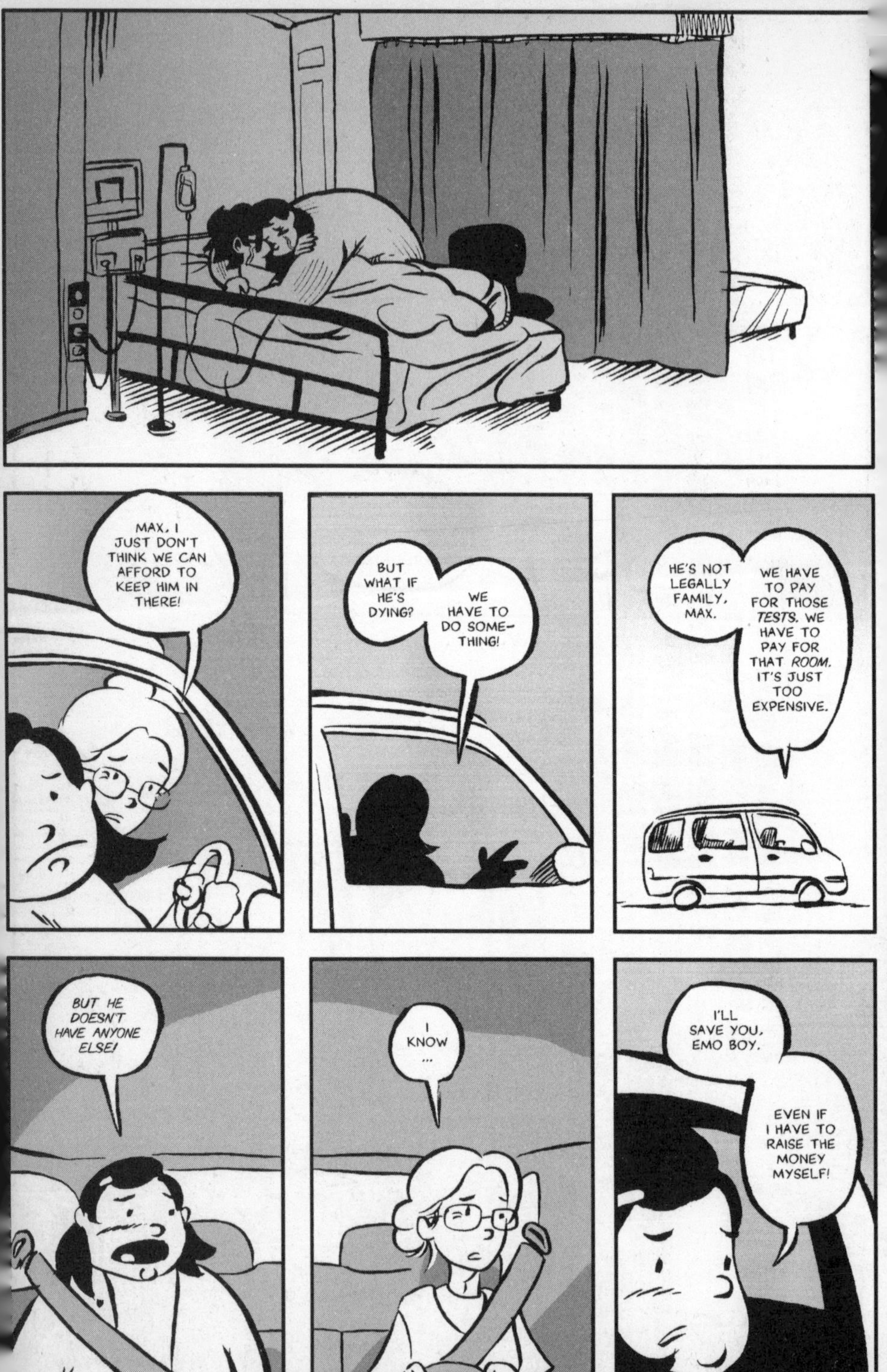
MAX, I JUST DON'T THINK WE CAN AFFORD TO KEEP HIM IN THERE!
BUT WHAT IF HE'S DYING?
WE HAVE TO DO SOME-THING!
HE'S NOT LEGALLY FAMILY, MAX.
WE HAVE TO PAY FOR THOSE *TESTS*. WE HAVE TO PAY FOR THAT *ROOM*. IT'S JUST TOO EXPENSIVE.
*BUT HE DOESN'T HAVE ANYONE ELSE!*
I KNOW ...
I'LL SAVE YOU, EMO BOY.
EVEN IF I HAVE TO RAISE THE MONEY MYSELF!

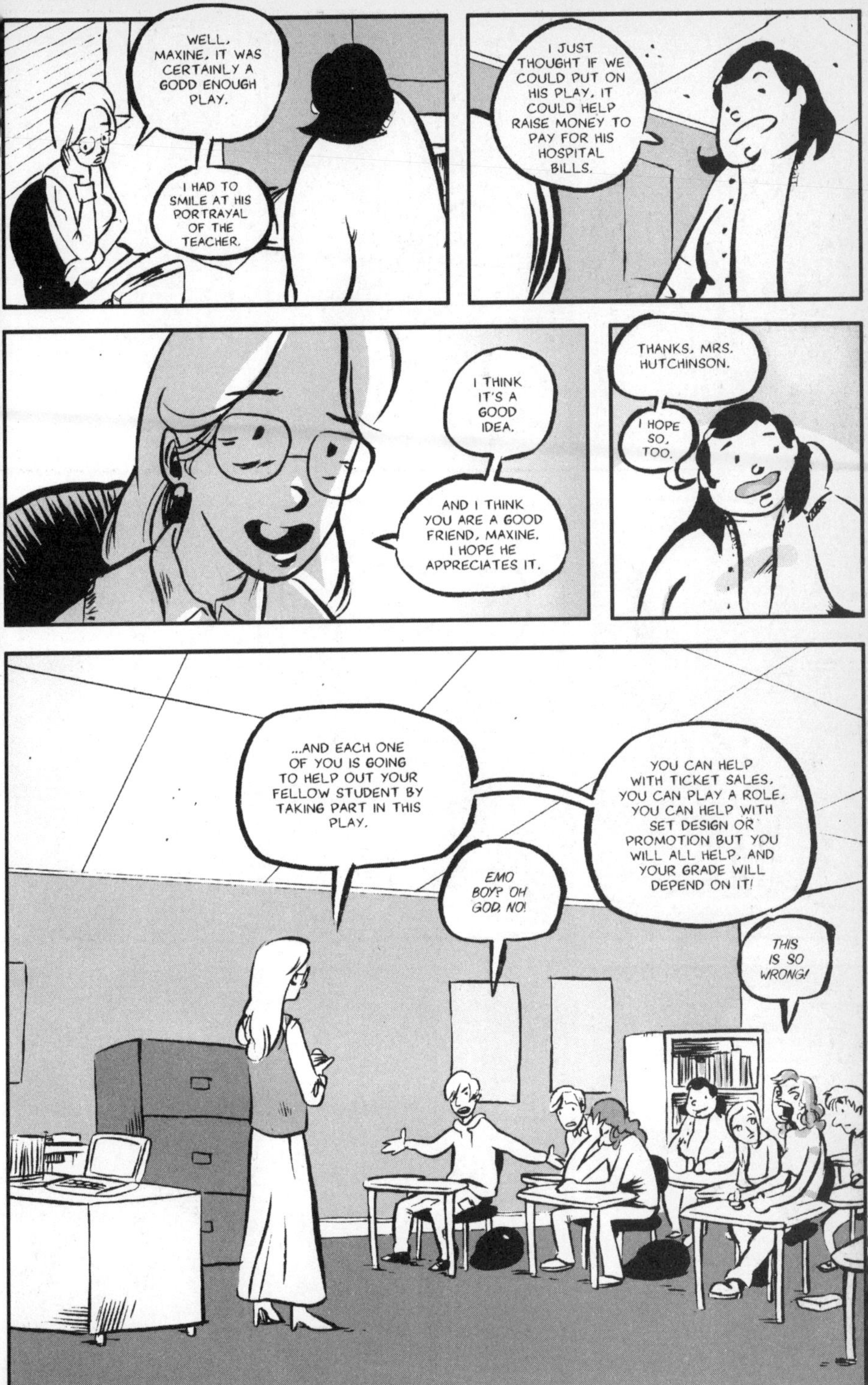
WELL, MAXINE, IT WAS CERTAINLY A GODD ENOUGH PLAY.
I HAD TO SMILE AT HIS PORTRAYAL OF THE TEACHER.
I JUST THOUGHT IF WE COULD PUT ON HIS PLAY, IT COULD HELP RAISE MONEY TO PAY FOR HIS HOSPITAL BILLS.
I THINK IT'S A GOOD IDEA.
AND I THINK YOU ARE A GOOD FRIEND, MAXINE. I HOPE HE APPRECIATES IT.
THANKS, MRS. HUTCHINSON.
I HOPE SO, TOO.
...AND EACH ONE OF YOU IS GOING TO HELP OUT YOUR FELLOW STUDENT BY TAKING PART IN THIS PLAY.
YOU CAN HELP WITH TICKET SALES, YOU CAN PLAY A ROLE, YOU CAN HELP WITH SET DESIGN OR PROMOTION BUT YOU WILL ALL HELP, AND YOUR GRADE WILL DEPEND ON IT!
EMO BOY? OH GOD, NO!
THIS IS SO WRONG!

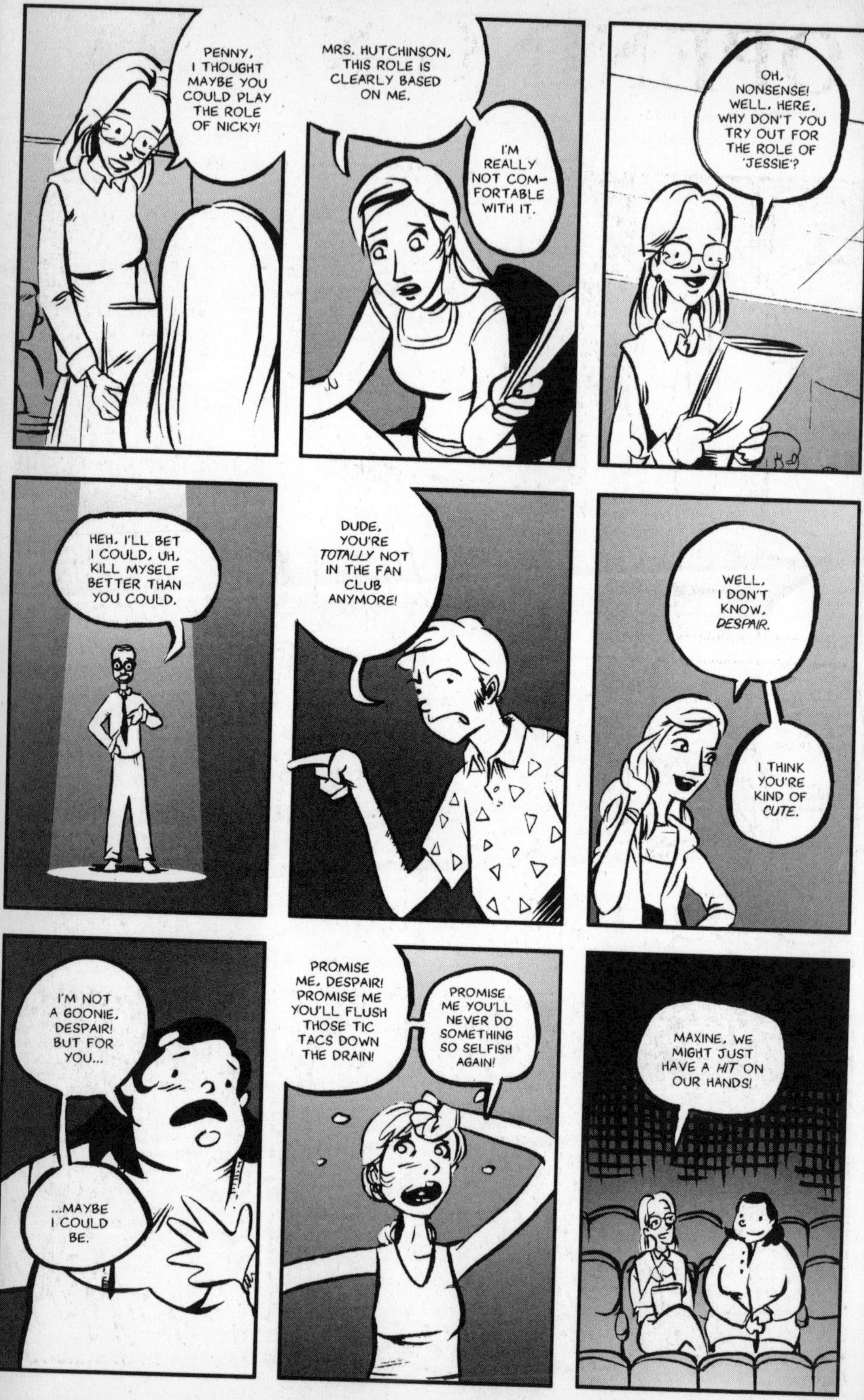
PENNY, I THOUGHT MAYBE YOU COULD PLAY THE ROLE OF NICKY!
MRS. HUTCHINSON, THIS ROLE IS CLEARLY BASED ON ME.
I'M REALLY NOT COM-FORTABLE WITH IT.
OH, NONSENSE! WELL, HERE, WHY DON'T YOU TRY OUT FOR THE ROLE OF 'JESSIE'?
HEH, I'LL BET I COULD, UH, KILL MYSELF BETTER THAN YOU COULD.
DUDE, YOU'RE *TOTALLY* NOT IN THE FAN CLUB ANYMORE!
WELL, I DON'T KNOW, *DESPAIR*.
I THINK YOU'RE KIND OF *CUTE*.
I'M NOT A GOONIE, DESPAIR! BUT FOR YOU...
...MAYBE I COULD BE.
PROMISE ME, DESPAIR! PROMISE ME YOU'LL FLUSH THOSE TIC TACS DOWN THE DRAIN!
PROMISE ME YOU'LL NEVER DO SOMETHING SO SELFISH AGAIN!
MAXINE, WE MIGHT JUST HAVE A *HIT* ON OUR HANDS!

# OPENING NIGHT

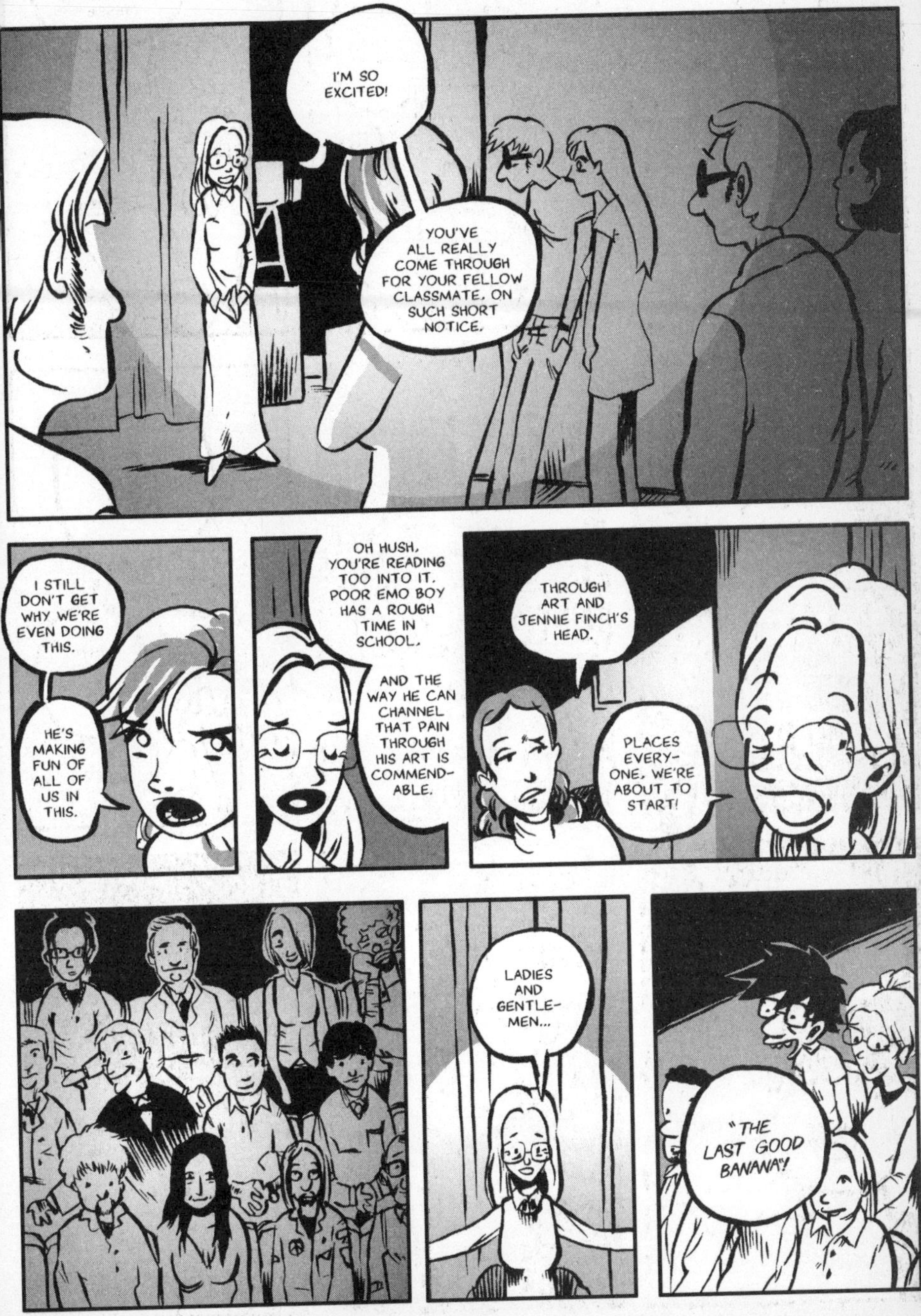
I'M SO EXCITED!
YOU'VE ALL REALLY COME THROUGH FOR YOUR FELLOW CLASSMATE, ON SUCH SHORT NOTICE.
I STILL DON'T GET WHY WE'RE EVEN DOING THIS.
HE'S MAKING FUN OF ALL OF US IN THIS.
OH HUSH, YOU'RE READING TOO INTO IT. POOR EMO BOY HAS A ROUGH TIME IN SCHOOL.
AND THE WAY HE CAN CHANNEL THAT PAIN THROUGH HIS ART IS COMMEND-ABLE.
THROUGH ART AND JENNIE FINCH'S HEAD.
PLACES EVERY-ONE, WE'RE ABOUT TO START!
LADIES AND GENTLE-MEN...
"THE LAST GOOD BANANA"!

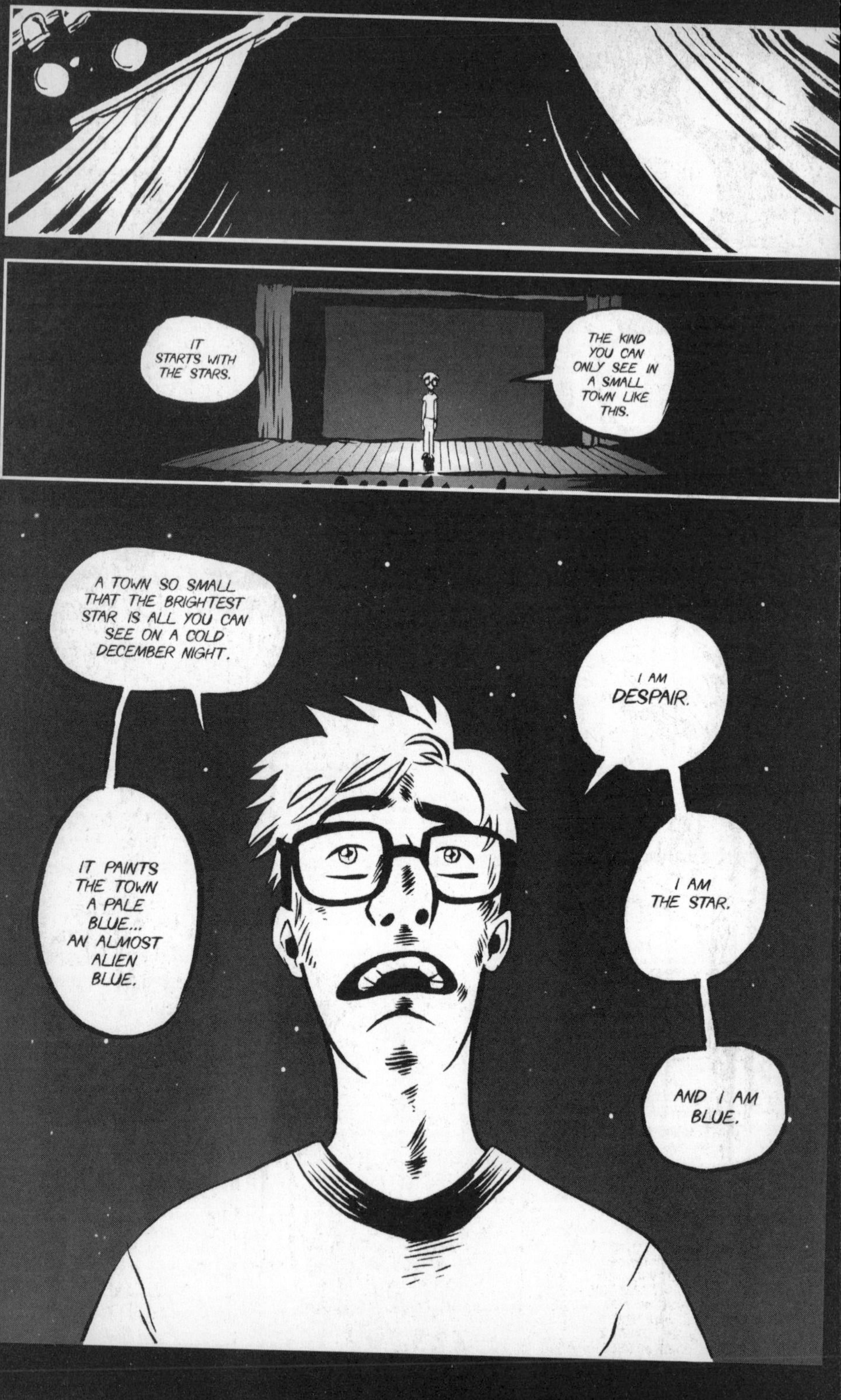
IT STARTS WITH THE STARS.
THE KIND YOU CAN ONLY SEE IN A SMALL TOWN LIKE THIS.
A TOWN SO SMALL THAT THE BRIGHTEST STAR IS ALL YOU CAN SEE ON A COLD DECEMBER NIGHT.
IT PAINTS THE TOWN A PALE BLUE... AN ALMOST ALIEN BLUE.
I AM DESPAIR.
I AM THE STAR.
AND I AM BLUE.

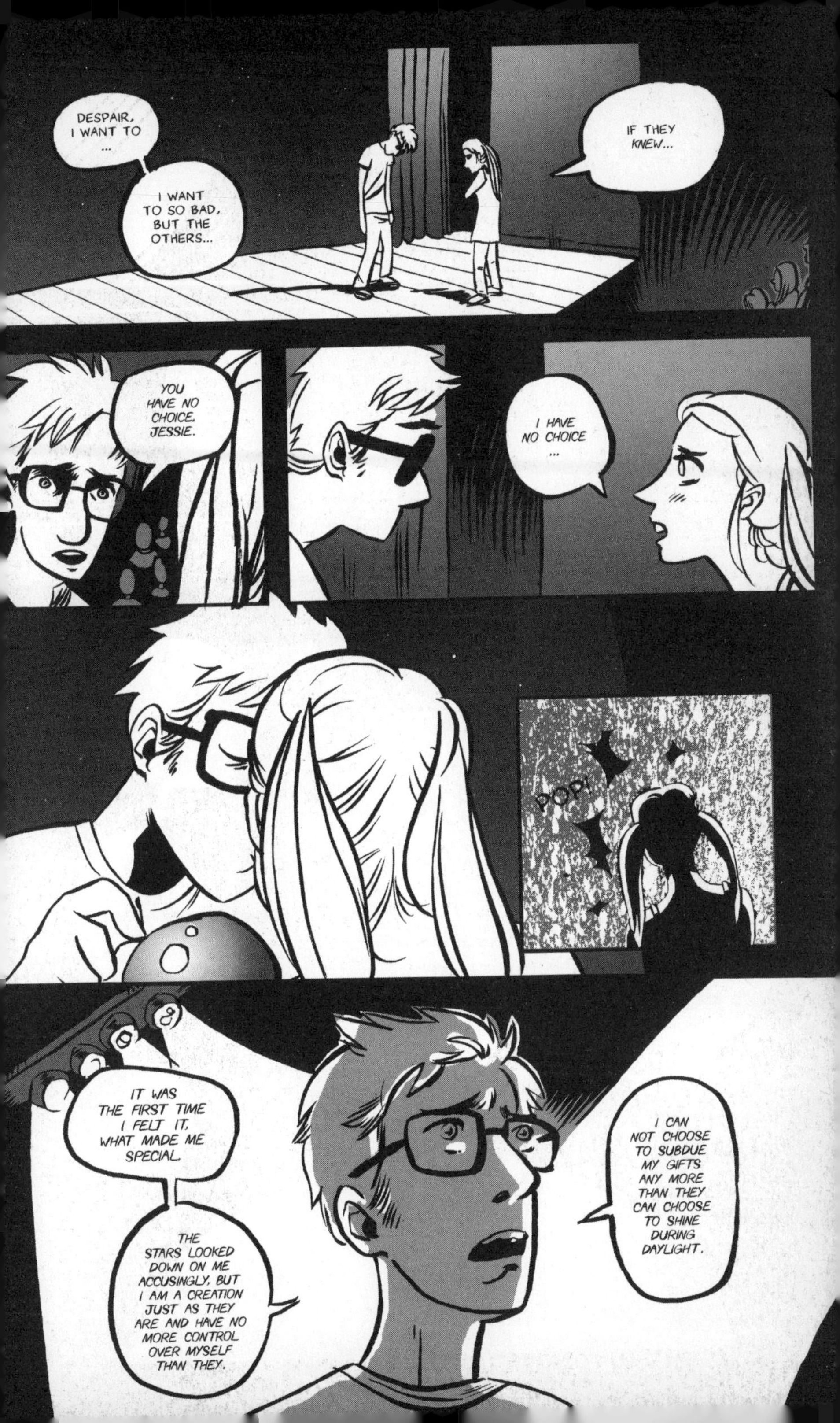
DESPAIR, I WANT TO ...
I WANT TO SO BAD, BUT THE OTHERS...
IF THEY KNEW...
YOU HAVE NO CHOICE, JESSIE.
I HAVE NO CHOICE ...
POP!
IT WAS THE FIRST TIME I FELT IT, WHAT MADE ME SPECIAL.
THE STARS LOOKED DOWN ON ME ACCUSINGLY, BUT I AM A CREATION JUST AS THEY ARE AND HAVE NO MORE CONTROL OVER MYSELF THAN THEY.
I CAN NOT CHOOSE TO SUBDUE MY GIFTS ANY MORE THAN THEY CAN CHOOSE TO SHINE DURING DAYLIGHT.

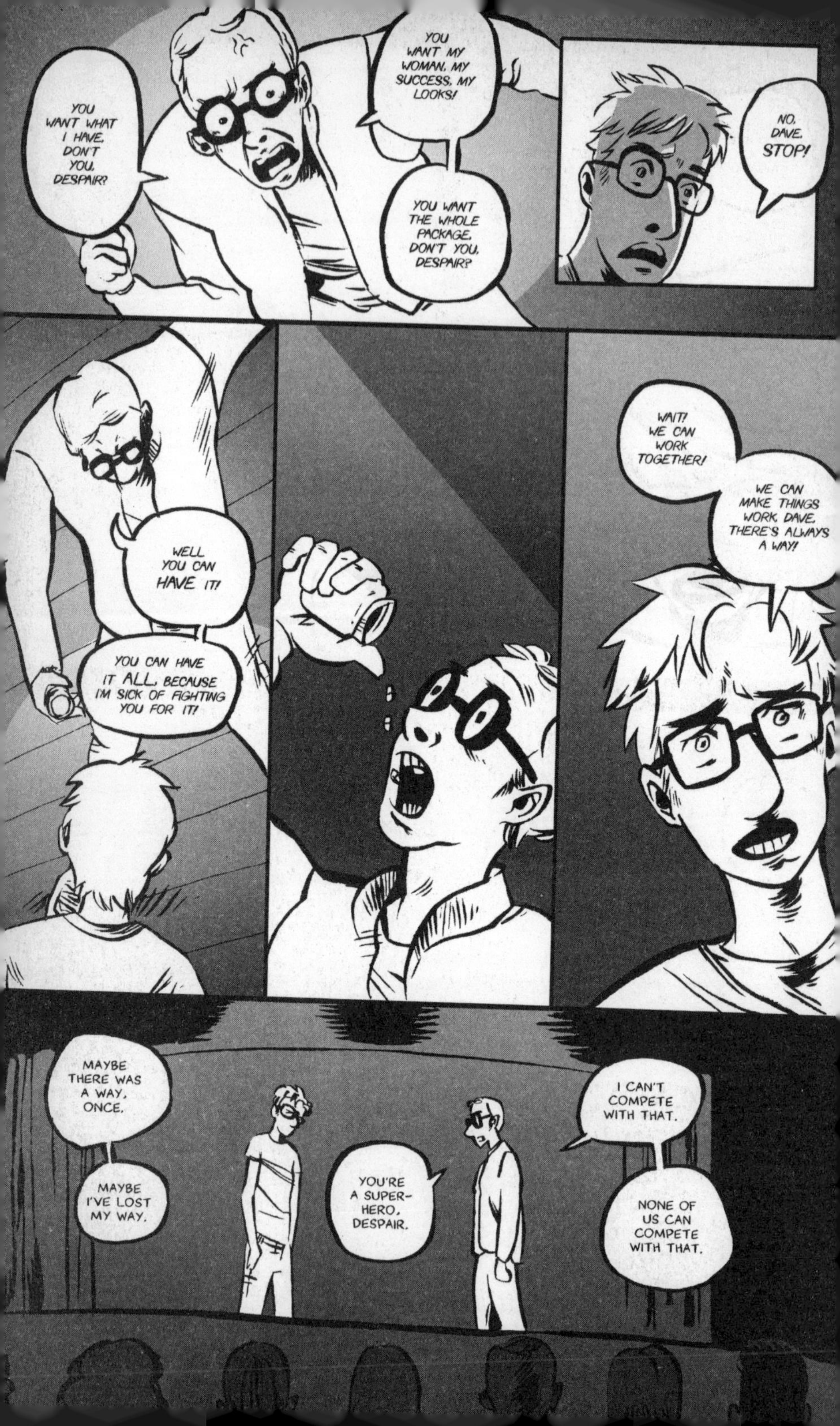
YOU WANT WHAT I HAVE, DON'T YOU, DESPAIR?
YOU WANT MY WOMAN, MY SUCCESS, MY LOOKS!
YOU WANT THE WHOLE PACKAGE, DON'T YOU, DESPAIR?
NO, DAVE. STOP!
WELL YOU CAN HAVE IT!
YOU CAN HAVE IT ALL, BECAUSE I'M SICK OF FIGHTING YOU FOR IT!
WAIT! WE CAN WORK TOGETHER!
WE CAN MAKE THINGS WORK, DAVE. THERE'S ALWAYS A WAY!
MAYBE THERE WAS A WAY, ONCE.
MAYBE I'VE LOST MY WAY.
YOU'RE A SUPER-HERO, DESPAIR.
I CAN'T COMPETE WITH THAT.
NONE OF US CAN COMPETE WITH THAT.

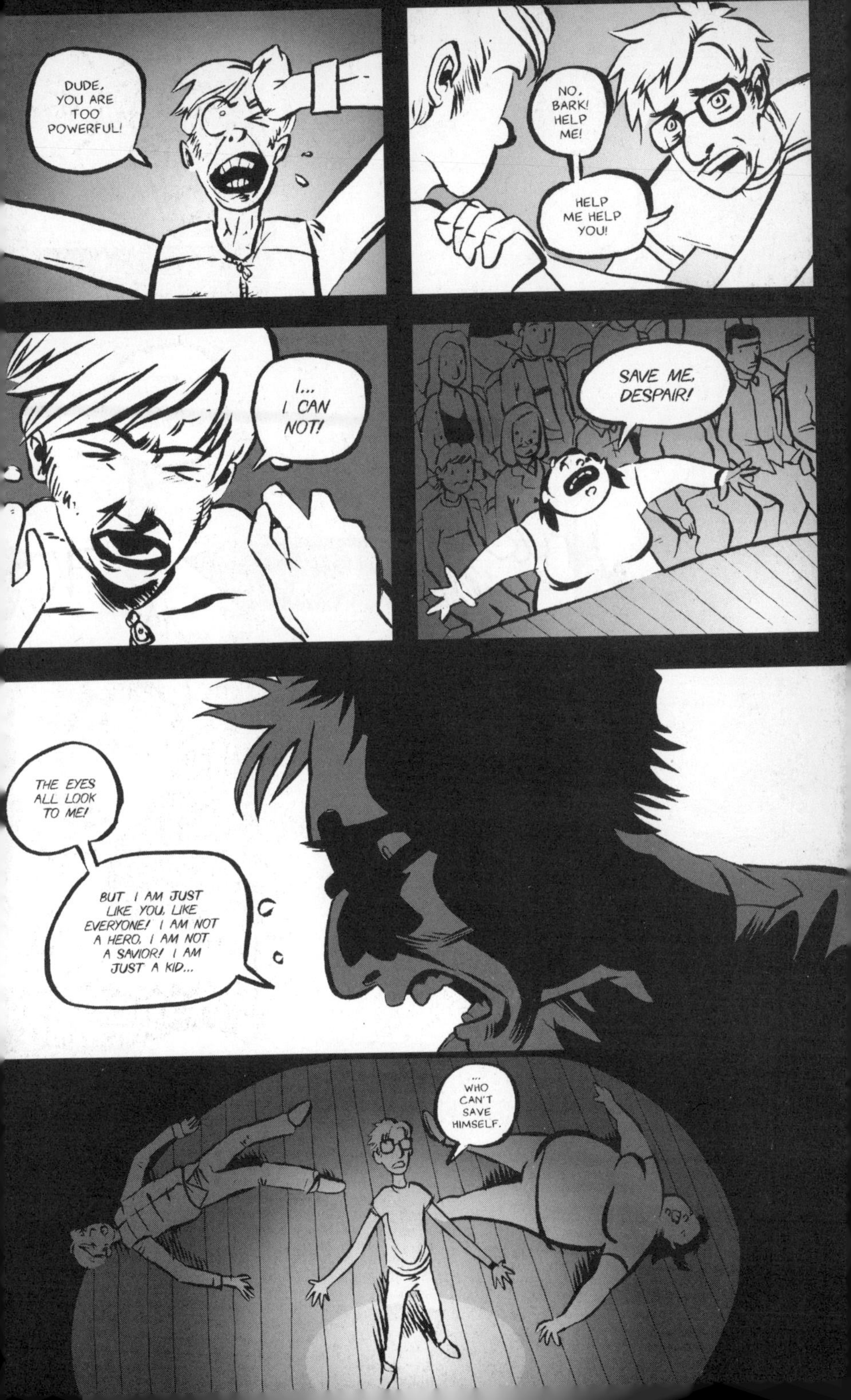
DUDE, YOU ARE TOO POWERFUL!
NO, BARK! HELP ME!
HELP ME HELP YOU!
I... I CAN NOT!
SAVE ME, DESPAIR!
THE EYES ALL LOOK TO ME!
BUT I AM JUST LIKE YOU, LIKE EVERYONE! I AM NOT A HERO, I AM NOT A SAVIOR! I AM JUST A KID...
... WHO CAN'T SAVE HIMSELF.

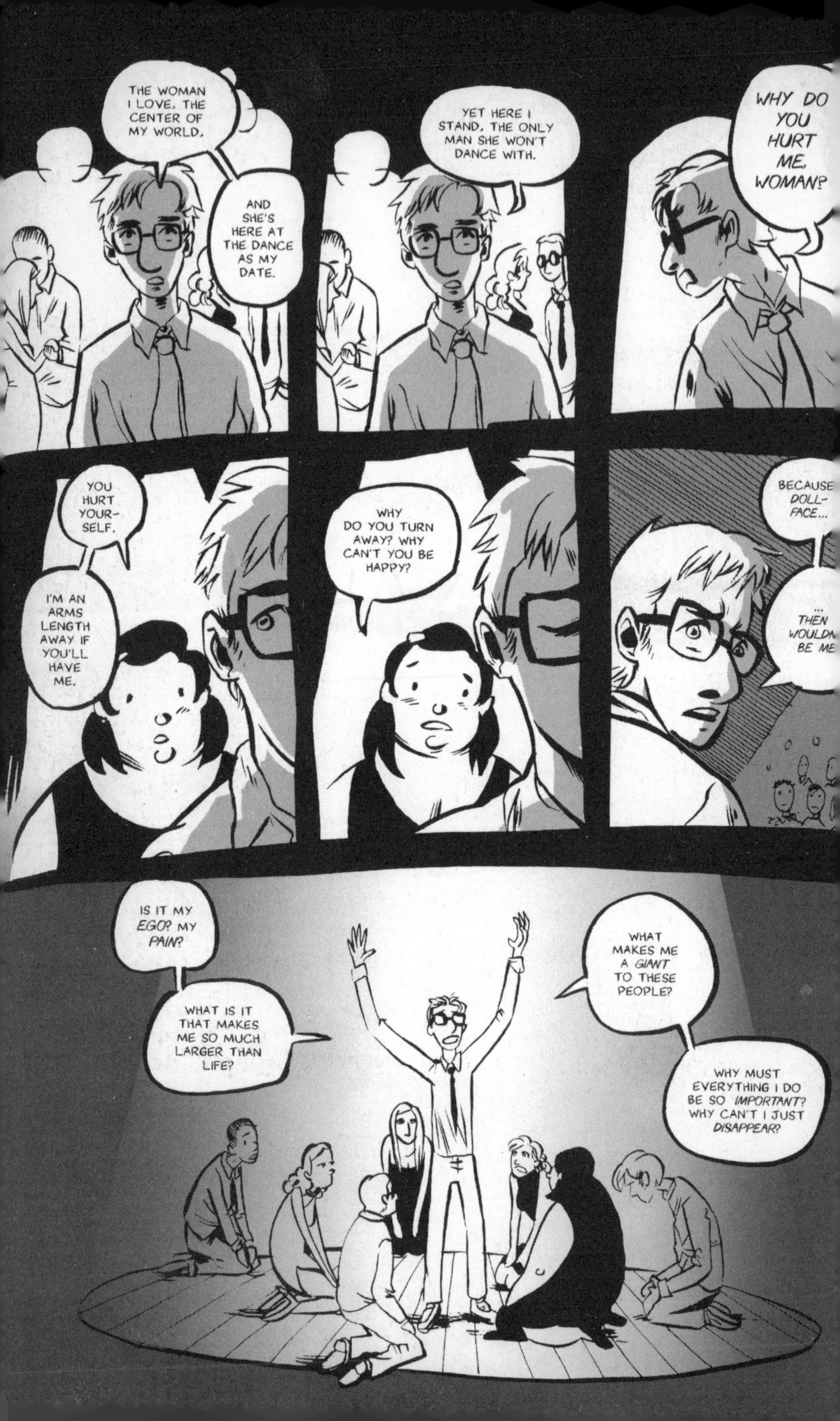
THE WOMAN I LOVE, THE CENTER OF MY WORLD,
AND SHE'S HERE AT THE DANCE AS MY DATE.
YET HERE I STAND, THE ONLY MAN SHE WON'T DANCE WITH.
WHY DO YOU HURT ME, WOMAN?
YOU HURT YOURSELF.
I'M AN ARMS LENGTH AWAY IF YOU'LL HAVE ME.
WHY DO YOU TURN AWAY? WHY CAN'T YOU BE HAPPY?
BECAUSE DOLL-FACE...
...THEN WOULDN BE ME
IS IT MY EGO? MY PAIN?
WHAT IS IT THAT MAKES ME SO MUCH LARGER THAN LIFE?
WHAT MAKES ME A GIANT TO THESE PEOPLE?
WHY MUST EVERYTHING I DO BE SO IMPORTANT? WHY CAN'T I JUST DISAPPEAR?

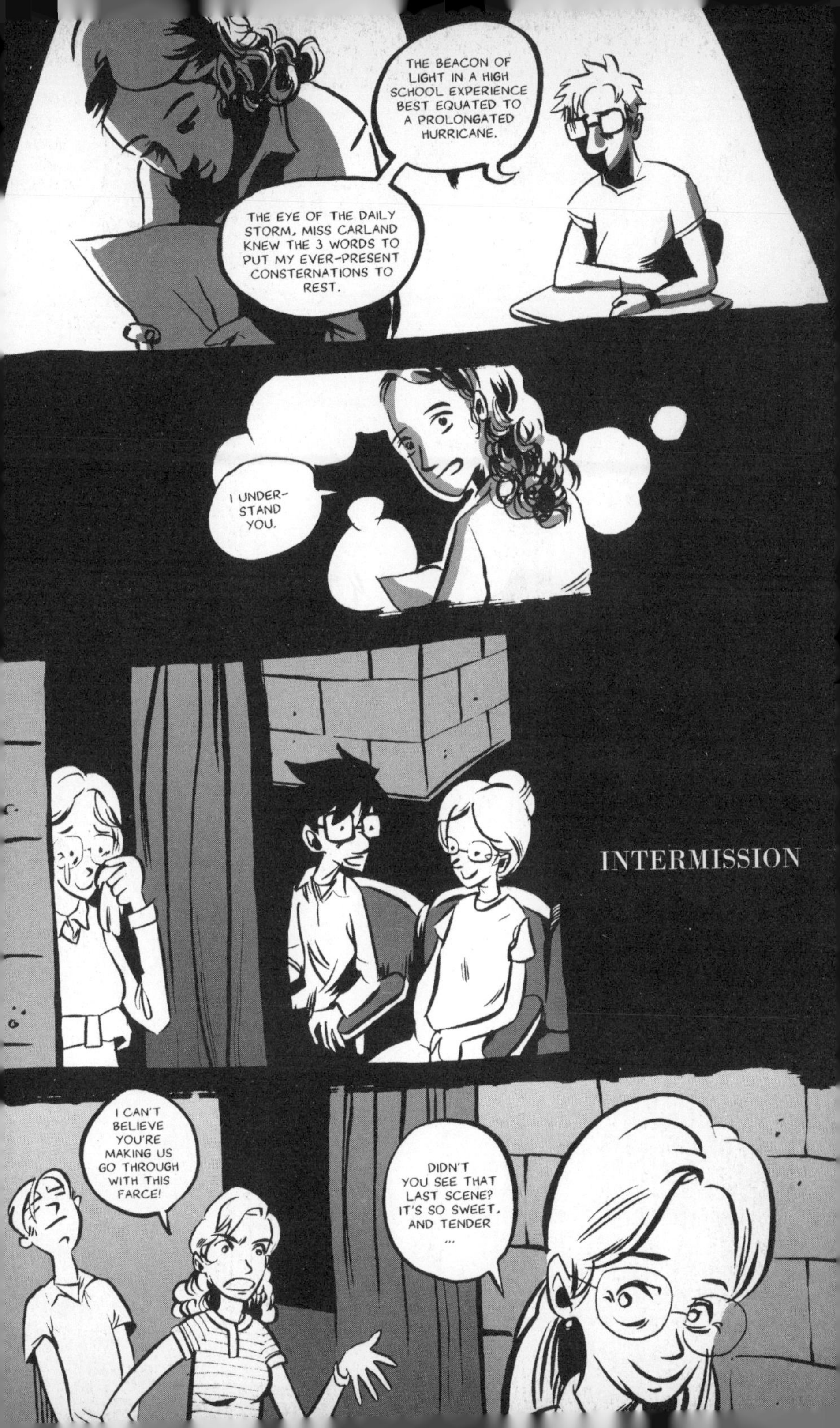
THE BEACON OF LIGHT IN A HIGH SCHOOL EXPERIENCE BEST EQUATED TO A PROLONGATED HURRICANE.
THE EYE OF THE DAILY STORM, MISS CARLAND KNEW THE 3 WORDS TO PUT MY EVER-PRESENT CONSTERNATIONS TO REST.
I UNDER-STAND YOU.
INTERMISSION
I CAN'T BELIEVE YOU'RE MAKING US GO THROUGH WITH THIS FARCE!
DIDN'T YOU SEE THAT LAST SCENE? IT'S SO SWEET, AND TENDER ...

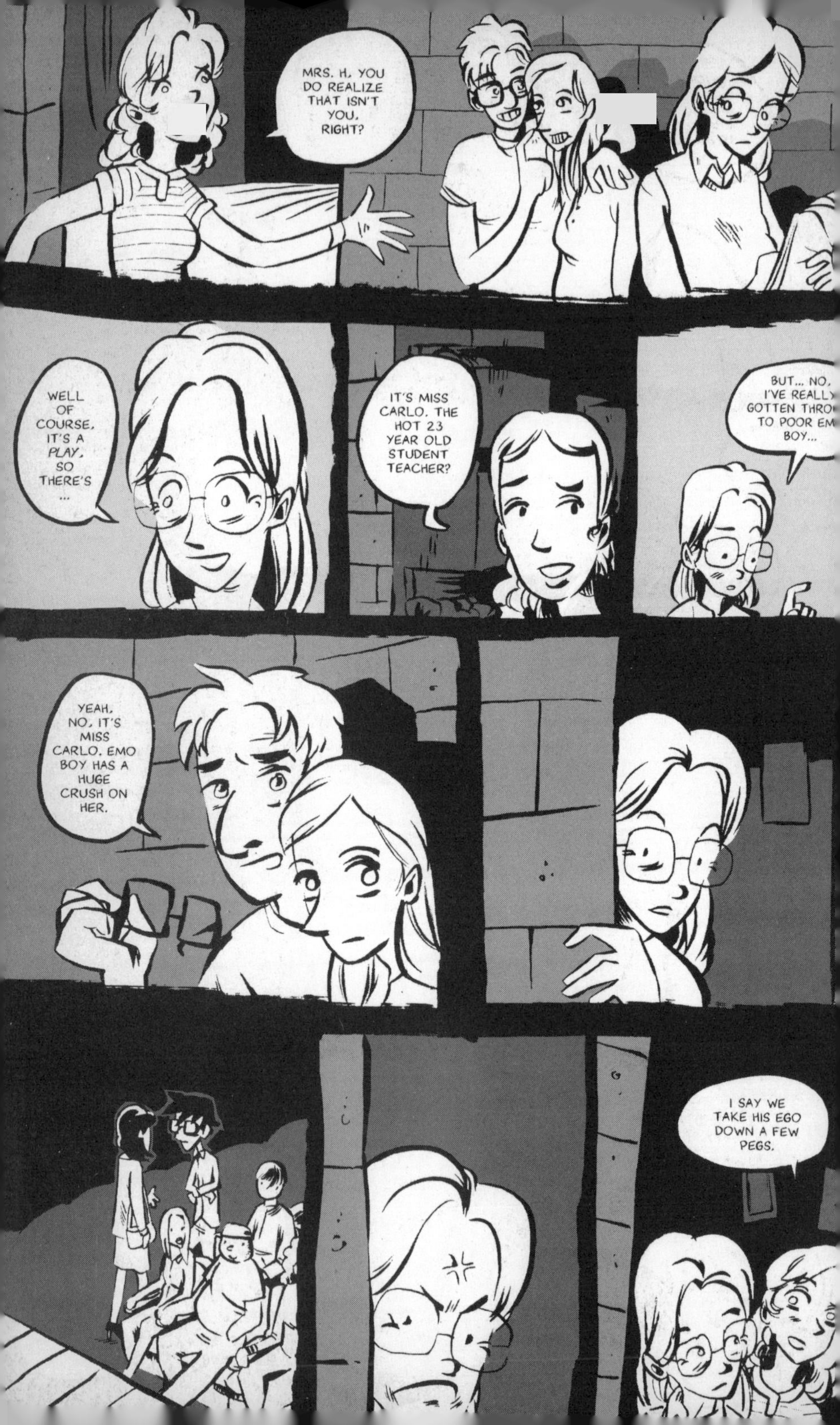
MRS. H, YOU DO REALIZE THAT ISN'T YOU, RIGHT?
WELL OF COURSE, IT'S A *PLAY*, SO THERE'S ...
IT'S MISS CARLO. THE HOT 23 YEAR OLD STUDENT TEACHER?
BUT... NO, I'VE REALLY GOTTEN THRO TO POOR EM BOY...
YEAH, NO, IT'S MISS CARLO. EMO BOY HAS A HUGE CRUSH ON HER.
I SAY WE TAKE HIS EGO DOWN A FEW PEGS.

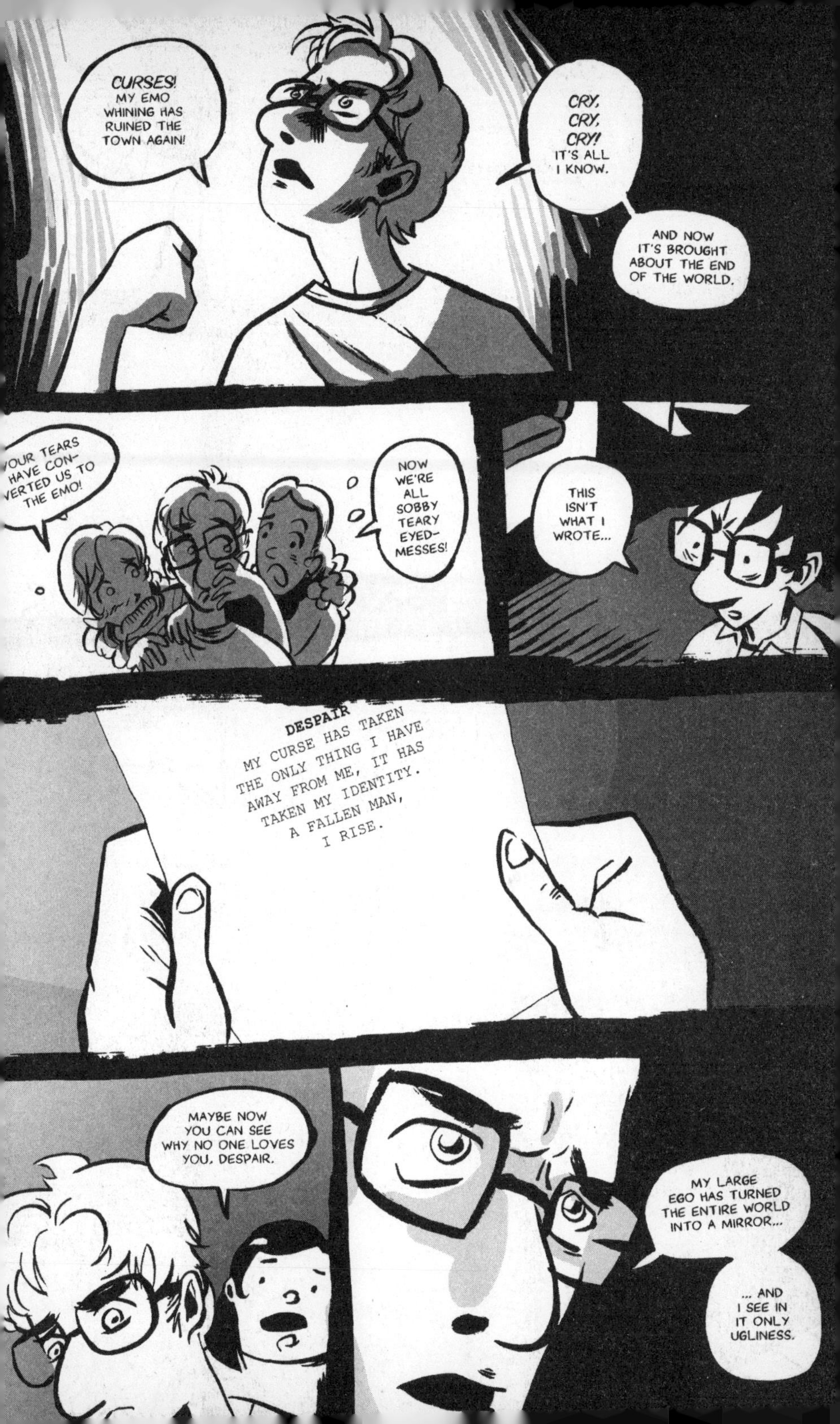
CURSES! MY EMO WHINING HAS RUINED THE TOWN AGAIN!
CRY, CRY, CRY! IT'S ALL I KNOW.
AND NOW IT'S BROUGHT ABOUT THE END OF THE WORLD.
YOUR TEARS HAVE CONVERTED US TO THE EMO!
NOW WE'RE ALL SOBBY TEARY EYED-MESSES!
THIS ISN'T WHAT I WROTE...
DESPAIR
MY CURSE HAS TAKEN THE ONLY THING I HAVE AWAY FROM ME, IT HAS TAKEN MY IDENTITY. A FALLEN MAN, I RISE.
MAYBE NOW YOU CAN SEE WHY NO ONE LOVES YOU, DESPAIR.
MY LARGE EGO HAS TURNED THE ENTIRE WORLD INTO A MIRROR...
... AND I SEE IN IT ONLY UGLINESS.

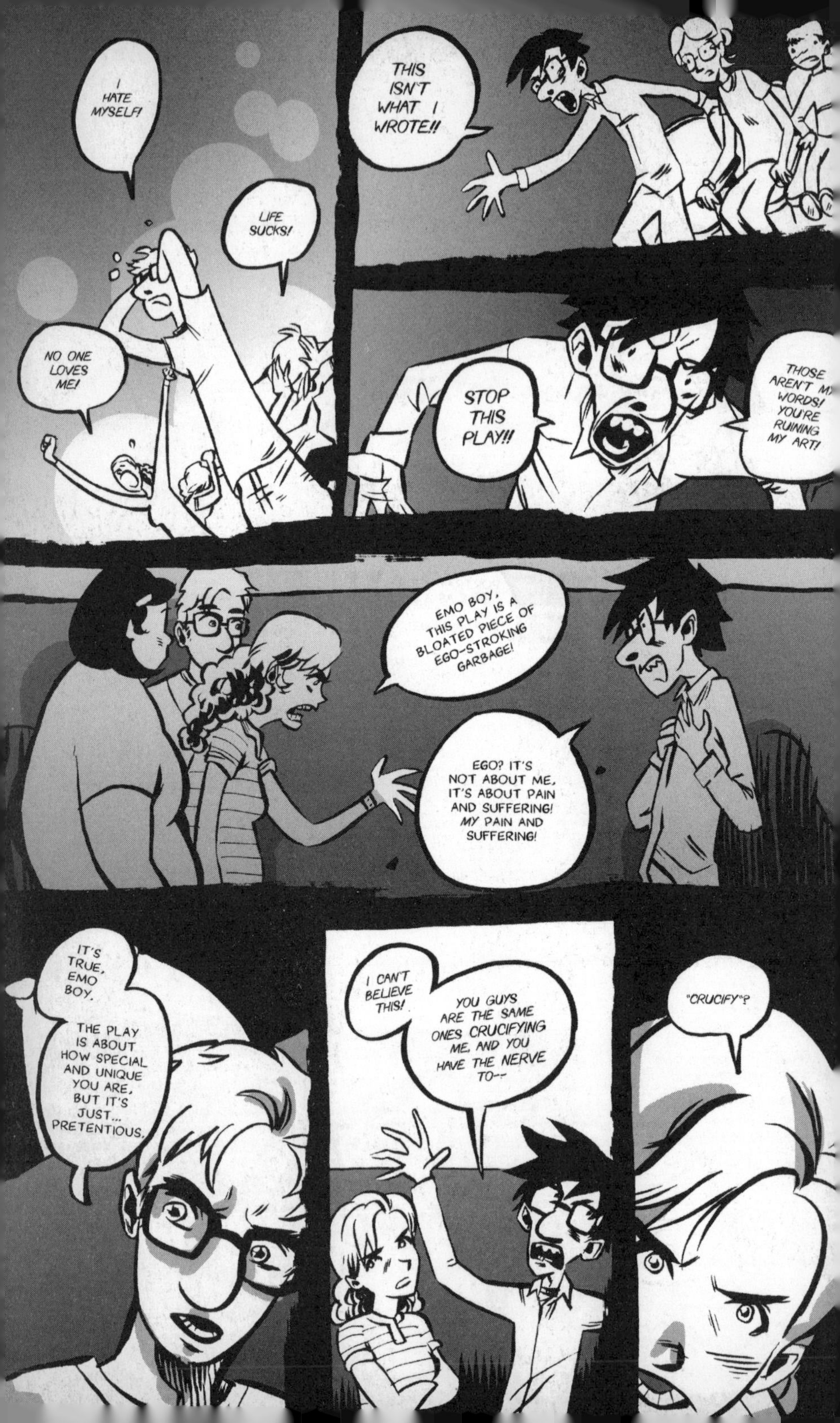
I HATE MYSELF!
LIFE SUCKS!
NO ONE LOVES ME!
THIS ISN'T WHAT I WROTE!!
STOP THIS PLAY!!
THOSE AREN'T MY WORDS! YOU'RE RUINING MY ART!
EMO BOY, THIS PLAY IS A BLOATED PIECE OF EGO-STROKING GARBAGE!
EGO? IT'S NOT ABOUT ME, IT'S ABOUT PAIN AND SUFFERING! MY PAIN AND SUFFERING!
IT'S TRUE, EMO BOY.
THE PLAY IS ABOUT HOW SPECIAL AND UNIQUE YOU ARE, BUT IT'S JUST... PRETENTIOUS.
I CAN'T BELIEVE THIS!
YOU GUYS ARE THE SAME ONES CRUCIFYING ME, AND YOU HAVE THE NERVE TO--
"CRUCIFY"?

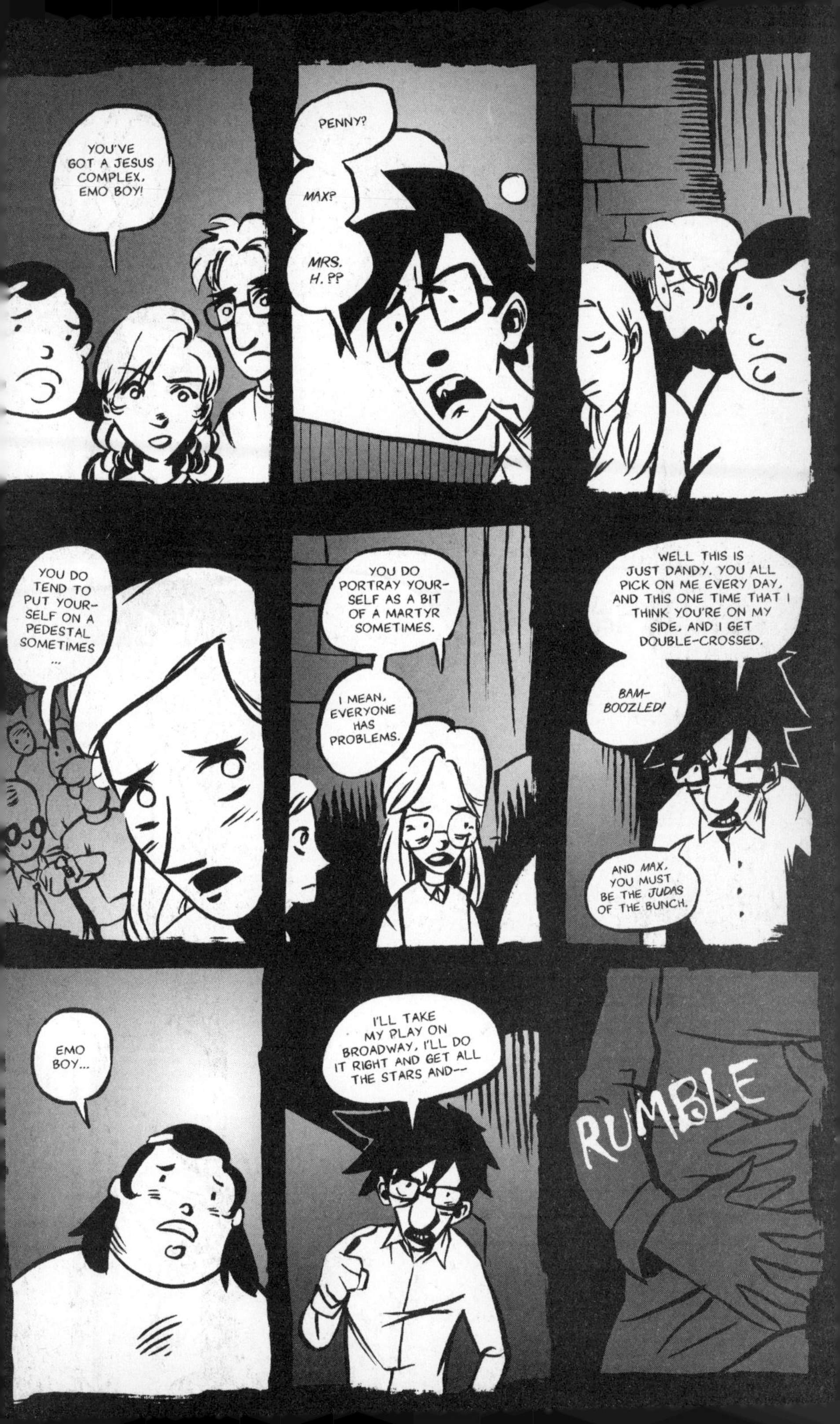
YOU'VE GOT A JESUS COMPLEX, EMO BOY!
PENNY?
MAX?
MRS. H.??
YOU DO TEND TO PUT YOURSELF ON A PEDESTAL SOMETIMES ...
YOU DO PORTRAY YOURSELF AS A BIT OF A MARTYR SOMETIMES.
I MEAN, EVERYONE HAS PROBLEMS.
WELL THIS IS JUST DANDY. YOU ALL PICK ON ME EVERY DAY, AND THIS ONE TIME THAT I THINK YOU'RE ON MY SIDE, AND I GET DOUBLE-CROSSED.
BAMBOOZLED!
AND MAX, YOU MUST BE THE JUDAS OF THE BUNCH.
EMO BOY...
I'LL TAKE MY PLAY ON BROADWAY, I'LL DO IT RIGHT AND GET ALL THE STARS AND--
RUMBLE

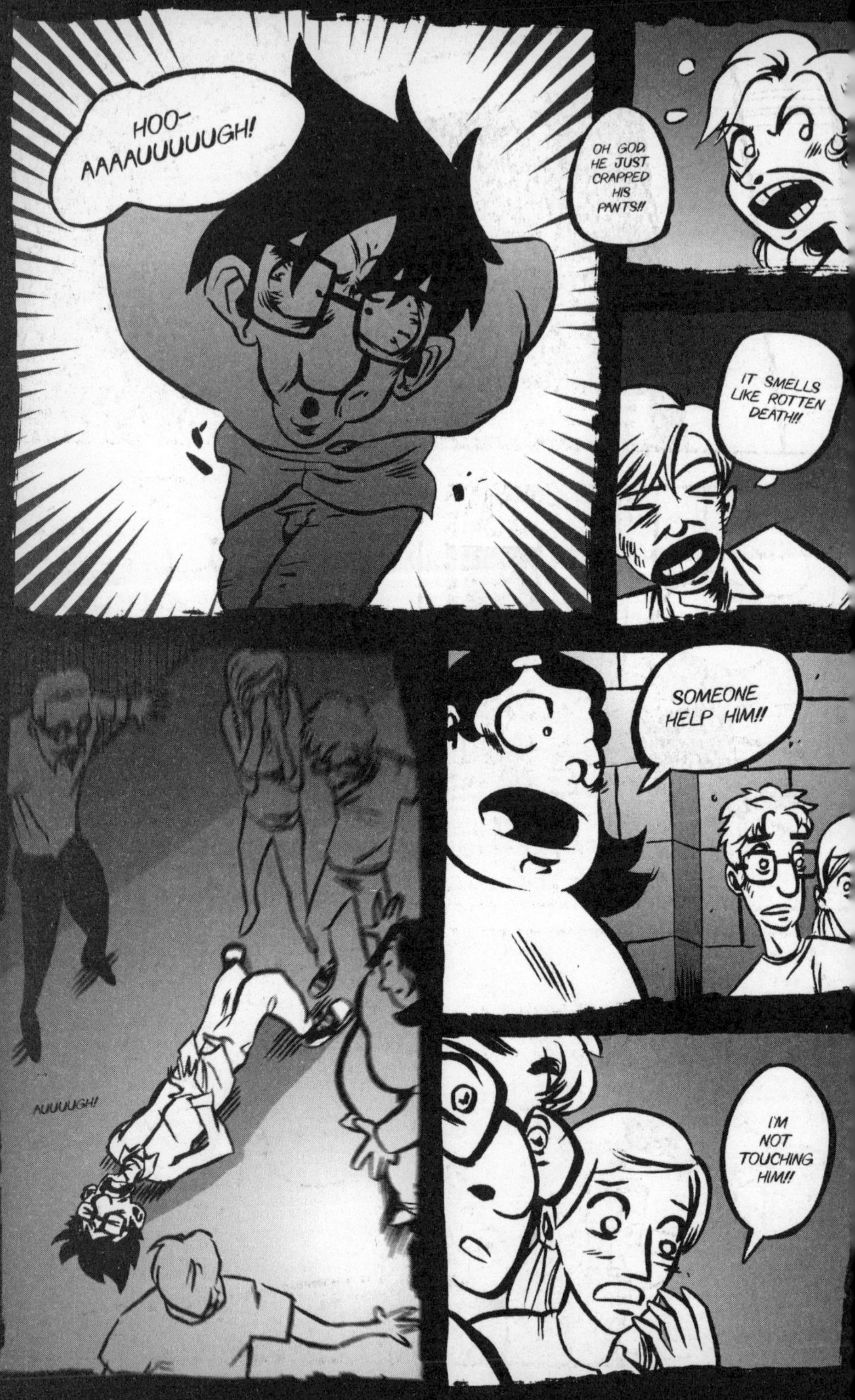
HOO-AAAAUUUUUGH!
OH GOD, HE JUST CRAPPED HIS PANTS!!
IT SMELLS LIKE ROTTEN DEATH!!
AUUUUGH!
SOMEONE HELP HIM!!
I'M NOT TOUCHING HIM!!

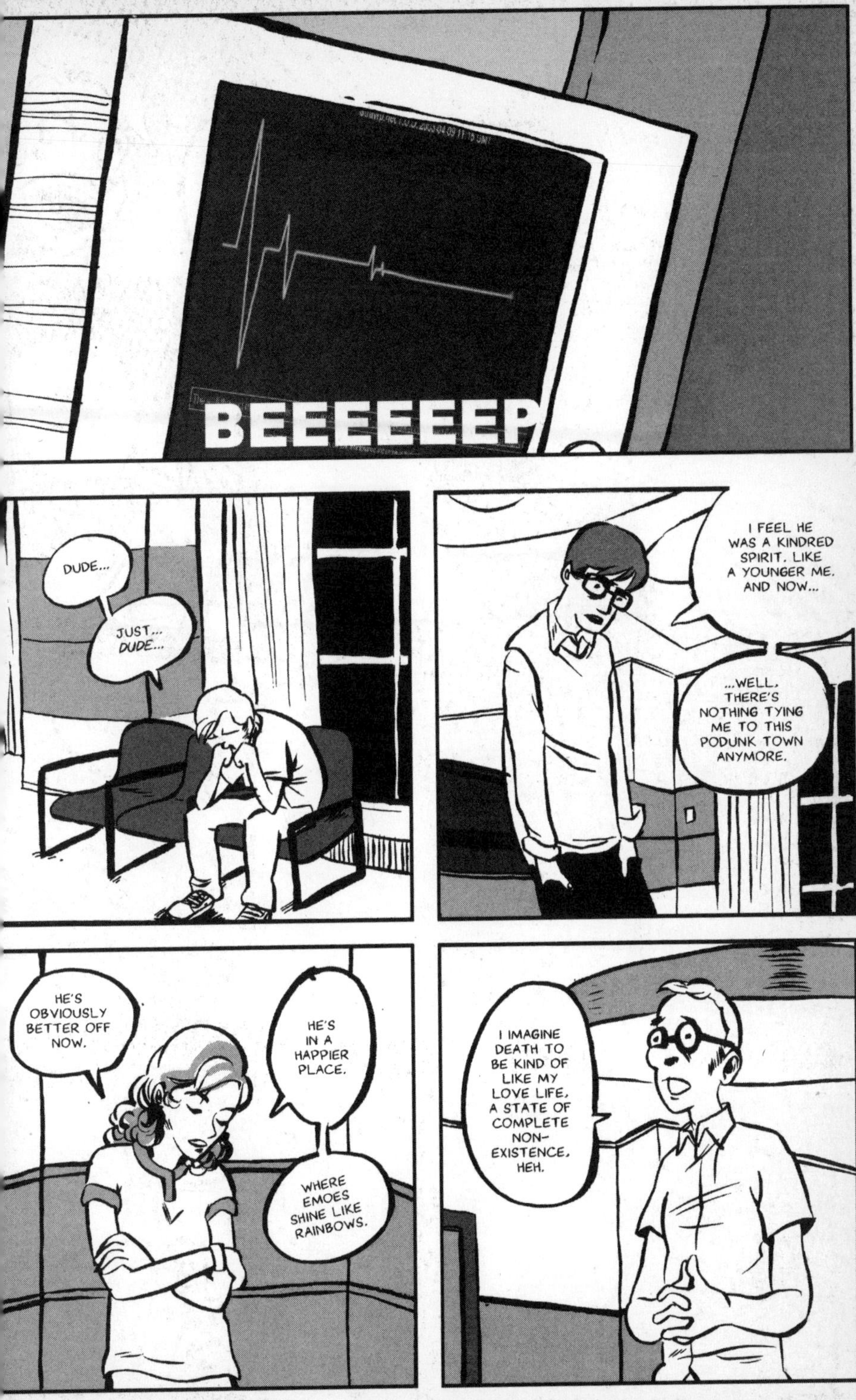
BEEEEEEP
DUDE...
JUST... DUDE...
I FEEL HE WAS A KINDRED SPIRIT. LIKE A YOUNGER ME. AND NOW...
...WELL, THERE'S NOTHING TYING ME TO THIS PODUNK TOWN ANYMORE.
HE'S OBVIOUSLY BETTER OFF NOW.
HE'S IN A HAPPIER PLACE.
WHERE EMOES SHINE LIKE RAINBOWS.
I IMAGINE DEATH TO BE KIND OF LIKE MY LOVE LIFE, A STATE OF COMPLETE NON-EXISTENCE, HEH.

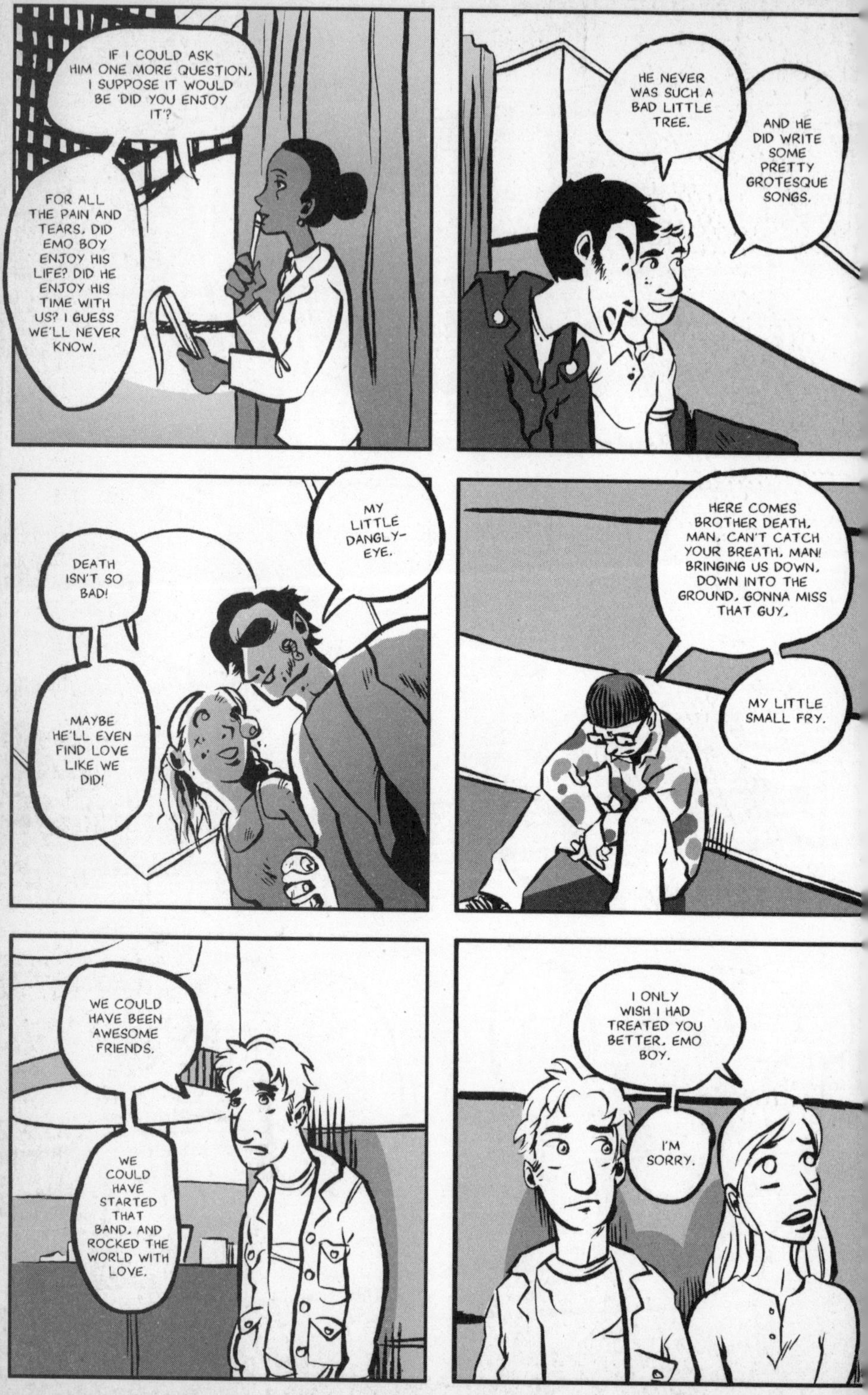
IF I COULD ASK HIM ONE MORE QUESTION, I SUPPOSE IT WOULD BE 'DID YOU ENJOY IT'?
FOR ALL THE PAIN AND TEARS, DID EMO BOY ENJOY HIS LIFE? DID HE ENJOY HIS TIME WITH US? I GUESS WE'LL NEVER KNOW.
HE NEVER WAS SUCH A BAD LITTLE TREE.
AND HE DID WRITE SOME PRETTY GROTESQUE SONGS.
DEATH ISN'T SO BAD!
MAYBE HE'LL EVEN FIND LOVE LIKE WE DID!
MY LITTLE DANGLY-EYE.
HERE COMES BROTHER DEATH, MAN, CAN'T CATCH YOUR BREATH, MAN! BRINGING US DOWN, DOWN INTO THE GROUND, GONNA MISS THAT GUY,
MY LITTLE SMALL FRY.
WE COULD HAVE BEEN AWESOME FRIENDS.
WE COULD HAVE STARTED THAT BAND, AND ROCKED THE WORLD WITH LOVE.
I ONLY WISH I HAD TREATED YOU BETTER, EMO BOY.
I'M SORRY.

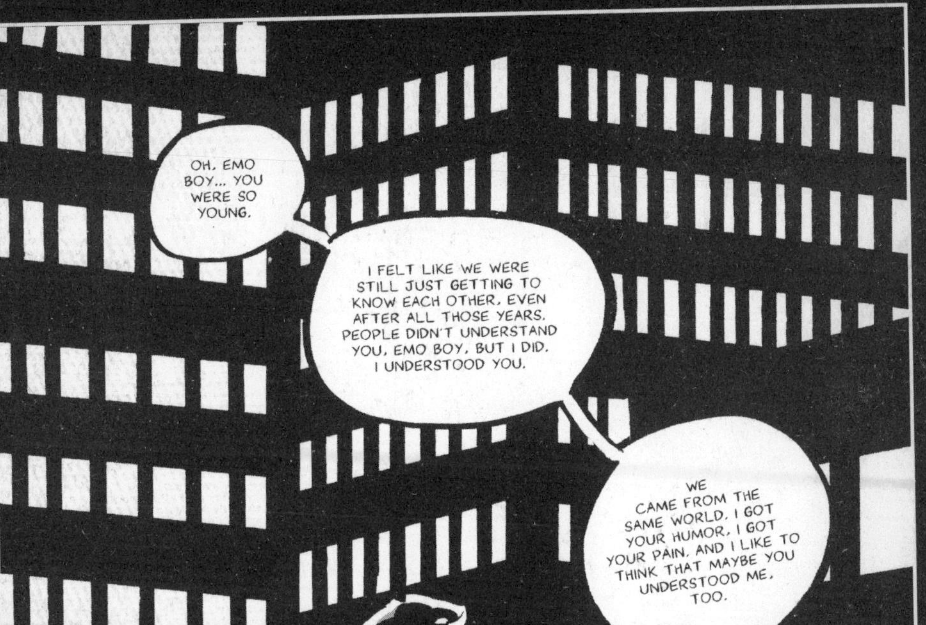
OH, EMO BOY... YOU WERE SO YOUNG.
I FELT LIKE WE WERE STILL JUST GETTING TO KNOW EACH OTHER, EVEN AFTER ALL THOSE YEARS. PEOPLE DIDN'T UNDERSTAND YOU, EMO BOY, BUT I DID. I UNDERSTOOD YOU.
WE CAME FROM THE SAME WORLD. I GOT YOUR HUMOR, I GOT YOUR PAIN. AND I LIKE TO THINK THAT MAYBE YOU UNDERSTOOD ME, TOO.
I CAN'T HELP BUT THINK THAT THIS WAS JUST THE BEGINNING OF THE ADVENTURES WE WERE GOING TO HAVE TOGETHER.

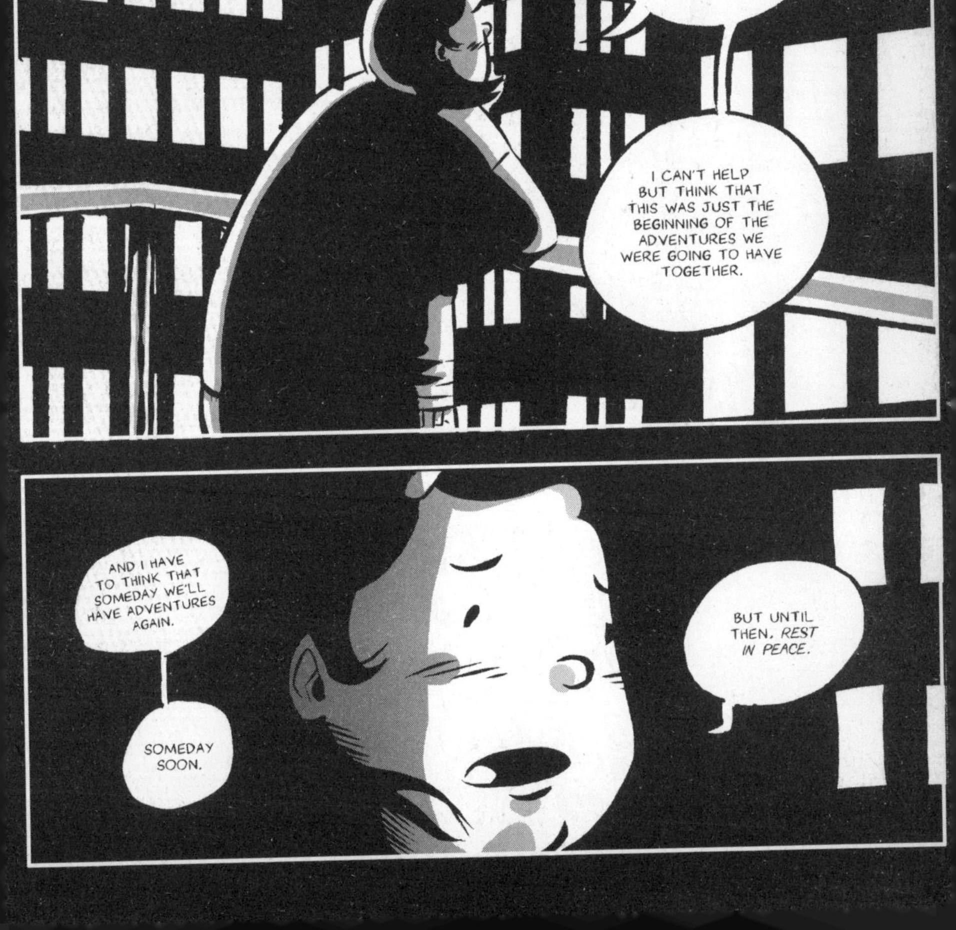
AND I HAVE TO THINK THAT SOMEDAY WE'LL HAVE ADVENTURES AGAIN.
SOMEDAY SOON.
BUT UNTIL THEN, *REST IN PEACE.*

# 3 DAYS LATER

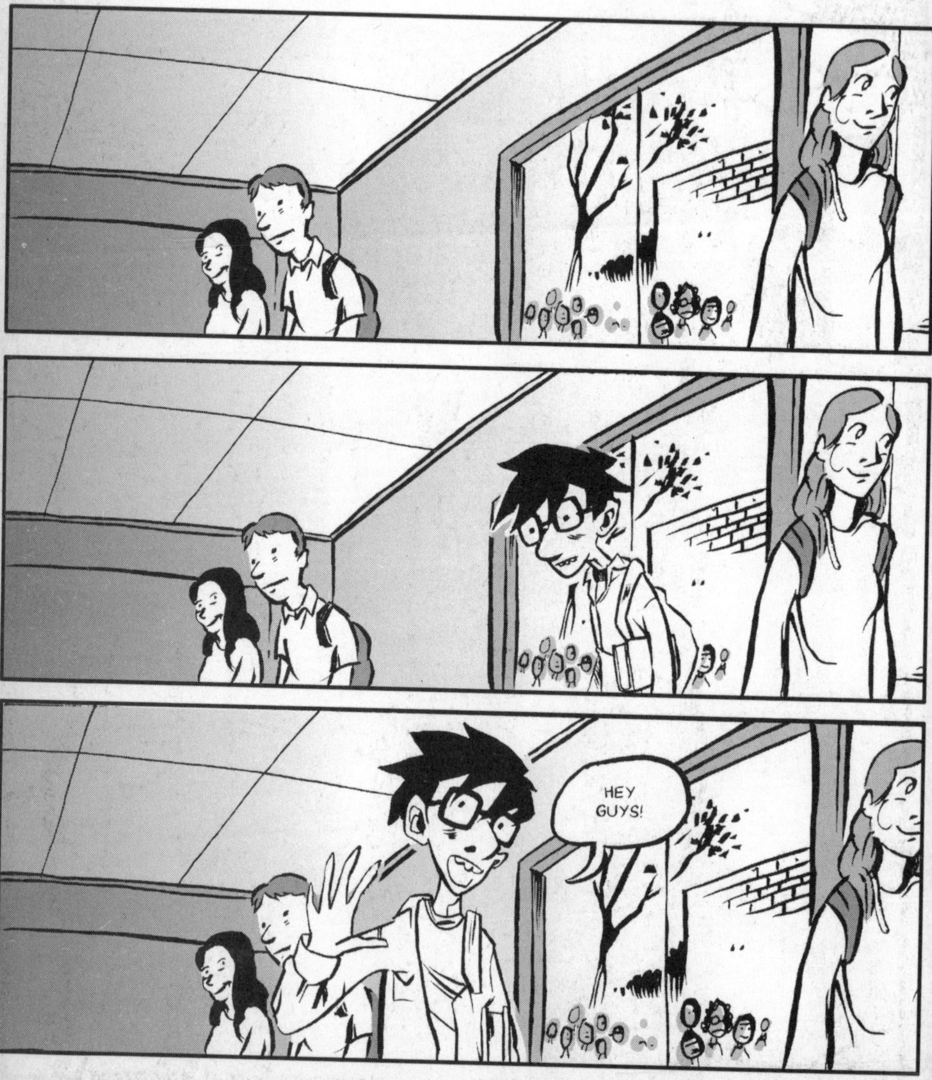
HEY GUYS!

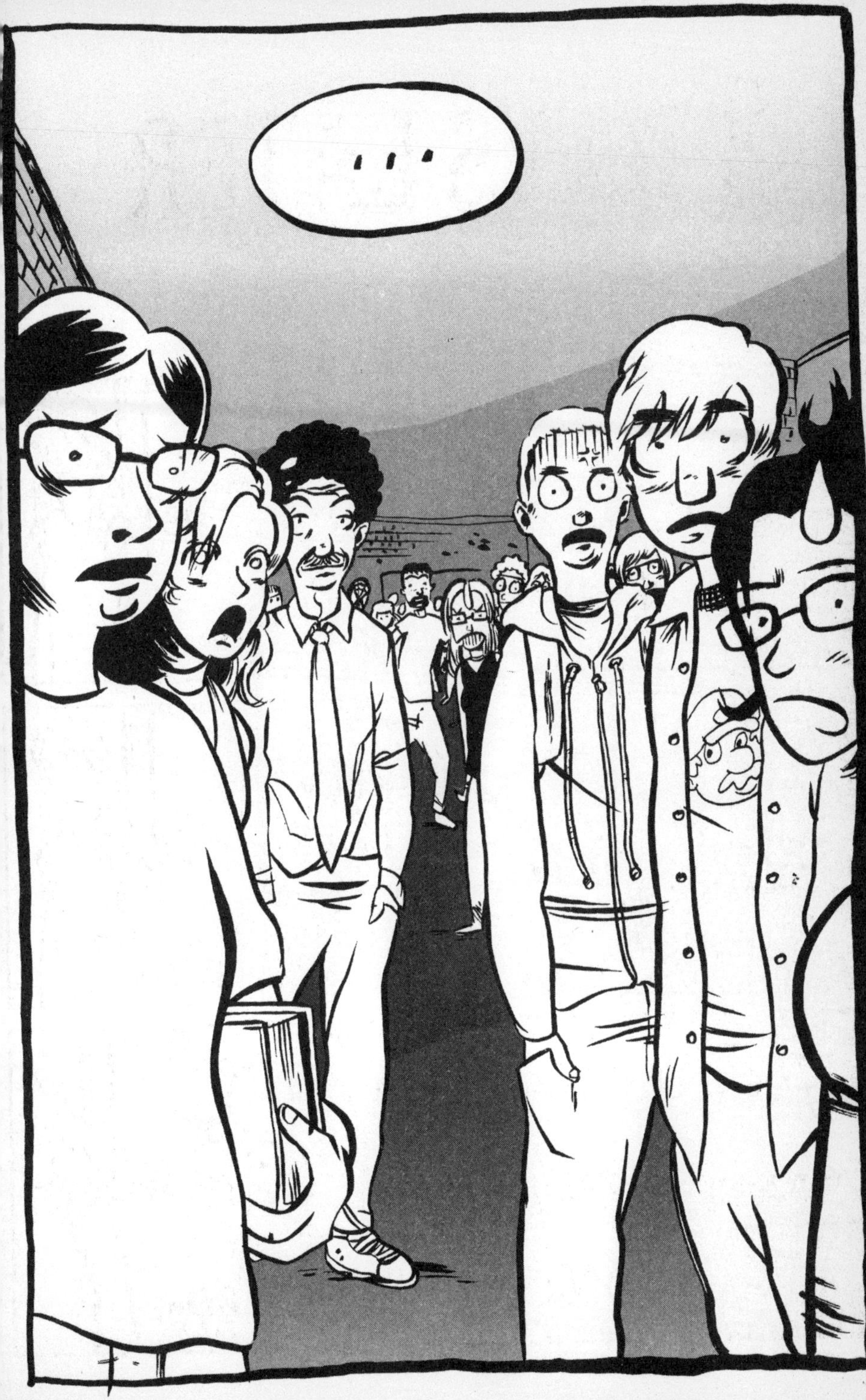
...

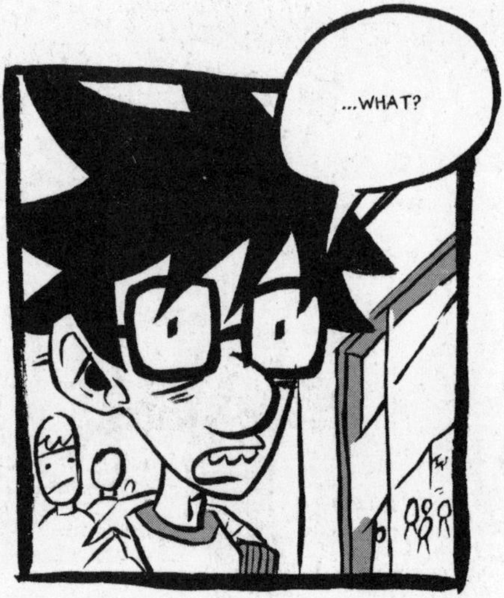
...WHAT?

THE END!

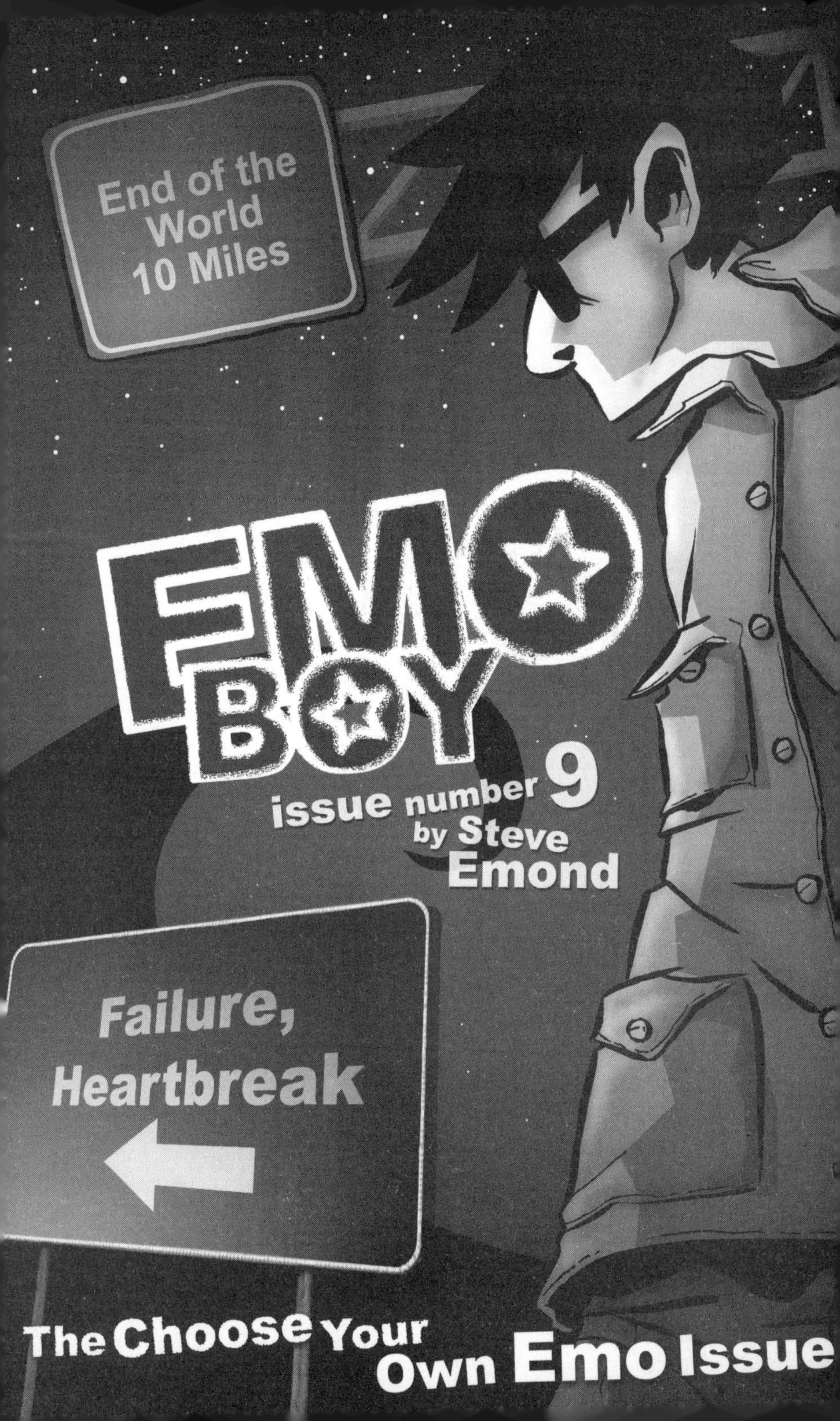
End of the World 10 Miles
EMO BOY
issue number 9
by Steve Emond
Failure, Heartbreak
The Choose Your Own Emo Issue

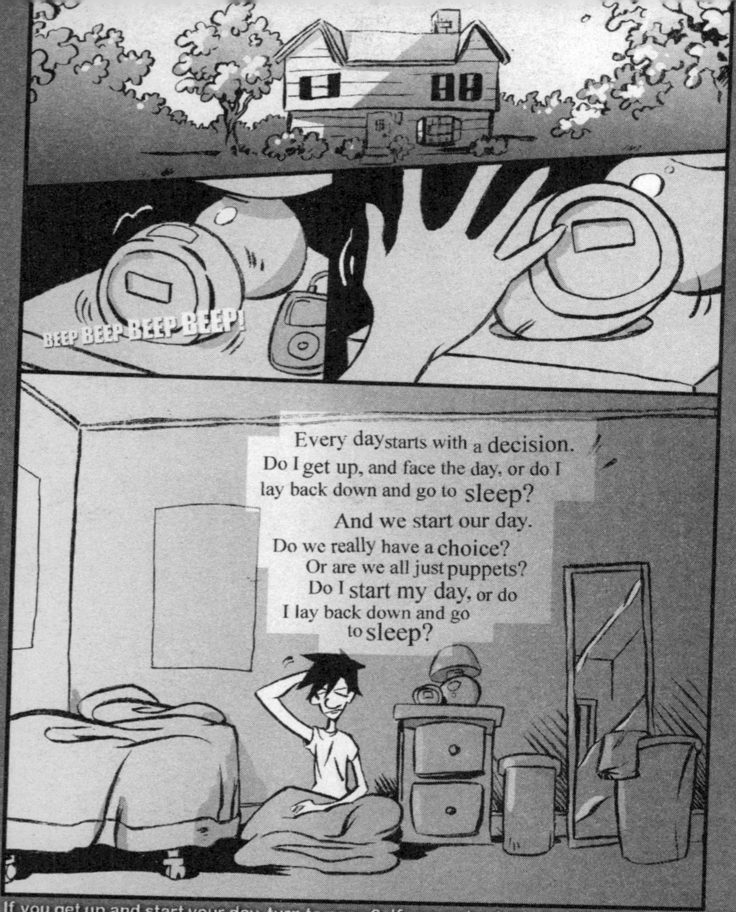
BEEP BEEP BEEP BEEP!
Every day starts with a decision.
Do I get up, and face the day, or do I lay back down and go to sleep?
And we start our day.
Do we really have a choice?
Or are we all just puppets?
Do I start my day, or do I lay back down and go to sleep?

If you get up and start your day, turn to page 9. If you go back to sleep, turn to page 3.



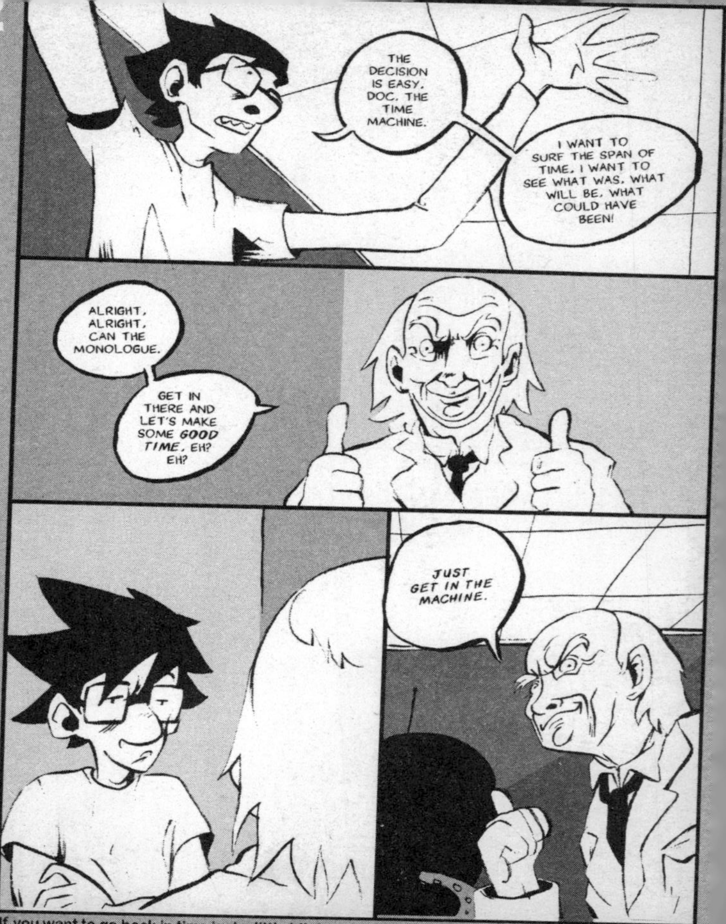
THE DECISION IS EASY, DOC. THE TIME MACHINE.
I WANT TO SURF THE SPAN OF TIME. I WANT TO SEE WHAT WAS, WHAT WILL BE, WHAT COULD HAVE BEEN!
ALRIGHT, ALRIGHT, CAN THE MONOLOGUE.
GET IN THERE AND LET'S MAKE SOME GOOD TIME, EH? EH?
JUST GET IN THE MACHINE.

If you want to go back in time just a little bit, turn to page 1. If you want to go back to childhood, turn to page 41. If you want

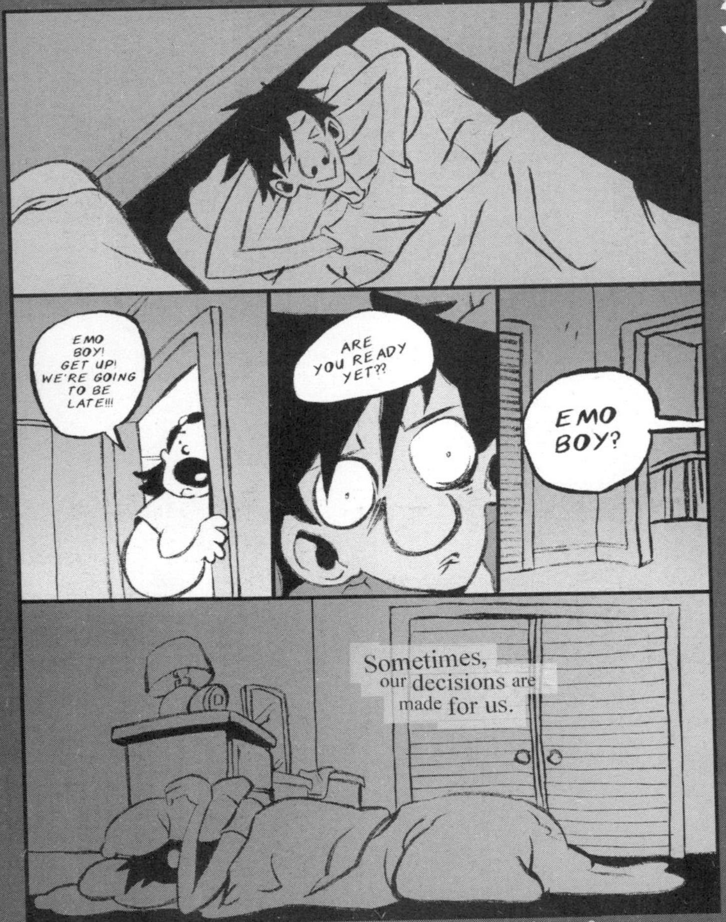
EMO BOY! GET UP! WE'RE GOING TO BE LATE!!!
ARE YOU READY YET??
EMO BOY?
Sometimes, our decisions are made for us.

If you want to stay in bed, turn to page 13. If you want to wake up, turn to page 9.



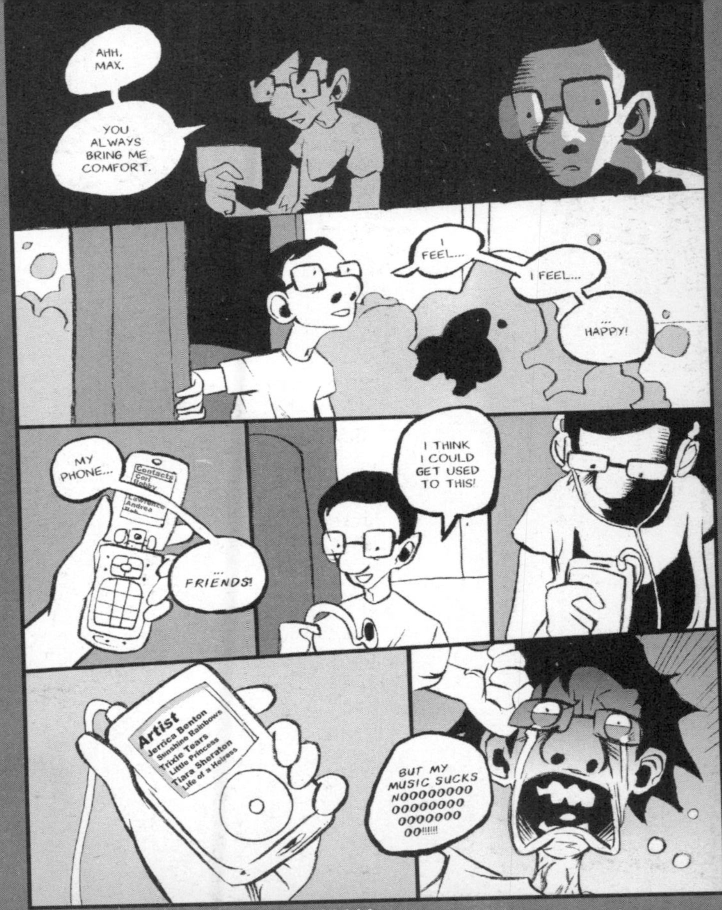
AHH. MAX.
YOU ALWAYS BRING ME COMFORT.
I FEEL...
I FEEL...
... HAPPY!
MY PHONE...
... FRIENDS!
I THINK I COULD GET USED TO THIS!
Artist
Jerrica Benton
Sunshine Rainbows
Trixie Tears
Little Princess
Tiara Sheraton
Life of a Heiress
BUT MY MUSIC SUCKS NOOOOOOOOOOOOOOOOOOOOOO!!!!!!

BAD ENDING!!!!!!!!!!!

5

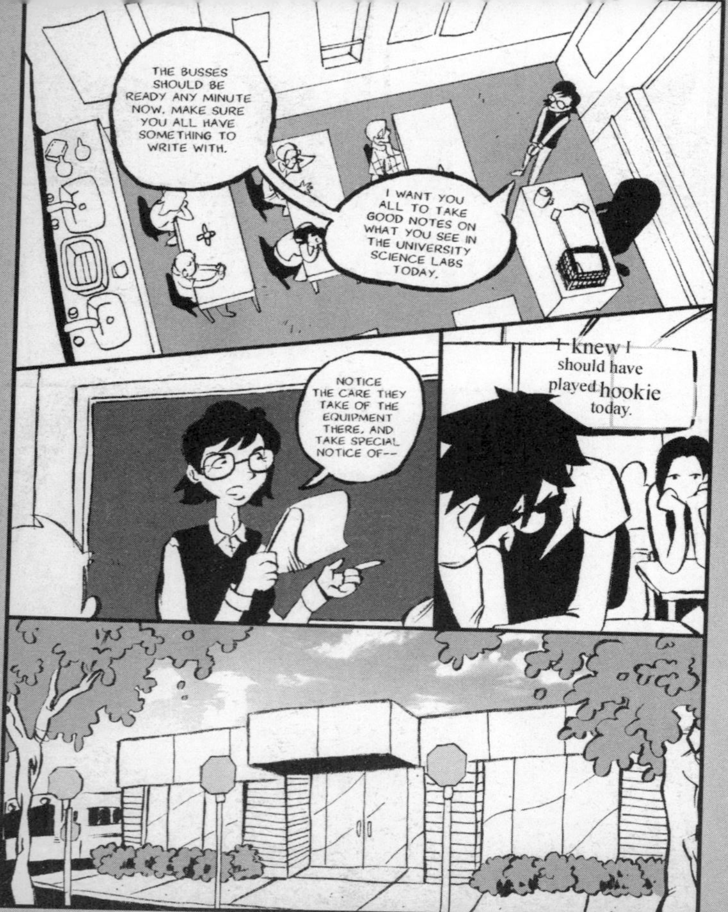
THE BUSSES SHOULD BE READY ANY MINUTE NOW. MAKE SURE YOU ALL HAVE SOMETHING TO WRITE WITH.
I WANT YOU ALL TO TAKE GOOD NOTES ON WHAT YOU SEE IN THE UNIVERSITY SCIENCE LABS TODAY.
NOTICE THE CARE THEY TAKE OF THE EQUIPMENT THERE, AND TAKE SPECIAL NOTICE OF--
I knew I should have played hookie today.

Turn to page 30.

6

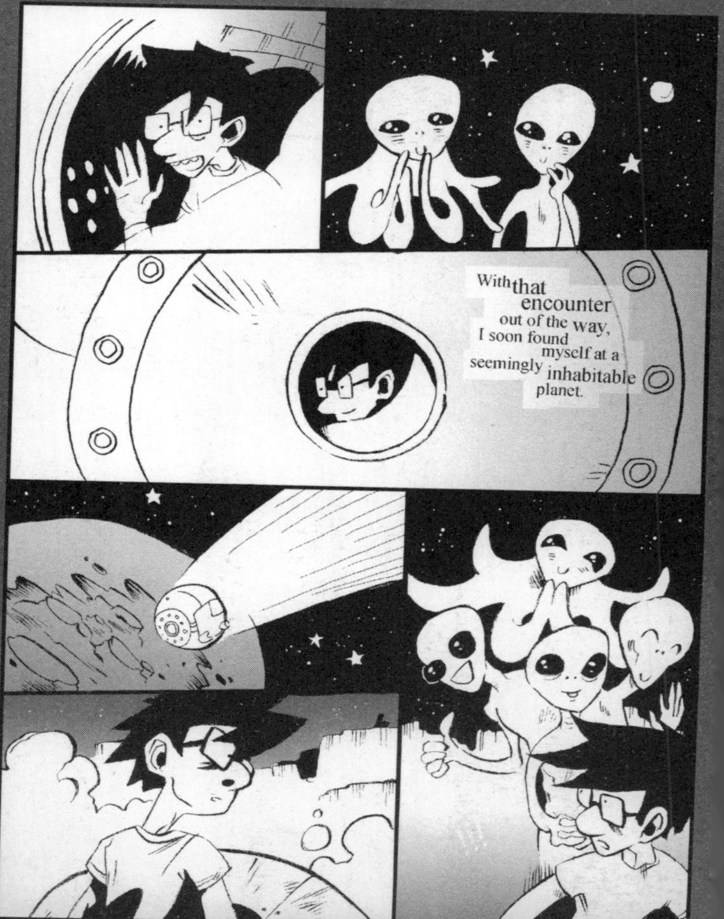
With that encounter out of the way, I soon found myself at a seemingly inhabitable planet.

Turn to page 12

7

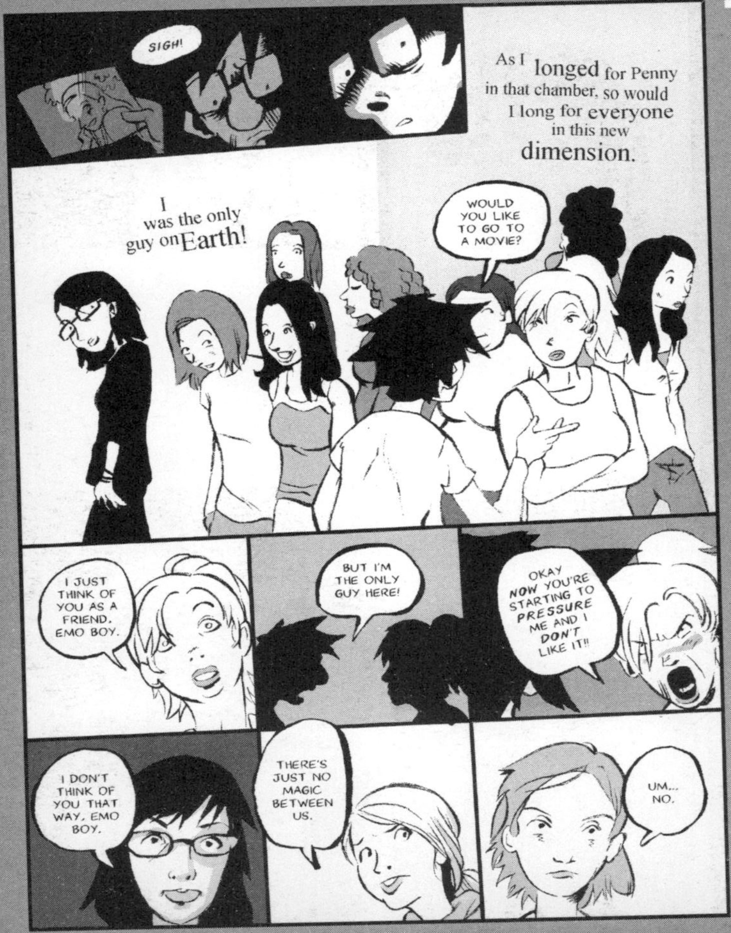
SIGH!
As I longed for Penny in that chamber, so would I long for everyone in this new dimension.
I was the only guy on Earth!
WOULD YOU LIKE TO GO TO A MOVIE?
I JUST THINK OF YOU AS A FRIEND, EMO BOY.
BUT I'M THE ONLY GUY HERE!
OKAY NOW YOU'RE STARTING TO PRESSURE ME AND I DON'T LIKE IT!!
I DON'T THINK OF YOU THAT WAY, EMO BOY.
THERE'S JUST NO MAGIC BETWEEN US.
UM... NO.

8

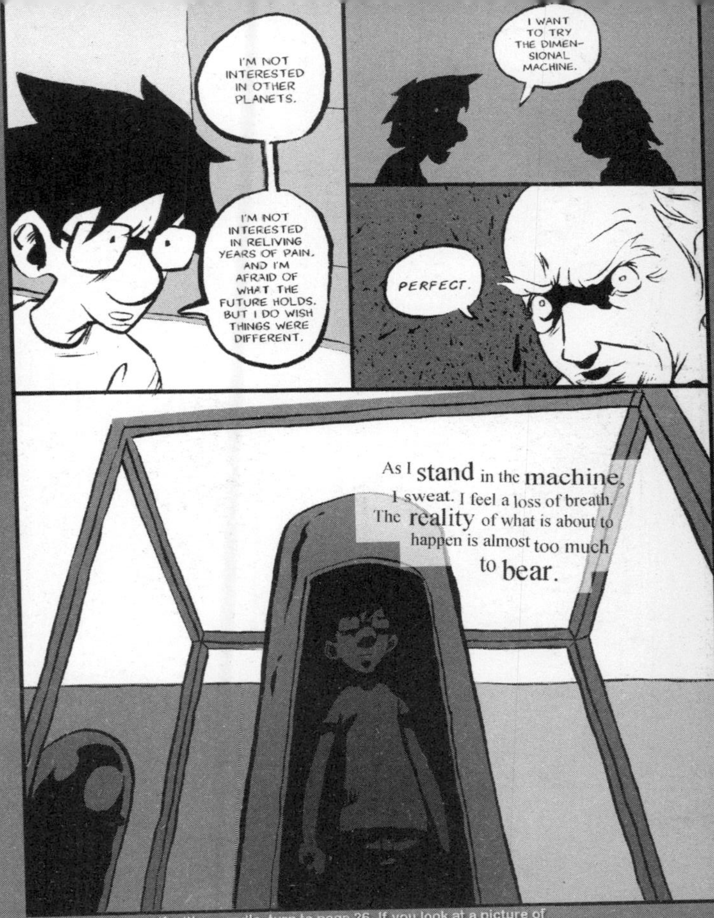
I'M NOT INTERESTED IN OTHER PLANETS.
I'M NOT INTERESTED IN RELIVING YEARS OF PAIN, AND I'M AFRAID OF WHAT THE FUTURE HOLDS. BUT I DO WISH THINGS WERE DIFFERENT.
I WANT TO TRY THE DIMENSIONAL MACHINE.
PERFECT.
As I stand in the machine, I sweat. I feel a loss of breath. The reality of what is about to happen is almost too much to bear.

If you prick yourself with a needle, turn to page 26. If you look at a picture of Maxine, turn to page 4. If you look at a picture of Penny, turn to page 7.

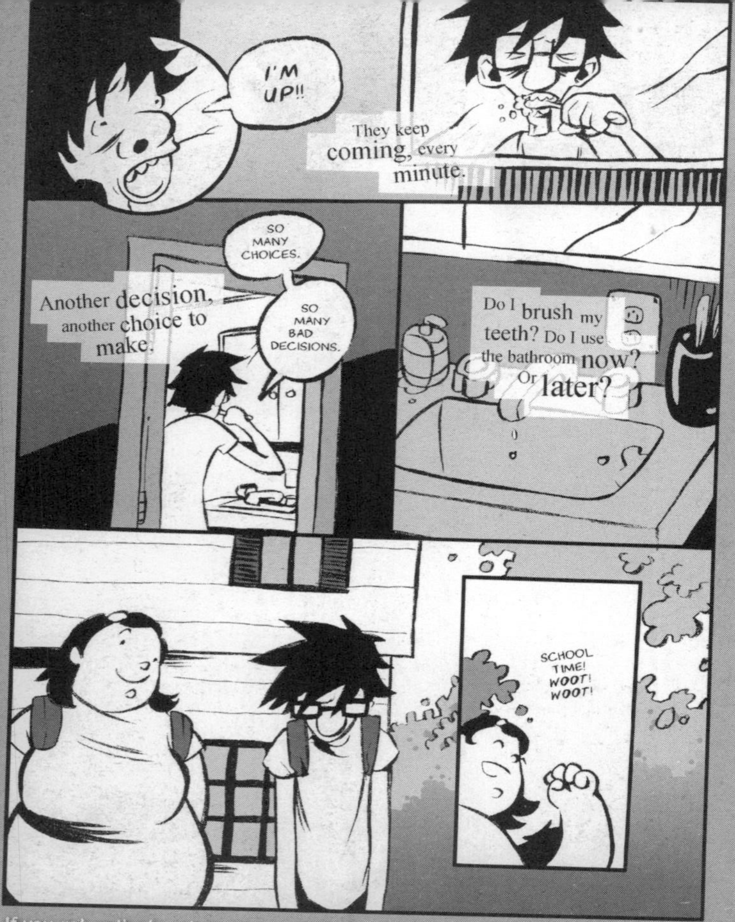
I'M UP!!
They keep coming, every minute.
SO MANY CHOICES.
SO MANY BAD DECISIONS.
Another decision, another choice to make.
Do I brush my teeth? Do I use the bathroom now? Or later?
SCHOOL TIME! WOOT! WOOT!

If you get on the bus, turn to page 5. If you play hookie, turn to page 14.



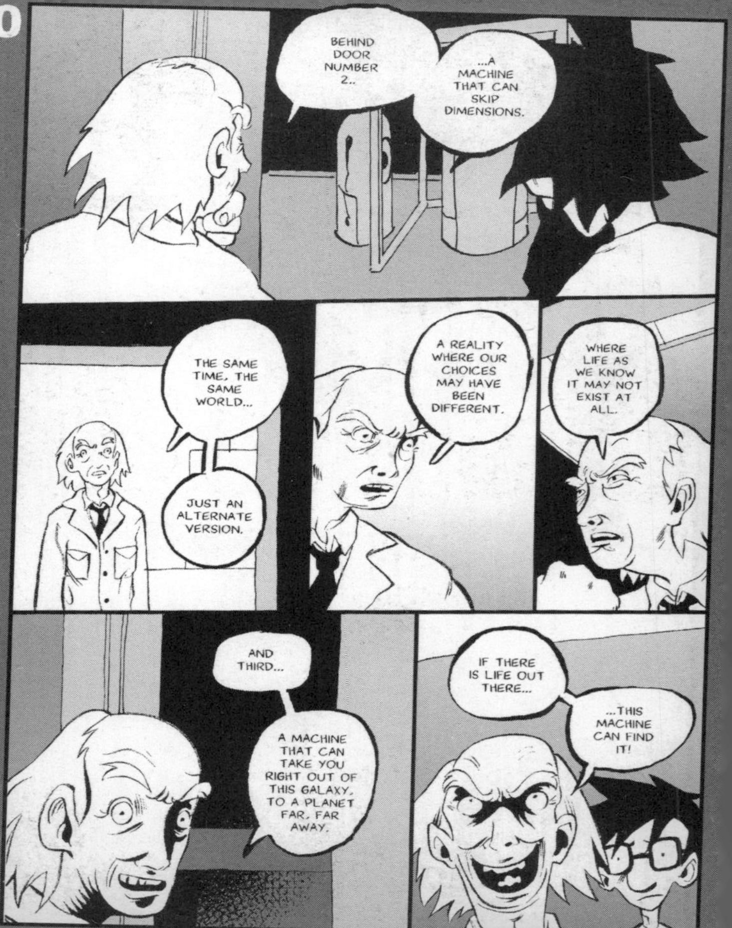
BEHIND DOOR NUMBER 2..
...A MACHINE THAT CAN SKIP DIMENSIONS.
THE SAME TIME, THE SAME WORLD...
JUST AN ALTERNATE VERSION.
A REALITY WHERE OUR CHOICES MAY HAVE BEEN DIFFERENT.
WHERE LIFE AS WE KNOW IT MAY NOT EXIST AT ALL.
AND THIRD...
A MACHINE THAT CAN TAKE YOU RIGHT OUT OF THIS GALAXY, TO A PLANET FAR, FAR AWAY.
IF THERE IS LIFE OUT THERE...
...THIS MACHINE CAN FIND IT!

Turn to page 22

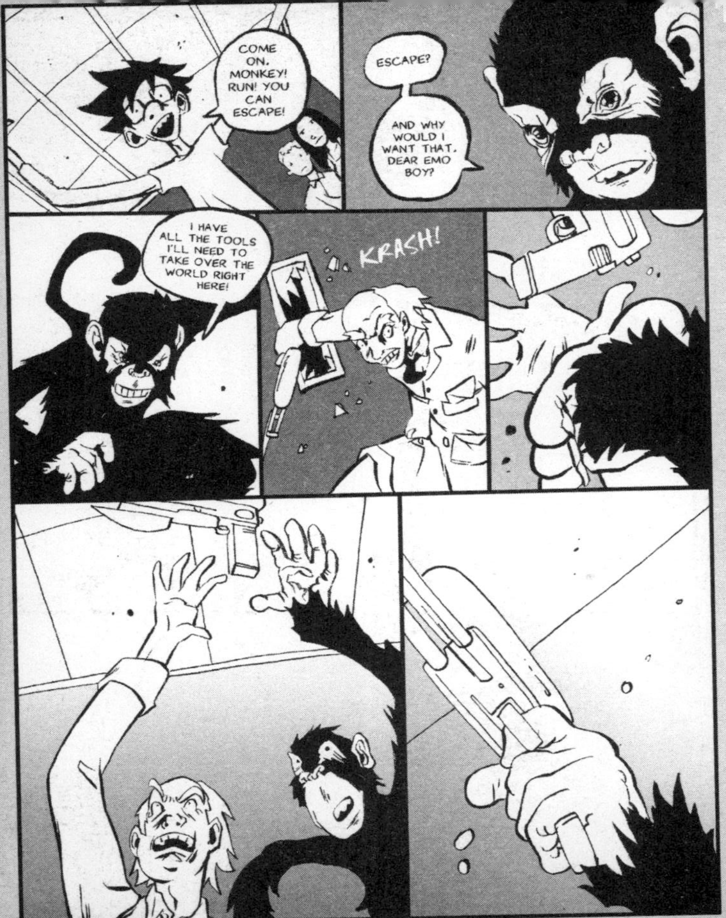
COME ON, MONKEY! RUN! YOU CAN ESCAPE!
ESCAPE?
AND WHY WOULD I WANT THAT, DEAR EMO BOY?
I HAVE ALL THE TOOLS I'LL NEED TO TAKE OVER THE WORLD RIGHT HERE!
KRASH!

Turn to page 42



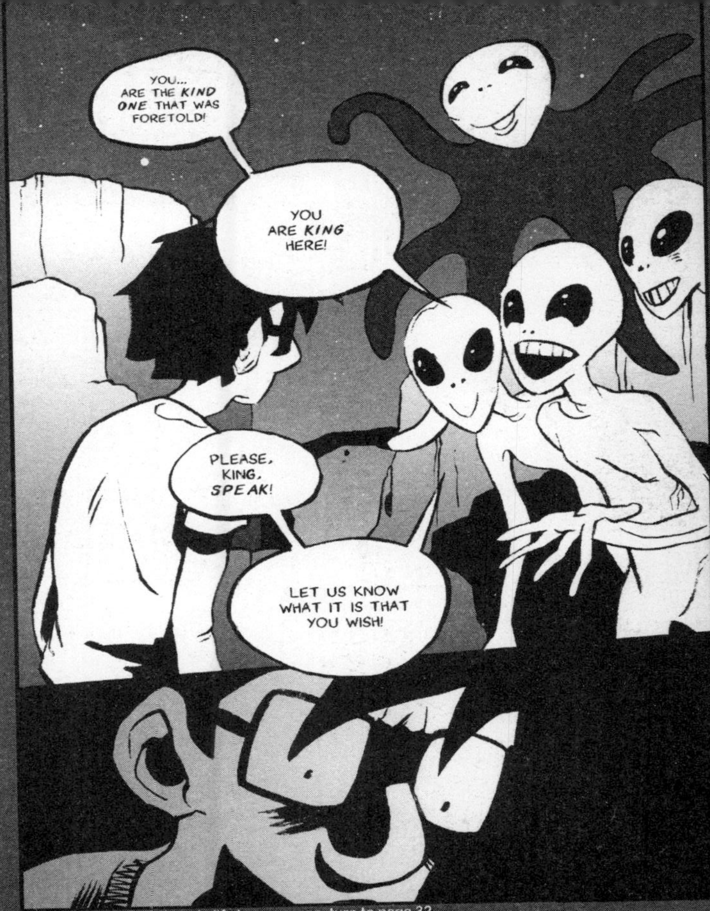
YOU... ARE THE KIND ONE THAT WAS FORETOLD!
YOU ARE KING HERE!
PLEASE, KING, SPEAK!
LET US KNOW WHAT IT IS THAT YOU WISH!

If you believe everything in life has purpose, turn to page 32.
If you believe the world is pointless, turn to page 35.

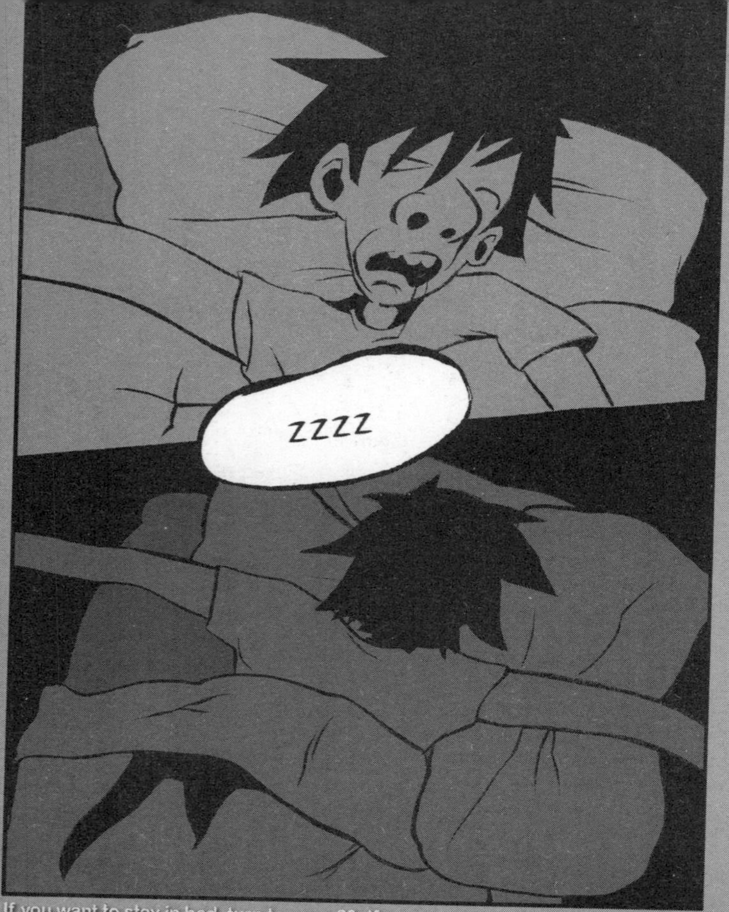
ZZZZ

If you want to stay in bed, turn to page 39. If you want to wake up, turn to page 9.



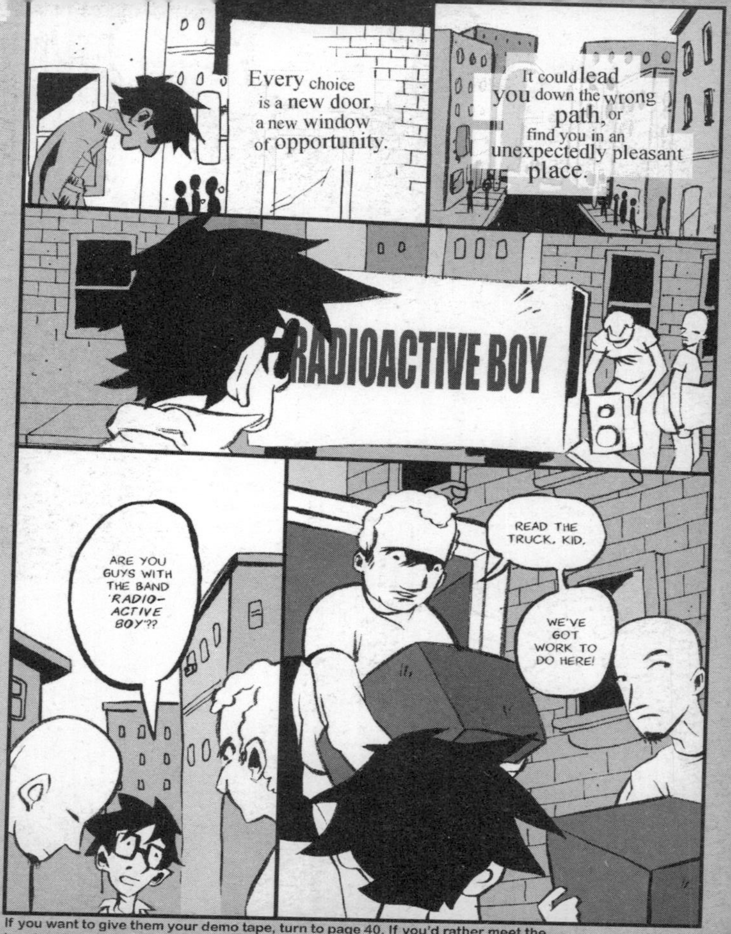
Every choice is a new door, a new window of opportunity.
It could lead you down the wrong path, or find you in an unexpectedly pleasant place.
RADIOACTIVE BOY
ARE YOU GUYS WITH THE BAND 'RADIO-ACTIVE BOY'??
READ THE TRUCK, KID.
WE'VE GOT WORK TO DO HERE!

If you want to give them your demo tape, turn to page 40. If you'd rather meet the band, turn to page 23.

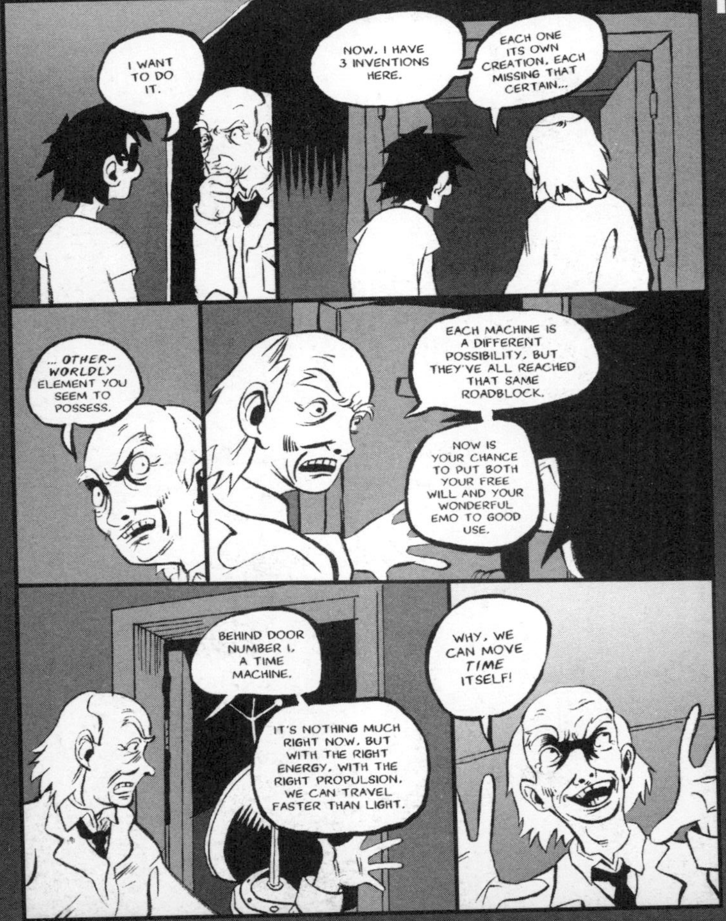
I WANT TO DO IT.
NOW, I HAVE 3 INVENTIONS HERE.
EACH ONE ITS OWN CREATION, EACH MISSING THAT CERTAIN...
...OTHER-WORLDLY ELEMENT YOU SEEM TO POSSESS.
EACH MACHINE IS A DIFFERENT POSSIBILITY, BUT THEY'VE ALL REACHED THAT SAME ROADBLOCK.
NOW IS YOUR CHANCE TO PUT BOTH YOUR FREE WILL AND YOUR WONDERFUL EMO TO GOOD USE.
BEHIND DOOR NUMBER 1, A TIME MACHINE.
IT'S NOTHING MUCH RIGHT NOW, BUT WITH THE RIGHT ENERGY, WITH THE RIGHT PROPULSION, WE CAN TRAVEL FASTER THAN LIGHT.
WHY, WE CAN MOVE *TIME* ITSELF!

Turn to page 10.

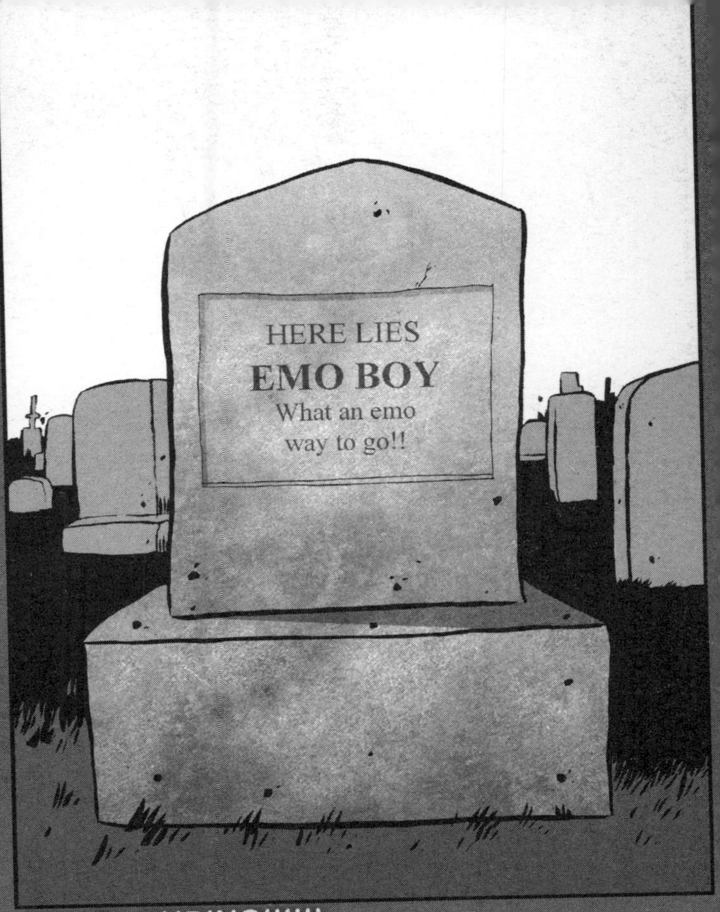
HERE LIES
EMO BOY
What an emo way to go!!

DEATH ENDING!!!!!!

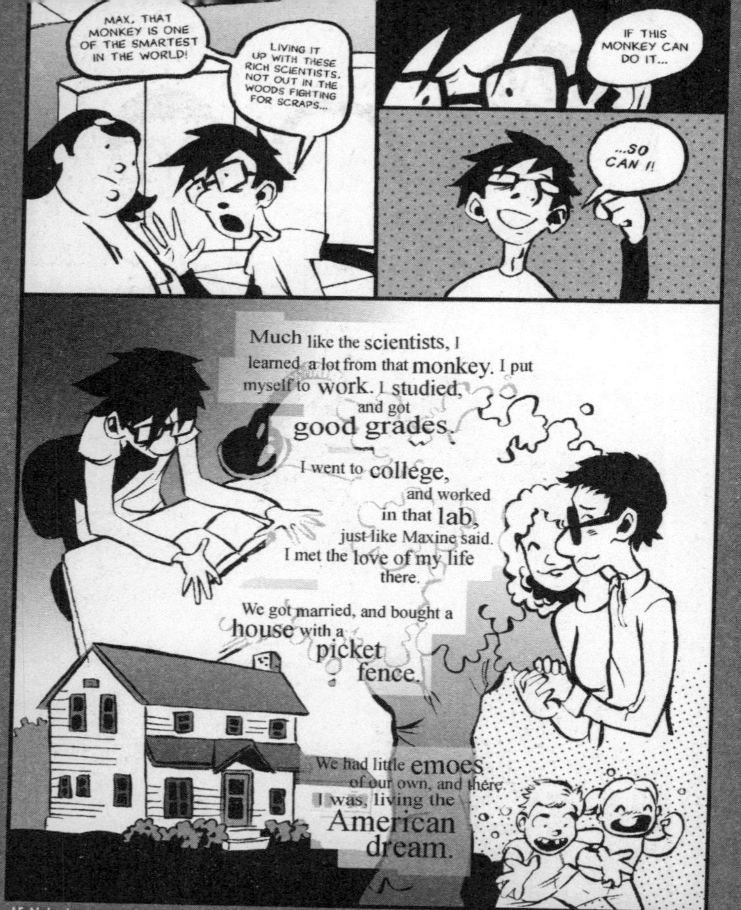
MAX, THAT MONKEY IS ONE OF THE SMARTEST IN THE WORLD!
LIVING IT UP WITH THESE RICH SCIENTISTS, NOT OUT IN THE WOODS FIGHTING FOR SCRAPS...
IF THIS MONKEY CAN DO IT...
...SO CAN I!
Much like the scientists, I learned a lot from that monkey. I put myself to work. I studied, and got good grades.
I went to college, and worked in that lab, just like Maxine said. I met the love of my life there.
We got married, and bought a house with a picket fence.
We had little emoes of our own, and there I was, living the American dream.

If this is your dream, turn to page 29. If this is your nightmare, turn to page 36.

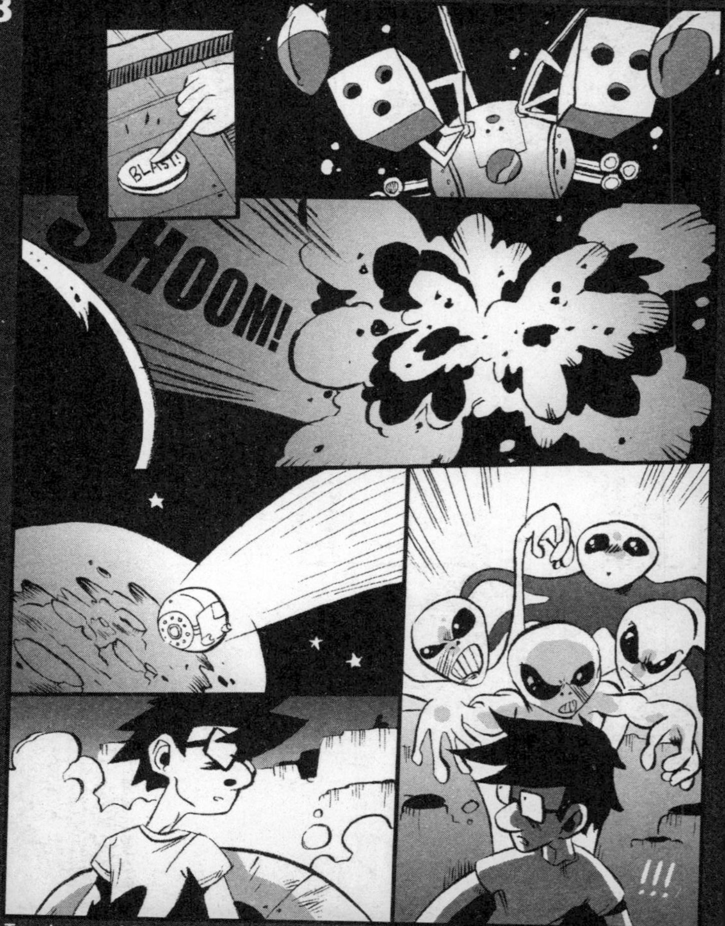
BLAST!
SHOOM!
!!!

Turn to page 33.

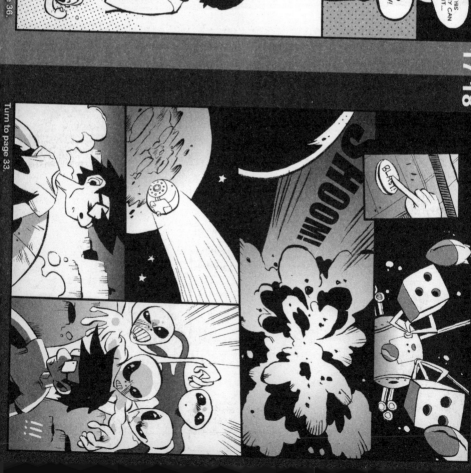

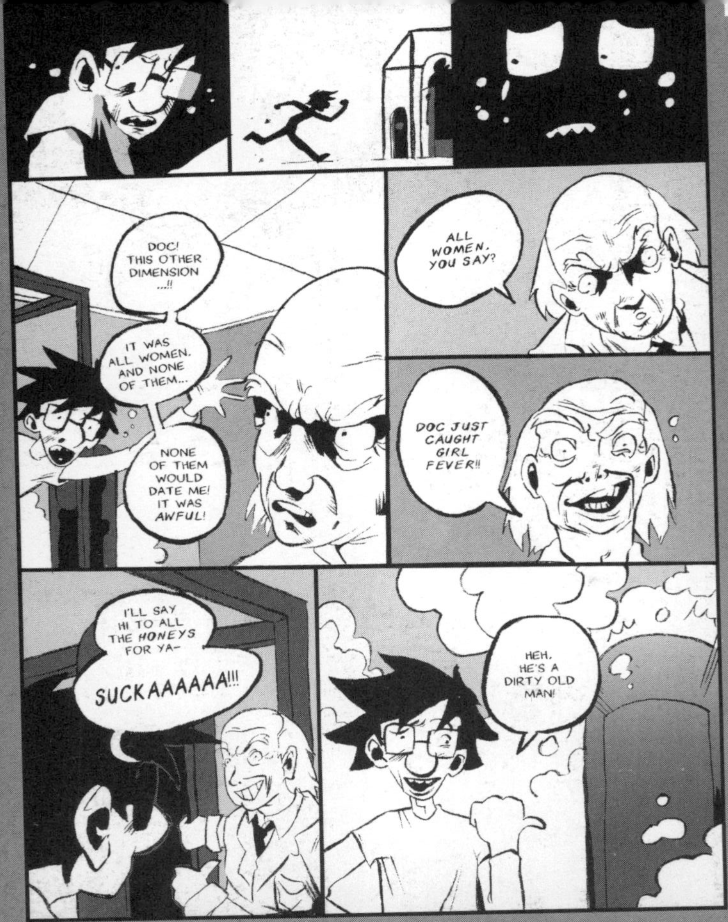
DOC! THIS OTHER DIMENSION ...!!
IT WAS ALL WOMEN. AND NONE OF THEM...
NONE OF THEM WOULD DATE ME! IT WAS *AWFUL!*
ALL *WOMEN,* YOU SAY?
DOC JUST CAUGHT GIRL FEVER!!
I'LL SAY HI TO ALL THE *HONEYS* FOR YA-
SUCKAAAAAA!!!
HEH, HE'S A DIRTY OLD MAN!

PERVY ENDING!!!!!!!!

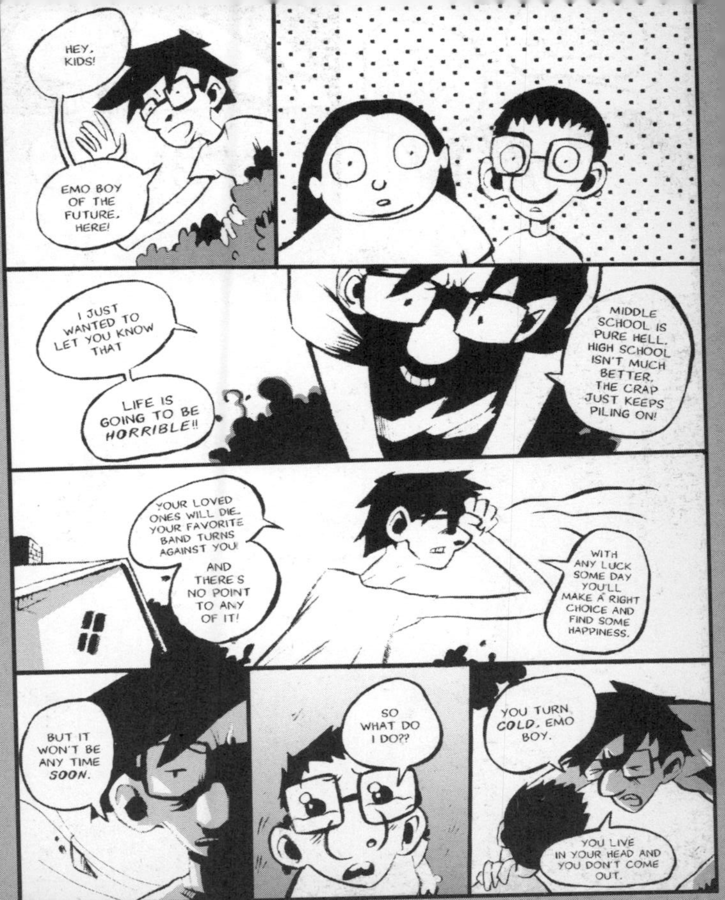
HEY, KIDS!
EMO BOY OF THE FUTURE, HERE!
I JUST WANTED TO LET YOU KNOW THAT
LIFE IS GOING TO BE *HORRIBLE!!*
MIDDLE SCHOOL IS PURE HELL. HIGH SCHOOL ISN'T MUCH BETTER. THE CRAP JUST KEEPS PILING ON!
YOUR LOVED ONES WILL DIE. YOUR FAVORITE BAND TURNS AGAINST YOU!
AND THERE'S NO POINT TO ANY OF IT!
WITH ANY LUCK SOME DAY YOU'LL MAKE A RIGHT CHOICE AND FIND SOME HAPPINESS.
BUT IT WON'T BE ANY TIME *SOON.*
SO WHAT DO I DO??
YOU TURN *COLD,* EMO BOY.
YOU LIVE IN YOUR HEAD AND YOU DON'T COME OUT.

Turn to page 16.

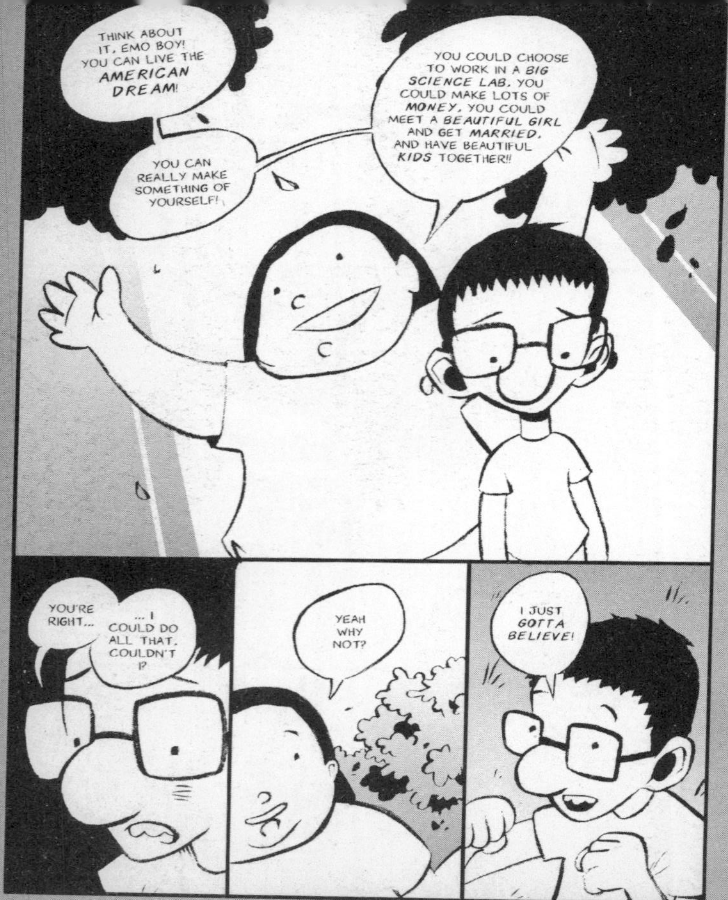
THINK ABOUT IT, EMO BOY! YOU CAN LIVE THE AMERICAN DREAM!
YOU CAN REALLY MAKE SOMETHING OF YOURSELF!
YOU COULD CHOOSE TO WORK IN A BIG SCIENCE LAB. YOU COULD MAKE LOTS OF MONEY. YOU COULD MEET A BEAUTIFUL GIRL AND GET MARRIED. AND HAVE BEAUTIFUL KIDS TOGETHER!!
YOU'RE RIGHT...
... I COULD DO ALL THAT, COULDN'T I?
YEAH WHY NOT?
I JUST GOTTA BELIEVE!

Turn to page 45.

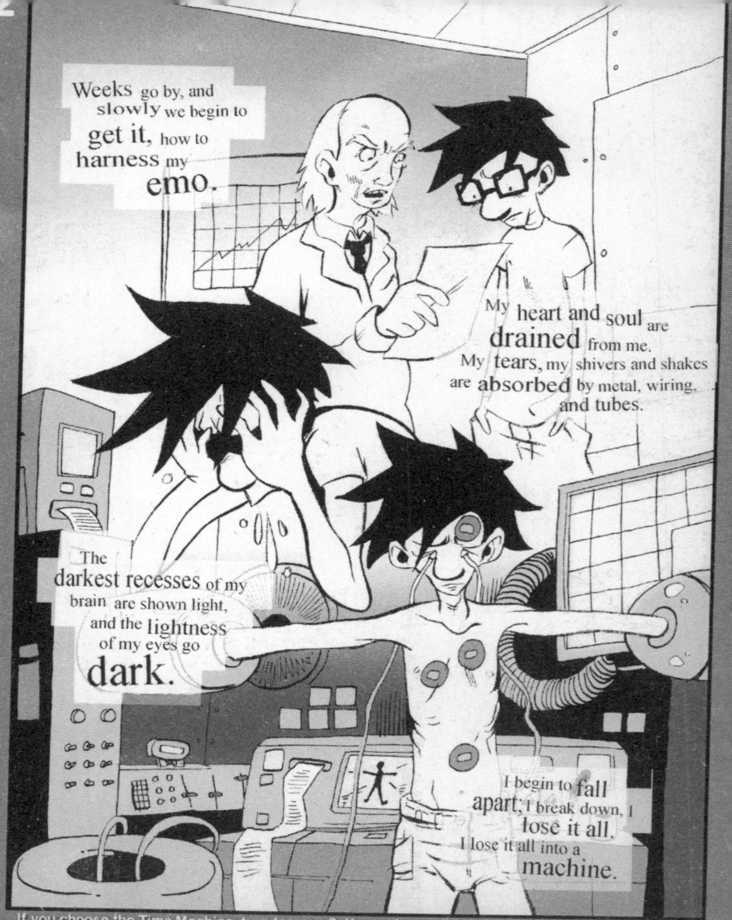
Weeks go by, and slowly we begin to get it, how to harness my emo.
My heart and soul are drained from me. My tears, my shivers and shakes are absorbed by metal, wiring, and tubes.
The darkest recesses of my brain are shown light, and the lightness of my eyes go dark.
I begin to fall apart; I break down, I lose it all. I lose it all into a machine.

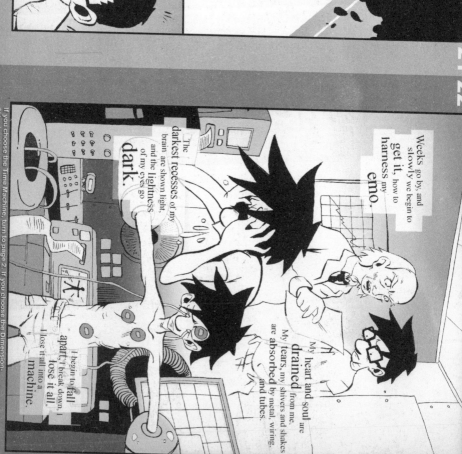

If you choose the Time Machine, turn to page 2. If you choose the Dimension-Skipping Machine, turn to page 8. If you choose the Space Ship, turn to page 34.

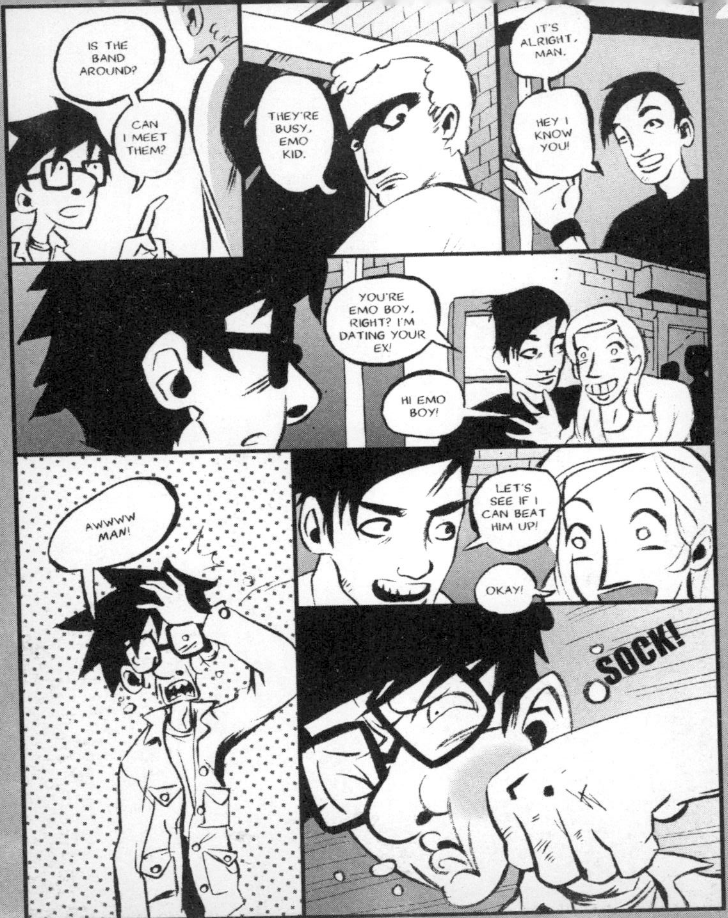
IS THE BAND AROUND?
CAN I MEET THEM?
THEY'RE BUSY, EMO KID.
IT'S ALRIGHT, MAN.
HEY I KNOW YOU!
YOU'RE EMO BOY, RIGHT? I'M DATING YOUR EX!
HI EMO BOY!
AWWWW MAN!
LET'S SEE IF I CAN BEAT HIM UP!
OKAY!
SOCK!

BAD ENDING!!!!!!!!!!!

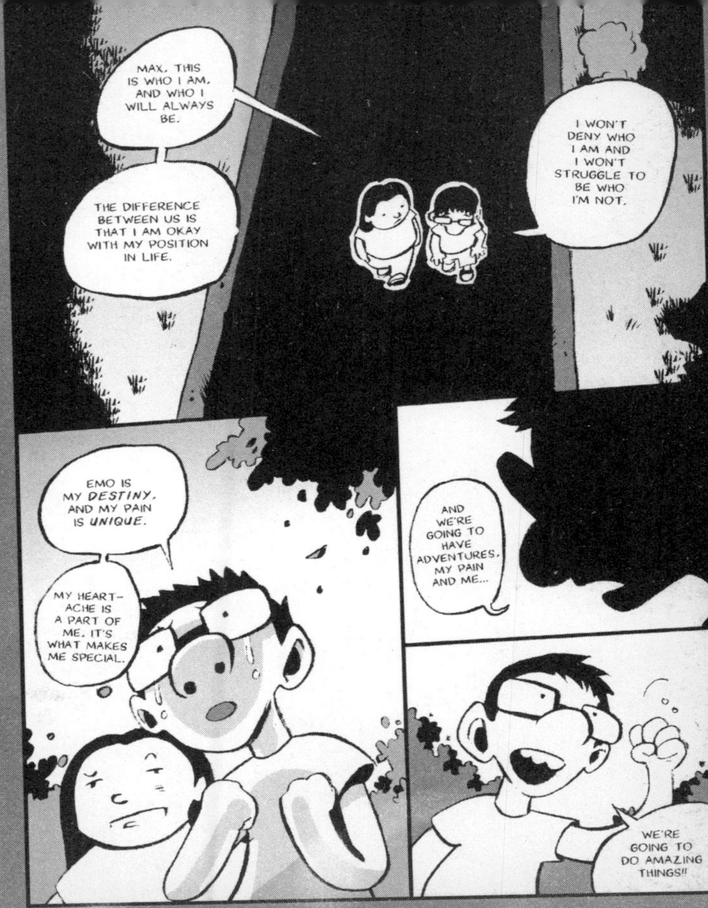
MAX, THIS IS WHO I AM, AND WHO I WILL ALWAYS BE.
THE DIFFERENCE BETWEEN US IS THAT I AM OKAY WITH MY POSITION IN LIFE.
I WON'T DENY WHO I AM AND I WON'T STRUGGLE TO BE WHO I'M NOT.
EMO IS MY DESTINY, AND MY PAIN IS UNIQUE.
MY HEART-ACHE IS A PART OF ME. IT'S WHAT MAKES ME SPECIAL.
AND WE'RE GOING TO HAVE ADVENTURES, MY PAIN AND ME...
WE'RE GOING TO DO AMAZING THINGS!!

Turn to page 1. Of Issue 1!!!

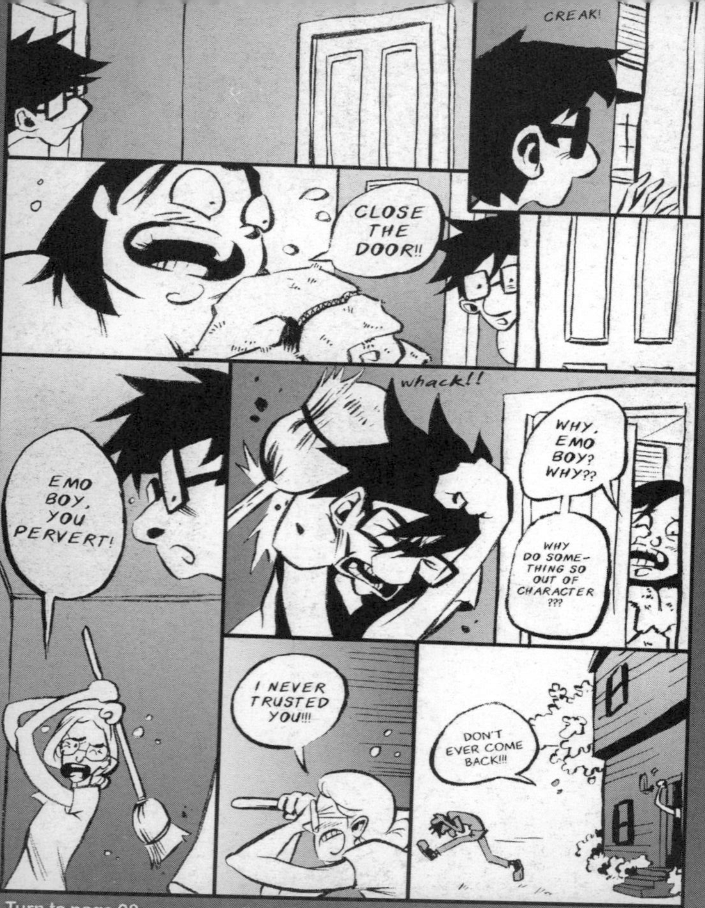
CREAK!
CLOSE THE DOOR!!
EMO BOY, YOU PERVERT!
whack!!
WHY, EMO BOY? WHY??
WHY DO SOMETHING SO OUT OF CHARACTER ???
I NEVER TRUSTED YOU!!!
DON'T EVER COME BACK!!!

Turn to page 28.



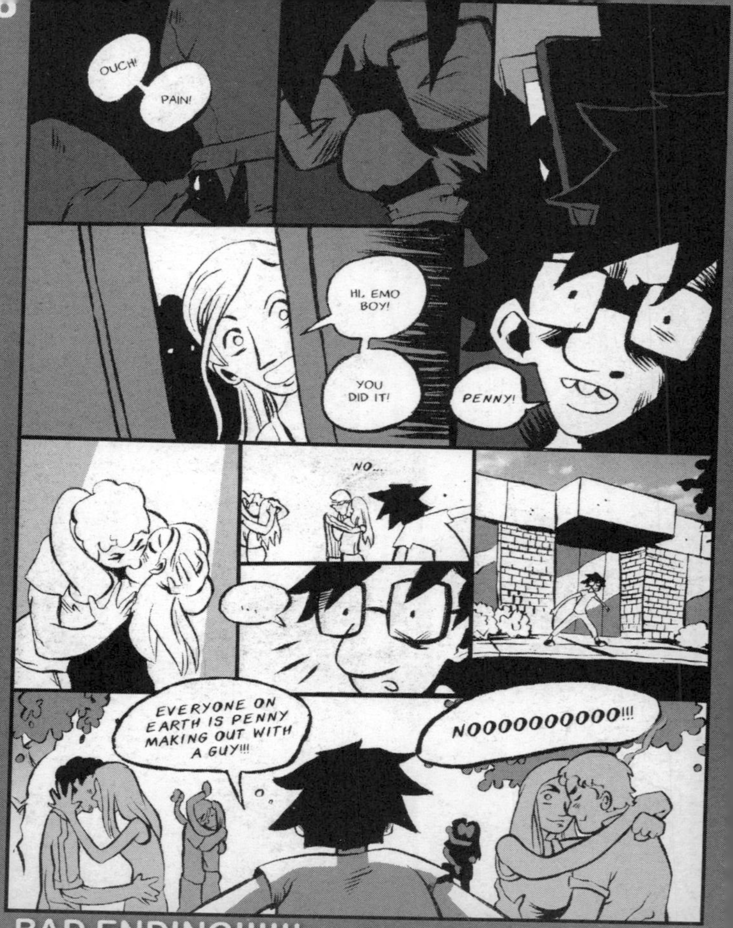
OUCH!
PAIN!
HI, EMO BOY!
YOU DID IT!
PENNY!
NO...
EVERYONE ON EARTH IS PENNY MAKING OUT WITH A GUY!!!
NOOOOOOOOOO!!!

BAD ENDING!!!!!!

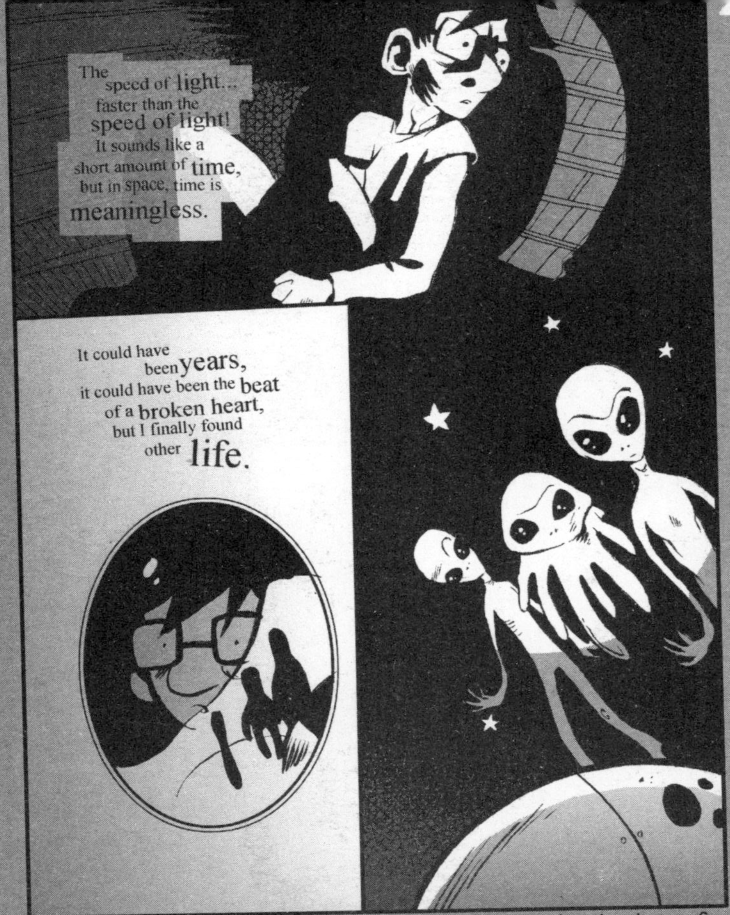

The speed of light... faster than the speed of light! It sounds like a short amount of time, but in space, time is meaningless.
It could have been years, it could have been the beat of a broken heart, but I finally found other life.


If you are afraid of aliens, turn to page 18. If the aliens seem harmless, turn to page 6.

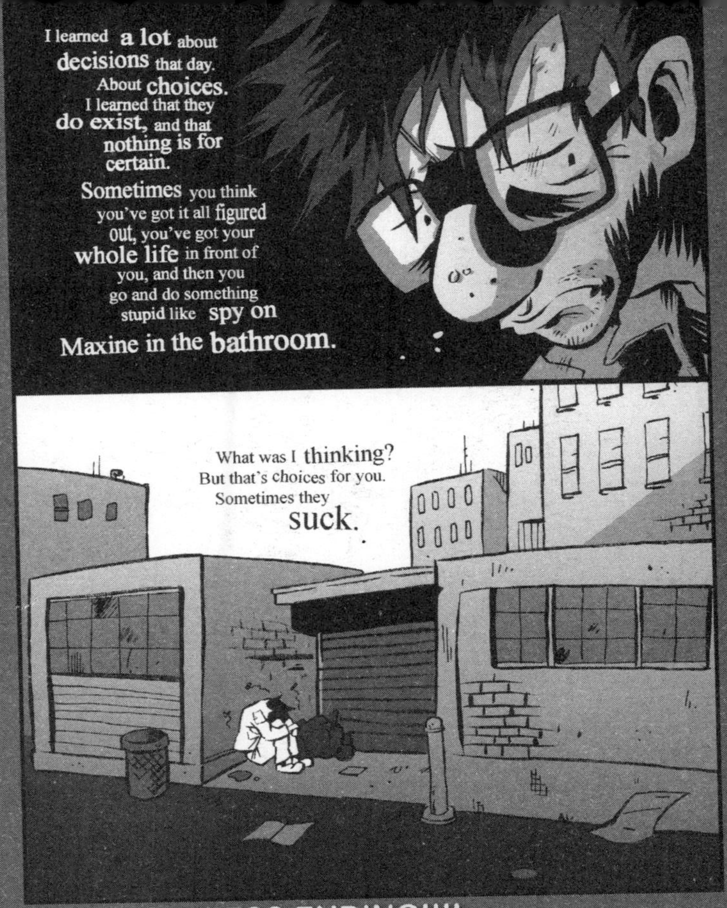

I learned a lot about decisions that day. About choices. I learned that they do exist, and that nothing is for certain.
Sometimes you think you've got it all figured out, you've got your whole life in front of you, and then you go and do something stupid like spy on Maxine in the bathroom.
What was I thinking? But that's choices for you. Sometimes they suck.


BAD HOMELESS ENDING!!!!

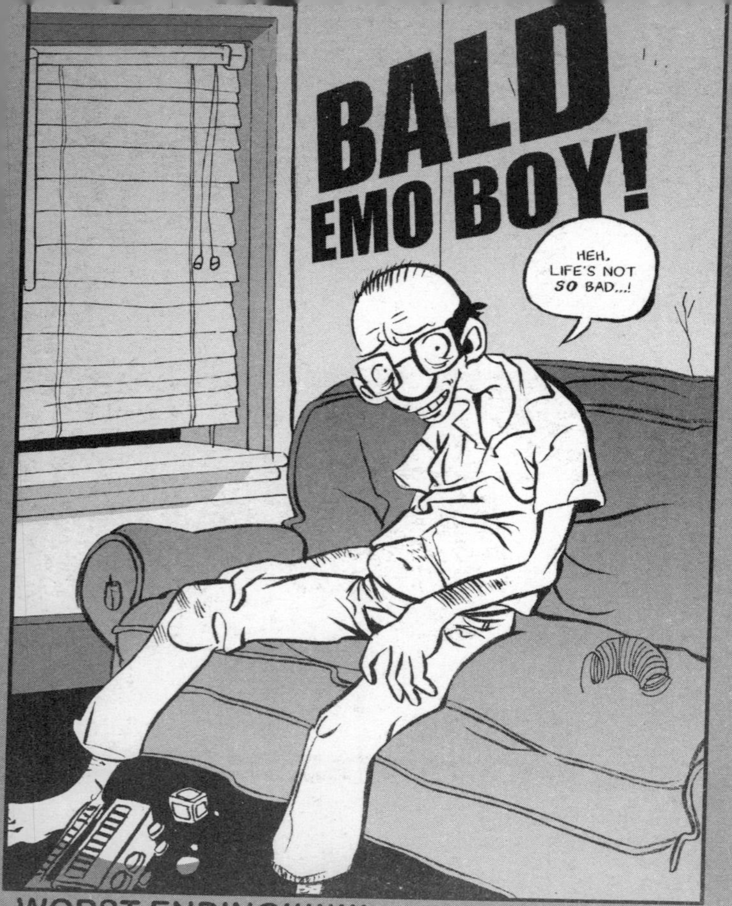
BALD EMO BOY!
HEH, LIFE'S NOT SO BAD...!

WORST ENDING!!!!!!!!

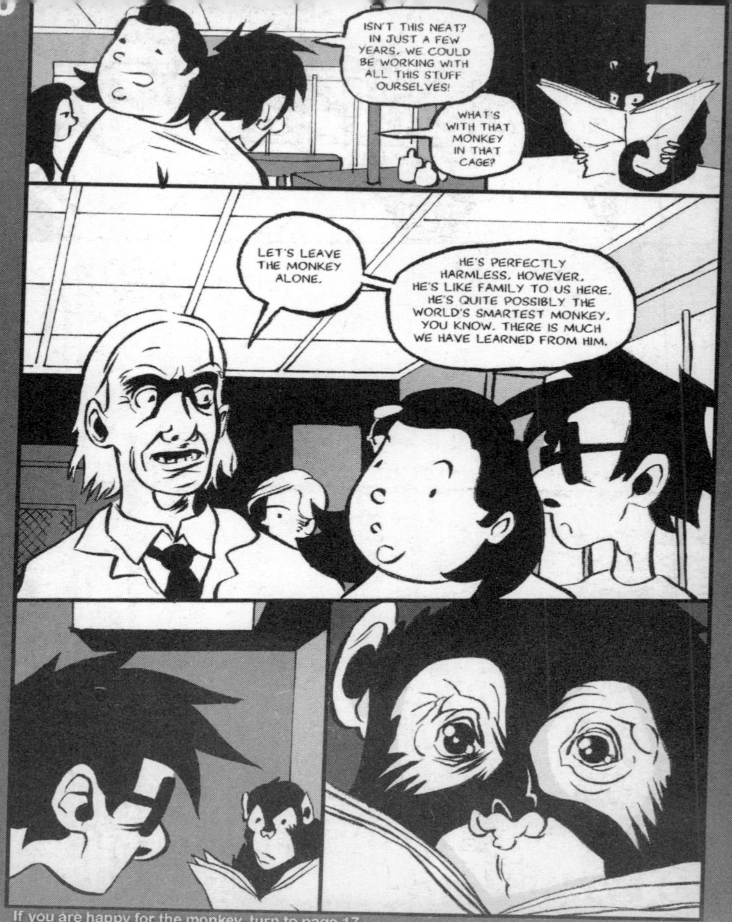
ISN'T THIS NEAT? IN JUST A FEW YEARS, WE COULD BE WORKING WITH ALL THIS STUFF OURSELVES!
WHAT'S WITH THAT MONKEY IN THAT CAGE?
LET'S LEAVE THE MONKEY ALONE.
HE'S PERFECTLY HARMLESS, HOWEVER. HE'S LIKE FAMILY TO US HERE. HE'S QUITE POSSIBLY THE WORLD'S SMARTEST MONKEY, YOU KNOW. THERE IS MUCH WE HAVE LEARNED FROM HIM.

If you are happy for the monkey, turn to page 17.
If the monkey saddens you, turn to page 38.

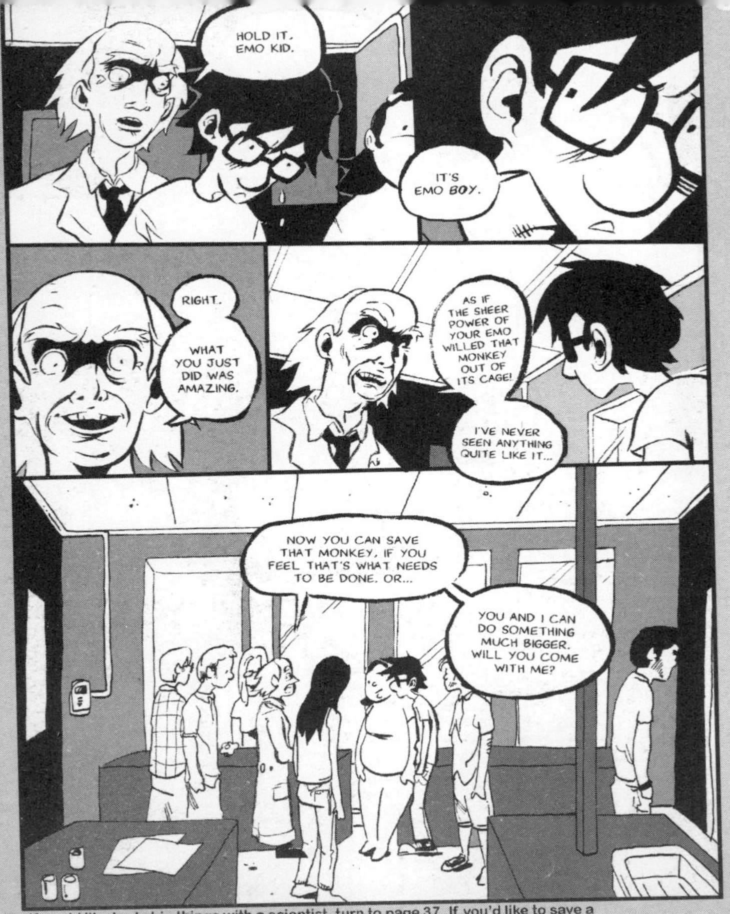
HOLD IT, EMO KID.
IT'S EMO BOY.
RIGHT.
WHAT YOU JUST DID WAS AMAZING.
AS IF THE SHEER POWER OF YOUR EMO WILLED THAT MONKEY OUT OF ITS CAGE!
I'VE NEVER SEEN ANYTHING QUITE LIKE IT...
NOW YOU CAN SAVE THAT MONKEY, IF YOU FEEL THAT'S WHAT NEEDS TO BE DONE. OR...
YOU AND I CAN DO SOMETHING MUCH BIGGER. WILL YOU COME WITH ME?

If you'd like to do big things with a scientist, turn to page 37. If you'd like to save a monkey, turn to page 11.

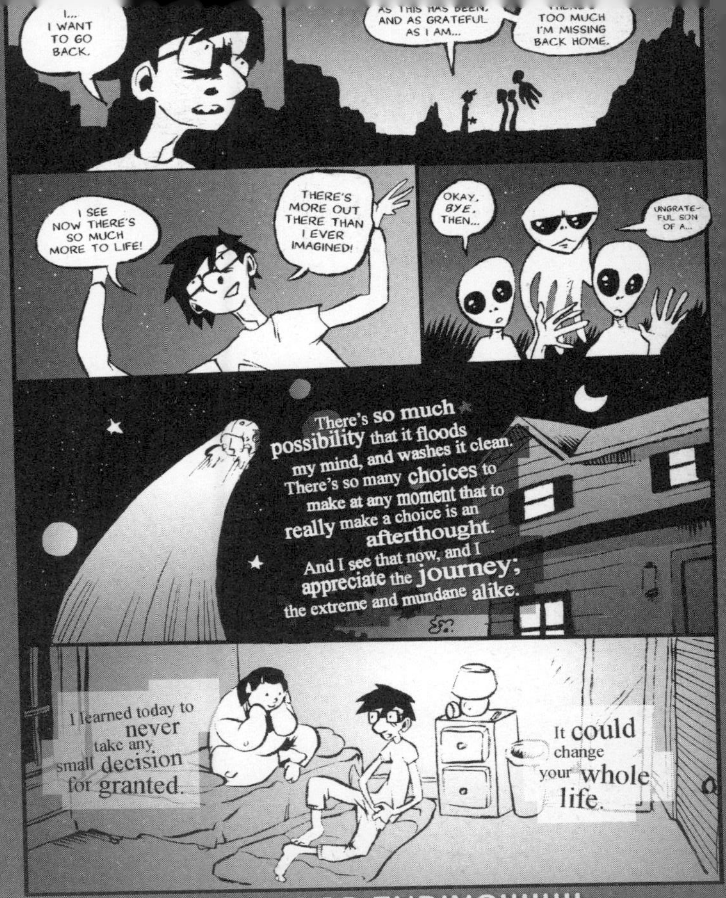
I... I WANT TO GO BACK.
AND AS GRATEFUL AS I AM...
TOO MUCH I'M MISSING BACK HOME.
I SEE NOW THERE'S SO MUCH MORE TO LIFE!
THERE'S MORE OUT THERE THAN I EVER IMAGINED!
OKAY, BYE, THEN...
UNGRATE-FUL SON OF A...
There's so much possibility that it floods my mind, and washes it clean. There's so many choices to make at any moment that to really make a choice is an afterthought.
And I see that now, and I appreciate the journey; the extreme and mundane alike.
I learned today to never take any small decision for granted.
It could change your whole life.

SENTIMENTAL GOOD ENDING!!!!!!!!

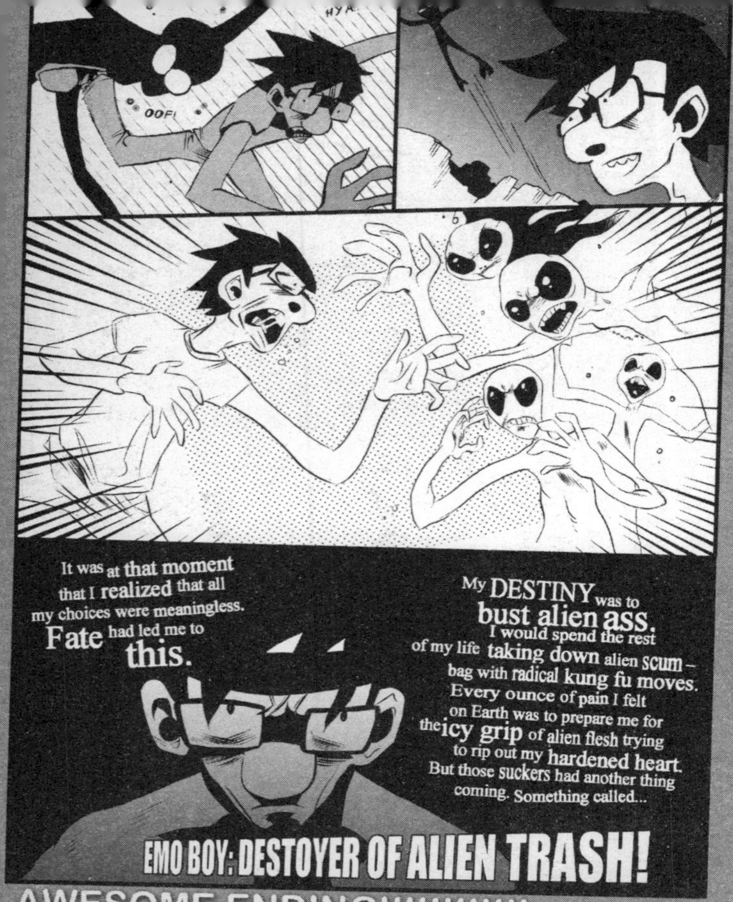
HYA
OOF!
It was at that moment that I realized that all my choices were meaningless. Fate had led me to this.
My DESTINY was to bust alien ass. I would spend the rest of my life taking down alien scum–bag with radical kung fu moves. Every ounce of pain I felt on Earth was to prepare me for the icy grip of alien flesh trying to rip out my hardened heart. But those suckers had another thing coming. Something called...
EMO BOY: DESTOYER OF ALIEN TRASH!

AWESOME ENDING!!!!!!!!!!!!

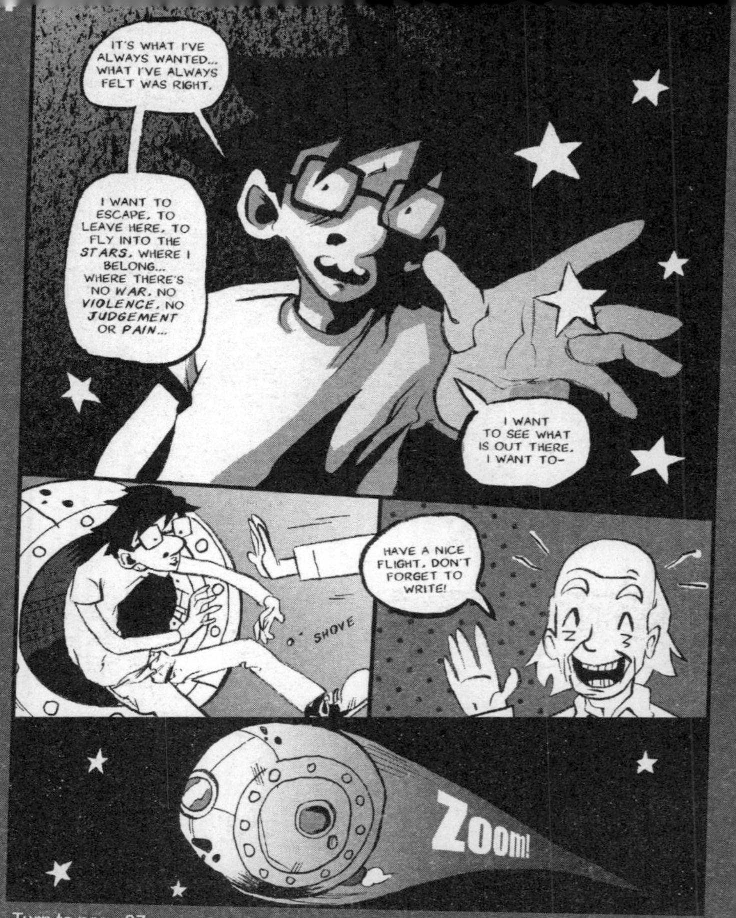
IT'S WHAT I'VE ALWAYS WANTED... WHAT I'VE ALWAYS FELT WAS RIGHT.
I WANT TO ESCAPE, TO LEAVE HERE, TO FLY INTO THE STARS, WHERE I BELONG... WHERE THERE'S NO WAR, NO VIOLENCE, NO JUDGEMENT OR PAIN...
I WANT TO SEE WHAT IS OUT THERE. I WANT TO–
SHOVE
HAVE A NICE FLIGHT, DON'T FORGET TO WRITE!
Zoom!

Turn to page 27.

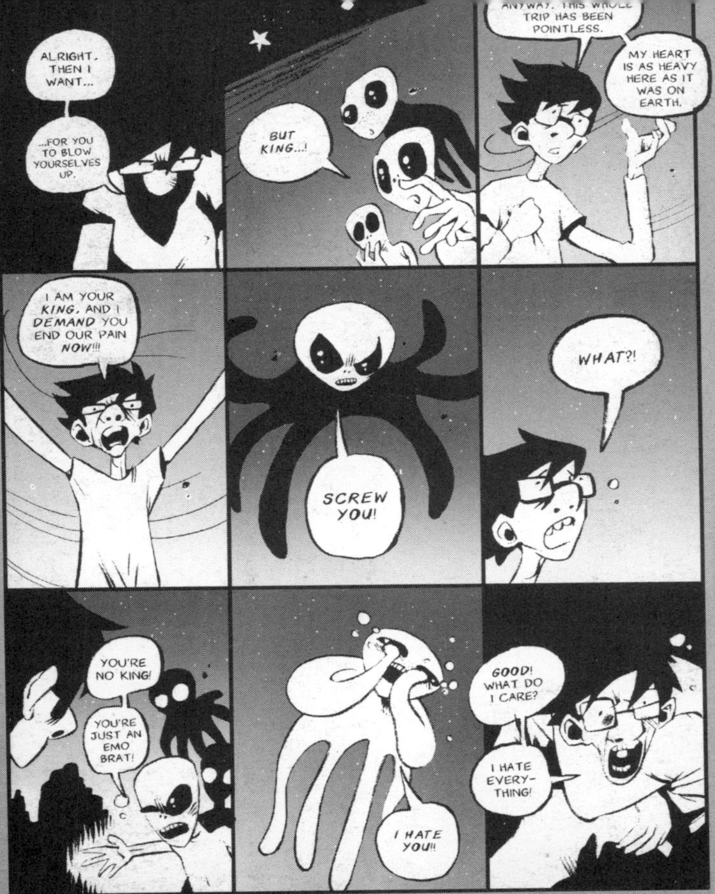
ALRIGHT, THEN I WANT...
...FOR YOU TO BLOW YOURSELVES UP.
BUT KING...!
ANYWAY, THIS WHOLE TRIP HAS BEEN POINTLESS.
MY HEART IS AS HEAVY HERE AS IT WAS ON EARTH.
I AM YOUR KING, AND I DEMAND YOU END OUR PAIN NOW!!!
SCREW YOU!
WHAT?!
YOU'RE NO KING!
YOU'RE JUST AN EMO BRAT!
I HATE YOU!!
GOOD! WHAT DO I CARE?
I HATE EVERY-THING!

# BAD ENDING!!!!!!!!!

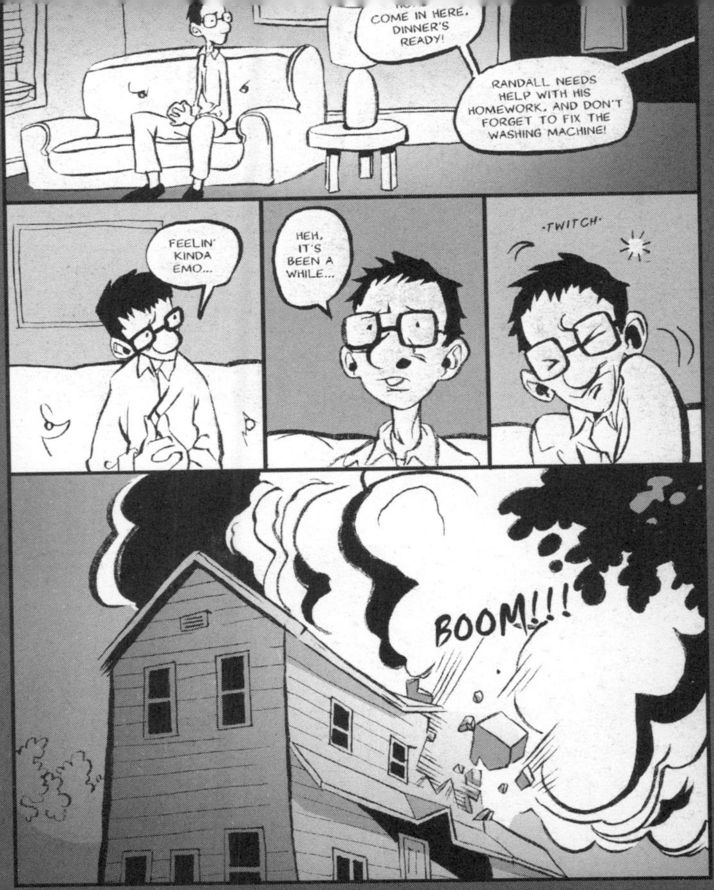
COME IN HERE, DINNER'S READY!
RANDALL NEEDS HELP WITH HIS HOMEWORK, AND DON'T FORGET TO FIX THE WASHING MACHINE!
FEELIN' KINDA EMO...
HEH, IT'S BEEN A WHILE...
·TWITCH·
BOOM!!!

Turn to page 16.

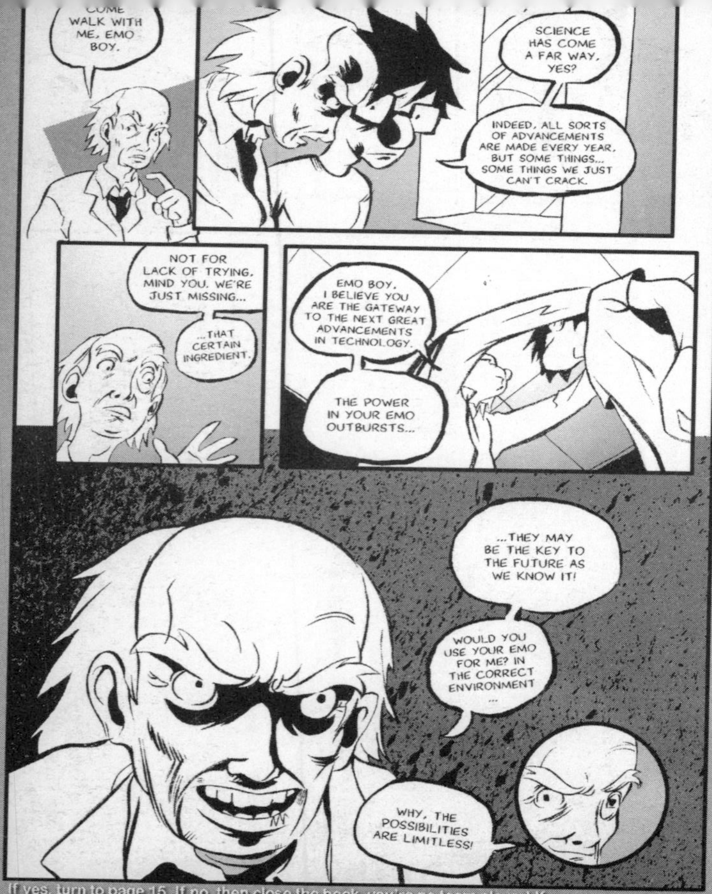
COME WALK WITH ME, EMO BOY.
SCIENCE HAS COME A FAR WAY, YES?
INDEED, ALL SORTS OF ADVANCEMENTS ARE MADE EVERY YEAR, BUT SOME THINGS... SOME THINGS WE JUST CAN'T CRACK.
NOT FOR LACK OF TRYING, MIND YOU. WE'RE JUST MISSING...
...THAT CERTAIN INGREDIENT.
EMO BOY, I BELIEVE YOU ARE THE GATEWAY TO THE NEXT GREAT ADVANCEMENTS IN TECHNOLOGY.
THE POWER IN YOUR EMO OUTBURSTS...
...THEY MAY BE THE KEY TO THE FUTURE AS WE KNOW IT!
WOULD YOU USE YOUR EMO FOR ME? IN THE CORRECT ENVIRONMENT ...
WHY, THE POSSIBILITIES ARE LIMITLESS!

If yes, turn to page 15. If no, then close the book, you're no team player! If you think he should trim his nose hairs, then turn to page 43.

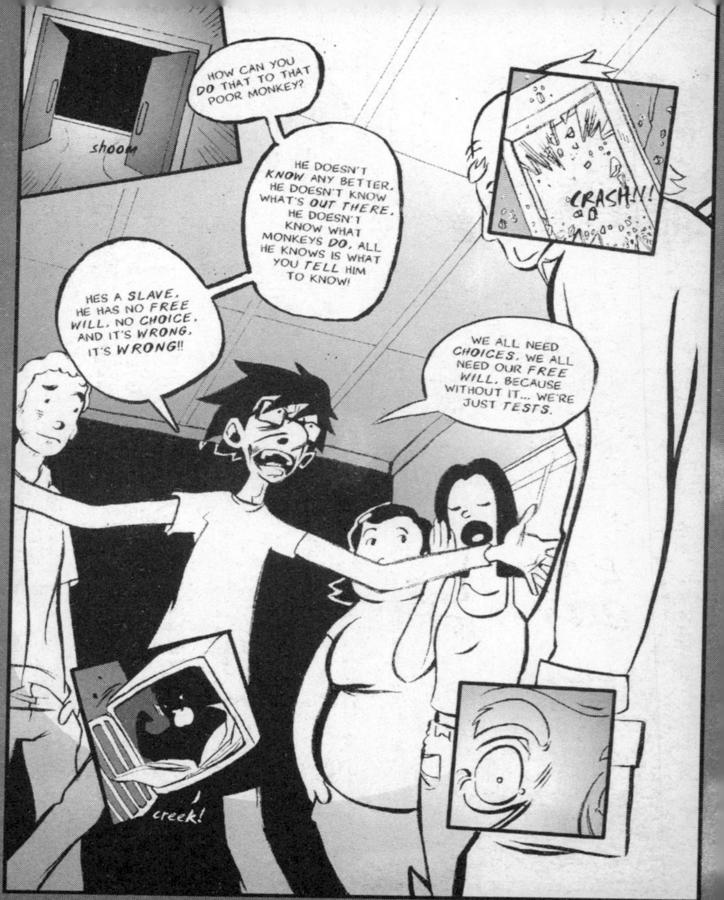
HOW CAN YOU DO THAT TO THAT POOR MONKEY?
shoom
CRASH!!!
HE DOESN'T KNOW ANY BETTER, HE DOESN'T KNOW WHAT'S OUT THERE. HE DOESN'T KNOW WHAT MONKEYS DO. ALL HE KNOWS IS WHAT YOU TELL HIM TO KNOW!
HES A SLAVE. HE HAS NO FREE WILL, NO CHOICE, AND IT'S WRONG, IT'S WRONG!!
WE ALL NEED CHOICES. WE ALL NEED OUR FREE WILL, BECAUSE WITHOUT IT... WE'RE JUST TESTS.
creek!

Turn to page 31.

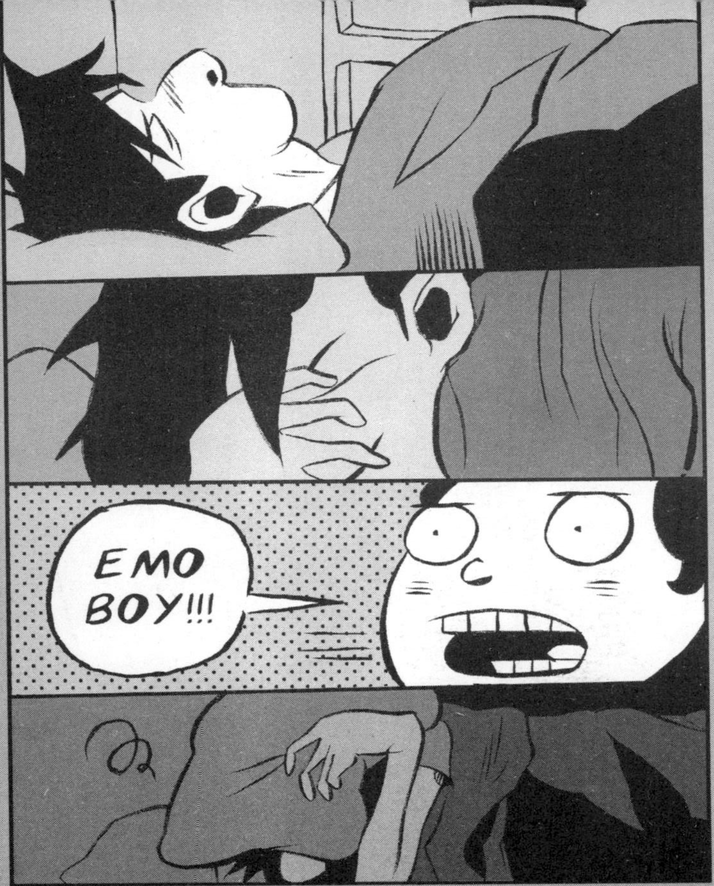
EMO BOY!!!

Turn to page 44.

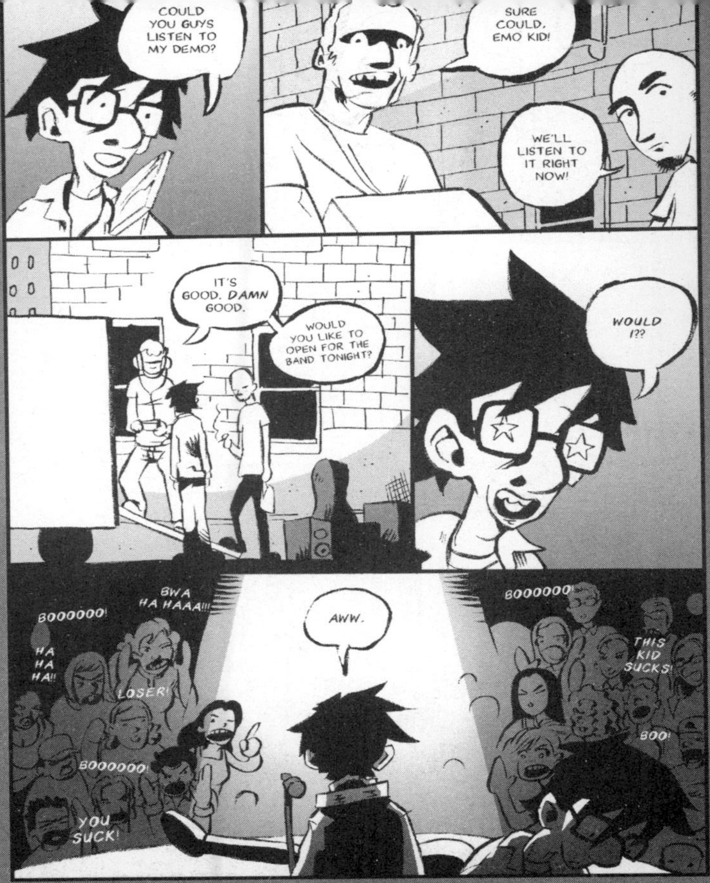
COULD YOU GUYS LISTEN TO MY DEMO?
SURE COULD, EMO KID!
WE'LL LISTEN TO IT RIGHT NOW!
IT'S GOOD. DAMN GOOD.
WOULD YOU LIKE TO OPEN FOR THE BAND TONIGHT?
WOULD I??
BOOOOOO!
HA HA HA!!
BWA HA HAAA!!!
LOSER!
BOOOOOO!
YOU SUCK!
AWW.
BOOOOOO!
THIS KID SUCKS!
BOO!

BAD SINGING ENDING!!!!!!!

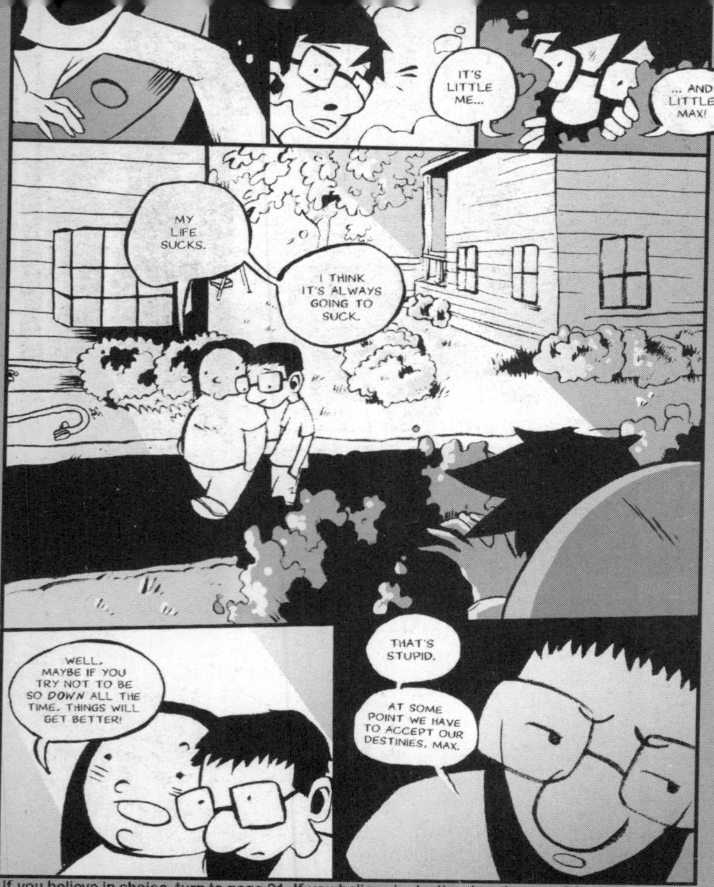

IT'S LITTLE ME...
... AND LITTLE MAX!
MY LIFE SUCKS.
I THINK IT'S ALWAYS GOING TO SUCK.
WELL, MAYBE IF YOU TRY NOT TO BE SO DOWN ALL THE TIME, THINGS WILL GET BETTER!
THAT'S STUPID.
AT SOME POINT WE HAVE TO ACCEPT OUR DESTINIES, MAX.


If you believe in choice, turn to page 21. If you believe in destiny, turn to page 24.
If you want to say hello to little you, turn to page 20.

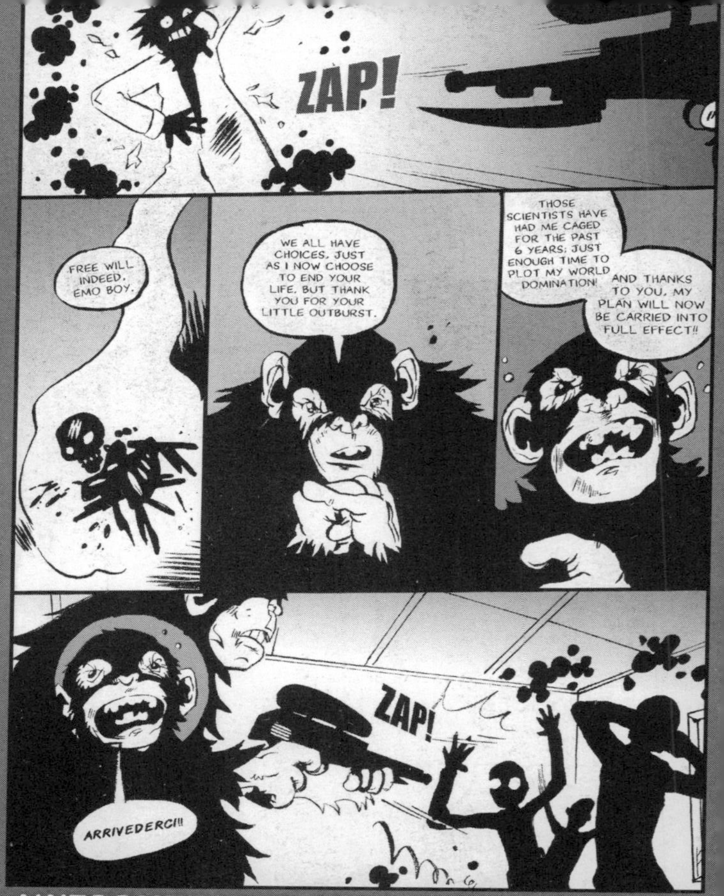

ZAP!
FREE WILL INDEED, EMO BOY.
WE ALL HAVE CHOICES. JUST AS I NOW CHOOSE TO END YOUR LIFE. BUT THANK YOU FOR YOUR LITTLE OUTBURST.
THOSE SCIENTISTS HAVE HAD ME CAGED FOR THE PAST 6 YEARS; JUST ENOUGH TIME TO PLOT MY WORLD DOMINATION!
AND THANKS TO YOU, MY PLAN WILL NOW BE CARRIED INTO FULL EFFECT!!
ARRIVEDERCI!!
ZAP!


AWESOMELY BAD ENDING!!!!!!!!

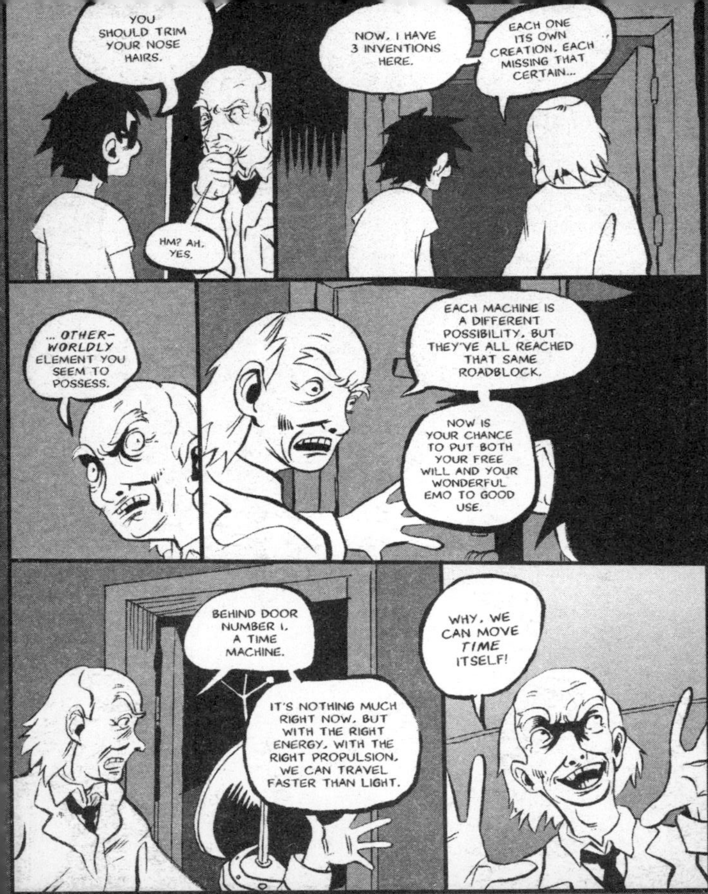
YOU SHOULD TRIM YOUR NOSE HAIRS.
HM? AH. YES.
NOW, I HAVE 3 INVENTIONS HERE.
EACH ONE ITS OWN CREATION, EACH MISSING THAT CERTAIN...
... *OTHER-WORLDLY* ELEMENT YOU SEEM TO POSSESS.
EACH MACHINE IS A DIFFERENT POSSIBILITY, BUT THEY'VE ALL REACHED THAT SAME ROADBLOCK.
NOW IS YOUR CHANCE TO PUT BOTH YOUR FREE WILL AND YOUR WONDERFUL EMO TO GOOD USE.
BEHIND DOOR NUMBER 1, A TIME MACHINE.
IT'S NOTHING MUCH RIGHT NOW, BUT WITH THE RIGHT ENERGY, WITH THE RIGHT PROPULSION, WE CAN TRAVEL FASTER THAN LIGHT.
WHY, WE CAN MOVE *TIME* ITSELF!

Turn to page 10.

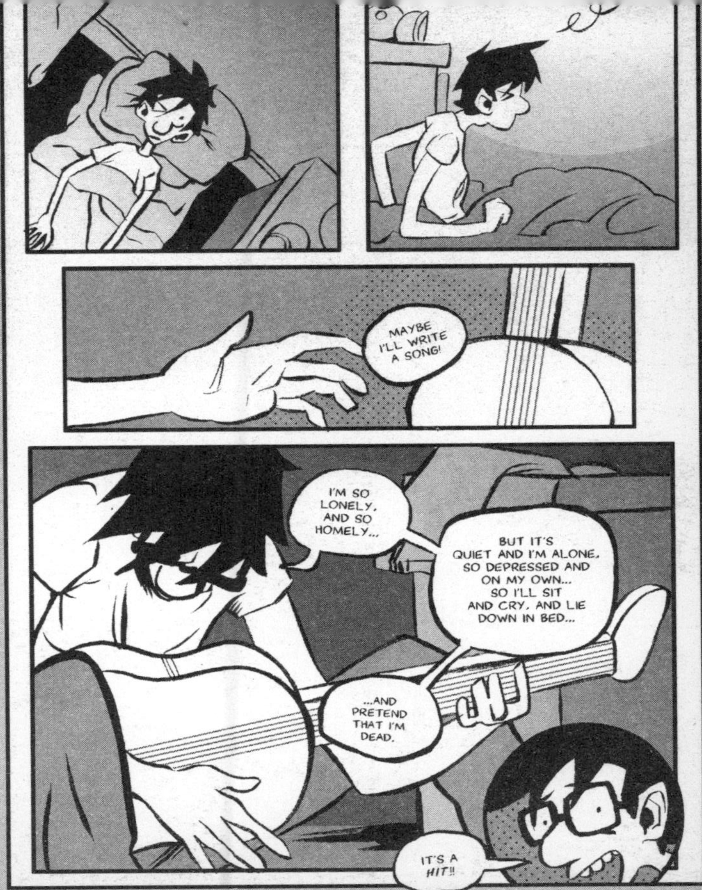
MAYBE I'LL WRITE A SONG!
I'M SO LONELY, AND SO HOMELY...
BUT IT'S QUIET AND I'M ALONE, SO DEPRESSED AND ON MY OWN... SO I'LL SIT AND CRY, AND LIE DOWN IN BED...
...AND PRETEND THAT I'M DEAD.
IT'S A *HIT*!!

**BEST** ENDING!!!!!!!!!!!!!!!!!! Congratulations!!!!

If this is your dream, turn to page 29. If this is your nightmare, turn to page 36.

Maxine was right! My life decisions were mine to make. I put myself to **work**. I studied and got **good grades**. I went to **college**, and worked in that **lab**, just like Maxine said. I met the love of my life there.

We got married, and bought a **house with a picket fence**.

We had little emoes of our own, and there, I was living the great **American dream**.

**Emo Boy Pin Up by Benjamin Roman**

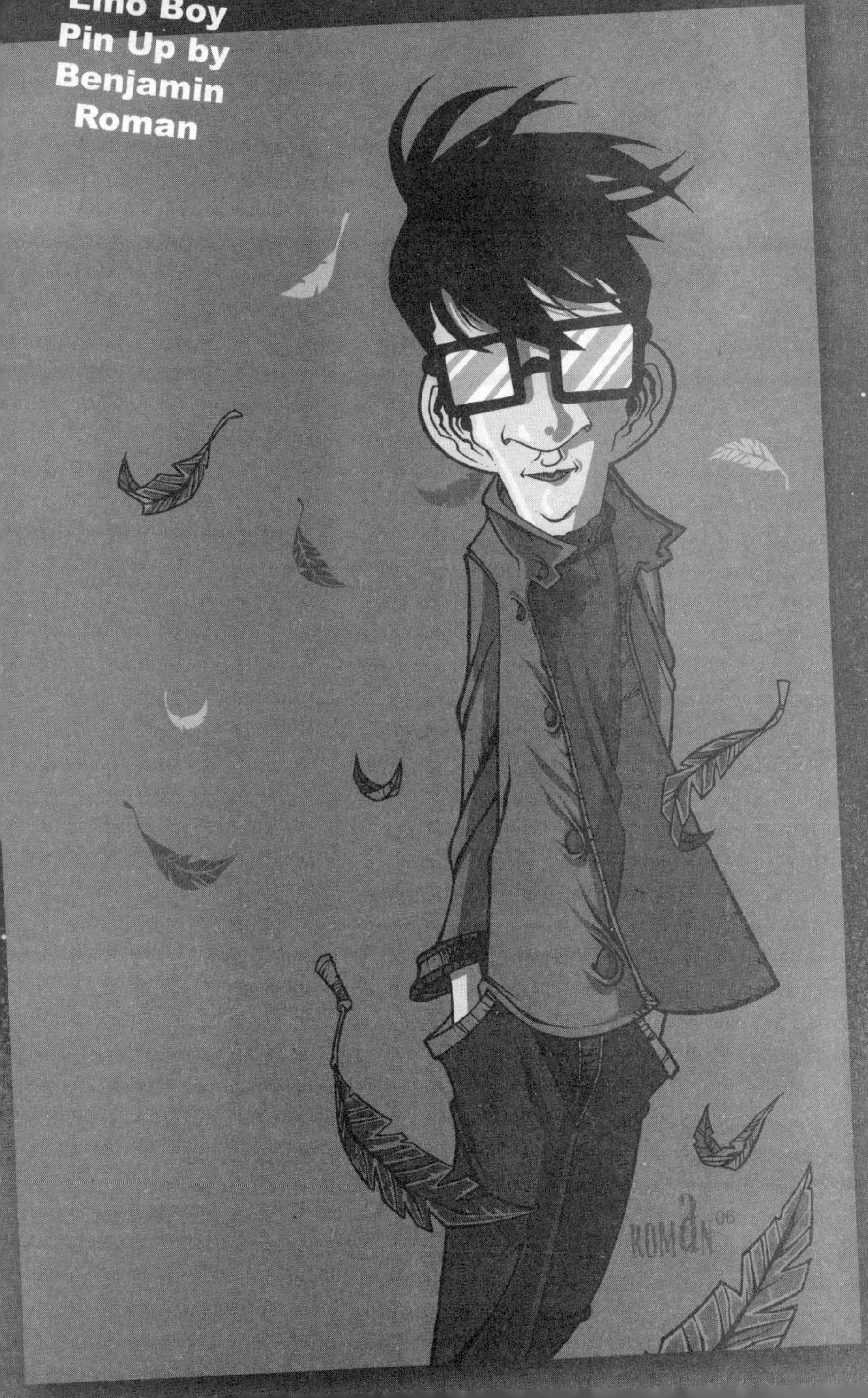
ROMAN '06

**Emo Boy Sculpture by Laura Beaumont**

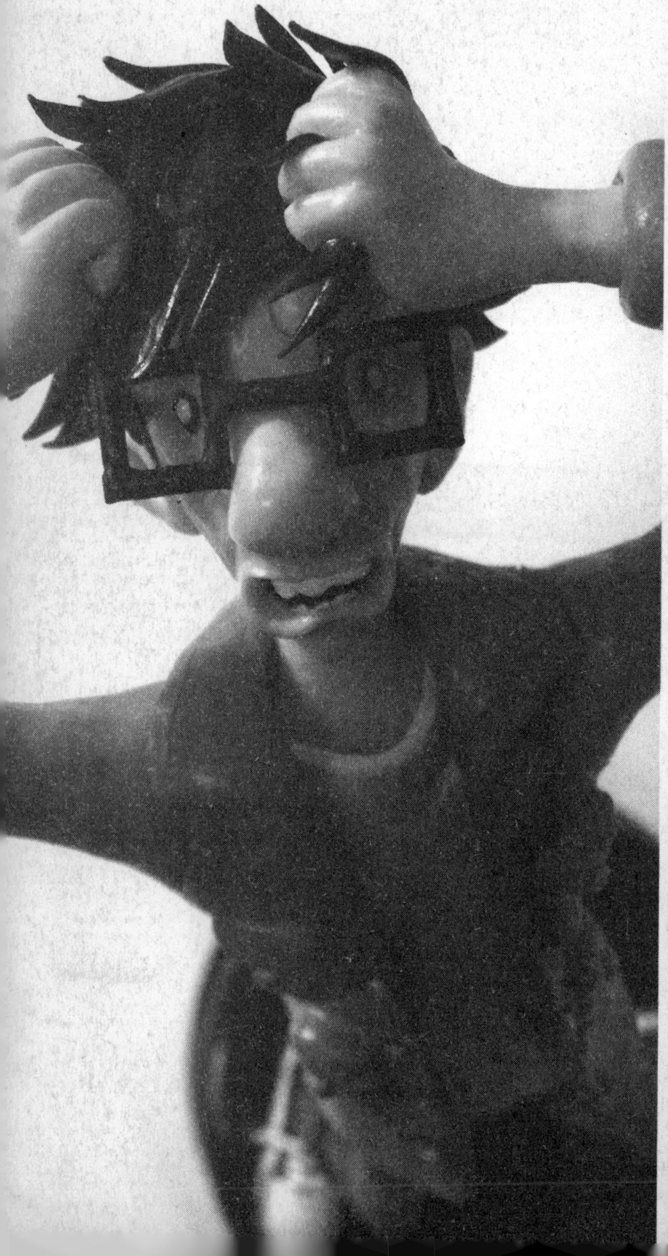

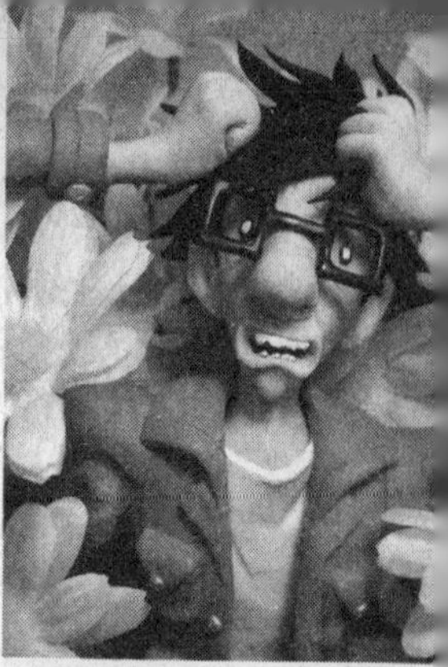

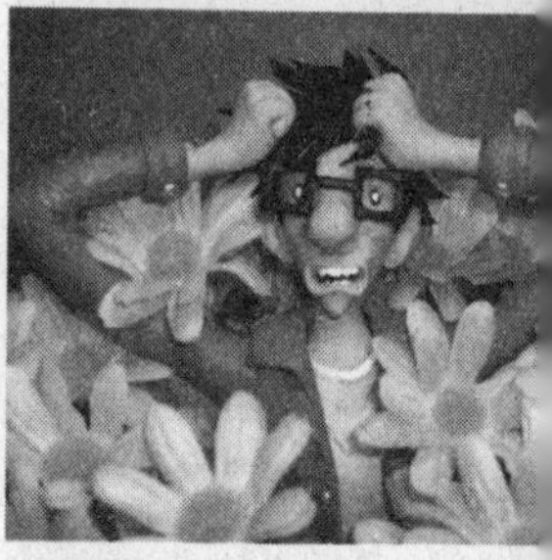

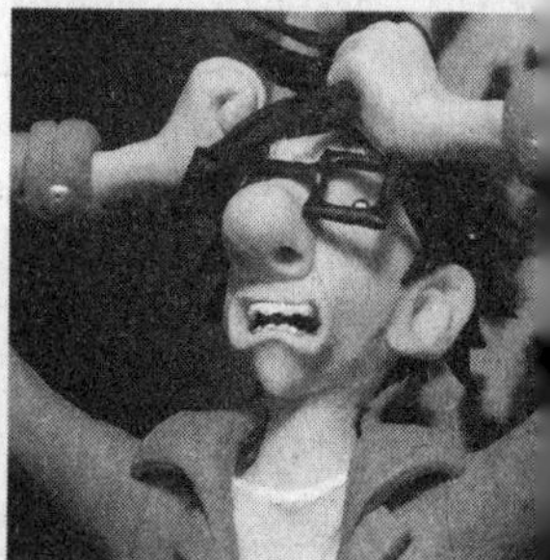

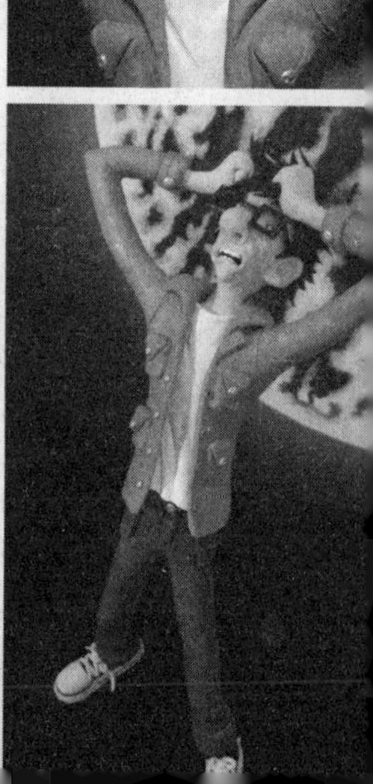

**Emo Boy Pin Up by Tara Billinger**

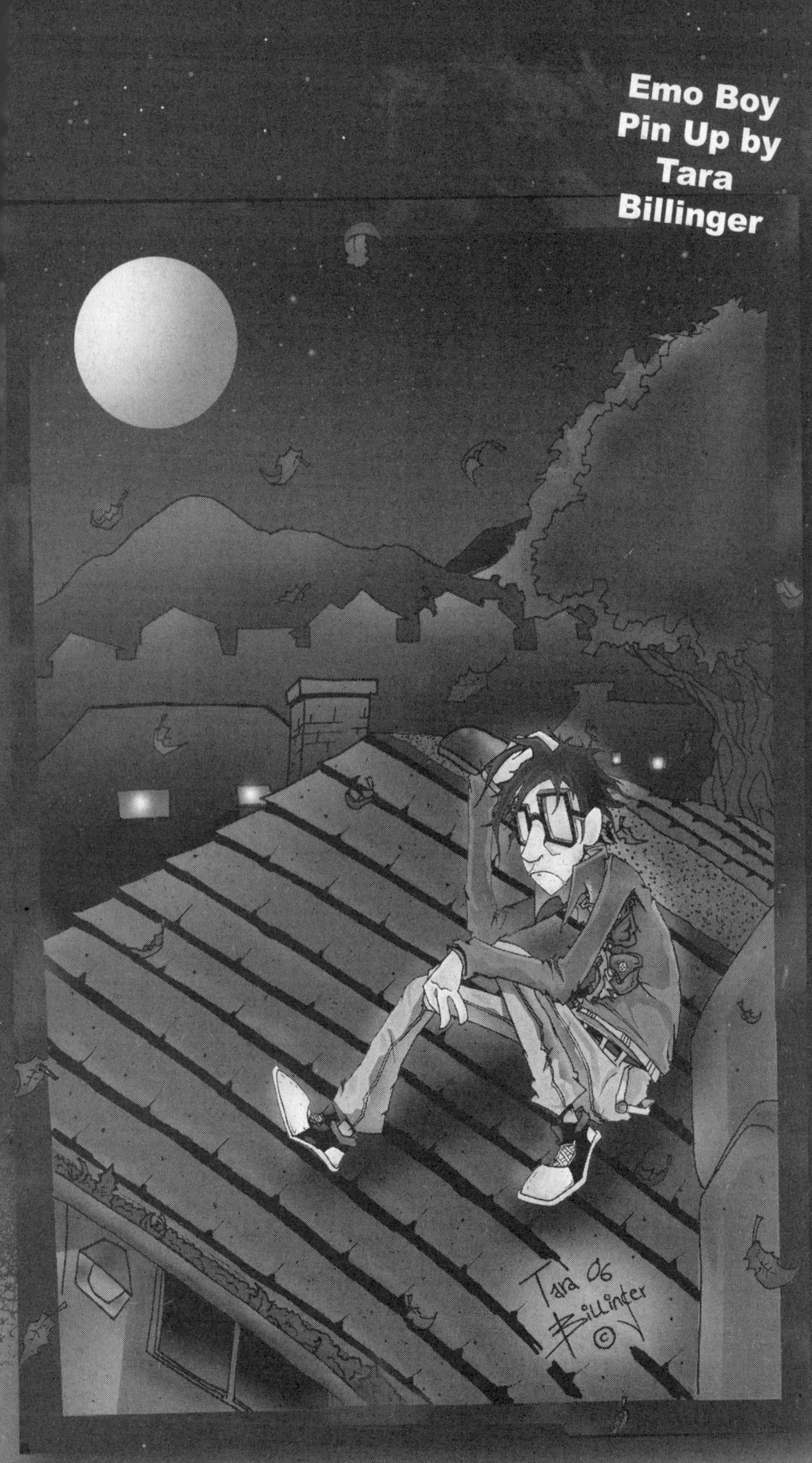
Tara 06
Billinger ©

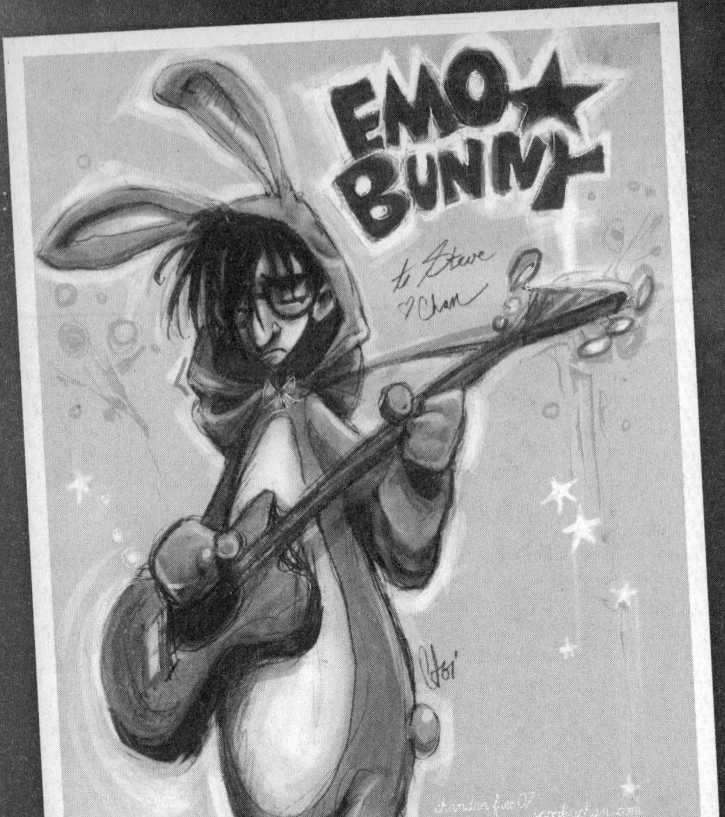
EMO
BUNNY

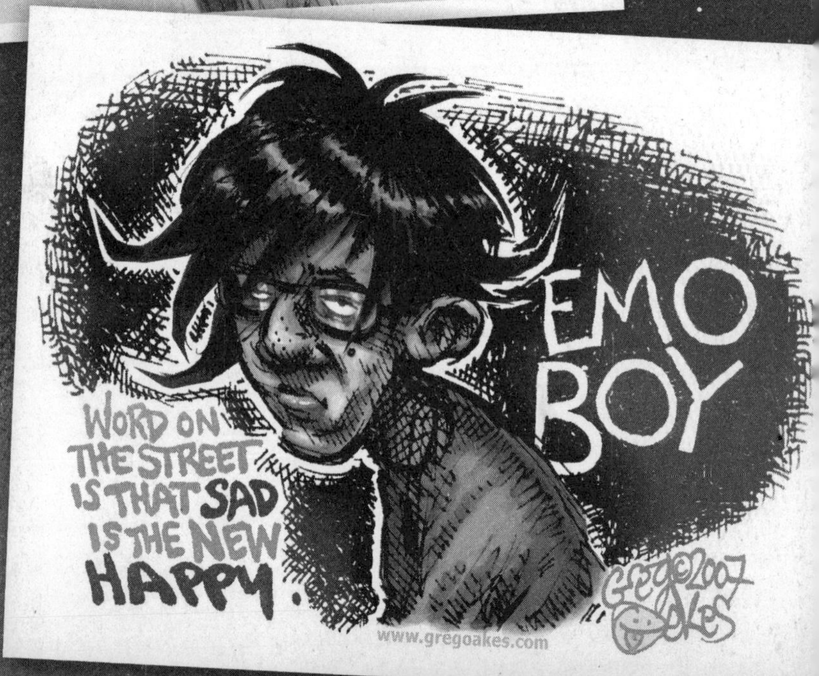
EMO
BOY
WORD ON THE STREET IS THAT SAD IS THE NEW HAPPY.
Greg Oakes 2007
www.gregoakes.com

Emo Boy Pin Ups by Chandra Free and Greg Oakes